Dear Catharine, Dear Taylor

Dear Catharine, Dear Taylor

The Civil War Letters of
a Union Soldier and His Wife

Edited by Richard L. Kiper

Letters transcribed by Donna B. Vaughn

University Press of Kansas

Published by the University Press of Kansas
(Lawrence, Kansas 66049), which was
organized by the Kansas Board of Regents
and is operated and funded by Emporia State
University, Fort Hays State University,
Kansas State University, Pittsburg State
University, the University of Kansas, and
Wichita State University

British Library Cataloguing in Publication
Data is available.

Printed in the United States of America

10 9 8 7 6 5 4 3 2 1

The paper used in this publication meets the
minimum requirements of the American
National Standard for Permanence of Paper
for Printed Library Materials Z39.48-1984.

Library of Congress
Cataloging-in-Publication Data

Peirce, Taylor, 1822–1901.
Dear Catharine, Dear Taylor : the Civil War
letters of a Union Soldier and his wife /
edited by Richard L. Kiper ; letters
transcribed by Donna Vaughn.
    p. cm. — (Modern war studies)
Includes bibliographical references and
index.
    ISBN 0-7006-1205-X (cloth : alk. paper)
    1. Peirce, Taylor, 1822–1901 — Corre-
spondence. 2. Peirce, Catherine L., d. 1867
— Correspondence. 3. United States. Army.
Iowa Infantry Regiment, 22nd (1862–1865)
4. United States — History — Civil War,
1861–1865 — Personal narratives. 5. United
States — History — Civil War, 1861–1865 —
Social aspects. 6. Iowa — History — Civil
War, 1861–1865 — Personal narratives. 7.
Iowa — History — Civil War, 1861–1865 —
Social aspects. 8. Soldiers — United States —
Correspondence. 9. Army spouses — Iowa
— Des Moines — Correspondence. 10. Des
Moines (Iowa) — Biography. I. Peirce,
Catherine L., d. 1867. II. Kiper, Richard L.,
1945–. III. Vaughn, Donna. IV. Title. V.
Series.
    E507.5 22nd .P54 2002
    973.7′77 — dc21   2002006389

To "The Greatest Generation"

SERGEANT R. LESLIE KIPER
United States Army, 1942–1945

FIRST LIEUTENANT RALPH O. KIPER
United States Army, 1942–1953

STAFF SERGEANT DONALD G. KIPER
United States Army, 1943–1946

STAFF SERGEANT E. B. HALLEY
United States Army, 1940–1945

Contents

Preface

In March 1997 Professor Ted Wilson of the University of Kansas asked me to evaluate a collection of letters between a Civil War soldier and his wife—Taylor and Catharine Peirce. The collection had come to Ted by way of Dick Himes, emeritus professor of biological sciences at the University of Kansas. Dick's wife, Sue, and her brother, Jack Vaughn, are descendants of the uncle of Taylor Peirce. Sue and Jack's father, Walter Vaughn, had grown up in Marion, Iowa, and knew Taylor's daughter Catharine (sometimes spelled Katherine) as "Cousin Kitty." About 1918 Catharine moved to California but stored much of her furniture and some of her belongings in the Vaughns' barn. Walter married in 1929, and Catharine told him and his wife, Marjorie, to take whatever they needed from what she had left behind. While sorting through the boxes, Walter came across the letters in this collection. The letters then passed to Jack and Sue. Jack's wife, Donna, was the driving force behind this project. She undertook the arduous task of transcribing the letters from the handwritten form. After I provided Professor Wilson with my analysis, he put me in touch with Donna at her home in California, and I began the process of editing the collection.

Although several collections of letters from Civil War soldiers to loved ones at home have survived and been published, this collection of 178 letters is unique in that it includes 51 letters from Catharine to Taylor and 17 from their daughter Sarah (sometimes called Sallie) to Taylor. It is rare for a collection to contain such a large number of letters from the home front to the soldier. One can only imagine the lengths to which Taylor went to protect those letters and ensure that they were returned home. Mail has always been a precious commodity to soldiers, and the fact that Taylor kept and preserved the letters from his wife and daughter, as well as eight letters from his sister and brother-in-law (Mary and Cyrus Milner), indicates the depth of his desire to maintain close contact with those far away.

Taylor and Catharine faithfully wrote to each other almost weekly. Because of Taylor's literacy, his letters provide an exceptional view of army life from the perspective of an enlisted soldier and husband who was trying to do his duty to his country and to his family. Catharine's letters are an intimate look into the life and trials of a soldier's wife. Her story is one of coping with loneliness and the responsibility of caring for her children while longing for her husband's safe return.

Taylor's first letter is dated August 20, 1862, shortly after he enlisted. His last letter is dated July 14, 1865, as he and the 22nd Iowa Volunteer Infantry are preparing to depart Savannah, Georgia, for Iowa. Although there are numerous references to letters from Catharine, the first surviving letters from her begin in January 1863, while Taylor is with his regiment in Missouri. Her final letter is written in August 1865, while Taylor is en route home.

Taylor and Catharine were not famous. They were ordinary people whose lives were interrupted by war. As such, they reflect the thousands of families—both Union and Confederate—who sent men to battle while the women remained at home to take care of the children, mind the farm or store, pay the bills, and worry whether their husbands would see the next dawn or they would receive word that they were widows.

The book is organized according to major operational deployments of the 22nd Iowa Infantry. Each section begins with a summary of events during the particular period and includes maps to identify sites mentioned in the letters. Most letters have been annotated to include biographical information about named individuals. I attempted to identify all the soldiers mentioned in these letters, but when that was not possible, there is no notation. Although there are many other individuals mentioned in the letters, with few exceptions, I made no attempt to identify them. Also included in the notes are comments on specific military movements conducted by the unit and clarification of obscure or esoteric terms.

Only in cases in which confusion could occur has grammar been altered. Sentences in the original letters are rarely separated by periods. For clarity, though, sentence breaks using periods and capital letters have been inserted. An effort was made to adhere as closely as possible to spellings in the original letters. The correct spellings of words that are unclear are included in brackets. Illegible words are noted as such. Note that Taylor's last name is spelled both as "Peirce" and "Pierce." He and Catharine use the former spelling, while various military records use both spellings. Taylor's second wife, Eliza, used "Peirce" as her signature. Their marriage certificate and Taylor's death certificate, however, spell his name "Pierce," as do many of the federal census records. I have chosen to adopt the spelling used by Taylor, Catharine, and Eliza. When an alternative spelling appears, it is because that is the spelling in the original letter or document. Catharine and Taylor spell her name "Catharine," but Taylor's sister Mary always spells it "Catherine." Other relatives also spell her name "Catherine" or occasionally "Cathrine." In one letter dated February 15, 1865, Taylor spells her name "Catherine" twice while also clearly spelling it "Catharine" at other points in the letter.

In no case have racist remarks (by today's standards) been changed; such terms reflect the times in which Taylor lived. Portions of letters that have been omitted are indicated by asterisks.

In July 1999 I located the graves of Taylor, Catharine, Cyrus, and Mary in Des Moines. (In 1901 Taylor was buried in a grave marked only by a rectangular iron marker that measured two inches by three inches. Over time the marker had become covered with several inches of earth. In October 2001 the Veterans Administration placed a permanent granite marker on Taylor's grave.) That visit was a deeply moving experience because of the privilege of sharing such an intimate part of their lives. I walked the streets where they had lived during and after the war. On another occasion I visited the house where Catharine (Taylor and Catharine's daughter) and Mary lived in 1900. These visits were full of both sadness and joy. There was sadness because photographs of these individuals no longer exist, and I wanted to picture them on those streets and in that house. There was sadness that relatives other than those mentioned earlier could not be located. I wanted them to know the kind of people their ancestors had been. The joy was in knowing that the story of two ordinary people caught up in a cataclysmic event would be told. These two people are indicative of millions of other men and women who lived during times of war. Theirs is a story of life, of hardship, of war, of loneliness, of fear—but the story of Taylor and Catharine is, above all, a love story of a husband and wife separated by the tragedy of the American Civil War.

This work could not have been completed without Donna Vaughn's tedious efforts to transcribe the handwritten letters. I also owe a debt of thanks to the staff of the Combined Arms Research Library at Fort Leavenworth, Kansas, particularly Dorothy Rogers, who willingly acquired numerous works through Inter-Library Loan. I am especially grateful to Ellen Westhafer of the State Historical Society of Iowa for her assistance with records of the 22nd Iowa Infantry. Linda Roskins at the Woodlawn Cemetery in Las Vegas, Nevada, sent me photographs of Eliza's headstone. Others who provided assistance include Georgia Spellman from the Savannah Diocese; Bill Meltzer from the Chester County, Pennsylvania, Historical Society; Richard Raymond from Harpers Ferry National Historical Park; John Albert from the Georgia Historical Society; Pat Deaton from the Jasper County Genealogical Society; and the staffs of the Iowa Genealogical Society in Des Moines, the Mid-Continent Library in Independence, Missouri, and Glendale Cemetery in Des Moines. Two close friends, Jack Ogren and Bob Cassella, assisted me with many of the technical aspects of computers and genealogies. Once again, Barbara Baeuchle provided her considerable artistic talents as evidenced by the quality of the maps.

As she has been for thirty-four years, my wife, Diane, was an ardent supporter during this project. In the more than five-year journey from lunch with Ted Wilson to publication, our two youngest children graduated from college, three of our children were married, our first grandchild was born, and Diane completed her master's degree. Throughout the turmoil and excitement of those years she remained a steadfast encouragement to me. Truly, "she is worth far more than rubies."

Dear Catharine, Dear Taylor

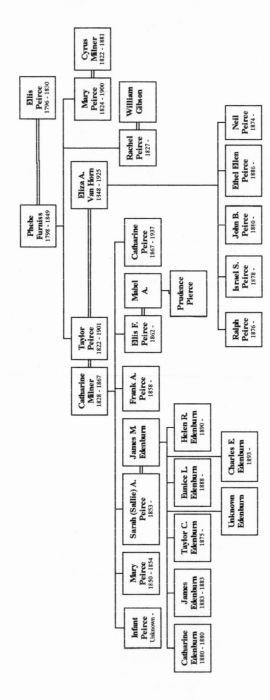

Family tree of Taylor Peirce

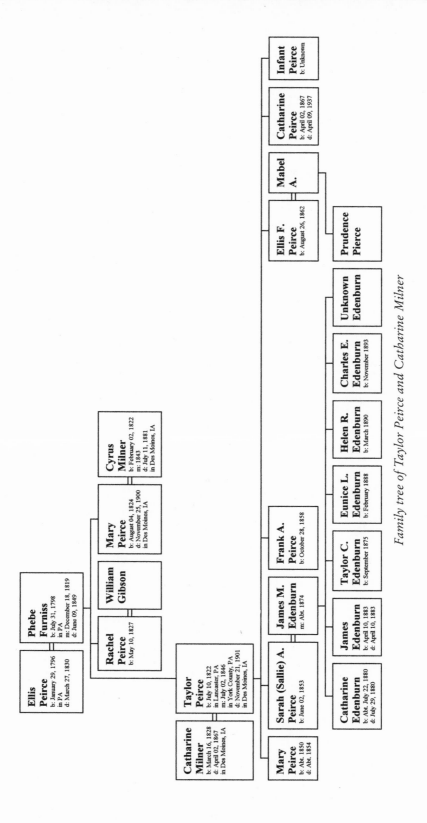

Family tree of Taylor Peirce and Catharine Milner

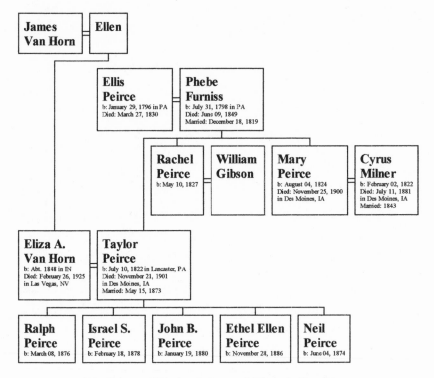

James
Van Horn

Ellen

Ellis
Peirce
b: January 29, 1796 in PA
Died: March 27, 1830

Phebe
Furniss
b: July 31, 1798 in PA
Died: June 09, 1849
Married: December 18, 1819

Rachel
Peirce
b: May 10, 1827

William
Gibson

Mary
Peirce
b: August 04, 1824
Died: November 25, 1900
in Des Moines, IA

Cyrus
Milner
b: February 02, 1822
Died: July 11, 1881
in Des Moines, IA
Married: 1843

Eliza A.
Van Horn
b: Abt. 1848 in IN
Died: February 26, 1925
in Las Vegas, NV

Taylor
Peirce
b: July 10, 1822 in Lancaster, PA
Died: November 21, 1901
in Des Moines, IA
Married: May 15, 1873

Ralph
Peirce
b: March 08, 1876

Israel S.
Peirce
b: February 18, 1878

John B.
Peirce
b: January 19, 1880

Ethel Ellen
Peirce
b: November 28, 1886

Neil
Peirce
b: June 04, 1874

Family tree of Taylor Peirce and Eliza A. Van Horn

Introduction

President Abraham Lincoln's April 15, 1861, appeal for 75,000 soldiers to join the Union cause brought the American Civil War to Iowa. Although as early as January several militia organizations had offered their services to Governor Samuel J. Kirkwood, it was not until April 17 that he called for the formation of one regiment. By the end of July nine regiments were assembling. Iowa's quota for 1861 was 19,316 men, but the state would furnish 21,987. A subsequent call by Lincoln for 300,000 troops on July 1, 1862, established a quota of 10,570 Iowa soldiers. Again the state exceeded that number by furnishing 24,438 men. Among the 824 volunteers for the 22nd Iowa Infantry Regiment was Taylor Peirce.[1]

On August 2, 1862, Taylor was enrolled in Company C, 22nd Iowa Infantry Regiment, at Newton, Iowa. He was mustered into federal service with the rank of third sergeant on September 9 for a period of three years and received an enlistment bonus of $25. At age forty, Taylor was one of the oldest members of a company whose age averaged twenty-five. Members of the company were primarily from Jasper County, but only two of the enlistees were Iowa natives. The diversity of home states reflected the westward migration that occurred in the United States during the early nineteenth century. The most represented state of birth was Ohio, with thirty-six soldiers in the company; next was Indiana with seventeen and Pennsylvania with nine. The remaining native-born troops were from Virginia, New York, Missouri, New Jersey, Illinois, Wisconsin, Tennessee, New Hampshire, Maine, Maryland, Kentucky, and Michigan. Four were foreign born: one each from Canada and England, and two from Germany. Until mustered out in July 1865, Taylor and his fellow soldiers would travel from Iowa to campaign in Missouri, Louisiana, Mississippi, Texas, Virginia, Georgia, North Carolina, and South Carolina.

Taylor was born July 10, 1822, in Chester County, Pennsylvania,

---

1. *Roster and Record of Iowa Soldiers in the War of the Rebellion,* 6 vols. (Des Moines, Iowa: Emory H. English, 1908–1911), 3:638.

to Ellis Peirce and Phebe Furniss Peirce.[2] Ellis died at age thirty-four of typhoid fever, and Phebe died at age fifty. Nothing is known of Taylor's childhood. It appears that he was well educated, for he was familiar with European history, could recite poems he had memorized, and apparently authored several of the poems that appear in his letters. He was politically aware and able to articulate his views on the war, the Union, and slavery, among other issues.

Taylor had two sisters—Rachel, who married William Gibson, and Mary, who married Cyrus Milner. Cyrus had a sister, Catharine, whom Taylor married on July 2, 1846, in York County, Pennsylvania. Taylor and Catharine first lived with Cyrus and Mary in Lancaster County. A daughter, Mary, was born to the Peirces probably in 1850 and died at the age of four from a fever.[3] Cyrus worked as a cattle drover, a job that in 1850 took him as far as London, Ohio. Mary accompanied him and lived there at least through March of that year.

According to the authors of *The History of Polk County, Iowa,* Taylor was in the Des Moines area in the mid-1840s. They say they spoke to Taylor, whom they described as "an old trader among the Fox and Sac Indians before the white people came to Des Moines and who spoke their language fluently." Fort Des Moines opened in May 1843, and on October 11, 1845, Indian claims to the Des Moines area expired, and settlement by whites began in earnest.[4]

In January 1850 Taylor was at Parkersburg, Iowa (approximately twenty-five miles west of Waterloo), while Catharine remained in Pennsylvania. In a letter to his wife he expresses his desire for her to

2. Taylor's military records state that he was born in Lancaster, but his oath of office as first lieutenant states that he was born in Chester County. The records of the Church of Jesus Christ of Latter-day Saints indicate that he was born in Goshen, Chester County, Pennsylvania. Because Taylor signed the oath of office, it is reasonable to conclude that the oath contains his correct birthplace. The reason for the discrepancy cannot be determined.

3. This daughter is not mentioned in the 1850 census, but a daughter is included in the 1852 census. One letter dated July 21, 1850, from Taylor to Catharine asks that she "tell Mary that her Poppa sends her a kiss." A letter from Mary Milner to Catharine dated March 8, 1850, also makes a reference to "little Mary." A letter from Mary's aunt, D. Speakman, dated July 17, 1854, states that Mary had recently died.

4. *The History of Polk County, Iowa* (Des Moines, Iowa: Union Historical Company, 1880), 717.

join him in the summer. Apparently, he had fallen on hard times in Pennsylvania and was working in Iowa as a farm and mill manager with the intention of buying land to allay his debts. The job paid $1,000 annually, plus he was able to earn extra money by farming 900 acres and raising ninety hogs. He wore buckskin trousers and moccasins, ate venison, and lived in a ten- by twelve-foot log hut, sleeping on bearskins and covering himself with wolf and buffalo skins. By July, however, he had returned to London, Ohio (approximately twenty miles west of Columbus), and Cyrus had returned to Pennsylvania. Taylor wrote to Catharine that he would be home soon, but whether he actually made the trip is uncertain.

In March 1851 Taylor and Catharine arranged for her to move to Iowa, along with Cyrus and Mary. By May the Milners and the Peirces were living in Union, Iowa. Mary's obituary states that she and Cyrus moved to Iowa in 1852, although a personal letter indicates that they were living in Union in 1851. Soon afterward, Taylor and Cyrus began a trip to Oregon; for what purpose and how far they went are not known. One letter in this collection states that Cyrus had once visited Pike's Peak, presumably during this trip. By 1852 both families had moved to Poweshick Township, Jasper County, Iowa, where Taylor worked a farm and served on the grand jury. The next year a daughter, Sarah A. (also called Sallie), was born to Taylor and Catharine.

Over the next several years Taylor and Catharine bought and sold numerous pieces of property in the county. From 1853 until 1861 they were involved in at least fourteen real estate transactions. During this time they apparently moved several times within the county, because in a letter dated February 10, 1865, Catharine writes that she had not lived anywhere longer than three years since they had been married. One letter dated April 17, 1856, states that she had no house, and Mary offered to let her come live with her and Cyrus in Des Moines.

By 1856 Taylor had become a member of the militia and owned eighty acres of corn that produced 1,500 bushels, as well as sixty-six acres of unimproved land. Apparently he was a leading citizen, because that year he was one of four citizens called on to sign a measure that increased the bond of the county treasurer from $16,000 to $30,000. In October 1858 Catharine gave birth to a son, Frank A.

The 1860 federal census recorded Taylor as a commercial laborer (as distinguished from a farm laborer) who owned real estate valued at $6,000. Taylor's obituary in the *Newton Journal* states that prior to his enlistment in 1862, he operated a sawmill near Colfax, about nine miles west of Newton.[5]

By 1856 Cyrus and Mary had moved from Jasper County to Des Moines, where he worked as a millwright. Mary was described by Taylor and Catharine's daughter as being "slight," "delicate," and "sensative," about five feet tall with brown eyes and brown hair. She described Cyrus as "iritable." He and Mary lived in a large brick house—"one of the most pretentious dwellings in the growing city" —on the northeast corner of Front and Washington Streets near the end of the bridge across the Raccoon River.[6] In August 1862 another son, Ellis F., was born to the Peirces, and Catharine and the children moved in with Cyrus and Mary when Taylor left for the war. Cyrus attempted to enlist, but he fell while drilling—presumably from the seriousness of his asthma—and was taken home on a stretcher. He remained an invalid the remainder of his life. Cyrus and Mary had no children, and Catharine once expressed her fear to Taylor that she and the children were a bother to them. In their letters to Taylor, however, the Milners express only their concern for Catharine and the children.

In August 1863 the town provost marshal approached Cyrus about opening the home as a boarding house for transient soldiers. The next day Cyrus talked with Mary, and the house, known as Washington House, was opened. Soldiers were charged fifteen cents a day for room and board. Catharine and Mary were assisted by Cyrus and two female borders—Anna Kelly and, presumably, Sallie Mohnrern, who is mentioned in one letter.

Taylor was able to return home twice during the war. His first furlough was in late August 1862 after the regiment was mustered, and the second was in September 1863. He was promoted to first sergeant on December 15, 1863, and was commissioned first lieutenant on April 25, 1865 (April 22 according to the oath of office).

Although the letters make numerous references to "likenesses" being made of Taylor, Catharine, and the children, none have survived. The only description of Taylor is from the muster roll, which

5. *Newton Journal*, November 27, 1901, 2.

6. These descriptions are from notes made by Catharine, the daughter of Taylor and Catharine, about events in her life.

indicates that he was five feet, six inches tall and had brown hair, brown eyes, and a light complexion.

The salutations give no hint of the depth of the relationship between Taylor and his wife. All letters to him begin "Dear Taylor," and almost all to her begin either "Dear Catharine" or "Dear Catharine and all the rest." Two are addressed simply as "Dear Folks." Occasionally a letter is addressed "Dear Wife," and one is addressed "My Dear Wife." In two letters he uses a pet name for Catharine—Kate—and in seven others he addresses her as Kitty.

Taylor's and Catharine's letters follow a pattern consistent with many written during the war.[7] The first line of Civil War letters often begins with "I sit down to write," "I seat myself," or similar words. These words are found in the opening lines of most of the Peirces' letters.

The letters then follow the format of many letters between spouses in the nineteenth century. A study of such letters by Karen Lystra concludes that "spouses, after several years of cohabitation, generally expected less self-revelation from each other and paid more attention to the details of day-to-day living."[8] This is certainly the case with this collection. Catharine never writes what could be considered a love letter, although she clearly expresses her affection. For example, in the body of one she addresses him as "Dear one." Taylor expresses his love for Catharine in only eight letters, four of which were written soon after his enlistment. In one he says, "I love you as well a man can," and in another, "my love for you all has increased." He writes of their future life being "one blissful dream of love and affection." In a fourth he recalls being "cheered with thy love and companionship." Although in his letter of February 15, 1865, Taylor claims, "I have got to old to write love letters to Catharine," probably the actual reason for not being too intimate is that he intended his letters to be shared with Mary and Cyrus. Indeed, in one letter in which Taylor begins to express "the intensity of love we felt for each other," he immediately apologizes for his words and fears that she will be ashamed to show it to the others. Clearly, he misses his wife, for in a letter of Sep-

7. James I. Robertson, *Soldiers Blue and Gray* (Columbia: University of South Carolina Press, 1988), 105.

8. Karen Lystra, *Searching the Heart: Women, Men, and Romantic Love in Nineteenth Century America* (New York: Oxford University Press, 1989), 10.

tember 13, 1862, he writes, "I would like to take thee in my arm once more." Again on December 19, 1864, he writes, "Oh how I wish I could once more be with you." In his letter of March 25, 1865, Taylor jokes that he longs for the caresses of his children "and some older ones too but I must not make so much fuss about that or I shall have you all crazy for my return." Only in the letter of April 23, 1865, in which he states that he longs to "clasp thee once more," does Taylor specifically ask Catharine not to share it with the family.

In one particularly revealing letter Taylor confesses that often he has not given his wife the affection she needed. He admits that his "unfeeling acts" and "stubborn acts of unkindness" were born of a "hard heart." Remarkably, in an age when men were dominant, he asks for forgiveness and promises to try to repay her for "all the love lavished on my unworthy self." He adds, "I would give all I possessed to be with you again."

Taylor occasionally addresses letters specifically to his children. One particular salutation in a letter to his son — "My Dear Little Franky"—indicates the level of affection he feels for them. In that letter he writes that "it fellt as if I was tearing the last chain of affection from my heart when the day come to leave you all." He adds, "I could hardly keep my throat from choking right up."

Although many of Taylor's letters close with "give my love to all," only two contain the word "love" specifically addressed to his wife. Several others ask Catharine to give his love to Mary and Cyrus and "take a good share for thyself." Most of his closings use the word "affectionately" (sixty-eight times) or variations that include "Thy affectionate husband," "Affectionately your husband," "Thine affectionately," or "Yours affectionately," plus the abbreviations "aft" and "affty." Other letters close with "Yours," "Thine as ever," "Yours as ever," "I remain yours," "Your Taylor," and "Farewell." Twelve of his letters are signed "Taylor Peirce," and the remainder are signed "Taylor."

More frequently than Taylor — eighteen times — Catharine includes the word "love": "Thy loving wife," "with heartfelt love," "with love I remain," and "I close with love to thee." She uses "affectionately" fifteen times and adds the word "wife" in eighteen closings. She uses "Forever" or "ever" ("Forever thine," "Forever thine own," "As ever thine," "Thy ever affectionate wife") twelve times. She signs seventeen letters "Catharine," but the others are signed

"Catharine A. Peirce," "C A Peirce," or "Catharine Peirce." In one she signs her name "Cat Peirce."

There are several references to religion in the letters. Taylor and Catharine refer to God but never to Jesus Christ. In one letter Taylor hopes that the "Lord will stop the Effusion of blood," but whether he is referring to Jesus or using "Lord" as the translation for the Old Testament name for God is not clear. To them, He is a God "who rules all things," who "is just," who watches over them ("may god keep you in his own"), and in whom they should put their trust ("trust in the God that made us"), but who also "directs" hardships "to humble us." Taylor accepts the "immortality of the Soul," rewards and punishments, and the goodness of God. He is familiar with the concept of atonement and often writes of blood being shed to atone for the sin of slavery. He does not, however, accept the "Divine origin of the bible," does not place "blind faith in [the] book word of god," and concludes that there are theories and maxims in the Bible that are contrary to God's nature. Despite these views, he encourages his children to read the Bible and to judge for themselves its benefits. In March 1865 he sent some "religious books" to Frank and wrote: "I sent them along not because I thought them indispensible but because I wished that the children may not be prejudice against any one creed but contemplate calmly all the opinions expressed and judge for themselves which is right."

There is no reference either to the need for prayer and a personal relationship with God or to a specific denomination. Indeed, Taylor specifically writes that "I have always despised sectarianism of all kinds." In another he states that he is "partial" to Methodists, but the context indicates that the comment is sarcastic. Catharine is far more open about the presence of God in daily affairs. She often writes of putting her trust "in him who can take care of us all" and that she "must trust in the Lord." In one letter she mentions attending a Quaker service in Des Moines with Mary, and several times their daughter Sallie writes of attending Sunday school and that Mary and Catharine were at church.[9]

9. Although by 1860 there were forty-five Quaker settlements in eighteen Iowa counties, the first organized Society of Friends meeting in Des Moines was not until 1868. Apparently, Mary and Catharine attended a service conducted by an itinerant preacher. See *History of Polk County, Iowa,* 682, and William J. Petersen, *The*

The letters include numerous pronouns normally associated with the Quakers—"thy," "thine," "thee," "Friend." Between the founding of Pennsylvania in 1681 and 1720, when Germans began to arrive, Quakers held dominant influence in the original counties, which included Chester and Lancaster.[10] The name "Peirce" can be traced to Chester County through the records of the Nottingham Monthly Meeting and the Kennett Monthly Meeting. Additionally, Taylor's uncle and aunt (Isaac Peirce and Hannah Kirk Peirce) were members of the Society of Friends. It does not appear that Taylor actively practiced any religion, but undoubtedly there was a strong Quaker influence in his life. The only mention of religion in the census records is the 1895 census, which classifies Taylor as "Liberal."

Other than one mention of attending a Quaker meeting, Catharine says little about organized religion. As with Taylor, her use of "thee" indicates a probable Quaker background. While active support for the war effort was strongly discouraged by the Quaker meetings, prominent Quakers, such as poet John Greenleaf Whittier, implored fellow believers to "mitigate the sufferings of our countrymen, to visit and aid the sick and the wounded, to relieve the necessities of the widow and the orphan."[11] In response, Quaker women supported local aid societies or the Sanitary Commission by giving food or clothing or by assisting in gathering hospital supplies.[12] In one letter Catharine mentions the work of the Ladies' Loyal League but does not say that she attended a meeting. Her sister-in-law Mary (who presumably had the same exposure to the Society of Friends as her brother had) did make bandages and fill boxes for shipment to soldiers in a volunteer effort with the U.S. Sanitary Commission.

The collection includes seventeen letters from Sarah (or Sallie), who was nine when Taylor enlisted. She writes of events in the home, of her siblings, and of school, but she also writes of her love for her fa-

Story of Iowa: The Progress of an American State, 4 vols. (New York: Lewis Historical Publishing Co., 1952), 1:729.

10. George P. Donehoo, *Pennsylvania: A History,* 5 vols. (New York: Lewis Historical Publishing Co., 1926), 4:1617, 1621.

11. Samuel T. Pickard, ed., *Life and Letters of John Greenleaf Whittier,* 3 vols. (Cambridge: Harvard University Press, 1975), 2:441.

12. Jacquelyn S. Nelson, *Indiana Quakers Confront the Civil War* (Indianapolis: Indiana Historical Society, 1991), 63.

ther and how much she misses him. She asks him to send her his poems or money for a new dress, and once she asks for an accordion. In typical child fashion, she complains to him about being scolded and asks him to come and take her away. In one she begs him to allow her to get a job so she can earn money for herself, but she will, of course, use some of it to buy clothes for her brothers. Taylor asks Catharine to encourage Sallie to write in order to practice her "letters," but there is another reason. He misses his family and his children greatly, and letters from his daughter are an encouragement to him. "I am very much delighted in getting Sallie's Epistles," he writes.

Historian James McPherson and political scientist Joseph Frank have examined the motivation for Civil War soldiers both to enlist and to remain in the Union army after their initial terms of service. They conclude that patriotism, the fear that anarchy might result from disunion, a sense of duty, and, for some, a desire for adventure were the principal reasons soldiers went to war. Frank subsumes many of these reasons under the heading of "political awareness." For Northerners, slavery was rarely an initial reason to enlist. Indeed, there was often overt hostility to freeing the slaves as an objective for the war.[13] With the issuance of the Emancipation Proclamation, however, soldiers began to write more frequently of their support for or opposition to a wartime objective of freeing the slaves. By the end of the war, that objective had become accepted by the majority of Union soldiers.

Taylor's first letter on August 20, 1862, provides a clue to his motivation to enlist: "the happiness and prosperity of our children depend on the Suppression of this rebellion." In a letter dated September 13, not only does he continue to share his views about ending the rebellion—"labouring to save our country and government"—but he, unlike many other Union soldiers, declares that slavery must be wiped out. He writes, "it is my duty . . . to put down this rebellion and blot out the institution of slavery." This is particularly remarkable because the preliminary Emancipation Proclamation was not issued until September 22.

13. James M. McPherson, *For Cause and Comrades: Why Men Fought in the Civil War* (New York: Oxford University Press, 1997), 6, 18–28; Joseph A. Frank, "Measuring the Political Articulateness of United States Civil War Soldiers: The Wisconsin Militia," *Journal of Military History* 64 (January 2000): 75–76.

Taylor's views on slavery often parallel those of Abraham Lincoln, although there is no evidence that Taylor read any of Lincoln's speeches. In an 1854 speech in Peoria, Illinois, Lincoln proclaimed that there was no "moral right in the enslaving of one man by another," and in Chicago in 1858 he quoted Scripture to advocate against imposing slavery. Taylor, too, views slavery as a moral issue and often refers to it as a "sin" that "swolowed up" "every vestige of human rights." To him it is a "pernicious doctrine" and "heinous curse"—a clear reflection of Lincoln's 1858 characterization of slavery as "wrong." Taylor believes that the nation as a whole is responsible for slavery—"sins of the nation" he calls it. Because the institution had existed since before the Revolution, Taylor concludes that the nation permitted it to "lay and fester" and was now having to make a blood atonement for "its crimes." This echoes a sentiment expressed by Lincoln in April 1864, when he declared that God may will the North and the South to pay for their "complicity in that wrong" by giving to both sections "this terrible war, as the woe due to those by whom the offence came."[14]

Taylor and Catharine use the word "nigger" several times. Bell Wiley concludes in his classic *The Life of Billy Yank* that anti-Negro feeling in the Union army was most prevalent among soldiers from border states or those with limited education.[15] Taylor was in neither of those categories, so whether he had some antipathy toward blacks or was merely using a term common to the vernacular of the period cannot be accurately determined. Occasionally he uses both "nigger" and "negro" in the same sentence and once expresses sorrow over the "suffering of the poor African." In several instances he compares the Negroes to others, proclaiming that "negroes are the best part of the southern population," that "negroes are better than southern whites," and that "eastern officers are less moral and religious than the major-

14. Lincoln speech at Peoria, Illinois, October 16, 1854; Lincoln speech at Chicago, Illinois, July 10, 1858; seventh debate with Stephen Douglas, Alton, Illinois, October 15, 1858; letter from Lincoln to Albert G. Hodges, April 4, 1864; Lincoln's Second Inaugural Address, March 4, 1865—all quoted in Arthur Zilversmit, ed., *Lincoln on Black and White: A Documentary History* (Malabar, Fla: Robert E. Krieger, 1983), 20, 38–39, 56–57, 165, 181.

15. Bell I. Wiley, *The Life of Billy Yank: The Common Soldier of the Union* (Baton Rouge: Louisiana State University Press, 1978), 321–23.

ity of the negroes." Catharine writes approvingly of Lincoln's policies toward the race: "Father Abraham is all right on the Niggar."

Although initial Union policy toward the Confederacy has been described as conciliatory, by the time Taylor was mustered into service (following Union defeats at First and Second Manassas and near Richmond), support for such a policy had essentially disappeared.[16] As early as September 1862 Taylor's letters convey his outrage toward the slaveholder. He has only contempt for slaveholders, who had "been raised in idleness and tyranny" and had "no concientious scruples." In his view, their slaves are of a higher "moral class" than they. That they would have to "either beg, Starve, Steal or work" is of little concern to him.

Of the Confederate soldiers he has a different view. He feels a deep sympathy for them, "many of them crippled for life," who must return to a ruined land. "My heart bleeds for them in spite of myself," he writes.

During the Vicksburg campaign he expresses sorrow for the Southern people who were driven off their land and had their homes destroyed, but he concludes, "they have brought it on themselves." He views many Southerners as "an indolent race of poor whites," an "extremely ignorant" lot who had succumbed to the treason of their leaders. With obvious compassion he writes of "hundreds of the poor creatures" who obtained food from the Union commissaries. Following the assassination of Lincoln his feelings harden and he wishes for "a clean shucking of the South."

As did many soldiers on both sides during the war, Taylor feels a strong sense of duty to join the Union army and to remain with it throughout the war. His earliest letters are filled with his conviction that he has a duty to his country and his children to put down the rebellion. He confides to Catharine that his conscience requires him to do his duty. Once he makes a direct connection between doing his duty and his religious beliefs by declaring that if he does his duty, he will "be cared for by him who attends to all." There is a strong sense of pride in Taylor that he is serving his country honorably. In one letter to his son he writes at length about duty, telling Frank that he did

16. Mark Grimsley, *The Hard Hand of War: Union Military Policy toward Southern Civilians, 1861–1865* (New York: Cambridge University Press, 1995), 67–68.

what he did because it was "the right principle." After two years of service he wrestles with whether to reenlist or to return home: "Selfishness says do not reenlist. Patriotism says reenlist." The war ended before he had to decide.

Taylor's motivation is particularly interesting in light of the probability that he had a Quaker upbringing. In her book *Indiana Quakers Confront the Civil War,* Jacquelyn Nelson notes that a statement similar to the following—"Friends maintain a testimony against . . . bearing arms and all military service"—appears consistently in the minutes of Quaker monthly meetings. Taylor's presumed Quaker background forced him to choose between a belief that slavery is wrong and the Quaker tenet that violence, even to resist evil, is itself evil. Since the 1600s Quakers had expressed concern about slavery, and by 1800 most, if not all, Quakers had freed their slaves. Although Quakers had strong anti-slavery convictions, those convictions did not extend to taking up arms to abolish the institution. Nor was patriotism a justification for military service. One meeting proclaimed in no uncertain terms that "we love our country . . . , but we . . . cannot believe that any cause is sufficient to . . . warrant us in violating what we believe to be the law of our Lord." Nevertheless, men were not automatically disowned if they did serve.[17]

Although the letters do not indicate that Taylor was concerned about violating a Quaker principle by enlisting in the army, there is the strong probability that a Quaker background caused him to justify his military service several times. The letters show clearly that patriotism and disdain for slavery prompted him to serve. In the former regard he was no different from thousands of non-Quakers who joined. Nelson's study concludes that few soldiers stated that freeing slaves was a motivation to enlist.[18] What makes Taylor different is that he writes often that freedom for the enslaved had motivated him to enlist.

Taylor's fervor for the Union cause did not diminish during the

17. Nelson, *Indiana Quakers Confront the Civil War,* 9–10; minutes of the Indiana Yearly Meeting of Friends, 1862, as quoted in ibid., 14; J. G. Randall and David Donald, *The Civil War and Reconstruction* (Lexington, Mass.: D. C. Heath, 1969), 25; Thomas E. Drake, *Quakers and Slavery in America* (New Haven, Conn.: Yale University Press, 1950), 24–25, 197.

18. Nelson, *Indiana Quakers Confront the Civil War,* 38.

war. His letters clearly convey that his motivation for remaining in the army continued to be his desire to put down "this cursed this wicked rebellion," "the Old Serpent of Rebellion." Indeed, he uses the word "rebellion" fifty-three times in his writings and refers to those who support secession as "traitors"—a word he uses five times. Taylor's continued use of the word "rebellion" indicates the depth of his ideological motivation. He uses the word seventeen times in letters written between August 20, 1862, and March 22, 1863 (seven months); twelve times in letters between October 4, 1863, and July 24, 1864 (ten months); and eleven times between January 9 and July 14, 1865 (six months). His fear was that if the South were allowed to secede, the West would leave the Union, and anarchy would result.

It is not unusual for soldiers, especially those who face the difficulties of camp life and the horror of battle, to resent those not in the army. In one letter Taylor verbally attacks those who are not serving. He regrets "that there is no way to compell the cowards and Secish Sympathisers to come to the war." In September 1864 he declares that "selfishness has taken the place of Patriotism" and that "cowardice and averice" are the leading principles. The following month Catharine expresses her disdain for Copperheads by referring to them as "cowards [who] love money more than any thing else." In another letter Taylor complains about the paltry Thanksgiving dinner served to the men. He writes that men at home sent food to the army so that they would have something "to brag about," but in Taylor's view such men "are a set of cowards who are afraid to come out and help us fight."

Few soldiers in the Civil War wrote of their fears, but Taylor was an exception. In three letters he mentions his fears, and in the first, following the battle of Port Gibson in May 1863, he writes that he "did not suffer from that sickning failing called fear." Later that year, however, he acknowledges the emotions that swept over him as he thought of his family prior to battle. He writes of the reality of the danger and the possibility of death but adds that he does not fear death: "love of country and right is strong enough to enable me to face the enemy without murmuring." In April 1864 he confesses in a lengthy letter to his son Frank that he does have a "fear of being killed" but that his greatest fear is to "be called a coward." Taylor, as did many Civil War soldiers, has a particular antipathy toward officers who showed cowardice, and he wastes no words in condemning them to those back in Iowa: Captain Ault and Major Atherton "are both cowards," and "there is men here who swears they will kill [Ault]."

As James McPherson and Gerald Linderman point out in their studies of Civil War combat experience, many soldiers either put their fate in God's hands or bargained to renounce a particular vice if God would spare them in battle.[19] Taylor's ambivalence toward God's protection is captured in the few words mentioned earlier—"feeling certain that if I do right . . . I will be cared for by him who attends to all." His addition, however, "if I get through these trials safe," indicates that doing "right" might not guarantee that he will live through the war.

Taylor writes to Catharine of battles but generally spares her the horror of the sights and sounds of the battlefield. He writes only that he has seen "comrades torn and mangled on the battle field" and is "sick of blood and slaughter." He describes the battle of Port Gibson, the assault on Vicksburg, skirmishes in south Texas, and encounters with Confederates in the Shenandoah Valley (although several pages that describe the battles are missing). In none of his letters does he indicate any specific danger to himself. He was wounded on October 19, 1864, but there is no mention of that incident in his next letter to Catharine. That letter, however, is missing the last page or pages. Undoubtedly, Taylor's reluctance to convey the danger of battle to his wife, children, and relatives was meant to spare them worry.

Pride in his regiment is a frequent topic in Taylor's letters. Civil War units were quite different from those in today's army. Companies and often entire regiments were recruited from the same town or county, and the men served together for the entire period of enlistment, usually three years. The men had a common bond with one another and with the community that resulted in pride in their origin and in their military accomplishments. "The brave 22n" Taylor calls the regiment on the day that Vicksburg surrendered. That pride often extended beyond the regiment to any unit from their home state. "No better or brave men exist than the 22 & 23 rgts of Iowa Vol," he writes in June 1863. Taylor has only contempt for eastern regiments, and he

---

19. McPherson, *For Cause and Comrades;* Gerald F. Linderman, *Embattled Courage: The Experience of Combat in the American Civil War* (New York: Free Press, 1987).

is not hesitant to share that contempt with his Iowa family: "The western Armys are drawn from the bone and sinue of the Population," while the Army of the Potomac "is made up of the most doless and worthless part of the Population." Their officers, he writes, "are superanuated politicians and Editors or something of that kind." As Bell Wiley points out, such opinions ran both ways.[20]

Taylor's letters contain subjects typical of those in letters from soldiers in wartime. There are complaints about the food, lack of mail, infrequency of pay, and quality of the officers. There are descriptions of camp life, the weather, and amusements such as snowball fights, music, and gambling. He tells of the ravages of disease and assures his wife that he is abstaining from alcohol, although in one letter he writes that he "took a good slug of whiskey and slept soundly all night." Taylor's letters are especially vivid in their description of the regions through which he passed. He writes at great length of the people and the quality of the farmland. His narratives of the South are particularly interesting as he describes the suffering of the civilians and the fertility of the soil. The letters of both Taylor and Catharine contain instructions and questions about finances, debts, and other transactions—the day-to-day business that has to be conducted even in the midst of a war.

Catharine's letters are full of news of the children, the weather, the condition of the crops, events and politics in Des Moines and Newton, and the cost of goods; talk of relatives; and her views on the war. Despite her expressions of loneliness and even the use of the word "gloomy" to describe herself, the letters are notable in their attempt to set an upbeat tone. October 1864 was a particularly difficult month for Catharine. There were numerous battles in the Shenandoah Valley that involved the 22nd Iowa, and Catharine expresses the fears that soldiers' wives throughout the ages have expressed. She wonders whether she is "one of the number that [may] have to mourn for thee" and asks God "for help to bare my load of trouble in this my hour of trial. I can not help but feel sad," she writes. Three weeks later she confesses to "being some what anxious all the time" and eight days later again expresses her anxiety as to Taylor's fate.

Catharine tells Taylor about the children's progress in school, their

20. Wiley, *The Life of Billy Yank*, 109.

antics, and their illnesses, but also of her need for them to fill the void left by his absence. She bares her fears that the children could die of disease and her despair should that happen, but she adds, "Do not be uneasy or troubled about us" and twice urges him not "to think I want thee to give up untill the war is over." She also expresses her desires for their life together after the war ends and he returns home: "then we will for get all the troubles and trials we have had and settle down in our old days and be happy." She yearns for them to be able to "settle down in some little corner of this great republic at peace with all mankind and enjoy life as it comes along quietly" and longs to be "in a humble home of our own."

The relationship between Taylor and Catharine is typical of that between many husbands and wives during the mid-nineteenth century. Women were taught to restrict themselves to the domestic sphere, to be submissive and obedient, and to accept their dependence on their husbands. Although the Seneca Falls Convention of 1848 had attempted to enhance the status of women in society, by the Civil War they were generally still barred from politics and even from commenting on public affairs. Mary Massey has concluded that although women would not dare offer political opinions in public, many of their letters and diaries of midcentury contain such commentary because of the personal way they were affected by the war. Their writings include both criticism and praise of political leaders.[21] Catharine is no different from the women of Massey's study. She writes frequently of her dislike for the Copperheads and her admiration for "Old Abe" and the "glorious cause." She also expresses her hope that the Union army will "make a bold strike" to annihilate the rebellion quickly and that "Jeff Daviss and some more of the big ones of the South can be got and hung." Possibly the Quaker influence in her life —a group that allowed women equality in worship—also gave her the boldness to comment on national affairs.[22] Never did Taylor rebuke her for that boldness.

21. Arthur W. Calhoun, *A Social History of the American Family from Colonial Times to the Present*, 3 vols. (Cleveland, Ohio: Arthur H. Clark, 1918), 2:83–84; Mary Elizabeth Massey, *Women in the Civil War* (Lincoln: University of Nebraska Press, 1966), 161.

22. *Encyclopedia Britannica*, 15th ed., s.v. "Friends."

The Civil War also forced women to become more independent and to take a more active role in all the affairs involving the home.[23] Taylor's "progressive" thinking concerning Catharine is best reflected in a letter he wrote to her in September 1862. "I want thee to take hold and do for thyself and use thy own judgment about matters and lirn to lean on thyself so that If I should be called away thee will have a knowledge of business to make a living for thyself." This is a remarkable statement, since women generally were neither found in the business world nor entrusted with the family's finances.

Taylor has great confidence in Catharine's ability to handle financial affairs and gives her a considerable amount of responsibility for taking care of their debts. At first glance, one could conclude that this was done because he was away. But Catharine was living with Mary and Cyrus, and although Taylor sometimes asks her to consult with Cyrus, he tells Catharine to decide whether to sell the livestock, to arrange the details of selling property, and to collect on a judgment obtained against someone who owed them money. In the matter of paying taxes, he leaves the decision to Catharine whether to pay them, keep the money, or let Cyrus handle it.

Catharine's sympathy for the South manifests itself only with regard to the freed slaves and the children. She desires "to be down there to administer to the wants of the poor ignorant freed people." Of the children she writes, "I think a pity of the poor little children but the just must suffer with the unjust if the parents had not been such foul traitors they might still of enjoyed peace and plenty."

In a number of letters Catharine apologizes for having nothing to write about — "I can not think of any thing new to say." Or she writes, "I expect thee thinks my letters are very poor ones." She should not have worried. Any soldier who has been away from his loved ones will attest to the fact that any letter, no matter how seemingly dull to the writer, is a possession to be treasured.

Taylor was mustered out on July 25, 1865. At that time he owed the U.S. government $24.24. Records dated April 30, 1865, state that he was due a clothing allowance of $42 but had drawn $69.14 in clothing since December 3, 1863. Presumably, the amount he owed the gov-

23. Massey, *Women in the Civil War*, xxii; Barbara Welter, *The Woman Question in American History* (Hinsdale, Ill.: Dryden Press, 1973), 159, 161.

ernment was for the value of the clothing he had drawn that exceeded his allowance.

After the war Taylor returned to Des Moines, where he was employed as an engineer. He and Catharine and the children continued to live with Cyrus and Mary at the Washington House. Several times during the war Taylor had written to Catharine that he might open a butcher shop in Des Moines after his return. A letter from an acquaintance in December 1865 mentions such a shop, but there is no indication in city records that he actually had such an enterprise. Taylor served on the organizing committee of the Grand Reunion of Iowa Veterans held in Des Moines on August 31, 1870. William Tecumseh Sherman was the honored speaker. The next year Taylor became city clerk of Des Moines and served in that position until 1879 (from 1874 to 1877 he was also city auditor), after which he worked in the grain business and at a plow factory. Although the exact date cannot be determined, while living in Des Moines after the war, Taylor was the victim of a theft of $600 by a man named Rain. The thief was convicted and sentenced to five years in jail, but he escaped on the night of his sentencing.[24]

On December 19, 1864, Taylor writes to Catharine that he "could be content to wear out the remainder of [his] life in [her] company without any other wish." Although he survived the war, he and his wife would have less than two years together. Sadly, on April 2, 1867, Catharine died while giving birth to a daughter, also named Catharine.[25]

Little is known of the four surviving children born to Catharine.[26] Sallie married James Edenburn and gave birth to seven children. In 1892 she and James were living in Taylorville, Iowa. In 1918 Frank was living in Billings, Montana. Ellis, his wife Mabel, and their daughter Prudence were living at 1357 Pennsylvania Avenue, Des Moines, in 1920. Catharine never married. She was the librarian at the Carnegie Public Library in Marion, Iowa, was active in the women's rights movement, and edited a publication entitled *Women's Standard.* She

24. *History of Polk County, Iowa,* 674–75, 682, 737.

25. The daughter died in 1937. On the death certificate her name is spelled Katherine.

26. An insurance application completed by Frank Peirce in 1895 states that one brother died in infancy. This is the only reference to this brother in any record. Possibly Frank was referring to his sister Mary, who died at about age four.

moved to California about 1918, became the city librarian in Porterville, and died there on April 9, 1937. Prior to her death she was a resident of Mrs. Sauce's Rest Home in the town.

On May 15, 1873, Taylor married Eliza Ann Van Horn in Indianola, Iowa, in a service performed by Reverend Alexander Burns. Eliza was born in 1848, and her family had moved from Howard County, Indiana, to Iowa around 1857. In 1870 Eliza was living in the same ward of Des Moines as Taylor, and perhaps that explains their meeting. The couple, with Taylor's children, established a home at 100 Front Street. In 1876 they were living at 100 Jefferson Street, one block from their previous home. By 1900 five children (Neil, Ralph, Israel L., John B., and Ethel Ellen) had been born to Taylor and Eliza, and the family was then living at 103 Jefferson Street. A 1902 declaration for a widow's pension listed Eliza's address as 101 South Jefferson Street.

Cyrus Milner died in 1881 and was buried in Woodland Cemetery in Des Moines. Neither Cyrus nor Mary is listed in the 1880 federal census, but Mary is in the 1895 and 1900 censuses. At that time she was living in a house she owned free of a mortgage at 1520 Center Street in Des Moines with her niece Catharine M. Peirce—the daughter born to Taylor and Catharine in 1867. Letters indicate that Catharine was living at that address as early as April 25, 1892. Mary died in November 1900 and was buried alongside Cyrus.

After his return from the war Taylor was not in good health. He was deaf in his right ear and had substantial hearing loss in his left. Taylor had mentioned a hearing loss in a letter to Catharine, and she had expressed her concern in a letter dated February 7, 1864. He suffered from hemorrhage of the bowel, a constant cough, catarrh (inflammation of mucous membranes in the throat or nose), and lung problems. He was able to perform limited manual labor until 1877 but was unable to do so after that. In October 1882 he was receiving a pension of $2 each month for the wound to his hand at the battle of Cedar Creek, Virginia. Presumably his poor health kept him from attending the first reunion of the 22nd Iowa Infantry Regiment held in Iowa City in September 1886. By 1895 he had suffered a stroke that severely affected his speech. He was able to get around only by using a cane or crutches. On November 21, 1901, Taylor died at the age of seventy-nine and was buried in Woodland Cemetery, Des Moines.

The cause was listed as chronic diarrhea and exhaustion. At the time of his death he had no life insurance and owned no property. On June 10, 1902, Eliza was granted a widow's pension of $8 a month plus an additional $2 because Ethel, who was under the age of sixteen, still lived at home. The pension was increased to $12 on April 19, 1908.

Eliza died on February 26, 1925, in Las Vegas, Nevada, where she had lived for four months. The cause of death was chronic bronchitis, which she had suffered with for five years. Contributing causes listed on the death certificate were a heart condition, which she had had for ten years, and senility. She was buried in Woodlawn Cemetery. During the last month of her life she was under the care of two town residents who served as nurses. Although it cannot be proved conclusively, she was probably living with Ethel Potthoff, who provided a statement regarding Eliza's condition, including the fact that she had known Eliza for thirty-five years. Ethel Peirce was born to Taylor and Eliza in 1886, so Ethel Potthoff was probably Eliza's daughter. Eliza's affairs were handled by her son Israel, who between 1900 and 1910 had moved to Oakland Township, Alameda County, California, where he was employed as a mail clerk.

Both John and Israel Peirce served in the Spanish-American War. In 1898 John enlisted in Company B, 51st Iowa Infantry. He served at the Presidio in San Francisco and was discharged on November 2, 1899. Israel enlisted in Company D, 49th Iowa Infantry, on May 26, 1898. He was discharged at Savannah, Georgia, on May 13, 1899. In 1920 Israel was a roomer in Lydia Hatch's boarding house at 365 Thomas Street, Pomona City, and at the time of Eliza's death in 1925 he was still living in Pomona.

Missouri

IOWA

● Parkersburg

● Union

Colfax ●Grinnell ● Iowa City
Des Moines ● ● Newton
Vandalia ● ● Davenport
Indianola ● ● Knoxville

St. Paul ●

● Keokuk

ILLINOIS

MISSOURI

St. Louis

Iron
Mountain ● St. Genevieve
Rolla ● RR
Waynesville ● Pocahontas
Salem ●
Pilot
Knob ● Cairo
Springfield ● Houston ● ● Patterson
Wilson's Hartville ● Eminence
Creek West Plains ● ● Thomasville

Pitman's Ferry ●
Pocahontas ●

ARKANSAS

EDITOR'S NOTE. Taylor enrolled in Company C, 22nd Iowa Infantry, on August 2, 1862, at Newton, Iowa, for a period of three years. Seven companies comprised men from Johnson County; there was one company each from Monroe and Wapello Counties, and Company C was from Jasper County. Captain Adam T. Ault of Newton was appointed company commander. The companies of the regiment assembled at Camp Pope, near Iowa City, where they were mustered into federal service in early September. Iowa Governor Samuel J. Kirkwood appointed Colonel William M. Stone as regimental commander. At the time, however, Stone was on parole after having been captured at Shiloh on April 6, 1862, and could not return to active duty until he was officially exchanged. In the meantime, Lieutenant Colonel Harvey Graham commanded the regiment. After his exchange, Stone would serve as regimental commander until he resigned in August 1863 to run for governor. He was elected and took office on January 14, 1864.

In late July Brigadier General John M. Schofield, commander of the Military District of Missouri, informed Major General Henry W. Halleck, commander of the Department of the Missouri, that a large Confederate force was approaching Rolla and that he needed troops to meet the threat. A few days later he told Halleck that "the rebels are rising all over Missouri," and two weeks later he again asked Halleck for reinforcements. Halleck then authorized Schofield to call on the governor of Iowa for two infantry regiments.

Accordingly, the 22nd Iowa Infantry left Camp Pope by rail on September 14 for Davenport. It then boarded the steamer *Metropolitan* and arrived in St. Louis on the eighteenth. The day prior, Schofield had warned Halleck that Rolla, Missouri, was "threatened by a pretty strong force." In response to an order from Schofield, Brigadier General John W. Davidson, commander of the District of St. Louis, ordered the regiment to Rolla. It arrived there on September 23 and went into camp about two miles west of town on the road to Springfield, Missouri. From that date until January 1863 the men protected commissary stores, guarded the railroad, and escorted supply trains.

On January 27 the regiment was ordered to march to West Plains, Missouri, where it joined the 21st and 23rd Iowa as part of the Army of Southeast Missouri. In February the brigade marched to the vicinity of Iron Mountain, where it arrived on the twenty-sixth. It remained there until ordered on March 9 to join Major General Ulysses S. Grant for the Vicksburg campaign.

Taylor's letters to Catharine begin on August 20, 1862.

> Camp Pope
> Aug 20 1862
> Dear Catharine

I am here and have got harnessed in and am well and feel in a great deal better Spirits than I expected to when I left you. We have a beautifule place here to drill in and plenty of good water.[1] We have not yet got to feeding ourselves. We have a Victuallin house that feeds us for 30 cts pr. day and as Uncle Sam pays they do not give us much that will sour on our stomachs but is prety good considering we have boiled beef and vegetables and good bread. The coffee is the hardest of all we get, I suppose that some people would like it, for it woud bear an Iron wedge and so strong that sugar will not sweeten it. This is a curious kind of life for one like me that has always been used to acting as he pleases and would bear no control. If we start to go 20 yards we have a man poke his sword in our face and if we have no pass we must turn back and the etiquett that is in use here is perfectly rediculous to one not initiated into military rules. Stone is our Colnel. I had a long talk with him and seemed glad to see me among the men and promised to come to our quarters and give us a speech to-night. Major is Harvey Graham[2] a sociable and brave officer. He used to live in davenport and sold me the belt and pipe for our mill. He seem to be always about seeing to the comfort of the men. Mrs Ault come down with us but she could get to cut much [illegible] as military wifes are such that officers lower than Generals can not come to camp to stay. I tell you that although a Captain has some authority over his men yet he is responsible for their good conduct and efficiency. I think I will like it very well for I can bear the regulations if I see all others having to submit. We had our election today. Ault is our Captain[3] Murrey 1st Lieutenant[4] and a man by the name of Mullin our 2nd Lieutenant.[5] I have the post of Sergent with the pay of $22 per month and plenty of work to do. You have no Idea of the feelings that is hid in a man by the sight of things here. There is now 8 companys here and we expect this regiment to be full this week. Then after a few weeks drill we will be off for dixie. The news from the south is alarming. Today the confederate is invading Kentucky at several points and Gen Morgan has fallen back with his forces toward Cumberland Gap.[6] Dear Catharine the happiness and prosperity of our Children depend on the Suppression of this rebellion and although you know that I love you and the children as well a man can and will probably have more concern for your present welfare than most men yet your future prosperity is of greater importance than anything else in this world. And if I had any choice I would not come back now if I was at Liberty to return with out seeing the last of this rebellion.

[afternoon] We have had a hot day of it and the drill has made me a little tired. We have to drill 5 hours per day at least no more than that and less if we get tired. I have just received notice of an appointment in the commisarys department where I will not have so much military duty to proform but a good bit more business and the meatings is a great time to me at present and the increase of pay is more. I can not tell what the pay is as it is an office of the regiment and not of the company. Our regiment will be mustered in this week and then I will draw my bounty and an increase of pay which I will send home as soon as I get it for I need nothing but what I have unless it is some towels.

I will be at home next week. Ault got me appointed as a recruiting officer to go after some men for his company with a weeks leave of absence.

Now if anything should happen that I would not get back, I settled with Anthony Minnick and forgot the amount I paid Dr Parks for him which I think was about fifteen dollars. Thee can find out by John Sumpter's docket in the suit where Parks sued Mrs Minnick. My account against Mrs Minns was 145 Dolls and when that is added it will make 160. So they owe me. Anthony acknowledged it was all right.

I want thee to write me on the receipt of this and let me know how thee stood the ride for I have been uneasy about it ever since I left home.

Bill Smith left this morning. He found he could not get an office and so his patriotism simmered down.

I send Cyrus and Mary my love and tell them that all is going well for me and of course for them. Tell Mary not to fret for me for I feel

I will live to see us united and happy. Kiss the children for me and tell them that I want them to be good and that will make me happy while I have to be away. Receive all my love and take good care of thyself. I remain thy affectionat husband.

Taylor

1. Samuel Jones of Company C described the camp location as "at the edge of town, and on a beautiful green."

2. Harvey Graham was a native of Pennsylvania but a resident of Iowa City. He was appointed major on August 2, 1862, promoted to lieutenant colonel on September 17, 1862, captured and paroled at Vicksburg on May 22, 1863, promoted to colonel on May 1, 1864, and served with the regiment until it was mustered out of service.

3. Adam T. Ault was an Ohio native and a resident of Newton when he was appointed captain on August 2, 1862. He resigned August 8, 1863.

4. Neill Murray was a Pennsylvania native and a resident of Vandalia, Iowa. He had been appointed second lieutenant of Company E, 14th Iowa Infantry, on November 4, 1861. He resigned May 24, 1862, and was then appointed first lieutenant of Company C, 22nd Iowa Infantry, on July 25, 1862. He was wounded on May 22, 1863, at Vicksburg and resigned on May 27, 1863.

5. Lafayette F. Mullins was a native of Kentucky and lived in Vandalia, Iowa, when he was appointed second lieutenant on July 25, 1862. He was wounded at Vicksburg on May 22, 1863; he was promoted to first lieutenant on May 28, 1863, and to captain on August 9, 1863. He was wounded again on October 19, 1864, at Cedar Creek, Virginia. He served with the regiment until it was mustered out of service.

6. On June 18, 1862, Union Brigadier General George W. Morgan occupied Cumberland Gap with about 10,000 men. A Confederate advance under Major General Edmund Kirby Smith in August 1862 forced Morgan to evacuate his position in mid-September.

Camp Pope Iowa City
Sep 12 1862
Dear Catharine

I received thy letter and was glad to hear of thy genuine good health and the childrens fine condition And I hope the rheumatism will not hinder thee from getting around. If thee can sell all the stock or fix it so that Cyrus can fat it and sell it and use the money to pay his debts with, thee may as well do it. About the money I paid Van. I paid it for Cyrus and Van promised to credit on the note and he shall either do it or pay thee back the money for I do not propose to pay money for those damd old cattle. And our article of agreement will not compell me to do it and by God I wont do it nor I will not allow him to take any such a drive on me. The 20 I paid him I sued Cyrus for Smith. I never settled with Cyrus for our board last winter but I paid him some sixteen dollars on it. I think thee can find out by asking Cyrus and if he has forgot it is down in my little book. I allow Cyrus to try and make the most out of the things and use it and give thee something to show for it so that if I should not get back thee can have something to go on for thyself. I will try and get home this fall. I may be home next week. The Col told me to day that he expected marching orders soon and did not like to let me off unless I was actually necesseated to go and then for not more than 4 days so I shall wait awhile. I send thee 25 dollars. I have some more but I think I had better keep it for fear we do not draw our state pay before we leave and if we do not it may be some time before we get it and I will need a pair of gloves and some other fixings for winter. We are in the department of Gen Pope.[1] His head Quarters is at St Pauls and it is supposed that he will go north instead of South. We have good news from Washington today. They say that the rebles has got so far north that the Federal lines has closed in on their rear and cut them off and will be likely to capture the whole force.[2] I hope next summer will see me at home and at my occupation again. I want thee to try and keep the things togather until spring and I will either be at home or be in my grave but I do not feel as if I was going to die yet and I feel just as if we were going to be victorious of fraud and wrong and establish our government on the principles of human rights. I want thee to teach the children that justice is the only road to happiness and prosperity and any other course must lead to violence and misery. Although a man may be poor and hard set to get along yet the course of strict integrity will eventually bring him out all right. I want thee to take hold and do for thyself and use thy own judgment about matters and lirn to lean on thyself so that If I should be called away thee will have a knowledge of business to make a living for thyself. I forgot about the oxen. I never paid Cyrus for the oxen and when I talked of going away I concluded not to take them as he wanted to use them and I did not need them so I sent them back. And all right I will write thee again in a few days and give thee some ideas.

Thine affectionately Taylor

1. Major General John Pope had been successful along the Mississippi River in the spring of 1862, but he was soundly defeated by Confederates under Robert E. Lee and Stonewall Jackson at Second Manassas in August. He was then sent to command the Department of the Northwest with headquarters at St. Paul, Minnesota.

2. By September 6 the Confederate Army of Northern Virginia had crossed into Maryland, with the Union Army of the Potomac moving slowly after it. The invasion ended with a Union victory at Antietam Creek on September 13.

Iowa City Sept 13 1862
Dear Catharine

Last night when I wrote I did not know what we would do next but we received notice to cook three days rations and be ready to march tomorrow night by 11 oclock.[1] So thee sees that we are on the wing and I hope when thee next hears of Company C thee will hear nothing to make thee blush. I believe every man of us feels as though we would rather lay down our lives than be defeated. The exitement in the camp is not of the noisy kind but men walk around with their lips compressed and brows drawn down as if they meant it. I do not think we have a man that would leave the rank if he could and the idea of getting into some place where we can help our fellow soldiers seems to be the prevailing wish. The 22nd regiment is a fine body of men and we have the name of being the finest company in it but also bear the name of having the most noisy and mischievous. However we have never of any very had nor I think no dishonest actions in the co yet.

Our 1st Lieutenant[2] a Pennsylvanian left to go home and said that he would call on thee if had time. He is a noble fellow and the finest looking man in the regiment. He and I are good friends and expect to fight it out together. I have written to Ingersole to night. I want thee to consult him with regard to the business as much as possible for I think he has the best view of business of any man I know of although he likes his money prety well but thee must lookout for that and be close for thee does not know. But thee will have to make thy own living from this time on.

Dear Catharine I would like to take thee in my arm once more and have the little children around me and have Mary and Cyrus by our side. It seems to me that my love for you all has increased since I left you but I know it is my duty to stay here and try and be one of the many that God has raised to put down this rebellion and blot out the institution of slavery. If I thought today that slavery could or would exist after the rebellion I would leave the army tomorrow but I believe that the close of this war human liberty will be established on a basis that will give happiness and prosperity to our children and this posterity. While on the other hand if they whip us and succeede in establishing slavery every vestige of human rights are swolowed up in brute force or the aristocracy of wealth and no man however inteligent or worthy if he is not either a brute in physical force or a notable in wealth will be a slave in the true senc of the word. Tell Mary that I want her to be a sister to thee and a second mother to the children and god will bless her through them. I will try and write to thee as soon as I can again. Cyrus can get into this co if he wants to but I can not promis him any position yet although I think in time he may get one.

May god keep you in his own and kiss the children for me. I have been very bussy all day and will have to beat it in the morning again so I guess I will have to close up. I wrote Ingersoll about the Parker sale. You can make any arrangements about it that you pleas. I send up by Col Gardner[3] to have that mortgage sent up. I forgot it when I was in Newton. Thee had better see Ritz Asher and have that judgment against Hurst collected as soon as thee can. The one in favour of Coleman & Ingham when collected is to lift a note that Ingersole holds against me for $60 and I want thee to see to getting it as soon as collected. The one in favor of Mitchell Elis and Co I assigned over to thee and get all the money and keep it.

I have mad out our pay rolls to day to draw our months pay and as soon as we draw it I will send it to thee as I do not need much. Give my love to Mary & Cyrus and keep a good share for thyself and the children.

Thine affty Taylor

1. The 22nd Iowa was ordered to depart Camp Pope for Davenport and then to continue on to St. Louis.

2. First Lieutenant Neill Murray.

3. There was no Colonel Gardner in any Iowa regiment. Taylor is probably referring to Colonel John A. Garrett, who was from Newton. Garrett was a lieutenant colonel in the 22nd Iowa and was appointed colonel of the 40th Iowa Infantry on August 22, 1862 (according to the 40th Iowa history) or September 17 (according to the 22nd Iowa history). The 40th Iowa assembled between September 1 and 22

at Camp Pope near Iowa City. As Garrett would have had to depart the 22nd Iowa to command the new regiment, it is probable that Taylor asked him to see Catharine in Newton.

Benton Barracks St Louis
September 21st 1862
Dear Catharine

This is Sunday morning and after a busy week I concluded to write to thee and let you all know how the week has passed. One week ago to-night we were marched to the cars at Eleven oclock and transported to Davenport. After staying there some 5 or 6 hours we were put on board the Metripolitan [*Metropolitan*] and taken to Keokuk where we arived on tuesday about noon when it commenced raining and rained all night. I was out on duty in the evening and got wet and went and laid in my wet clothes all night in the depot for there was so many of us there being about 3 regiments that we could not get in to a house. So I made the best of it and took a good slug of whiskey and slept soundly all night and have felt no bad effects from it yet except the usual effects of the liquor and to day I feel as if I could stand thunder. After the boat came in on Wednesday morning I and Ault went on board and took a room togather and had a good time of it to this place. We were guarded out of the cabin a part of the time while on bord which made some of the men mad but I seen the nessessity of the order and took it coolly for when there is so many men here must be some regulations or the good of the whole must be forfeited. I have had nothing to grumble at yet and have been treated with consideration at all times and am perfectly satisfied with the service for I find if a man will do his part he will always have friends.

Well we armed Thursday morning and about sun up a man lost his bayonet over board and offered a man a Dollar to get it for him. The man jumped in and dove for it and that was the last we ever seen of him. He was from Monroe Co[1] had a brother in the same Co and left a wife and two children. I thought that it might have been my own case and was thankfule that I was still alive for I had some thought of getting it myself and might have been lost but it may cure me from my venturesome spirit. After we armed and I was detached with 6 men to take care of our stores and was in town untill sunset and after seeing all safe on the wagons I took the horse railroad with 4 of the men and arived in the barrucks about dark. This is the place Fremont[2] fixed up at his own expence for the rendezvous of troops and a camp of instruction for the soldier which if he never done another good action ought to commend him the respect of the wives and relatives of the soldiers. It is about 3 miles from town. The Barrucks or lodgings are long rows of buildings about 32 feet wide and 10 ft high and in appartments large enough to hold 97 men with a room 10 by 16 at the end for the officers and long enough to hold one regiment each and behind each row there is a row of cook houses of the same size with a furnace to cook by and a hydrant to suply all the water wanted to be used with a row of sinks that passes into a sewer to convey of the offall of the camp and troughs on either side of the buildings to convey the water and drawings from the roofs of the houses into the common sewers. There is streets runing between the sleeping appartments and the cooking rooms about 40 feet wide and in front of each row of barracks is a Veranda or piassa 10 feet wide which covers the walk from one end of the Barracks to the others. The whole covers an area of 645 acres and contains several streets with a general centre for business such as sutters stores, Dageuratype galleries, gambling tables, restaurants and shoe shop and stationary store and all that the men needs and some that they do not need. There is no liquor allowed inside the guard nor gamering for money is not permitted but I see some of them at it. There is said to be 15,000 men here now and these buildings are erected to hold 40,000 men when all full. The parade ground for Infantry is in the centre and the buildings all around with the head Quarters of the Commander of the Post at the east end of it where I go every morning to make our morning reports and of cours get to see the big ones. The cavalry parade outside the picket and I have not yet seen them as I have been to busy to go to look at them.

The commander here now is Col Bonivill[3] a man after the fashion of Hudibras[4] or Falstaff[5] and if thee can form an Idea of their appearance I need not describe him. John Horine[6] of our county is adjutant of the post and I do not know the rest of the officers by name. Our men are all out on grand review, the most tiresome thing we have to go through with but as I had to Invoice our goods to day I was excused and took this time to write a letter.

We did not draw our pay from the state and so I could not send thee any more money. I hope thee got the $25 I sent for I have had no letters since I got one from thee before Roge left. I heard he left the day after I wrote to thee through J Shrech. I suppose he stole our blankets and whatever he had in his possesion, the d—d hound.

Niel Murrey came down this morning and tells me that John Sumpter told him that he would take care of my things which has been some relief to my mind as I now know that I will not be likely to get off from the army this fall for I understand that we will leave here on tuesday for Rolla[7] and Springfield. And the Major told Ault this morning that we would be likely to have a fight on the battle ground of Wilsons Creek[8] before 2 weeks as the rebles have concentrated 40,000 men there and we have force enough to meet them. And I think we will be very likely to do it as our officers are the right kind of grit and will not be likely to leave the secish longer than they can get at them. I feel anxious to try my hand and see whether I can do as much as I think I can. I hope we will all do our duty and get rid of this rebellion and once more enjoy the sweets of our homes in peace. I have no instructions to give today. I now trust in thy good judgment to see to our things and when thee is at fault consult either Cyrus, Ingersole or J Sumpter and when ever thee asks my advice I will give it. Kiss the children for me and give Mary and Cyrus my love and take a good share for thyself. I dream of thee every night and thought I was sowing oats and wheat last night and thee sifting looking at me and when I awok it was not so. I am in good heart and as happy as I can be under the circumstances. If I can get my picture taken to day I will send. I will write soon again.

Affectionately thine Taylor

1. This was Noble A. Rogers from Albia, Iowa. His brother, Henry F. Rogers, was captured at Vicksburg and died of disease on January 5, 1865, at Baltimore, Maryland.

2. Major General John C. Fremont commanded the Department of the West with headquarters at St. Louis, Missouri. He was relieved of command in November 1861 and was reassigned to command the Mountain Department, which included the Shenandoah Valley of Virginia.

3. Colonel Benjamin L. E. Bonneville was born in France and graduated from the U.S. Military Academy in 1815. He explored the West for several years and

fought in the Mexican War, where he was wounded. He was breveted brigadier general and served until 1866.

4. A satire written by English poet Samuel Butler in 1663 (part 1), 1664 (part 2), and 1678 (part 3).

5. Sir John Falstaff was a character created by William Shakespeare in *Henry IV*.

6. First Lieutenant John W. Horine, Company E, 14th Iowa Infantry, was from Vandalia, in the southwest corner of Jasper County. At the battle of Shiloh, April 6–7, 1862, the regiment had 236 men captured or listed as missing. Those captured were paroled in the fall of 1862 and returned to Benton Barracks at St. Louis. Horine is not listed as having been captured.

7. The 22nd Iowa departed St. Louis on September 22 and arrived in Rolla the next day.

8. The battle of Wilson's Creek, Missouri, was fought August 10, 1861. The outnumbered Federals were defeated by a Confederate force under Brigadier General Ben McCulloch. Union Brigadier General Nathaniel Lyon was killed, and the Union forces withdrew to Rolla. In September 1862 Confederate Major General Thomas C. Hindman concentrated 10,000 troops near Fort Smith, Arkansas. Any northern movement was precluded when Schofield began to assemble Union forces at Springfield. The 22nd Iowa would remain at Rolla to protect that point.

Sunday night Sep 21/1862
Dear Wife

John Deakin[1] is here and will take this up for me and since I wrote the other we have had marching orders and will leave here as soon as the cars comes in which will be sometime between now and tomorrow noon. We go to Rollo [Rolla]. The Secish is there 10,000 trying to cut off General Herron[2] who is from Iowa from the main thuroughfare of retreat. They have about 40,000 men and as herron only has about 8000 he is endangered of being surrounded and captured[3] and we start to hold the cusses in check until he gets his men around to Rollo. The 21st Iowa Reg[4] went off to-day and there is a Mo. reg here and ours will go in the course of 2 days and I understand that there is about 10 Reg going up by the Iron Mountains r.r.[5] So thee may expect to hear of a fight in a few days where I hope we will give a good account of ourselves and whip the rascals. Now if things all go off right thee will hear from me in a week or two and if I fall why then I am done and thee must trust in the God that made us all who is a husband to the widow and a Father to the orphan. If thee manages things right thee will have enough to live on by a little economy and the children can be schooled out of the public funds but I do not feel as if my time had come yet and I hope to live through this war and be able to take you all to my breast again and that before a great while. I want Sallie to learn her lessons and get a good education and tell Frank that he must grow up to be a man every inch of him and be good and industrious and honest and keep his mind on one thing and he will succeed in all he undertakes. Try to instill in him the spirit self government and a perfect reliance on his own abilities and lean on no one but himself for anything for that with a sound integrity will accomplish almost all things in this world but the preservation of life and that is in the hands of a power higher than man although man can do many things to preserve that or at least to lengthen it. And try to impress him with the love of virtue for that has been a great scource of happiness to me through all my troubles and has given me happiness when the cares of life pressed heavy on me. But for the love of my wife and feeling of security in that respect I would have had many days of happiness and even now I am happy although miles lay between us and a barrier greater than distance intervenes. I mean my duty to my country and my children in trying to crush out this rebellion.

I write this to thee as my convictions after a life of 40 years that has been one of continual warefare for a living and a position in the world and think I have had experiance enough to be able to give some advise if I have not always followed it myself. When I say to be good, I do not mean to be rigid but never to overstep the bounds of prudence and do that that will cause unhappiness to others for by causing unhappiness to others it must universally work an unhappiness to ourselves. That is with regard to our action where a second person is concerned and where ones self is the party injured or to be injured the bounds of prudence should never be oversteped. For if the passions or appetites are allowed to be divested of the guide that reason gives, it must bring pain and unhappiness and as we are social beings and can live seperate from others it must be a source of vexation to those that we come in contact with.

Now I have written this homily for fear that I may get a secesh pill in my stomach that I cannot digest and thee will have something to remember me by. Thee can not imagine the feelings I have on this Sunday evening on the expectation of having to go into battle in the course of the next 24 hours. I have no falterings like I expected to have when I enlisted but feel eager to join in the fray to try and help those that are labouring to save our country and government but I also know that many a brave heart will cease to beat and many a wife and child will morn a Husband Father or Brother slain in the cause that we all are trying to put down before this reaches thee. Oh God why could not man see that the laws that enslave men and make brutes of them must return on their own heads with ten fold violence and for every drop of blood drawn from the Back of the slave by the lash of the driver ten thousand times the amount must strain from the heart of the oppressor. And for every groan wrenched from the wretched father or mother or wife or husband by their inhuman separation ten thousand shrieks will rend the air from those that will be butchered in this most inhuman rebellion and widows and orphans will be turned out in the cold world to sate the avarice of the slave holder and their tyrannical lust for power. Dear Catharine try and instill the love of justice in the minds of our children and preach it to all that thee comes in contact with for injustice and tyrany must bring ruin to those that practice it. The night is growing late and I have been at the desk all day and must now get some rest to prepare for the coming labour and will have to close my letter. God bless thee and the little ones and keep you from all harm. Think of me and write to me often.

Farewell Taylor

1. John Q. Deakin was a judge and surveyor in Des Moines. He also operated a sawmill and owned 780 acres in Polk and Guthrie Counties.

2. Brigadier General Francis J. Herron had moved from Pittsburgh, Pennsylvania, to Dubuque, Iowa, in 1855. He served with both the 1st Iowa and the 9th Iowa Infantry and fought at Wilson's Creek and Elkhorn Tavern (Pea Ridge) in March 1862, where he was wounded and captured. He was exchanged and assigned to the District of Missouri.

3. In August Confederate Major General Thomas C. Hindman, commander of the District of Arkansas, began assembling troops near Fort Smith, Arkansas, in preparation for an invasion of southern Missouri. When he learned of the preparations, Schofield called for reinforcements.

4. The 21st Iowa Infantry Regiment marched from Benton Barracks to St. Louis and boarded a train for Rolla.

5. The Iron Mountain Railroad was chartered in 1851 as the St. Louis and Iron Mountain Railroad. By September 1862 it ran from St. Louis to Pilot Knob. Schofield had reports that Confederates were preparing to move against Springfield and Rolla. The Union army began to concentrate at those two locations, as well as at Pilot Knob.

Head Quarters 22nd Regiment of Iowa Volunteers Camp
Near Rolla
Oct 5th 1862
Dear Catharine

This is sunday again one week since I wrote and three weeks since I received anything from thee. Does thee intend to write or do I not get thy letters or does thee not get mine? I have written every week since I left home. I got a letter from Ingersoll since I wrote in which he stated thee was well but says that Cyrus has had a poorly spell which I am sorry to hear. How does thee get along? Has thee got my letter and picture? I sent them by John Q Deakin from St Louis. He said he would leave them with John Sumpter. I suppose that Joseph has returned before this. If he has get him to take charge of the mill and let the stock remain with some of the neighbors until I return home and do not give thyself any unnessary trouble about the affairs but go along and have the things attended to as though thee intende to have me at home in a short time. If Kuhn has not got home I want thee to have the boiler emptied and the belts put away and just let the mill stand untill I get back. Thee can do as thee pleases with the hogs and make any other arrangements about matters thee thinks best but do not pay out any money on any debts until thee has enough to keep thee and the children. I wrote to Ingersoll and enclose the letter. Thee can read it and it will give thee an Idea of what I want and what situation the things are in and thee can then hand it to Ingersoll and him and thee can make some arrangements in accordance with the instructions contained in it. This is about all concerning business.

We are still at Rolla and do not know when we will leave here. It is rumoured that we will be kept here to guard this post this winter. If so I will get to spend some time at home and if on the contrary we are ordered off South I will not get much time to spend at home nor do I wish to be away when there is a prospect of having anything to do. As the thing stands now I do not think the war will last longer than Spring for old Abe has at last set his foot in the right track and the thing has either got to stop or a total extermination of the southern rebles must take place so I think we are good for a discharge in less than a year. Dear Kate I would like to see thee and the children and if we stay here this winter and thee does not have too much to attend to I intend to send for thee and have you here for a week or two. It would only be 3 day trip and it would be a great satisfaction for me to have thee and the children here to see the movements of war and its accompanying bustle. I like it. It makes a mans blood tingle to see the men drawn out in martial array with their military dress and arms and accoutrements with the drum and fife playing some old and well remembered air. It makes me feel as if I was not more than 20 and as bouyant and full of fire as when thee used to see me round the hills of our childhoods home. But, ah, how different is the cause and its effects then it was the gush of youth with the desire for manhood and its duties and its privileges with a hope for the future that it might be enjoyed in peace and competince. Now it is the fire of stern determination either to sustain our position in the list of nations and be in a position to enjoy life or fall in the attempt. This is a great place that is our camp and its doings and the vicinity around it. We have had preaching here to day. While the preaching was going on before the Cols tent the boys were playing Euchre,[1] some cooking some swearing and some washing so that the whole thing seemed so ludicorous to me that I walked into the tent and commenced making out my company accounts so as to be ready to commence with Monday Morning and nothing behind. I have a great amount of business to do togather with my instruction for a soldier. It occupies all my time. I only get about one hour rest in the day but I do not have to be out much at nights which is a good thing for me. I never felt so well in my life as I have done since I come here. If the land was a little better this would be a good place to live as I think it must of nesessity be healthy for there is not vegitation enough to create a fever and it is so dry that I think weak lungs would not be much trouble. I have been busy all week learning the bayonet exersise and will commence to teach it to our company to morrow and of course will be occupied with it for 2 weeks and will not have much time to write only on sunday until I am done.

Col Stone[2] has not got his exchange yet but he is here. He has not yet taken the command but is expecting to get word every day so that he can. The officers is all very good to me and I have a very good time of it considering the camp life. I am cook for our mess at this time. I have a nigger to get wood, carry the water, grind coffee and run arrands. I do the cooking and see to getting the grubs. I have myself the three officers of this company and the Adjutant of the regiment to mess with. I get fifteen dollars extra for seeing to their affairs which makes $32 per month I am making now. I also get my clothes halled [hauled] when we march and have not got to be at any expence whatever. Our second Lieutenant has come from town with something like the fever to day. I think it is from eating to much trash. We get good living and plenty of it. We have fresh beef 3 times a week and good shoulder smoked side meat, mixed vegitables, beans and potatoes but the potatoes is not like the Iowa potatoes. They are watery and small. The mixed vegitables are all kinds dried and pressed togather into a kind of cake and when boiled they assume the appearance of the genuine article and make good soup. Did thee get the money I sent thee from Iowa City? Does thee know how to direct the letters? Thee must direct them to me to the care of Cap Ault Co. 22 regiment Iowa Volunteers Rolla Mo and they will come. I expect to get the rest of our pay in the course of a few days and then I will send thee home some more. I do not need much money here. I want thee to get thy picture and the two oldest childrens taken and send it to me as soon as thee can. Give my love to all. Kiss the children for me and tell Mary to keep up a good heart.

Thine affty Taylor

1. Euchre was a popular card game that could be played by two to six people. The most popular form was with four people using thirty-two cards — only sevens and above.

2. Colonel William M. Stone was born in New York in 1827. He moved to Knoxville, Iowa, and became owner and editor of the *Knoxville Journal.* He was then elected district judge. On June 10, 1861, he was appointed captain of Company B, 3rd Iowa Infantry, and was promoted to major on June 26, 1861. He was captured on April 6, 1862, at Shiloh while serving with the 3rd Iowa Infantry and paroled on May 30. The exact date of his exchange is unknown, although all prisoners taken at Shiloh were exchanged by November 17. The *Des Moines Register* reported on November 21, 1862, that Stone had been released from his parole and would join the 22nd Iowa. He had been designated commander of the 22nd Iowa Infantry on August 1, 1862, but did not take command until December 4, after his exchange. In 1863 he was elected governor of Iowa.

[partial letter, October 17 and 18, 1862] knows that I like good victuals and of cours I have what I like when I am not to lazy to cook it which does not occur excep on sunday and then all things stops with me unless I am on duty which has not occured but twice since I was in the service. We have a good company. I have never seen a lot of men togather that seemed to like one another so well. Their has hardly been an angry word passed since we left Newton and no Quarreles that amounted to anything at all. We have some sick but the diseases has been from neglect or exposure unnessarely or over eating so that it has not been fatal. We lost one man out of the regiment by drowning, one with consumption, and one with eating too much after haveing the measles[1] which all the deaths out of 970 men in two months of the most unhealthy part of the year which I think is remarkable. Our officers is all good to us and I think do all they can for us to make us comfortable and contented. We had an election this week and it was quite exiting to hear all hands spouting politics just like we used to do at home. We cut H T Winslow.[2] I showed the boys his note to Ingersoll and told them about the circumstance and he only got 19 votes. They Give old Grinnell[3] about 600. I suppose he is elected to Congress from that district. I wish thee to write me how it is. We have the Chaplain of the Regiment[4] boarding with us and thee may know he has a sweet time as he is a Methodist and thee knows how partial I have always been to that denomination. However he bears it with a good grace and I believe if he was not a preacher I would come to like him for he seems like a good fellow enough and seems to take an interest in the men and things about the regt and I guess if he dont pitch in to me we will get along pretty well after while. I am in the mess with the Captn, the two Lts, the Adjutant and the Chaplain and one nigger cook. I oversee the cooking and do the Company Clerking drill a squad in the morning and go out on drill in the afternoon.

I have just stoped writing to get the mail and distribute it. I was in hopes that I would get a letter from home but alas I am doomed to disappointment in this as well as in a great many other things in this world.

Dear Catharine if thee knew how bad I felt every night the mail comes in without a letter from thee thee would certainly write to me at least once in two weeks. I long to see thee and the children but I do not want to leave here and go home until the rebellion is put down and the time will come when we can enjoy ourselves in peace and quietness. Mary seems to think that thee is in such poor health that thee will not be able to do much towards helping thyself. Is thee in any worse condition that thee has been all along? If so I want to know it. If thee is not I want to know it. If thee is not able to do any labour thee can educate the children which will be one of the first things to do. Any how take good care of thyself I again repeat and let the things go if it exposes thee to attend to them. For I do not want to loose thee now when the light is beginning to dawn that I feel sure will give us all happiness.

The weather is mild here. It is so much like it is in Iowa in the fore part of Autumn. We have had two nights that made a little Ice and three or four frosts but the weather is still quite warm. This is a poor county, however it raises fruit. We have had peaches, apples and fox grape and all the chicken grapes one could wish. Tell Cyrus if he was here now he could make enough of wine to make him rich. If a man had wine here he could have all the money that the officers get.

I will stop now and wait untill to morrow night to finish this and may be something new will turn up to write about that will be interesting for I consider this a poor letter so far as I have not got anything from thee and I am in a poor fix to write a good letter for things pass unheeded that at other times would be a scourse of gratifycation and delight to me.

Saturday night 18th. I have to inform you of other things that has happened since I commenced my letter. Co. B. has left us to day to escort a train of 100 wagons to Springfield where Gen Herron has his head quarters but he and Skofield are further south and have been giving the rebels fits.[5]

We have good news to-night from the south. We get the news ever night by telegraph here and know all that is going on. If the union forces meets with no reverses we will not be likely to be needed longer then spring which I most hartily pray for. The regiments that lay around this post has began to mov off. The 33 Mo and the 21st Iowa left last night or rather this morning for salem a town about 35 mile south east of this. The 6 Mis Artilery left for springfield yesterday[6] and a part of the Dare Devils left yesterday in pursuit of 200 rebels that was seen makeing their way south at Waynsville the night before. We move on Monday to town and I suppose we are stuck for this winter and maybe during the war as this is the most valuable Post in the western department. We are all in good health. What men were in Hospital are discharged and no more getting sick and we all are in first rate spirits. If it was not for the Deer ones at home I would be as happy as a king. I am looking—Just [as] I began to write this sentence I got thy letter[7] and was glad to hear from thee and it has made me feel two Hundred per cent better than I have for two weeks. If Rog only stole the old tools and what he could take of that kind I do not care so much now but if I live to get back and can find out wher he is I will bet he returns them and some more. I must try and keep myself cool for there is no use in fumeing about it now for I have other things to think of that is more nessessary than money or property. I think John Sumpter will be a good friend to thee and will materially assis thee with advice for I look upon him as [last page missing].

1. Noble A. Rogers drowned on September 18, and Joel A. Priest died of disease on October 10. Priest was an Iowa native and Ashland resident when he enlisted August 7, 1862. The third soldier cannot be identified.

2. Horace Spencer Winslow was a lawyer originally from Vermont. He moved to Jasper County in 1856 and in 1862 was elected district attorney of the Sixth Judicial District.

3. In October 1862 Josiah B. Grinnell, a Republican Congregationalist minister from Iowa, was elected to the U.S. House of Representatives from the Fourth District. He served from March 4, 1863, to March 3, 1867.

4. The regimental chaplain was Richard B. Allendar, a resident of Knoxville, Iowa. He was mustered into federal service on September 9, 1862, and resigned on July 19, 1863.

5. On September 14 Herron was ordered to take four regiments from Rolla and march to Springfield. He then skirmished with Confederates in the vicinity of Cassville and Pineville, south of Springfield.

6. The 21st Iowa and 33rd Missouri left Rolla on October 18, 1862, for Salem, about twenty-five miles distant. Taylor is probably referring to Company F, 2nd Missouri Artillery. Incomplete records indicate that Company F was organized at Benton Barracks near St. Louis and was stationed in the vicinity of Rolla in September. In November this company was stationed at Hartville, along with the 33rd Missouri and 21st Iowa.

7. The letter from Catharine was not found.

> Head Quarters 22 reg Iowa Vol Inftry
> Rolla Missouri Nov 4th 1862
> Dear Catharine

I recived yours of various dates last evening[1] and am very much troubled about thee but I hope that ere this reaches thee, thee will be enjoying a better state of health. If it could be so I would like to come home a few weeks but I fear under the present state of things I will not be permitted to leave for some time yet as our regiment has a great deal of guard duty to proform. And unless some other regiment is quartered here it must continue untill the south Western army under Schofield advances as far south as the Arkansas River so that their supplies can be shipped to them by water.[2] I have just come back from a trip west. We went as an escort for a train 90 wagons and 600 mules going to Springfield. We were relieved from the command at Waynesvile[3] in Pulaski County and scorted another train back. It is not likely that we will have any more fighting in this state as we have got the rebels all rid out of these parts except now and then a small squad trying to pass south from Northern Missouri and they have to keep out of the way or Col Glover[4] lights on them with his cavalry and either kills all or takes them prisoners. I think that hereafter Government will establish military posts in all the Teritory and hold it as the army advances and will probable not have any more battles except where the rebels still continue hold large forces. I am well except a cold I caught about two weeks ago which I almost have got rid of and feel about as well as ever only low spirited about thee. I made out our Pay Rolls last night and we expect the paymaster here to pay us this week which I hope he will. I will send thee home the money. I have not had any money for nearly 2 months. I loaned what little I kept for myself to the sick boys to buy things to eat and as they never got it I concluded to confine myself strictly to Uncle Sams supplies for a living and find it just as good as if I had every thing I seen. So I will not keep much money for myself. I will have to get my boots half soled. I still wear my old boots and they look as if they would last me another year. My double breasted Jacket comes in good play now as Govt gives us none. I will have to buy me a pair of gloves to stand Guard in for I have to officiate about onc in two weeks in that duty and the nights are cold. We had a snow about 4 inches deep but it went off in two days and the weather has been fine ever since. The country west of here is the d—dest country I ever seen. It beats the worst mountains of Penna for roughness and poverty. There is not 10 acres of tillable land in anyone place for 125 miles and god knows how much further. As for the sunny South it is all in my eye. The weather here is just like Iowa so far and I think when the rain comes on it will be a great deal worse. We hear that Maddison Pearson[5] was sent for by the

Captain he enlisted with and then played sick and got a discharged. I hope to God the neighbours will run him out of the county. I have no mercy on any such men. Cap Ault and myself is just going to the Election to town this morning to see what kind of a set they have here. I want thee to write me often for thee does not know how I long for a letter from home. If I could hear every 5 or 6 days a line at least once a week. I will write again on Sunday. Give my lov to all and kiss the children for me. Farewell.

> Thine affty, Taylor Peirce

1. These letters were not found.

2. On October 22 Schofield began an advance into northwest Arkansas. Within a few days the Union army controlled the region north of Fayetteville. Fearing the possibility of a Confederate advance, though, Major General Samuel R. Curtis, commander of the Department of the Missouri, ordered Schofield to withdraw in order to defend Springfield, Missouri.

3. Waynesville is twenty-eight miles southwest of Rolla.

4. Union forces in the District of Rolla, Department of the Missouri, were commanded by Colonel John M. Glover from Knox County, Missouri. He was appointed colonel on August 5, 1861, and organized the 3rd Missouri Cavalry. Forces at Rolla were commanded by Lieutenant Colonel Harvey Graham. They consisted of the 22nd Iowa Infantry, four companies of the 3rd Missouri Cavalry, the 9th Missouri Cavalry, and three batteries of the 2nd Missouri Artillery. Eight companies of the 13th Cavalry, Missouri State Militia, were stationed at Waynesville.

5. No one by this name is listed in either Jasper or Polk County. It is possible the individual is M. Pierson from Polk County. He was a farmer and would have been age twenty-nine in 1862.

Head Quarters 22nd Regiment of Iowa Volunteers
Rolla Nov 9 1862
Dear Wife, Sister & Brother

I received your most welcome Letter of this day week[1] and you can not conceive how it elated me. Although Catharine has not wholly recovered yet I hope by careful attention to herself she will so far recover that she will ceace to be a burthen either to herself or you. You say that she has had no nurse. Why is this? I am sure that she might as well have for she can certainly get enough out of the things there to pay one. I do not wish you to think that I find fault with any thing that is done but Mary has so much to do and withall is not very stout.

I think she ought not to have so much to do. I did not intend for Catharine to be a burthan to you. I only wanted a place for her to stay and keep the children while I was away. I can make enough to keep her without you worrying yourselves more than is nessessay to keep her for I thought by letting my business all stop and letting her stay with you and use my means that you would all be happier and it makes me feel bad for us to be troublesome to you. There is a judgment I signed over to her against Alf Hurs for some 34 dols that she ought to collect and that would last her for money untill I get mine which I expect to in a few days as Col Stone told me last week that the money was on the way to pay us off and we have had our pay rolls sent to us and all made out.

The judgment I speak of is one I got from T Mitchell and is in Ashleys hands and if she will write to Ashley about it I think she will get the money. Now although I am away from you yet I feel it will not be long untill I will be at liberty to return and spend the remainder of my life in peac and quietness and then I think things will near a brighter aspect than they have done for a time past. Marys letter[2] was full of gladness to me for it spoke of plenty in Iowa and where there is plenty there must be some comfort. If you would once travel through this desolate and barran region made more desolate by the ravages of war and see the misery want and squallid poverty of the most of the inhabitants here you would feel joyful that you lot was cast in other lands.

My dear ones, for dear to me you are and how very dear you were I never felt so vividly as have done since I have been in this service. How glad would I be if I could take every shade of trial and sorrow from your paths so that we could togather walk down the path of life to the final close where the sorrows and troubles of this like end in an eternity of rest.

How glad it makes me feel to hear from you for night after night where all the camp is full of spirits reading letters from their friends I set lonesome and seem as if I had nothing in common with the rest of my comrades. So write often. If you could write me twice a week I would feel the better for it.

This is a most splendid Evening and all the camp is full of life and joy. We have had a quit Sunday. I have been to meeting to hear our old Chaplain preach And I must say that I have nothing to say against his sermon which is something for me to say. He made a very pilosopical speach speaking more to mens understanding of right and wrong than a blind faith in book word of god and he also made a good prayer, which has not often been my lot to hear. He divested it of all that superabundance of hell fire so in fashion with men of his stamp and was a pure suplication for our country and her soldiers.

I have had a good dinner to day. Made it myself and know it was all right. We have a little sheet Iron stove in the tent and as it was sunday we concluded that two meals pr day would do us. We got fresh beef yesterday and I made a beef stake and onions and had a baked apple pudding and sweet potatoes so you may think we all feel good over it. I tell you now I am getting my name up for cook if nothing else. I am still messing with the Captain and assist in the cooking and act as clerk for the company and am getting now about 33dl pr month [illegible]. Atherton[3] our former Adjutant has been promoted to Major and is boarding with us. He is much of a gentleman and is very kind to me and in fact all the officers is good to me and treat me with every respect due me and more too.

We will have an adjutant to appoint for the regiment now and may be something will grow out of it to my advantage but of that hereafter.

I am very well. Never was in better health in my life and have plenty to do. I think we will stay here all winter as the officers is sending for their wives. Mrs Ault is expected here in about two weeks and the major has sent for his so I expect there will be a good bit of fashion here this winter. We are looking to have to go west again in a few days with stores and as soon as we do I will drop you a line with the time of our return noted. Our company has 13 sick, two in the hospital and the rest able to go about. Not much the matter but overeating and some pretending to keep off duty for I tell you there is shirks in the army as well as anywhere.

As to my business affairs just let them stand untill I get back for unless I could be at the helm I do not expect in either Cyruss or Catharines state of health they could make much out at putting them along and I will have some money and then my things can be fixed up and I feel that I will be at home in the spring at least before the year is out. I know that this is not much of a letter for my mind is so constantly ocupied with the rebellion its opporations and it result that I am not in a situation to give any business advise but if Cyrus Can use any thing of mine that is there to his advantage let him do it. For the present hour only belongs to us and we know not what a day may bring forth.

My children the dear little things how I would like to clasp them to my bosom and sit and Sing Rogs Wife and Will Wastle [Willie Wastle] to them again. Tell auntie that she must learn Sallie to sing the Watchers [A Lass W' A Tocher] and Frank must sing Sctts wha hae [Scots, Wha Hae][4] and the two must sing the Star Spangled banner for me when I come back.

And oh teach them the rule of right and bid them to mind that although they may want many things yet others have rights that they must respect. Try and train thy young that virtue is the only true path to honor position and happiness. Teach them all thats manly good and fair and train them for the skyes.

You have no idea how changed this military service has made me. They all say that it is all that ever tamed the wild ass of Jasper.

I do not feel like doing any thing but trying to put down this rebellion and bringing our Country to a state that her citizens can again enjoy peace and prosperity.

I have just been out to roll call. I suppose you know something of the routine of duty by this time. The Drum and Fife plays the tattoo.[5] Imediately after they all collect for roll call before turning in for the night. Our boys are a gay set and such times for fun as they have. Poor fellows they do not seem to have a care for the future. To enjoy the present is for the most part the order of things. It is laughable to see them enjoying their meals. It seems all that some of them thinks about. They will get up and cook and eat in the morning then hurry the cooks at it again and by 11 oclock eat again and by 4 in the afternoon at it again and after dress parade[6] eat more. The eating is sufficient of itself to have the whole regiment in the hospital but their stomachs is very accomodating and after lying until morning the put them through again. The other morning one of our men a type of the hog comes in to our tent sick and wanted me to let him have something to eat. I knowing the fellow I refused to let him eat as he could get the same in his own mess if he would cook it. He went out looking as if he would never get enough again especially while sick in a short time. I had occasion to go to the sutters[7] when I found my friend leaning on the counter with two pies one in each hand to lazy to stand up first taking a bite of one piece and then off the other and winding up with a piece of cheese large enough to do me 3 day. So I felt my concience cleared of starving the poor sick creature and I have seen those that were on the sick list eat for two hours and then go to their quarters groaning, but these are only the shirks. We have many good men and this is the place to find them out for those that are men, it seems to dvest them of all else but their manliness and those that are not seems to loose all the principle they had.

If this war was over, I think there will be friendships formed here that will last through all time. It is in camp that men find out true friends and a similarity of situations and sympathies seem intuitively to draw men nearer to one another (of cours there is and will be exceptions). But as I said if this war was over I think men would be likely to enjoy one anothers society at home to a greater degree and with more satisfaction than before they went into the army. However it may be oweing to all being bent upon the same course that brings them closer here than they were at home and it might be that after they would return that they would naturally fall back in the old channels but I think not and I hope not for it is a great pleasure to receive and give sympathy to and from those we respect, and many acts of kindness are preformed here that would not be thought of at home.

This is sunday evening 10 oclock and I blieve I will wind up untill tomorrow for I feel as if I would like to write something more for I know this is a poor letter although I am in good spirits and contented. I can not get my mind on things that I think will be interesting to you and may be by tomorrow I will get tuned up or down so that I can put it on paper. I intend to write to Aunt Susan and see what news she can give me for I think the old dame will try and give me something of the news of the neighbourhood. I see by the paper Lord Lyons is in Washington.[8] It may be the government heads will stop this rebellion now as I see that many of the States have gone Democratic at the Election.[9]

Oh My Dear Wife I commence to write again this evening. I do not know wheather I am in any better condition to write this Evening or not. We have word this evening of the removal of Genl McClelland[10] and report of many changes to be made in the Cabinet. What this is all for I do not know but it does seem to me that there has been a lack of energy displayed somewhere. Where it is I can not tell for I am not conversant with the manner and the labour required to move large armies and therefore am not qualified to judge or hazard an opinion. We also hear to night of the removal of Col Millar[11] from the command of the 28th Iowa. Whether it is time or not I do not know but I do know that he was no more fit for the possisition than a dog and I will be glad if some more of Kirkwood[12] purps should meet with the same fate for Instance T G Smith and all other political appointees.

I have an Idea that the power that the Republican Party has wielded has made them so corrupt that it needs a purging to qualify it to manage the affairs of the government with propriety. So far this war has been a cource of revenue and little to the leaders of the people regardless of right and in which they have lost sight of the vital principal that the government stood upon and proceeded to fill their pockets and gain power.

For every day I see men in possitions that they either cannot fill or fill with disgrace to themselves and the cause which they pretend to fight for. And Whenever the time comes they must be huried from their possition with everlasting infamy for the right must triumph.

Nov 19th

Novembers wind howls oer the hills
The drifting mist rides down the sky
Our troops in Camp are Idle still
But still their Patriot hopes are high
Oh Would to God that we were free
To Spread abroad our banner fair
Then would expectant nations see
What freeborn men could do and dare.
But the welcome order soon will come
To March; then shouts will send the sky,
The marshaled host the sounding drum,
The horse, and horsemen, rushing by,
The bugles blast the drums long roll,
The squadron wheeling, into line,

Are Sights, and sounds, that fires the soul,
And vigour, lends to Manhoods prime
That Banner broad whose silken fold,
Our Fathers fought and bled to rear
Whose stars and stripes has oer us rold
Is still to every freeman dear.
The eagle the emblem of the free
Poised on the field of azure hue
Still loftur yet his flight shall be
In calmer skies of purer blue

You see I am still confident of the final sucsess of our arms and our principals. [last page missing]

1. This letter was not found.

2. This letter was not found.

3. John B. Atherton was a native Pennsylvanian and resident of Knoxville, Iowa. He was appointed adjutant on August 22, 1862, and was promoted to major on September 17, 1862. He was wounded at Vicksburg on May 22, 1863, and resigned June 8, 1863.

4. "Sic a Wife as Willie's Wife (Willie Wastle)," "A Lass W' A Tocher," and "Scots, Wha Hae" were three songs by Robert Burns. "Willie Wastle" was written in 1792 and was about a farmer's wife. Burns wrote "A Lass" in 1797 to accompany an Irish melody by the name of "Balinamona Ora." He wrote "Scots" in 1793 to celebrate the battle of Bannockburn.

5. Tattoo is an evening signal by drum or bugle to call soldiers to their quarters.

6. Camp life began with reveille at about five or six in the morning, followed by breakfast call. At about 8 A.M. drums or bugles signaled assembly for guards and details. This was followed by drill, lunch call, free time, more drill, and then retreat. Often retreat included a full dress parade in which uniforms, leather, and brass were inspected. Supper followed retreat, then tattoo, and finally taps.

7. Sutlers accompanied both the Union and Confederate armies and sold items not readily available through regular channels, such as fruit, stationery, pens, shirts, and liquor. Often the sutlers charged exorbitant rates, and their tents or wagons were favorite targets of soldiers who seized an enemy encampment.

8. Richard Bickerton Pemell, Lord Lyons, British minister to the United States, had been instrumental in negotiations over the *Trent* affair. On November 8, 1862, the Union warship *San Jacinto* stopped the British steamer *Trent* and removed two Confederate diplomats—John Slidell and James Mason. A crisis with England was avoided when Secretary of State William Seward ordered the two diplomats to be released.

9. In the 1862 election the Republicans lost in New York, Pennsylvania, Ohio,

Indiana, Illinois, and New Jersey, for a net gain of thirty-four Democratic seats in the House of Representatives. Nevertheless, the Republicans retained the governorships of seventeen states and gained five seats in the Senate.

10. Major General George Brinton McClellan succeeded Winfield Scott as general-in-chief of the Union armies. In the spring of 1862 he led the unsuccessful Peninsula Campaign to seize Richmond. He was replaced, but after the Union army was defeated at Second Manassas, he again assumed control and fought the Confederate Army of Northern Virginia under Robert E. Lee to a standstill at Antietam Creek. When he failed to pursue Lee vigorously, Lincoln lost patience and replaced him with Major General Ambrose Burnside on November 7, 1862.

11. Colonel William E. Miller, a Pennsylvania native and Iowa City resident, was appointed colonel of the 28th Iowa Infantry Regiment on August 10, 1862. He resigned March 13, 1863.

12. Samuel J. Kirkwood was born December 20, 1813, in Maryland, was admitted to the Ohio bar in 1843, and moved to Iowa in 1855. He was elected governor of Iowa in 1859 and to the U.S. Senate in 1866. He served a second term as governor in 1875 and in 1881 became secretary of the interior.

> Head Quarters 22 regiment Iowa Vol
> Rolla Nov 13/1862
> Dear Catharine

Col Stone is going to leave for Iowa this morning and I am going to send this by him. I have a letter partly written but I do not wish to send it until I get it finished. I am well and doing well. If Col Stone can he will call and see you and can tell you all about me and what I am doing and my future prospects. He is much of a Gentleman and is a splendid talker. If you can get him interested enough to take an interest in anything he will talk you all blind. He will not come back again untill he is exchanged and I suppose that we will stay here all winter. We have got a Major now and he is in Command. Our Lt Co¹ is in command of the post here and I suppose will remain so untill the regiment is removed. I want you to tell the Col all the words you wish to send to me and for there is sorry things that you can tell better than you can write I wish you to write me often for I feel very lonesome and when I can get a letter I feel better. I am still liveing with the Captain and clerking and cooking and drilling and doing all other things that is needed and am getting well paid for it and feel contented and happy. Give my love to Sallie and all the children and tell Mary that I shall never forget her for what she has done for me. And tell Cyrus that any thing he can use of thine to do it and if ever I get home he can allow me for it and if I do not live and thee can settle for it. This as all now as I am in a hurry so I remain

> Thy affectionate husband
> Taylor Peirce

I wish you would send me some postage stamps as I can not get them here.

1. This refers to Major John B. Atherton and Lieutenant Colonel Harvey Graham.

> Camp of 22nd Iowa Vol
> Rolla Missouri Nov 26 1862
> Dear Catharine

I commence again this evening to write thee again. When I will finish it I can not tell as I write when I have time and set down my ideas as they come along.

There is no new opperations in millitary matters with us nor is there any thing new with me. I am still in my old avocation Cooking drilling and clerking. I expect to quit the cooking and clerking in a few days as I find that I have too much to do now the weather is getting cold and my health is not quite so good as it has been although I am better than I usually am in the commencement of the cold weather. We have a good time of it here. We have nothing to do but cook and eat and get wood except about two hours a day we go on drill. We live pretty well. We have fresh beef ham bread fruit and potatoes and all other things needfull for our support. Our company sold $17 worth of over plus rations the other day and purchased dried fruit with it so we will live fine untill that is gone and by that time we will have some more to sell and we then can buy something else.

I am looking for a letter from thee this evening. It has been almost two weeks since I received one and am getting anxious about thee and the rest for when it goes over a week without getting one I fear there is something wrong and imagine all manner of bad things that keeps my mind so exited that I can not rest. So I wish you would write me every Sunday and while we stay here I can get them in about four days.

I am very well satisfied here except I am anxious to get this rebellion crushed and all the time we lie Idle here seems as so much time wasted but it maybe all for the best. We have cheering news now by the papers. We hear Burnside[1] has taken his way straight to Richmond and intends to fight his way through. We also hear that our forces has been makeing some important moves in the South and that there is a union Brigade forming in Alabama[2] and that the rebles are fleeing from the wrath to come. The Negroes is forming in various places and the thing must soon close up which I pray god it may. We are expecting Col Stone back again this evening[3] and we may move to St Louis. There is however nothing definate known about it.[4] We are much pleased with our new Major and think we are the most fortunate regiment in the field in the way of good and kind officers. I think in my last I wrote you that I was going to have a turkey roasted on Sunday for dinner and was going to have a lady for dinner. Well I had the turkey. You ought to have seen me with my sleeves rolld up stuffing the turkey. I got two onions and some light bread and pepper and went in. After I got it boiled till it was tender. I took him out and stuffed him and put him into a pan and into the stove he went and after he was done good and brown I called for dinner and the lady came and after the introduction was over I pitched in and carved and helped the guests and from the way they eat I come to the conclusion that I was some of a cook. The old Chaplain presented me with Three dollars as an earnest of his friendship. He is a good old man and is now out hunting trying to get another turkey and I reckon I will have it to cook if I will do it and if he asks me I am sure to go in.

I think one reason that I am not so well is that I have got billious[5] and cannot get any whiskey. I told the Surgeon about it to day and he sent me up ½ gallon but the steward set it down to do something and some one stole it and so I had to go without. I tell you it was a sore blow on me for my mouth was set for it and to loose it just as I thought I had it was too much for poor human nature to bear and you may believe I show some of it the first time I have been real mad since I come here.

There is a gay old time in camp to night. The violin Tamberine and bones are going it. The men are all enjoying themselves to the utmost. While I set here and write I hear the shouts and laughter of the men just as if they had no care but to be sad. They are a joyous set of boys and one to hear them and see them in their frolics they would think they never thought that they were on their way to mix in deadly strife where many a one might lay down his life ere another month rolls around. But so it is with human nature. No one thinks that he may be the first and all look forward with high hopes and a confidence in the future that cannot be shaken.

Mrs Ault has come but I have not seen her yet. But I must stop now and see if she knows ought of you but I expect not for self is the crowning principle with her and Doc too. So Il quit untill to morrow night.

Nov 30. I received thy letter of the 19th[6] last night and was glad to hear that thee was getting better for I have passed many sleepless night on thy account. But I am sorry that thee is so desponding about the recovery when thee ought to try and keep up thy spirits for thee has passed through much spells and has recovered and I hope thee will again. For the future looks bright to me if I can keep thee to enjoy it with me but O how dark without thee for thee knows that my whole life has been cheered with thy love and companionship so I conjure thee by the love I bear thee and the love of thy children to cheer up and rise above despondency. Mary wrote me[7] that the doctor said thee would be as well as thee had been and if thee will only keep up good heart all will be right. I want thee to write often once a week anyhow and if thee will only keep up I think I can get a furlough in January to come home a while. I did not want to go home untill next fall if the war continued untill then for it will cost me considerable and I want to save enough of money to fix us up when I come home and the men coming home to spend a few days and then having to undergo the hardship of parting again would give neither of us much enjoyment.

I got a letter from Rorabough last night.[8] He says that he is ready to pay what he owes thee but he thinks I have not used him right by charging him 75 cts for sawing when I agreed to saw for 60 cts for him. Now thee recollects the bargain. I was to saw for him and credit him and if he paid the money I was to saw for 60 cts and if he paid in produce at cash price it was to be 60 cts but if I had to take produce at the dicker price I was to have 73 cts. He also says that I have a charge on the book for 75 feet and 80 feet and have charge him \$2 32/100. I expect that he thinks it is for sawing and I suppose that it was for lumber. I let him have out of my own logs which would amount to that much exactly. Thee can do as thee pleases about taking Penticos note as thee has the Book assigned to thee and the note will not be an off-sett against the account. At any rate there is $14 of it that Shreck was to pay and I told Rorabough that I would not pay that nor the interest on it and if he pays in money thee can reduce 13 cts per hundred feet off of the sawing bill and if he wants more for his produce than thee can buy it for at cash thee need not take it. I will write to John Sumpter and thee can also write to him and have it fixed up to suit thyself. I do not want thee to expose thyself this winter in any way and try and regain thy health for I feel as if this war would be at an end so that I will be at work again next summer.

Tell Sallie that if I could get anything for her I would send her a present for being so good to her mother but there is nothing in this country for a person to get worth sending. So she must get a kiss from thee and Aunt Mary and that must do her untill I come home or can get something to send her. Tell Frank that he must learn his lesson and hurry and grow to be a man so that he can help pap to fight rebles or do anything else that there is for him to do.

From what thee says about the little one it is not probable that he will live unless thee gets better but if you can get him along untill warm weather he will be likely to get along. I do not feel the same love for him now that I do for the other children. I suppose it is because I have never been with him any[9] and of course I have not the same cause to love him that I have for the others. Such is human nature.

I have not got my pay yet nor do I expect to get it before the 9th of January now for the pay master has not come round and they think he will wait untill the end of this year when he will settle up for the whole time we shal have been in the service and as soon as I get it I will either send it or bring it. The Major told me yesterday that if thee did not get better by that time that I should have a furlough for 20 days but it will cost me nearly $30 to get home and back again and that would do the more good and bring thee more comforts than the mere enjoyment of my company for a few short days with a certainty of my having to leave thee again. Mrs Ault is here spreading herself and is the laughing stock of the company and the greater part of the regiment. She puts on the regular bawdy house airs and receves the attention of all that class of men that there is among the officers. We hear bad tales about old Shays and her at Newton. They say there that he has taken docs place and the better class have quit associating with her. I have quit living with the Captain for I did not wish to wait on her and so I quit and of course lost my surplus salary but $13 per month is not enough to buy me to wait on a whore. Doc is getting very unpopular here. He has been at his old trade playing off on his friends and lost the confidence of every officer in the regiment. However he has always used me well and I do not wish you to let this out either injure him or his wife and to get me into trouble.

I have some notion of trying to get the adjutancy of the regiment. I can get a petition with 100 siners for it to old Kirkwood and if Ingersole[10] and Frank Allen[11] would do anything for me I could get the place but I do not know whether it would pay for the trouble or not. If I do I will pitch in tomorrow and make the move and have all ready again Col Stone gets back. This is about all I can think of to night and as I have got the stamps now you may look for a letter often. Give my love to Mary and tell her that I can not tell her on paper how much I owe her. My love to all and write soon.

Taylor

1. By General Order 182, November 5, 1862, Burnside replaced McClellan as commander of the Union Army of the Potomac. He advanced south toward Fredericksburg, Virginia, and on December 13 launched a disastrous attack there against Lee, whose army occupied strong positions on the heights overlooking the town. He was relieved in January 1863 by Major General Joseph Hooker.

2. The 1st Alabama Volunteer Cavalry Regiment (Union) was organized at Huntsville, Alabama, in October 1862. This may be what Taylor is referring to.

3. Colonel Stone would not arrive until November 30.

4. The possibility of a move to St. Louis proved to be a false rumor.

5. Dysentery.

6. This letter was not found.

7. This letter was not found.

8. This letter was not found.

9. Ellis Peirce was born August 26, 1862.

10. In 1858 E. J. Ingersoll settled in Des Moines and opened a law practice. In 1865 he, Benjamin F. Allen, and others opened the Hawkeye Fire Insurance Company. Ingersoll became president of the company.

11. Benjamin F. Allen, a prominent citizen of Des Moines, was the nephew of Captain James Allen, who established Fort Des Moines in 1843. Initially he was in the dry goods business, but in 1851 he invested in a local steamboat company and in 1855 he started the Bank of Nebraska in Des Moines. In addition to founding the

Hawkeye Fire Insurance Company, he was treasurer and later president of the Iowa and Minnesota Railroad Company, organizer of the Capital City Bank, and founder of the Des Moines Water Works Company. In 1872 he served in the 14th General Assembly of Iowa. In 1874 he moved to Chicago; the following year he sold his interest in the Capital City Bank and eventually suffered financial failure.

> Camp of the 22 Regiment Iowa Vol Infantry
> Rolla Mo Dec 5 1862
> Dear Catharine

I looked long for a letter to night. I have heard nothing from thee since the 19th which is now near three weeks.[1] I am verry much worried about thy health. I fear thee is fretting about my absence and for fear that I will be killed or die before I get home but I do not feel as if I would die or be killed either during this war. I believe just as much that I will get home in the next year as I do that I am now allive.

Tomorrow morning Our Company starts for Waynsville to escort a train of 80 wagons loaded with stores for the army at Springfield[2] and I concluded to write to thee before I started so that I might have a letter from thee against I got back to Rolla. I am in good health and in good Spirits to-night as far as my military prospects are concerned and I feel as if I could fight rebles straight along if they would only let me at them. Capt Ault & Lady is cutting a stiff[3] and the captain has to stay behind to take care of her so we will have a good time of it for our Lieut[4] will command and he is as good a fellow as God ever made. We number now abut 65 effective men. There is some 30 shirks pretending sick. We have only one in the hospital and there is not much the matter with him now. We have about 2 or 3 that is not well enough to proform duty and the ballance is not fit for anything but food for powder. Col Stone took Command yesterday. He did not get to Des Moines and of course he did not get to see thee. He says that he will try to get me a furlough in January for two or three weeks and has promised me the first vacancy that occurs in the regiments that he has the control of. I am not getting but $20 per month now as I resigned my place in the officers family on the arrival of Madam and so my pride cut off my salary but I will get another birth before long and also maintain my self respect. I got the stamps and will send thee home the money as soon as U.S. pays over. This is about all to night. When

I get back I will expect a letter and will write thee another Epistle. Give my love to Mary Cyrus and Kiss the children for me. Farewell. Thy aft husband.

Taylor

1. This letter was not found.

2. The duty to escort wagons between Rolla and Waynesville was rotated among the companies of the 22nd Iowa.

3. *Stiff* was slang for liquor. The exact meaning of "cutting a stiff" cannot be determined.

4. First Lieutenant Neill Murray.

Camp 22nd regt Iowa Vol
Rolla Mo 7th 1862
Dear Catharine

I received thy letter one week ago and one last night from Mary written the 16th of November[1] and it made me feel quite happy to find out that you had been writing to me oftener than I had given you credit for. Why the letters are delayed is more than I can tell for it only takes one three days to come from there here and some of yours has come in that time but some has been 3 weeks and this one has been nearly two months on the road. I would have written last week but I was ordered to take 22 picked men and go off to act as provost Guard and did not wish to write untill I was relieved which took place yesterday, and so we have got back to camp again. We had a good time of it. I had my pick out of the whole company and a better set of men never set foot in leather or shouldered a musket. We have none of the disgraceful actions in our company that Mary speaks of Smith[2] writing about. Every mans property is safe from depredations while the men are in my charge and Col upholds me in it. When we arived at Camp I had the pleasure of knowing that no man had suffered in his property by any of our acts and of receiving the thanks of all parties both the men and the officers for our good conduct and the men thanked me for their good treatment. So you may think I felt proud and of course will have to write to thee about it. I am well in health and am as happy as I can be away from you and I hope now soon to hear the news that Liberty and right has resumed her sway over our beloved country and we will all be allowed to return to our homes and enjoy peace and prosperity. I thought this morning that I felt better in health and younger in spirits than I have at any time for the last 12 years if it will only last. We are expecting to go to Houston in a few days now[3] but it has been the talk for so long and if Col Stone can have his way we will not go at all but if we do I shall notify you. Mrs Ault is still here and will have to remain here untill we are paid off for they cannot get money to send her home.

I do not know when we will be paid but we are expecting the paymaster here every day now. I have over $100 due me but wheather I will get it all or not at this payment I cannot say. The Major and Chaplin[4] is trying to get me a better place and I hope will succeede not only for my own good but for yours also. It is thought here that Ault will resign his place and they wish me to hold on a while for the company wants me take the control of it for they say that I am the only man that has done any thing for them and they want me to be paid for it. You need not say anything about this as it is confidential among them. I expect you will get a letter from a colourd man some of these times whose son I helped out of some difficulty. He has written to me to know the address of my family together with a letter of thanks for my assistance. His name is Warwick and lives in Davenport Iowa and from his letter I have conceived a very good opinion of him. I do not know why he asked for your address but you can write me if you receive any thing from him.

We have a very good time of it here and I would as leave stay here as any place but Gen. Warren[5] is determined to have us if he can get Curtis[6] to let us go. We have good news from the army to night but bad news from the democratic legislators of Ilinois. It seems as if the pro Slavery men of the north was determined to ruin our country. The hounds are now trying to call home the soldiers now in the field. If they succeede in passing the resolution I hope the General Government will take it in hands and wipe every Vestige of State rights that is claimed rather than let Slavery exist longer.[7]

We are ordered to start for Waynsville tomorrow to escort a train through and all is hurry turmoil getting ready to move by daylight. This is a great business. We never know more than 6 hours ahead what we will have to do next. When I sit down to write this I supposed we would not have to leave here for two weeks but in a half hour the whole program was changed and we will start at six oclock for the west.

We are cleaning out the rebles here fast. We have from fifty to 100 prisoners daily brought in and sent to St Louis. If we have no bad luck the rebles will be as scarce here by spring as they are in Iowa. The Army of the frontier[8] is makeing good time and the rebles is deserting and comeing over by hundreds and the provost Marshalls office at this place is full from Morning till nigh administering the oath to returned rebles. If it was not for the fire in the rear I would feel confident of winding this thing up in three months but the d—d Democrats is determined to give us all all the trouble they can.

I wrote thee some time ago to send me your pictures if you can get thee and the children on one and Cyrus and Mary on another. I would like it but you can do as you think best. You can have them taken like I had mine and I can get them framed here. I would like C. find out my situation in regard to the lodge and see if I can pay up my dues and have a certificate. I have never knew what was done with my case and he can find out and let me know. I must close for I have a heap to do and must be at it. Give my love to all.

               I remain thy aft husband
               Taylor

1. These letters were not found.

2. Merion Smith, Company A, 23rd Iowa Infantry. Smith was an Ohio native and resident of Des Moines when he enlisted July 19, 1862. He was discharged for disability October 21, 1863. The letter from Mary Milner was not found.

3. Companies A, H, and I would march to Houston, Missouri, beginning December 21. Peirce and Company C remained at Rolla. On December 13 Brigadier General Herron, who had fought the battle of Prairie Grove, Arkansas, on December 7, requested that Curtis send him the 22nd Iowa, but Curtis did not approve the request.

4. The regimental chaplain was Richard B. Allender. He was a Pennsylvania native who resided in Knoxville, south of Newton, when he enlisted on September 4, 1862.

5. Fitz-Henry Warren was commissioned colonel of the 1st Iowa Cavalry in June 1861 and spent the next year chasing Confederate sympathizers in Missouri. He was promoted to brigadier general on July 16, 1862, and at the end of the year commanded the forces at Houston.

6. Major General Samuel R. Curtis.

7. The 1862 elections resulted in Democrat majorities in both the Illinois house and senate. The Democratic-controlled legislature in Illinois opposed the Emancipation Proclamation and urged Lincoln to withdraw it and declare an armistice. Many citizens opposed the proclamation and urged family members to desert the

army because of it. Republicans, however, won all six seats in the U.S. House of Representatives, thus confirming that most Iowans supported Lincoln and the proclamation.

8. The Army of the Frontier was formed on October 12, 1862, from forces in Kansas and Missouri. Brigadier General John M. Schofield was named commander.

Camp Near Rolla Mo
Dec 17 1862
Dear Catharine

I take this evening to write to thee and the rest of you. As the bearer of this Thomas Story[1] has been discharged on account of disability and is going straight to Des Moines and as I get but few letters I thought may be you do not get my letters. I have not had any word from you since the 1st of this month[2] and if you knew how lonesome I was you would write me once a week. At any rate the letters come in 4 days and when I get them I feel as if I was almost with you but it is so long between times that I get very tired waiting and conjure up all kinds of imaginations of what is the matter at home. I suppose that we will leave here in a few days now for some point for the 1st of Jany is near at hand[3] and I am satisfied that Lincoln means to see his proclimation put into effect. And I think the whole Federal Force will be put into Motion and the troops now in Missouri will not be likely to leave any rebles behind them to keep up a fire in the rear. They are completly aroused and I am of the oppinon that when our forces move we will devastate the country. For heretofore the rebles property has been protected and as soon as the Loyal forces were gone they would make their way around the army and as their property was spared to them they would just go to work and be as great rebles as ever and would rob the loyal citizens and devastate their estates and abuse their families till the soldiers sees that there is no use in fooling with them and are determined to wipe it out of Missouri. I am well this evening and would be in good heart if I could hear from home. All is going right here with me. The man who carries this can tell you more about my affairs than I can write and can also tell you how I get along in the Service and how I behave myself and what kind of a character I have here.

I told him that if he would carry this to you you would give him a good dinner and something to drink which last I wish you to be careful not to forget. I am looking for a letter daily and expect to get one to night but as Story leaves in the Morning I have to finish this before the mail gets in. Gen Herron has telegraphed for us to go to Springfield and we will either go there or to Houston our first destination. All things are so uncertain in the army that one can not tell what we will do from one day to another. Give my love to all. I sent you an epistle yesterday or I would write more. Give my love to all my friends and kiss the children for me and thee and Mary must keep in good heart.

       Taylor

1. Thomas Story was a native of Ohio but moved to Vandalia, Iowa. He was mustered into federal service on August 28, 1862, and was discharged for disability on December 20, 1862.

2. This letter was not found.

3. The 22nd Iowa would not leave Rolla until January 26, 1863.

       Camp of the 22nd Regiment Iowa Vol Inft
       Rolla Missouri Dec 28th 1862
       Dear Catharine Mary & Cyrus

I have been looking for a letter now for a week but alas in vain. The last one I had was dated the 11th Nearly three weeks ago and the letters come in 4 days. Why is it that I dont get any more? I have not had more than one letter in two weeks since I left home and once it was 5 weeks between letters. Do you write and they are detained or are you tired of writing to me? I have written once a week ever since I left home and some times oftener. I think you might write at least once a week and then I would feel as if I was treated like the rest of them for nearly all of them get letters once a week and some of them twice a week. I tell you that the life of a soldier is not so full of pleasure that he can bear to be absent from home and not hear from it either without feeling as if he was forgotten. But enough of this. If you cannot write oftener you can write as often as it suits you and I will have to be satisfied. I am well and very well contented here. I have been busy making out our pay rolls. We expect our pay now in a few days and we are makeing preperations to have all things ready to receive it. Our Chaplain is going to go home and will take our money and distribute it for us but I am counting chickens &c but live in hope that we will get it all write this time. I have not much news to write this time that will be of any importance to you. When I last wrote I believe that I wrote that we expected to go to Houston some 75 miles south of this but things have taken another turn since and I think we will now stay all winter without doubt. Col Stone has relieved Col Glover in command of the district[1] and our Lt Col is command of the post and the Major is now at home and Capt Ault is in command of the regiment and he has never learned anything yet that amt to any thing in the military lines. So I think we are booked for a winter campaign in our tents except a raid or two on some poor Devils hen roost or hog pen may occur to break the monotony.

Mrs Ault is here yet. They all had a grand ball at St Francis a little town about 7 miles from here on Christmas Eve. I understand that all hands got drunk and had a high old time of it. There was a Miss Harrington [Thorington] there who is a sister to the Harrington [Thorington] that run on the anti war ticket for State senator.[2] Col Stone was her partner and as the Col does not much like secesh if it is in crinolines plied her with the ardent[3] untill he got her so drunk that she could only just get round. He then left her for a while to sober off and some other fellow got her out to dance. The Col told him that he could not trot the whiskey out of this woman for it cost him a dollar and a half to get filled up and he would be d—d any other man should dance it out of her so he made the fellow let her go and the Galt Col had the pleasure of dancing the whiskey out of her himself what he could get out. But they say that she got water loged and could not sail and [had] to be put to bed. I and two others was out on a hunt for three days and did not get to any of the balls and am very glad of it. I do not think I would have went if I had been at camp but I am contented to stay at home for I think when it comes to woman getting drunk I would rather be excused and I understand that it quite a common occurrance with the upper tendom of seceshia to imbibe untill they do not know their own husbands from any other man. It is said that our Capt lady played him false with some star shaped Gentleman but I can not tell how true it is. But I know that there was hell to pay some where or other but as the Cap has another woman living with them I guess he consoled himself by this time as all things seem to be going on right again.

We have a lot of dutch in our regiment now that have been rebelious or at least have laid down their arms and Gen Curtis has broke up the regiment and divided it up so as to compell them to come in again but we have not been able to do much with them as yet. They have them out trying to make them work some to day but I do not know how they are makeing it with them. But a dutchman is the devil to drive. You might as well try to drive a Jack Ass and I beliv the sooner we get shut of them the better we will be off.[4] I was afraid that we would have to shoot some of them last week and to shoot ones friends seems horrible to me although I could shoot an enemy as easily as any body yet I do not want ever to have to shoot our own men let them be ever so mutinous. We are all looking anxiously for the 1st of Jany and the workings of Old Abes proclimation. We all feel that it will end the war and that it is the only thing that will give us a chance of seeing our homes very soon since Burnsides defeat on the rappahanock.[5] However we have good new from the south and west and I hope to hear good news from the east when the sign gets right again.

I have nothing more I believe to write at this time except to the children. I want them to learn their lessons and be good children till papa gets home again and then they can help him to get along with his business again. For as soon as this war is over I think things will go along all right and times will be more prosperous than ever and with what little we can raise we can do something. Tell Frank that he must hurry and learn to read and write so that he can take care of Mother & sis and baby if pap does not get home and if he does he can help him keep his books and write for him and be a man.

This is a poor letter. I feel out of sorts to day not hearing from home and of course you cannot expect a bright letter from a blue man. I would not have written at all but I have always wrote once a week and will continue to unless hindered from some circumstance that is not under my control. If we move from here I will write you so that you will know it. In the mean time you can write to me as usual. There is one thing I forgot. I sent a letter by B McPherson[6] who was discharged on account of stiff knee but since he has got home he says he was playing off sick to get his discharge. Now if he comes around with both knees limber just tell him that I have wrote to you that I would rather he would make himself scarce for I do not wish my family to associate with a liar or a coward and if he does not move off put the hot water to him. Old Story was actually sick and I have some lenity for him as he was of no earthly use here it was as well to let him off. I give my love to all my friends. When thee writes I want to know if you have heard of Kirks boys and the young Peirces and whether these battles in Virginia has rubbed any of them out or not.

I remain affty your Husband Brother and father

Taylor Peirce

1. Colonel John M. Glover, commander of the 3rd Missouri Cavalry, took command of the District of Rolla, Department of the Missouri, on November 2, 1862. Stone took command of the district on December 21. Glover resumed command on January 16, 1863, but his location between December 21 and January 16 cannot be determined. A letter from Sergeant Walter Lee, 22nd Iowa, states that Glover left Rolla with his regiment, so he probably accompanied Companies A, B, F, and K on scouting expeditions in the vicinity of Rolla, Salem, and Waynesville.

2. Taylor is probably referring to James Thorington, who, from 1855 to 1857, represented Iowa in the U.S. Congress. He was supported by Free-Soilers and abolitionists. He lost a bid for the U.S. Senate in 1858 when former Iowa governor James W. Grimes, a Republican, received the nomination.

3. "Ardent" spirits is strong liquor.

4. Soldiers in the regiment were from at least sixteen foreign countries. The largest contingent consisted of fifty-two natives of Germany. One identified himself as a native of Baden, two as natives of Hanover, and four as natives of Prussia. Twenty-five were from Bohemia, and three from Austria. It is possible that Taylor categorized all these soldiers as "dutch," the common Americanization of "Deutsch." One soldier simply stated that he was from Europe, and one, Joseph D. Smith of Company G, said that he was a native of the Atlantic Ocean. Taylor's account of difficulties with German soldiers cannot be verified.

5. This refers to the battle of Fredericksburg.

6. James B. McPherson, originally from New York, was a resident of Newton, Iowa, and was mustered into federal service on August 28, 1862. He was discharged for disability on November 14, 1862.

Camp 22 Regiment Rolla Missouri

Jany 18th 1863

Dear Wife, Sister, Brother, & friends

I receved Marys letter of the 11th inst[1] and was slightly gratified to hear that you were all as well as you were. But I feel sorry to hear that Cyrus has had another bad spell for I was in hopes that now he had got the deed for the house he would be better for I know that trouble has always had a bad effect on his health. Indeed it has on every one as far as I know.

This is sunday evening and is quite pleasant but we have had quite a cold week of it. It snowed on tuesday and wednesday and Thursday was quite like Iowa but it is now quite moderate and looks like raining again. When I wrote last things looked like fighting but I am happy to say that the rebles under their great Genl Marmaduke[2] who made a raid on our lines with 4,000 to 6,000 men was gloriously whipped by Col Sigle and Brown[3] with about 1,200 vol and 100 state malitia and they were compelled to skedaddle across the arkansas as fast as their legs could carry them leaving about 500 dead and wounded and 300 prisoners.[4] This virtually winds up the rebellion north of the arkansas and west of the missippi for we hold a chain of posts clear across the country from Pilot Knob to the Indian Reserve on which the rebles can not make much impression.

We also have dispatches here today of a victory won on white River in Arkansas by Genl McClernand in which he took from 600 to 7,000 prisoners and all their camp equipage and stores valued at 2 million[5] which if correct winds up the war west of the Mississippi and will confine it exclusively to the territory embraced between the Missi and the Atlantic and south of Tennasee and north of Louisianna. And I think if old Abe will arm the Negros and precipitate the whole mass of available bone and sinus of the North they can either put down the rebellion or exterminate the accursed Traitors. I feel in better spirits to night concerning the final termination of the war than I have since the failure of McClellen before Richmond, however I never had any doubt about the final triumph of the men who fought for liberty and right. We may have some hard fights yet but if the 1st of May does not see the Government triumphant I miss my guess. The troops that were sent here last week was not wanted as Sigle and Brown had routed the rebles before they got to them & they now lay encamped around us as thick as hops. I suppose they will be ordered to St Louis in a day or two and we may probably go with them. I do not know what will be our next mov but Col Glover has returned to this place haveing cleaned out the Gurrillas in the upper part of Missouri and restored quiet in them parts and as there was nothing more to do.[6] So I suppose he will relieve Col Stone and then the 22nd will be likely to have a chance to show what kind of stuff it is made of. There is a great many men here both officers and privates here who I have known in former years. Some of them are good men and true and some are just the reverse. There is a great many officers that are very ineficient and only seems to stay here to get the money and do as little as they possibly can not careing wheather they do any thing for the benefit of their men and country or not. There is however some of them that have their whole heart fixed on their duty among which I am happy to say stands Our Field officers and some of our Company officers and may be all of them although I think some of them might do more than they do. I think we have the best regimental officers in the field or as good as any for if god ever made a man it is our Col and Major. They are both up right honest and sincere and beside that they have the virtue of humanity which is said to be a rare quality among military men. This week when it was cold and the weather bad the Col took all the men off duty except a few pickets and sent them to their tents untill the weather became mild again. Catharine asked me in her letter what we done for amusement when off duty.[7] For my part I always have enough to do but the boys as we call them play five cent poker, fiddle and dance, sing, write to their friends, and visit one another tents, and laugh and talk about their friends at home and relate the reports of the day that are continually circulating through a camp. Our Company composed of over 90 men has never had a fight in it yet they all agree like brothers and it would be impossible to collect the same amt of men at home and keep them togather for one week without having three or four fights. Thee wants to know how we spent the Christmas. On the Sunday before, I went to the Col and got his permission to take three men and go on a three days hunt which we did and visited many of the families of the loyal men for some 12 or 15 miles around who seemed glad to extend all the hospitality they could to us and we had a very nice time of it and for Soldiers behaved ourselves quite genteelily. I met some very genteel men among them and was very much pleased with the treatment I received.

I am in good health and am spending my time in cooking for the Officers. The Major the Chaplain the Captain the two Lts and Madam they got out of a Cook and was like to starve out so I turned out and am into it now untill they can get another cook which I hope they will get soon for I do not like to play waiter to a woman but I do not do that so I am so far right. Mary says Story thinks I am turned democrat but if he means by that that I am changed in my views from what I was he is mistaken for I would sooner loose my right arm than to be a northern democrat in the sence in which I understand it by. When the democrats are willing to give all men an equal chance in the broadest in which the term is used then I am a Democrat but untill that I am an Abolitionist. I endorse the Proclimation to the fullest extent and love the instutions of our country and the old Flag as well as any man ever did and am willing to lay down my life if need be to defend them. But I would not vote for Grinnell last fall for I did not consider him an honest man although he has professed to be an abolitionist. Yet I have watched his course for several years and have come to the conclusion that he would sell his vote for the benefit of obtaining place and power so I let him up.

I do not know of much more to write to night so I will conclude by saying that I am in good health and good spirits and hope to enjoy both for a long time.

I expect I will be paid off this week and will be able to send you some of the needfull.

Tell the children that I think of them every night when I lay down to rest and if it was not for their future welfare I would not stay here and lay out in the cold to fight for our country but would soon be with them and their dear mother.

19th. I have been so busy that I could not get time to finish this letter untill to night. It is raining and snowing just like it used to do in Pa but is not cold. The boys is all in their tents to night. The Col has taken the guard in and all is quiet. The troops that were brought here last week is again ordered to St Louis and will start in the morning. I think now we will remain here until March and maybe longer. I had a whiskey stew this morning. J Cole[8] had a bad cold and him and I made a requisition on the Hospital for ½ pint and took our stew and of course I am better than well to night. I have no news of importance and will close. I will write again in a few days and try and write a more interesting letter than this for it seems as if I had lost the art of expressing my ideas on paper. Give my love to the Children and retain the same for yourselves.

      Affty yours
      Taylor

1. This letter was not found. *Inst* is short for *instant,* meaning "of the current month."

2. John S. Marmaduke was a West Point graduate who resigned to fight for the Confederacy. He fought at Shiloh and was promoted to brigadier general on November 15, 1862. In September 1863 he fought a duel with Confederate Brigadier General Lucius M. Walker in which Walker was mortally wounded.

3. Egbert Benson Brown was a St. Louis businessman when he was commissioned lieutenant colonel of the 7th Missouri Infantry in August 1861. In May 1862 he was appointed brigadier general of the Missouri state militia and in November as brigadier general of the United States Volunteers. He was wounded during the January battle at Springfield. He commanded the District of Central Missouri, participated in the battle of Westport in October 1864, and in January 1865 commanded the District of Rolla. Taylor's handwriting is difficult to decipher regarding the other name, but both here and later in this letter it appears to be Sigle. Neither Brigadier General Franz Sigel nor anyone whose name is similar in spelling was present during this battle. Early in the war Sigle had been appointed colonel of the 3rd Missouri Infantry and became brigadier general in August 1861. He fought at Pea Ridge in March 1862 and was transferred to Virginia in June 1862. He was a native of Baden, Germany, and had fled to New York in 1852 in the wake of the Prussian reaction to attempts to establish a constitutional monarchy in several German states.

4. On January 8, 1863, Marmaduke attacked Springfield, Missouri, with 2,300 soldiers. Union forces there were commanded by Brigadier General Egbert B. Brown. Marmaduke broke off the battle and moved southeast toward West Plains. On January 11 he encountered Union troops at Hartville. That evening they withdrew, and Marmaduke, fearing Federal reinforcements, withdrew into Arkansas.

5. On January 11, 1863, Union forces under Major General John A. McClernand and naval forces under Admiral David Porter assaulted and defeated Confederates at Fort Hindman, also known as Arkansas Post, on the Arkansas River. Major General Ulysses Grant initially disapproved of the operation and considered relieving McClernand of his command. McClernand's men took 4,791 Confederate prisoners.

6. On November 30 Colonel John Glover led a force of about 130 cavalrymen from Rolla into the Ozark Mountains. On December 2 they encountered a Confederate force that they defeated. Glover and his men returned to Rolla on December 6. On January 10 the 21st Iowa, the 99th Illinois, the 3rd Iowa Cavalry, and the 3rd Missouri Cavalry were sent to reinforce Springfield. On January 11 they encountered and defeated Marmaduke near Hartville, Missouri. Glover did not accompany this expedition.

7. This letter was not found.

8. James A. Cole, a Tennessee native, resided in Newton and was mustered into federal service on August 28, 1862. He was mustered out of service on July 25, 1865.

Camp of the 22nd Regt of Iowa Vol Infty
Rolla Missouri Jany 23/63
Dear Catharine Mary & Cyrus

I received your letter of 11th[1] last Sunday evening and now set down to answer it and let you know how I am and what we are doing. There has not been any thing of special moment transpired since my last. Our Col has been relieved of his command of this district. Col Glover having ended his services in the north part of the state has returned and taken his place.[2] Lt Col Graham is still commander of the post and I suppose we will not be likely to move from here for a month yet if we do at all. Major Atherton is very unwell but is on the mend. Capt Ault is in command of the regiment during the majors illness Col Stone not having resumed the command since he was relieved. The troops that were sent here to help fight the rebles when they made their raid on Springfield and Hartsville hav all been ordered back to St Louis and the 8th and 12 and 14 Iowa regts will be sent to Davenport to reorganize having lost so many men in one way or another[3] that it is thought best to reorganise and make out full regiments and put them under the most efficient officers and relieve the inefficient ones. I seen many men amongst them that I have been acquainted with formerly and it seemd like seeing old friends for all soldiers seem glad to see any one that they have ever known. Our Company is in good health. I think there is only two in the Hospital William McKeever[4] and Lewis Smithhart.[5] McKeever has something the matter with his back and the Hipps and wants a discharge. The other one has the inflamatory Rheumatism. There is some few in quarters that is not very well but nothing dangerous. We have not lost a man by death yet. There has been 4 discharges and I think there will be two or three more before we go from here.[6] I however hope there will for a poor Soldier is of no manner of account in the army and is a burthen to the good ones—they having to wait on them.

We have had a snow storm this week but it is all gone now and this is a splendid evening clear and pleasant. The wind just cold enough to feel good and the ground drying off. We had an engagement the other day. After the snow fell the bugle Sounded at 1 oclock and the drums beat the long roll and soon the men was all hurrying towards their respective company parade grounds with their arms wondering what was the meaning of the call. After forming the regiment in line we were ordered to stack arms and the first division of the regiment was marched off to the top of a rising piece of ground about a quarter of a mile off. The second division was marched around a piece of brush and after we were halted on the top of the hill our adjutant who was in command of the whole informed us that we were to be attacked by the other party armed with snow balls and told us if they succeeded in driving us back to a little house about 200 yards in the rear that our renown as warriors would be forever lost. At it we went making snow balls and putting ourselves in a situation to defend ourselves against the enemy. We had the colours and of course we had them to defend. Lt Murray took a detachment and advanced as skirmishers. At the sound of the bugle we could hear them comeing but being under the hill we could not see them untill they commenced on the Lts party. They soon drove in the skirmishers and on they come, the snow ball flying as thick as you ever seen snow flakes. As soon as they got close enough we pitched in to them and having a good supply of ammunition on hand we give them thunder and after about ten minutes we got them started and routed them. The bugle sounded the call and we all returned to our lines thinking it was over and was congratulating ourselves on our victory when they suddenly made their appearance again and sailed into us with great fury. And after they had got us fairly into their commander took one half of his men and while we were at work with the rest and before we took notice of it he had out flanked and got in the rear and took the colours and such a time as we had you never seen. Some of the boys got mad but for most part it was the greatest fun I ever seen and has done for the men more to liven them up than anything that could have happened to them. Col Stone is a good officer and shows that he understands human nature. When he is here he is always getting up something to cheer up the mens spirits and trys to make them happy and contented. While he is a good disciplinarian he is a good and humane officer.

I do not know of much news to write about that would interest you. Our regiment is in good health and spirits and have had a very comfortable time of it. You would not believe how warm the tents with the stove in them. I live with the Lieutenants. We have a tent about 12 feet square and about 3½ feet high to where the roof commences. They have a bunk fixed up as high as the Eaves and I have my bed under theirs. I get 4 lbs straw a month and by laying that down in some boards and putting some old Gunny bags over it and lying one blanket down single and doubling the other one and throwing my over coat on it and getting in on top of the under blanket and putting the whole over me I sleep quite comfortable except some very cold night and then I have to get up and warm up the stove and go back to bed again. On the whole I have no cause of complaint for I am well dressed, well fed and have not much hard labour and would not have so much as I have if I did not chose to do it. But I find I am better satisfied when I am busy than I am when Idle.

I suppose you will make some fun of me when I tell you that I have sent a petition to old Abe signed by all the officers of the regiment recommending me for a commission authorising me to rais organize and discipline a negro company for the military service.[7] Whether I will get it or not I can not tell but it is the general belief that I will. If I do you will see the blackest set of soldiers out and who will need no uniform to make them all alike. If I should get it I will be likely to get home for a few days before entering on my duty unless old Abe should order me to propell at once.

There is many changes takeing place in the regiment among the officers and if I were to stay here I would stand a good chance for promotion. But if I can get into the negro regiments I will get to go into garrison and can then have some of you come and see me once and awhile.

There is news here by telegraph that General Herron has captured the reble Genl Marmaduke and 800 of his men but wheather it is so or not I am unable to say. I however think it is likely to be true.[8]

We have good news from Virginia again to night if it does not turn out like it has done heretofore but I hope not and amid all the news we hear that the God damd proslavery Democrats in Illinois are trying to sell that State to the Southren Confederacy.[9] I hope to God that Old Abe will send a detachment out there and hang the whole crew and burn their houses and I tell you that if they do not put a stop to their treachery the army will turn back and make a clean shucking of them for they are exicted wonderfully at the prospect of things there and will not stand to have their state brought into such a fix without makeing an effort to save it. And woe be to the traitors if they soldery takes them in hands and I think the secesh sympathysers in Iowa knows what is good for them they will keep a close lip on their sentiments.

I understand that the pay master is in town tonight. I can not tell wheather it is true or not. I will know by Monday. If he is not he will be soon as I seen by last nights paper that he had received $500,000 to pay out this district and I hope we will get some soon as I would like to send mine home before I leave here.

Tell the children that I send my love to thine and want them to be good and try and learn their lessons so that if I get crippled in the war and get old they can help me to work. The dear little things how I would like to set them on my knee and sing to them again. I often think what the little one is like and what is the reason I do not love him like I do the others but I suppose it is because I have not been with him and my affections have not been called in that way and I wonder whether he will ever learn to love me if I should get back again. I would rather have had him called something else for both the names have belonged to misfortune and without being superstitious I yet have an antypathy to any thing that brings to mind any thing that tinges the thought with unhappiness. It is tattoo and I must close.

> I remain yours
> Taylor Peirce

1. This letter was not found.

2. Colonel John M. Glover resumed command of the District of Rolla on January 16, 1863.

3. The 8th Iowa Infantry sustained 493 casualties at the battle of Shiloh, April 6–7, 1862. Those captured were exchanged on November 10, 1862. The 12th Iowa Infantry suffered 479 casualties, of whom about 400 were captured. Eventually they too were exchanged. The 14th Iowa Infantry lost 273 killed, wounded, and missing. Those captured were exchanged on November 19, 1862, and reached St. Louis in early December. The returnees then rejoined the remnants on their old regiments.

4. William McKeever was a native of Virgina but lived in Newton when mustered into federal service on August 28, 1862. He was wounded at Vicksburg on May 22, 1863, and died of those wounds on June 15.

5. Lewis W. Smithhart, a Kentucky native but resident of Newton, was mustered into federal service on August 28, 1862. He was wounded October 19, 1864, at Cedar Creek, Virginia, and was mustered out July 25, 1865.

6. By the date of this letter, four privates had been discharged for disease according to company records: William H. Brown, James B. McPherson, Elisha Shipp, and Thomas Story. Private John Linn was discharged for disease on February 11, 1863, shortly after the 22nd Iowa marched for Rolla. Brown, McPherson, and Shipp were Newton residents who enlisted on August 2, 1862, and were mustered on August 28. Story and Linn were Vandalia residents who enlisted on July

28 and 25, respectively, and were mustered on August 28. *Roster and Records of Iowa Soldiers* lists all as having been discharged for disability.

7. In July 1862 Congress authorized the enlistment of "persons of African descent." The War Department then authorized the arming of 5,000 "colored persons of African descent" on August 25, 1862. The order was limited to South Carolina. Lincoln's Emancipation Proclamation of January 1, 1863, authorized free blacks to be inducted into the armed forces. During the war, approximately 180,000 blacks would serve in the Union army. Peirce would not be appointed an officer to command black troops.

8. Marmaduke and his command retreated successfully and occupied winter quarters near Batesville, Arkansas.

9. On January 7 and 8, 1863, the Illinois legislature condemned Lincoln and the Emancipation Proclamation and called for the suspension of hostilities. The legislature went into recess on February 14, and Governor Richard Yates, a strong supporter of the proclamation, refused to reconvene it in June.

> Camp of the 22nd Regt Iowa Vol Infty
> Rolla Mo Jany 24th 1863
> Dear Brother

I received your letter of the 18th[1] this evening and was glad to hear that the family was all well but was sorry to hear that your were out of grubs and money for it seems as if the paymaster had forgoton us altogether but I live in hopes we will get our mony next week as I see by the paper that our paymaster Genl has received within the last few days the sum of $500,000 and is ordered to pay us off up to the 1st of November. I have over $100 coming to me now and was in hopes that I could get it all and get home for a week or so but I am afraid that I will have to forego that pleasure untill I get more money. For it would cost me $30 to make the trip and maybe more and I had better save that now than to spend it for the sake of a few days pleasure in the society of my friend from whom I would have to tear myself in a few short days. I wrote yesterday and gave you all the news that is of importance except we have been ordered to March as soon as we can get ready now and by the middle of next week we will be wending our way to the Ozark Mountains on our way to that most delectable country called Arkansaw[2] then to hunt of the travelers of that nice land. The next letter you will get from me will be mailed at Houston. We will then go to West Plains along with Genl Warrans[3] Brigade and I suppose we will then move on Pochohontos where there is said to be a small rebel force station. If we succeed in getting that place we are to form a junction with Genl Davidson[4] and march to Little Rock where the whole army of the Frontier is ordered to go[5] and then we will either fight or the rebles will run. I have no idea how soon I will get home now but I think the war is going to be put through now about as fast as it can be done so that we can take care of the Northern sympathisers and woe be to them if the soldier gets hold of them. About the Mill, I do not know what to say about the sale of it. If I could get home a little while I could tell better what to do with it but it is impossible for me to know what is best to do. If you cannot use the mortgage for your own benefit you had better let Ingersole have it if he will take it for the debt. I made writings with Miller Cole for his share and he has received some of the pay on it. Ingersole has the article and can give you all the information about it you need. I allow you to do just as you think best. If I could get home next summer I would like to keep it but may be you could do better for yourself by selling it and useing the means to help you fix up your affairs for I can work some way to start if I get home and if I do not I will not need it. However I feel as if I would not get killed in this campaign but God only knows and in him I put my trust. If I succeed in getting my commission to raise a nigger company I can put you in a way of making a nice thing of it and it will be easy work and I think would probably be as healthy as to go to the mountains. At least I would like for you to wait untill the 1st of March before you conclude to go certain. I will certainly hear from my petition in the course of three weeks and can then let you know wheather I can get home this spring or not.

I want you to do with my affairs just what you think is the best for yourself and that will be the best for me for our interests as so nearly linked togather that what is good for one is good for both. And you know that I am not one that reflects on things past if they should not turn out to have been the best that might have been done. I want you to take care of your health and keep yourself just as quiet as you possibly can and I hope you may live a long time to enjoy life and the society of those you love. For my part if it was not for the welfare of those that are to live after me and will be probably of more use in the world then I will be I would not be absent a day from my home and your society.

Little does a man know what the warmest of attachments are untill he is in a situation that renders the certainty of again rejoining those he loves doubtfull.

It seems to me that I would give all I had to once more see peace spread her golden wings over our belovd country and I could be relieved from my services here and be at liberty once more to rejoin you and pass the ballance of my life in the heart of my family and home.

Dear Brother I wish you to instill into the minds of my children that virtue is the only true path to happiness and the slightest deviation from it will as surely bring its punishment as that the sun shines.

The night is getting late and as we will be busy in makeing preperations to commence our march I will have to close. Give my respects to all and my love to Mary and Catharine and the Children.

> I remain you afft brother
> Taylor Peirce

1. This letter was not found.

2. On January 24 Colonel Stone was ordered by Major General Curtis to move the 22nd Iowa toward Houston, Missouri. The unit began moving on January 26.

3. Brigadier General Fitz-Henry Warren.

4. John W. Davidson graduated from West Point in 1845, served in the Mexican War, and fought Indians in New Mexico and California. He was appointed brigadier general in February 1862 and participated in the Peninsula Campaign. He was appointed to command of the District of St. Louis on November 2, 1862, and the Army of Southeastern Missouri on February 23, 1863. He spent the remainder of his Civil War career in Arkansas and Missouri.

5. On January 24 Schofield reported to Curtis that two divisions had crossed the White River and could start toward Little Rock in a few days. The next day Curtis halted Scholfield's movement.

> Des Moines Jan 24th
> Dear Taylor

I have commenced to write again and do not know what to write. The young ones pester me so that I can not think of any thing that would be worth writing about. We have the nicest winter this year that we have had since the year we lived at the Old coon mill. We have not had snow enough yet for a sleigh to run on. There was about twelve hour rain fell Thursday night and Friday morning and today the mud is some and the rivers are quite full and what little ice there was made last week has gone out. I think the wether must be sent to accomodate the poor war widows that have their own stock to take care of for there surely has been agreat many left to take care of themselves throughout the union that would of sufferd severely if the winter had of snowed and cold like last was. I wrote to John Sumpter two week ago about the pork and Rorabough account but have not heard from them since John was up after the [pile] driver. I have not received any thing from there since I was down in the fall. Cyrus talks some of going down this week to see about the things for me if the wether keeps good. C is better in health now than he has been since he came home the last time from the peek.[1]

Dear Taylor I am as well off as I can be with out thee but I tell thee that I am not contented yet. I thought when thee first went that I would get over the lonesome feeling in a little time but it is better yet or I do not know wether I ever will satisfied on this or not. The Children are such a care to me that I do not know how I will get along with them. I think I will send Sallie to school in the spring for I can not teach her properly myself. She has learn to read very well and is doing pretty well in her other study. Frank has learnd his letters and can spell and pronounce words of two and three letters and is much of a mischiff as ever. He is up in the morning by day light and keeps the house in an uproar from that untill seven oclock in the evening. I have got them a new spelling book and thay are learning to spell verey well. We are all well this week. As usual I have little use of my left arm yet but I am able to go about and do some little work for myself and tend the baby. The baby is growing some now. He was five months old on tuesday and waits twelve pounds which is better than any of us ever expected him to do. If thee had of seen him as we have thee would be surprised to think he is still alive. He did not grow any till he was three months old.

I must close as my baby is awake.

> With love to thee I sign myself
> Catharine A Peirce

1. In a March 23, 1862, letter from Rachel Speakman to either Catharine or Mary she refers to a trip that Cyrus took to Pike's Peak. Rachel is Mary Milner's cousin and was then living in New York.

West Plaines Mo Feby 5th 1863
Dear Catharine and all the rest

I set down this morning to write again to let you know what we are doing and how we got along. In my last I wrote you that we were ordered to Houston. But like all things in the army the men is not presumed to be in the secrets of the war department and instead of going to Houston we marched to this place which is 55 miles south of Houston. We left Houston about 8 mile west of us and come straight through. We had a very pleasant march. The weather was rough the day we started but it cleared off pleasant and we got along about 20 miles a day and got here all right with the exception of some sore feet. But the Shirks growled terribly the whole time about haveing to carry their knapsacks and guns and the ambulances was full all the time with them and all that could get on the wagons beside. I was fortunate in getting my knapsack and Blanket hauled and could assist the tired ones in getting their things along. I walked all the way and felt better when I got here than I did when I left. We were 7 days on the road and got here about noon of the [illegible] which was 2nd of February. When we found the 21st & 23rd Iowa who had come up here from Pilot Knot and had got up here 3 days before us. We Here found Genl Davidson with 17 regiment[1] but I am not allowed to say how many men we have or what is our destination if I knew. Suffice it to say that this army will make its mark and you will hear of this country being cleaned out as we move south. The Federal lines has advanced to the state line of Arkansas and in another month will hold all the Territory north of the Arkansas river. I see by last nights paper dated Feby 3d that Grant is moving on Vicksburg[2] and if they succeed in taking that which they will do eventually the reble cause in the west is gone up. Although some of our northern croakes is howling that the war is no nearer ended now than it was one year ago. Yet one year ago there was 7 states that the union Flag was not seen to wave over and 6 or 7 more that it only floated over by a kind of force. Now the ones that ware doubtful at that time have become subject to the Federal Government and assist to quell the rebellion in the others. And there is no state but what has the old Flag hoisted in some part of it and the area of rebellion is gradually and surely diminishing and from the appearance of things now the rebles cannot possibly hold out another six months. I see from the Richmond dispatch that they themselves own that if they do not get foreign assistance they can not hold out till the next crop is gathered and I know from my own observation that it will be impossible for them to subsist until they get assistance from the outside. For our army used every thing up as it goes and we are on half feed now not withstanding we can bring a great part of our supplies from the north where it is in abundance. So you see that they must have short allowances where they have to depend wholly on their own resorces for subsistance. It is reported that part of our division have a fight day before yesterday at salem in Ark abot 25 miles south of this and took a great many prisoners and defeated the rebles with great loss while our loss is only one or two. But I can not say as to the truth of the detailes[3] but the prisoners will be in to day and I will hear more about it.

The weather commenced getting cold the day we come here and last night it snowed about 7 inches and is very cold this morning. The 23rd has no stoves in their tents and they are very uncomfortable although I believe their health is as good if not better than our own. Frank McConnell[4] was in to see me this morning and Marion Smith[5] spent the day with me yesterday and it seems almost like getting home to see so many of my old friends around. J Scarbrough[6] come down and a great many others from our neighborhood and we had quite a good time of it. Frank McConnell is going to get a discharge on account of his back being so weak that he cannot get along. He has good health otherwise. Smith is the same old Smith. He pilosphises on the life of a soldier with great emphasis and seemed perfectly contented with himself and all the surrounding circumstances.

Our company was ordered out on a forageing expedition yesterday and as I was not well I was left behind to take charge of the camp and the sick untill the Co returned. I caught cold the day we came here. I had left my overcoat in the wagon and after we had marched abot 7 or 8 miles we had to halt to let a train pass which took an hour or more and being warm walking I stood untill I was chilled through and was quite unwell for two days but am better now. The cold is broke up and I think I will be all right in a day or two. It was lucky that I was not able to go with the company for they took nothing but their blankets with them and the weather has turned out so bad that I think they will suffer with the cold.

The paymaster is here to pay us 4 months wages and when He goes back he is going to take our money and express it for us so you will get mine in about two or three weeks. If I get all that is comeing to me I will be able to send you $90. If not it will be less. We have the Best Field officers out. Our Col has done more to make us comfortable than any other that I know of in the field and has seen to our wants better than any one could expect from a stranger. Yet there is some hounds that still howls and curses because he does not do more. He is now in command of a brigade being the ranking Col. He has an Iowa brigade and one that any commander might be proud of and the most of us feel proud of him. Graham is in command of the regiment and Major Atherton is now out with 6 companies out of the 3 Iowa rgt foraging. Mrs Ault has gone home. She started when we left Rolla and I think Capt will not remain long with us if I can see straight. If we do not get too far into the interior this winter I intend to come home in the Spring about the 1st of April and straighten things up before I leave again. For I am satisfied that the condition of things are such that if we do whip the rebles out the Govt must keep a heavy force in the field for some time to keep things quiet. And of course I will have to remain until I am not needed before I will be mustered out unless I get a commission and resign as soon as the war is over for I do not intend to leave the service untill the last reble has been forced to yield and peace is established on a full basis.

I hope old Abe will give me a commission in the negro regiments. I would like to lead them against their former masters and make them give up some of their luxurys to them who earned them and also to give them a taste of the tyranny which they have exersised so long until they would be willing to do unto others as they would have others do to them.

I am out of stamps and will have to get this letter sent by certificate. I loaned some of the stamps thee sent me but I can not get them back again as so you will have to pay for it there. Tell the children that I send each one of them a kiss which they are to get from Mother and when the money gets home they are to have some nice present such as Mother and Auntie thinks the most suitable for them. I send my love to all of you and my respects to all my acquaintances. I think the next letters you send you had better direct to St Louis for Genl Curtis always knows where we are and of course is always communicating with us and we will get our mail more direct from there and more certain than by any other rout. I will now close as the noon is come and I must get dinner and the sheet is about covered.

I remain affectionately
Yours Taylor Peirce

1. Davidson concentrated his forces at White Plains on January 31. By February 1863 Schofield was convinced the war in Missouri was over and requested that his forces, along with those of Davidson and Warren, be used in the offensive against Vicksburg. Curtis was reluctant to release troops to Grant. While the matter was raised to Halleck, Union forces remained concentrated at Springfield and West Plains.

2. Grant's two-pronged movement against Vicksburg had failed in December when both elements were forced to withdraw because of Confederate actions. In February the Union army was concentrated in Louisiana across from Vicksburg while Grant searched for a route either to bypass the city and ferry his army across the Mississippi or to utilize the bayous north of the city to move against the Confederate fortress.

3. Davidson ordered Colonel George E. Waring to conduct a reconnaissance toward Batesville, Arkansas, with a cavalry brigade. An infantry brigade was to accompany the expedition as far as Salem, Arkansas. On February 4 Waring encountered a Confederate force near Batesville and took several prisoners. Waring was then ordered to return to West Plains.

4. Alexander F. McConnell, Company G, 23rd Iowa Infantry, was a native of Indiana and resident of Prairie City when he was mustered into federal service on August 22, 1862. He was discharged for disability on July 20, 1863.

5. Merion Smith, Company A, 23rd Iowa Infantry.

6. James Scarbrough, Company C, 23rd Iowa Infantry, was a native of Pennsylvania and a resident of Mitchellville when he was mustered into federal service on August 23, 1862. He was wounded at the battle of Big Black River, Mississippi, on May 17, 1863, and died July 24, 1863, at Memphis, Tennessee.

Eminince, Mo Feby 16 1863
Dear Catharine

I again set down to write you all again. I wrote you last week but the mails are so irregular in this region that I do not know how long it will take this to reach you but Col Stone and the Chaplain leaves this for Rolla to-morrow and I think you will get it in about 6 or 7 days. I am well and in good heart. We have been on the move for 3 weeks except 3 or 4 days that we lay at West Plains. We are now about 60 miles from Rolla and will Either go to Rolla or to Pilot Knob.[1] One Division of the army started this morning to the Knob and we will either start for that place or Rolla to morrow. The rebles are all gone from this country except some few Gurrillas and them we gather up as we go along and shoot them. They are a set of murderers and are not fit to live to encumber society. Some of the cavalry took one yesterday morning who has shot at Gen Bentons[2] Courier the night before not knowing that the cavalry was about. So yesterday morning they caught him in his house and took him out about a mile and shot him. When we came along he was lying by the side of the road and his wife crying over him but she was no better than he for she kept on swearing vengence against the Federals and said she would make them kiss his blood and so we left her. It looks hard to me to see a man shot and his wife and children left alone but these men are the ones that keep up the cruelties that are continually being practiced in this part of Missouri.

We have been traveling through the Ozark mountain ever since the 1st of this month and a rough country it is. There is some pretty vallies in through them and now and then a very good settlement along some stream but the land is generally stony and poor covered with oak and yellow Pine. Some of the timber is very good and some day will be valuable. We are now on the Currant [Current] River some 25 miles from the Arkansas line and 3 miles from Eminence a town with one house and a court house and jail [in] it and an old mill which constitutes the whole town. I have been running a mile for two or three days grinding corn for the brigade as our rations have run short and the roads are so bad that our supplies can not reach us and we have been on ½ rations for some time. But I have enough to eat all the time and more than I need but some of the large eaters grow terribly about it. I expect that we will have short allowances until we get to the Rail Road for the trains can not reach us through this god forsaken country.

Lieutenant Murray starts home in the morning and has promised to call and see you and tell you how I get along and what I am doing. And if it is possible for you to get your pictures taken I mean Cyrus & Mary & thine and the babys I would like you to send it by him. The paymaster has come and has paid me my money and as soon as I get to the Express office I will express it home.

I would send it by Murray but the Col thinks that it will be safer to keep it until we get to the office as they might be attacked by a forrageing party and robed as they will only have a small escort with them. So I concluded to keep it with me untill we get to the Rail Road. Cap Ault and I have fell out and I do not hold any communication with him any more than just what is nessessary for me to have to do my duty. He has shown himself just as damned a dog as lives and if he was not afraid of me he would be overbearing as the devil himself but I have the upper hand and he has to keep mum. The Lt can tell you about it and so you need not fear for me but I will get along all right. I must now close for we will have to march in the morning and of course the time is precious with me. Give my love to all. Tell the children to be good and Pap will try and get home to see them this spring. Give Cyrus my best respects and tell him he could make some money following the army and buying up the worn out horses and mules and if I get my commission to raise the negroes I will come home and put him on the track.

> I remain affect your husband father and brother.
> Taylor Peirce

1. The regiment's destination was Iron Mountain, Missouri, about five miles north of Pilot Knob.

2. Brigadier General William P. Benton commanded the First Division, Army of Southeastern Missouri. Benton served in the Mexican War as a private, was commissioned a captain in the 8th Indiana Infantry in 1861, and was promoted to brigadier general April 28, 1862. He commanded a brigade throughout the Vicksburg campaign and was mustered out July 1865.

Des Moines Feb 27th 1863
Dear Brother

It is some time since I have written to thee. Since Catherine has got well she has written every week and Cyrus also wrote several times so I concluded to wait till they got tierd or till I had something to write that I though would interest thee. Captain Housten[1] is here and I though I wuld embrace the oppertunity of writing to thee. Catherine wrote the beginning of this week but I was afraid as thee is on the wing thee might not get the letter.

We are all well at present. Catherine is better than usual and the babe begins to look verry fat and healthy and the other children are well and enjoy themselves verry well. They often talk of thee and wish thee at home. Sallie often cryes abut it but I never fail to incourage her to think thee will come home all right when the war is over. They bothe learn their lessons every day except sunday and both are learning verry well.

Cyrus is well at this time much better than I ever expected to see him. He had one Bad spell of asthma a few weeks ago but is as well as usual now. We have not had one cold day in Iowa this winter. We have had a little snow but nothing to amount to any thing. We have had a great deal of cloudy weather lately some rain and any amount of mud the roads are nearly impassible at this time. The river has not been frozen over this winter. I consider this winter a perfect blessing to the poor lonely war widdow at home and also to the brave soldiers in the field. How often when I laid down in my good bed in a warm room this winter has my mind wandered away off to thee and thought how I would like to know if thee had a comfortable place to sleep or wheather thee was out in the cold and guard duty. But the great Father of all is kind to all his children and he tempers the wind to the shorn lamb. Oh that we could put our trust in his mercy and loveing kindness. It seems as if I loose sight of God and the good principals that a good Mother instilled into me but when trouble comes I find that is my only refuge the place to look for help in this life and mercy in the life to come. But I will chance the subject for thee used to dislike sermonizing and perhaps thee will throw the letter away without reading further.

*   *   *

I do not expect it is worth while to write to thee abut the business for Catherine has kept thee posted if thee gets the letters. William Scarborough was here this week. He says the cows are all right and every thing is going on the same slow way. The people are talking down in that neighbourhood of resisting the draft and think the proclamation of the first [illegible] a perfect outrage. Ingersoll is verry uneasy about the mill and Catherine and him has been trying to fire up matters but he is not willing to give the face for the Hurst mortgage and believe she has concluded to let the matter rest till thee comes home in the spring. She has not received any money yet from the army.

We have lived verry comfortable this winter. I feel better contented since we got the deed. If Cyrus gets able to work he will get a roof on the house this summer I hope. I think carpenters wages will be high this summer. Their has over a hundred mechanics been taken out of this place for the 17th regiment of cavelry.[2] Add Michel[3] went as a taylor. Among the rest Henry Smith has returned from the mountains and he and Fred are going back. So it seems as if every one is going somewhare.

* * *

Their is a great many secess here. Ingersoll is one of the worst. Some of the people fear that we will have civil war here but I have never felt as if their was much danger.

I hope before I write agen to have some better ink. Please give my best respects to Mr. Smith. Cyrus wrote to Smith[4] about one week ago. Please write soon and after. The last letter we received from thee was dated the second of Feb. I must close. Catherine and the children send their love. I remain thy ever affectionate sister.

Mary F. Milner

1. Leonard B. Houston was a native of Indiana and a resident of Des Moines when he enlisted in the 2nd Iowa Infantry on May 4, 1861. H was appointed captain, 23rd Iowa Infantry, on August 10, 1862; was promoted to major on May 19, 1863, and was mustered out on July 26, 1865.

2. Actually this was the 7th Regiment Iowa Volunteer Cavalry Reorganized. Between April 27 and July 13, 1863, eight companies were mustered. Regimental organization was completed when one independent company and three others from the 41st Iowa Infantry that had been serving on the frontier were added.

3. Addison Michael, who resided in Centerville, originally enlisted in the 7th Regiment Iowa Volunteer Cavalry on February 24, 1863, and was then transferred to Company A, 7th Cavalry Reorganized. He was mustered out May 17, 1866, at Fort Leavenworth, Kansas.

4. Presumably Merion Smith. Smith had written to Cyrus on February 24. There are four letters in the collection from Smith to Cyrus, but none are included in this book.

Des Moines Mar 8 1863
Dear Father

I am well and hope these lines will find thee the same. Mother said all is well. I can read part of thy letter [illegible]. I made a mistake. I feel bad. I [illegible] my cousin went app. I intend to go down to see them when the [illegible] come up here. Frank I do belev will never get over his mischieviousness be cus he is as bad as ever. I think of going to start to chool the medell of April. The baby grows fast. He will soon be seven months old. It snowd some last night. Just because I wanted to go to see Mrs Smith and Frank has been wanten to go down tow or three days but something turned up that we culdnat go. Fred was hear day before yesterday I bleve. [illegible] It is not very hard to write. I want to see him very much. I am not like that little girl that I read in a book. She spelt dear deer. I spilt the ink yesterday only a little. I beleve that uncle thinks the war will soon be over. I was Jos now making Frank pictare on a pace of paper.

Dear Taylor

I let Sallie send this more to encorage her to write than with the expectation of thee being able to read it. The child is verry anxious to learn to write to thee so I think it best to let her do so some times. She often writes letters on her slate to thee. Frank is very good to say his lessons and says he wants to do what his papa wants him to. Dear little things they talk of thee everday and seem to love thee well.

thy aff Catharine

Des Moines, Iowa
Mar 22nd 1863
Dear Taylor

I have lookd for thee home for these two days but have lookd in vain so I sit down to write thee to let thee know how we all are. We are all well except Cyrus. He is quite unwell at this time again. I have not receved any letter since the one of the 8th[1] and feel a little disappointed at not geting one or seeing thee by this time. I suppose that Lt Murrey has got to camp by this time and told thee how we ware at the time he was here. I am sorry to hear of Aults ill treatment of Murrey for I was rather predisposed to think him very much of a gentleman but Ault is so mean that I am not surprised to hear of him treating his very best friend the meanest of all. I wrote to John Sumpter last week to get Aults account ether sent to thee or to me so I could send it to thee but I have not receved any thing from him yet. If John should send it I want thee to let me know of it. Cyrus has still talked of going down to the grove[2] but I do not think he will be able to go to the mill to do anything this spring. I want to go down as soon as the weather becomes settled and warm enough to take Ellis. I want to see how they all feel down there. I think from what I can learn that there are a good many Copperheads[3] in the community there. W Scarborough was up some time ago to see about geting some rails out of the timber and he told me that the most of them said they would resist the Draft to thair utmost. I do not know what luck I would have a mongst them at collecting any thing or not. I have not had any thing from there this winter but 25 Dollars of the hog money and that I paid to Cyrus. So if thee was to get home any time soon thee would have all the accounts to fix up with for it will take a good bit to set us up again if thee should get home again this fall or when the war shall end. I do not think thee will be much please with this letter for I feel rather blue and of corse do not feel much like writing of any thing but the sturn realty. Mary would like to know if thee got the letter she sent by a Captain in the 23d that was here a week or so ago. She has got her and Franks picture taken and will send them as soon as we hear from thee again. The Children are learning their lessons verey well and are verry good considing who they belong to. The baby grows now and is get to be verry good and knows his sister and seems to love her and She loves him dearly and Frank can never do enough for his brother baby. I remain thine forever.

    Cath

1. This letter was not found.
2. Catharine is probably referring to Lamb's Grove, which is near Newton.
3. Copperheads were northern Democrats who opposed Republican war aims.

Vicksburg Campaign

EDITOR'S NOTE. On March 9, 1863, the 22nd Iowa was ordered to march from Iron Mountain to St. Genevieve, Missouri, where it was to board transports to steam south on the Mississippi River to participate in the Vicksburg campaign. The regiment reached St. Genevieve on March 12 and embarked on the transport *Black Hawk* on March 22. On March 27 the unit disembarked at Milliken's Bend. The 21st, 22nd, and 23rd Iowa and the 11th Wisconsin were organized as the Second Brigade, Fourteenth Division, Thirteenth Corps, of the Army of the Tennessee. Colonel Charles L. Harris was named brigade commander. The division was commanded by Brigadier General Eugene A. Carr, the corps by Major General John A. McClernand, and the army by Major General Ulysses S. Grant.

Until April 30 the regiment conducted operations on the Louisiana side of the Mississippi River as Grant attempted to find a route by which he could move his army south of the city and then ferry it across the river. On April 16 and again a few days later boats from Admiral David Porter's fleet successfully steamed past the Vicksburg batteries. On April 30 Grant conducted a river-crossing operation with McClernand's corps in the lead. There then followed a succession of battles at Port Gibson, Raymond, Champion Hill, and Big Black River. By May 21, the Union army was firmly established facing the fortifications of Vicksburg. Assaults on May 19 and 22 were unsuccessful, and the Union army settled down for a siege. The fortress surrendered on July 4, 1863. The 22nd Iowa participated in all major battles of the campaign. After the surrender the regiment moved to the vicinity of Jackson to protect the Union rear from attack by Confederates near that town.

On August 13 the regiment embarked on the *Baltic* and moved to the vicinity of New Orleans. Taylor had received a furlough and returned to Iowa during part of August and September, apparently departing Des Moines on September 19. He rejoined the regiment near Brashear City, Louisiana, in early October.

> Head Quarters 22 Regt Iowa Vol
> Milligans [Milliken's] Bend Louisiana March 28/63
> Dear Catharine and all the rest

We are here in Dixie 20 miles from Vicksburg along with some 40,000 troops and I suppose destined to play a part in the drama of this war in the takeing of the last stronghold of the rebellion in this regime. I think we will not have to fight much here. It seems to be the intention of those in command to take the town of Vicksburg by siege and I understand that our troops have it nearly surrounded at this time but I do not know what the prospect is of our final capture of the place. It struck me as a favourable sign of the final crushing of this rebellion to see what amount of territory we have wrested from the traitors in the last year. One year ago the rebles held the river from Orleans to island No 10 a distance of 1,000 miles. They now only hold from Port Hudson to Vicksburg, a distance of some 25 miles and that is besieged above and below by 160,000 men and must eventually fall.[1] There is gun boats continually running past the reble batteries and communicating with our forces below which makes me think that they will soon have to evacuate both of those places and leave us masters of the Miss' Valley.

This is a nice country here but I would not like to live here on account of the water. The land is flat and low. And at this time if it were not for the levees thrown up along the river it would all be under water the surface of the river being higher than the surrounding county.

The whole farming country here seems deserted. I do not think there will be enough raised here this year to support anything. The negroes are all run off and the plantations deserted and are fast being laid waste by the soldiers. It seem terrible to think of to see fine houses and large plantations that were once the seat of wealth and luxury and probably happiness wholly destroyed and the inhabitants cast out without even a home to go to. But they have brought it on themselves by their inhuman conduct and thirst for power and they must reap their reward.

Our whole brigade is not yet here. We are looking for Col Stone down to-day or to-morrow with the 21st and 23 and three companys of our regiment. We left him at Memphis and we passed the 23rd at Helena. I seen a member of the 28th at Helena[2] John Aikins Wils Butters J. W. Wilson[3] and I also seen a Lt Baldwin from Chester Co Pa who I used to know and a great number of friends and acquaintance. Jo Powell and Boliver[4] was at Helena a few days before we got there but their regiment had gone down the Yazoo pass and I did not get to see them. I have not much of importance to write about today.

I am well and I feel very well contented but we have been so much on the wing that I have not got my letters and am beginning to feel as if I would like to hear from home. The weather here is very warm. While I set here writing the sweat just drops off me. The trees are out in leaf and some of the boys had a mess of lettice last evening but with all the signs of natural life there is no activity in the signs of peaceful occupations. Not a plow nor a wagon except what belongs to the army is seen in this whole country. What a contrast to the states of the North at this season of the year.

Our Court Martial is adjourned for the time being until Col Stone arrives and Col Graham gets better so as to attend to it.

I got word that Old Bob Dixon has broke up and of course I will have to loose what I have paid Ault for that land as he will never be able to pay ten cents on the Dollar in what he owes. But still I want thee to send me my book account and look over my old notes and thee will find a note signed by Ault and G. T. Anderson and given to Frank Allen for $625 which I paid off now. I want that note and if Ault will not pay it I will make G Anderson antie on it. As soon as the things assume an aspect here that will admit of it I will come home and see to my things and fix them in a shop that they will be in a safer condition than at present. I think of sending a lot of clothing home by express as we have got down here when we do not need them now and I think they will be safer at home than here. If we should get far enough north to need them I can have them sent to me next fall and it will save me buying more. And if I do not need them thee can make them up for Frank or let Cyrus have them. We do not get as much news here about what is going on as we used to when we were in Rolla and further up the river but we may be able to learn something in a few days that may give us some better feelings than we possess now. I do not know what the defences around Vicksburg is nor do I have any Idea how long it will be before we will leave here but I think we will lay here some time before we move. For we will not be able to do much untill the water goes down and the roads drys up so that our transportation can go along with us.

I believe I have not much more to write now and as I will keep you posted once a week I will close.

Give my love to the children and tell them to be good little children and give them all a kiss for me and take one for thyself. Write me soon and let me know what is going on.

> I remain thy affectionate husband and Brother Taylor Peirce

1. New Orleans was captured by Captain David Farragut on April 25, 1862. Confederates began to evacuate Island Number 10 the night of April 7, 1862, and the garrison surrendered at Tiptonville, Tennessee, the next day. Port Hudson is about 25 miles north of Baton Rouge and, by river, about 150 miles south of Vicksburg.

2. The brigade commanded by Colonel Stone consisted of the 21st, 22nd, and 23rd Iowa Infantry Regiments. On March 20 the 23rd Iowa embarked for Milliken's Bend from New Madrid, Missouri. The 28th Iowa had been encamped at Helena, Arkansas, since November 20, 1862. In April it would reach Milliken's Bend.

3. John Aikins was an Ohio native who lived in Prairie City, Iowa, when he enlisted August 7, 1862. He was discharged March 11, 1864. Wilson H. Butters, another Ohio native who lived in Prairie City, also enlisted August 7. He died of disease on April 23 at Helena. J. Wright Wilson was a Pennsylvania native but was living in Newton when he enlisted August 5, 1862. He was promoted to regimental adjutant October 20, 1864, and was mustered out July 31, 1865.

4. Joseph Powell, 10th Iowa Infantry, was also from Newton. He enlisted August 28, 1861, was wounded May 16, 1863, at Champion Hill, and died of those wounds on May 25. Although the original handwriting of both Taylor and Catharine indicates that the second name is Boliver, no soldier by that name served from Iowa. The soldier is probably William F. Bodley from Jasper County, a member of Company B, 5th Iowa Infantry. He is mentioned in future letters, and the dates coincide with the locations of that regiment. Also, Catharine mentions in a letter dated November 20, 1864, that he had come home "with out a scratch" and would not return to the army. William F. Bodley was discharged July 30, 1864. Several other soldiers named Bodley served from either Newton or Jasper County, but they were wounded or killed, or their discharge dates and regiments do not coincide with dates mentioned in the letters. Leutenant Baldwin cannot be identified. Four Pennsylvania regiments participated in the Vicksburg campaign, but none had reached Milliken's Bend by the date of this letter.

Des Moines March 29th 1863

Dear Taylor

I am only going to write so as to let thee know how we all are. We are all well but Cyrus he is quite unwell yet but has not got to be as bad yet as he was this time last year. He is not so much out of heart as he was last spring and I hope when the weathe gets warm he will get better again. We are haveing pretty good wether but not as good as there was prospect of two weeks ago. But the farmers have commenced their spring work to sow wheat & with a good hearty grain and all kinds of produce bring a better price now than there has been for two or three years. All manner of things have gone up here. Calico is from thirty to thirty five cents per yard and all othere dry goods are at the same rait. Wages are better than for some time back and more work to be done and not hands enough to do it. W Minson says that there are more building enguaged to be done this summer in town than he knows of than has been done for the last two years. It seemes as if money is plenty or more plenty at least than for some time back for the Catholic have got money and subscription to the amount of five thousand Dollars to build a new church with. [page missing]

      Catharine A. Peirce

[undated][1] We are lying on the levee on the Missi with a mile of water on each side of us and it rained nearly all night last night and such rain as it puts down here. It is none of your fine northern rains driving before the wind in fine drops and taking a half hour to wet you through but it comes down just like pouring it out of a tub.

I do not know how long we will lay here but I suppose not longer than tomorrow morning. Col Stone took dinner with me to-day and he said he was going to try and move us this evening down to a plantation where we would be comfortable. He is certainly the best man in the army and if I live to get home I will never cease to love and respect him for his manly and humane conduct to the Soldiers under his command. He is more like an older brother than any thing else I can compare him to.

Well I have stoped twice before and now I have run clean out but when you write to me again I want you to be sure to inform me how much money the Lt left with you and also wheather you get the cloths by express that I sent you.

Give My love to Cyrus and Mary and tell them to write to me and when you write to Rachel[2] give her my love and tell her I do not forget her but I am so accupied that I seem to have not time to write and you must do it for me. Kiss the Children and tell them I will bring them presents when I come home and they must be good.

      Taylor

1. This letter was probably written on April 4. Taylor's letters in late March and early April were written on Saturday, and April 4 was a Saturday. Also, in late March and early April rain fell heavily in the area. The 22nd Iowa left Milliken's Bend on April 12, and this letter was written while the regiment remained near the Mississippi River.

2. Rachel Gibson was Taylor's sister.

     Des Moines April 6th
     Dear Taylor

I and the children are well and feel verey well contented for the present but lonesome without thee. The children talk dayly about thee and wish for thee to be at home so they could get a kiss and talk to thee. They both have so much to say to thee that I can not write the half. So I will leave thee to guess the most of their talk. Frank is a very good boy and says he love his papa well and all the rest of us 16 bushels. Sallie she thinks if ever a child loved a papa she loves hers and her little baby brother. She is never to busy playing to do what I want her to for the baby and he the Dear little thing seems to love her too. If any thing was to hapen to him I do not know what she would do, for there has so maney children died of late with the Deiptheria that I feel fereful of it. Hannah Silverman lost two with it last week and several others that I am not accuanted with. I try to take the best care of children that I possible can and then if they get it I can not help it. I have staid at home all winter on account of the baby and I have not been any place but at (T) W Johnsons yesterday. W has give out going to the peak now. I believe he was only talking to make us think that he did not want to be Draft in to the war or somethink of that kind. He sent his best respects to thee and wished thee a suscesful time and our own troups generally. But we can not tell any thing by what we hear these times for thare are so many that say one thing and do another and are trying to make times worse for us that do wish the soldiers good luck and a successful peace. I can not writt of for the baby is so cros that I have to rock him all the time.

Mary is not verey well but I guse that it is nothing but cold and she will be better by tomorrow. Cyrus is better again and is in good spirits for him to be thou he is not satisfied. He wants to go to the mountains or some other place to see if he will get well. He thinks he can not get entirely well here and I do not think he will ever be real well here or there or any where in the world. I do not know any thing write much for we get no war news those day on any thing of account. I saw in a paper at Johnson a great account of the weding of the Prince of wales and the Princese of Denmark[1] but I expect thee has seen more of it than I have. So I will close with respect all the boys and love to thee I remain thine

   Catharine

 1. On March 10, 1863, Edward VII, Prince of Wales and eldest son of Queen Victoria, married Alexandra, daughter of Prince Christian (later King Christian IX) of Denmark.

   Camp 22nd Reg Iowa Vol
   Millikins Bend La April 11 1863
   Dear Catharine and the rest of my relations & Friends
I again set down this evening to write to you. Our division which is the 14th division of the 13th Army Corps Department of Tennasee and under General Eugene A Carr Division Commander,[1] Genl John A McClernand Corps Commander,[2] and Genl U.S.Grant General in Chief[3] is now under marching orders for the country opposite Vicksburg on the west side of the river. For what purpose I know not but I suppose to assist in taking that nest of Traitors Which we are bound to do if it takes us all summer. If you look on the map you will see a town called Richmond[4] about 15 or 20 miles from V which is our destination at present I suppose to be ready to march and cooperate with the troops in the rear of V. We have reliable information that the rebles have nearly all left the City. For what purpose it is impossible to say. I have heard it said by some of the head officers that We would be in V in less than two weeks or else we would know that we could not take it. So you may look out to hear by my next letter of either a victory or a bloody defeat for I will not be likely to have a chance to write another untill after the battle. I know you will be under great suspense untill you hear from me again. But you must keep in good heart for the Father of all is watching over me and if I should fall in defence of the country and its laws I will bequeath to my family the name of a good soldier and a benevolent man to my comrades. And for the rest I will trust to fame to keep from being destroyed in the

General avalanch. I do not think I have an enemy in the regiment except Cap Ault and I would rather have his enmity than his friendship. There was Ten of our Co Expressed our overcoats home this evening and Have consigned them to Cyrus to have him write to Vandalia Jasper County to A M Smith so that he can come to your house and get them. I put in an overcoat one pair of Pants my old vest and dress coat and a cap for Frank. If it is to large for him you can take out a piece and let him wear it. The bundles are all tied up separately and labeled with Each mans name on a piece of paper. The Names of the men sending are John L Chiles Asa E Burtch H.W. Chiles William Irwin Joseph T Cushatt G. W. McCall G.W. Shawhan M.H. Falkner O E Vanhorn D.M.Vanhorn[5] Taylor Peirce. There is one whip in the package which is to go to A.M. Smith and as soon as the package shall arrive if Cyrus is not at home I want Mary to take this letter and go to the Express office and take them out and send word down to Vandalia as soon as you can so that Each one will get his clothes as soon as possible. The charges are all paid on them but if there is any Extra charge you may pay it and the boys will make it all right with me. I transmit the receipt from the Express Co here which you can present them. This is all about the cloths. About our business I have nothing to say but to let it go untill I get home for I do not wish to be bothered at this time about my business untill I get out of this fight and then I will come home and stay a short time to fix up things. I shall not say much abot things now except I am well and have made a barrell of beer to day to drink while the weather is so hot and the water not good. I think that by takeing care of myself that I can keep well here as I can in Iowa but I may be deceived. However I will try. I want you to write to Rachel and tell her that I have not forgotten her but that I have had so much to occupy my time in the way of my duty that I could only find time to write to you that occupy my first thoughts. Give my love to Cyrus and Mary and the little ones and tell Frank that I would like him to be a man and live up to all that is honorable and He will always have friends in the walk of life. And above all if I should not live to return to not instill into his mind the love of money for that will grow fast enough but rather try to make him understand the time value of one cent than to hanker for thousands. For I have found that happiness will dwell as well with poverty as with riches. And well does thee know that the happiest hours we have spent has been when we were the hardest set to get along and for those old times I would risk every thing but my good name and conscience.

This letter is about done, the candle out and we are ordered to move at 6 oclock so I will end. I remain Affectionately your husband Brother and Father

Taylor Peirce

1. Eugene A. Carr graduated from West Point in 1850 and fought Indians in Texas before the Civil War. He fought at Wilson's Creek, Missouri, and Pea Ridge, Arkansas. He was promoted to brigadier general on March 7, 1862.

2. John A. McClernand was an Illinois congressman who was appointed brigadier general May 17, 1861. He fought at Belmont, Missouri; Forts Henry and Donelson; Shiloh; and Arkansas Post prior to the Vicksburg campaign. He would be relieved by Grant before the fall of Vicksburg.

3. Ulysses S. Grant graduated from West Point in 1843. He served in the Mexican War and then resigned from the army in 1854. In June 1861 he was appointed colonel of the 21st Illinois Infantry and in August was appointed brigadier general retroactive to May 17. He commanded at Belmont, Forts Henry and Donelson, and Shiloh before launching the ill-fated attempt to approach Vicksburg by land through northern Mississippi. On October 25, 1862, he was appointed commander of the Department of the Tennessee and took command of operations against Vicksburg on January 30, 1863.

4. On March 30 Grant ordered McClernand to send a force to occupy Richmond and secure a navigable water route from Milliken's Bend through the bayous to a point on the Mississippi south of Vicksburg.

5. John L. Chiles: Virginia native; Vandalia resident; mustered August 28, 1862; wounded May 1, 1863, at Port Gibson, Mississippi; mustered out July 25, 1865. Asa E. Burtch: Indiana native; Vandalia resident; mustered August 28, 1862; mustered out July 25, 1865. Henry W. Chiles: Virginia native; Vandalia resident; mustered August 28, 1862; mustered out July 25, 1865. William Irwin: Ohio native; Vandalia resident; mustered August 28, 1862; discharged June 8, 1865. Joseph T. Cushatt: Ohio native; Vandalia resident; mustered August 28, 1862; killed May 22, 1863, at Vicksburg. George W. McCall: Ohio native; Vandalia resident; mustered August 28, 1862; transferred to Invalid Corps February 2, 1864; no further information. George W. Shawhan: Indiana native; Vandalia resident; mustered August 28, 1862; wounded October 19, 1864, at Cedar Creek, Virginia; mustered out July 25, 1865. Mifflin H. Falkner: Ohio native; Vandalia resident; mustered August 28, 1862; captured and paroled May 22, 1863, at Vicksburg; mustered out July 25, 1865. Owen E. Vanhorn: Ohio native; Vandalia resident; mustered August 18, 1862; died of unknown cause on July 10, 1863, near Vicksburg. David M. Vanhorn: Ohio native; Vandalia resident; mustered August 28, 1862; mustered out July 25, 1865.

Des Moines April /12/63
Dear Taylor

I have not got much to communicate this morning but it is sunday and I write to let thee know how we all are. We are all well to day. Cyrus is better than he has been for some time at least better than he was this time last year and I hope he will get better as the spring advances.

Dear one I sit down to write to thee not knowing what I may find to say to thee. We get no war news at this time. I suppose that the heads of affairs are trying to keep thing quiet for the present so the rebles will not know what thair at. All I have to say about it is that I hope they will do something soon that will tell and that pritty loudly too for I think that now is the time to strike a blow that will make them squirm. From what I can hear the rebles are nearly starved out and if it is true they will have to give up before long. We heard last week that there had been a bread riot among the woman and Children in Savanna[1] and that they were in a starveing Steate and would set fire to the city if they did not get bread. It seems to me that is a big threat for woman to make but then a woman will do and dair a great deal for her starveing children. I think a pity of the poor little children but the just must suffer with the unjust. If the parents had not been such foul traitors they might still of enjoyed peace and plenty unless they belong to the class of men that are pressed into the war against their principals which I learned there are hundreds of such among the reble forces.

I can not help but feel thankful to the giver of all good that we have pleny here at the North and a fine prospect for more. The spring is opend but not as earley or as forward as it had the apperence of two or three weeks ago. But still the framework gos on gloriously. We have had no rain for some time and it is geting pritty dry so the grass is backward this season. We have had no boats up this spring and that has made teaming a good business here and wages are good generaly. The river was full enought at one time for boats to run up but I suppose that government has them all in her services to carrie provisions for the soldiers. It must take an awfull amount to supply the army that lay around Vicksburg with enough to eat.

Thee wanted me to send thy book account on Ault and a note. The note I inclose to thee. The book account I hope thee has receved before this time as I sent it some three weeks ago and also Mary's and

Franks pictures. I would get little Ellis picure if I thought I could get any thing like a good one to send to thee but the artists do not like to take the picture of a baby and it is a hard matter to get them still long enough to get any like a picture. So I will wait a while and hope that thee will get home soon to see the little thing. I think he looks very much like the old [hoss?] himself. The other Children say they want thee to come home so that they can kiss and hugg thee. They both have to kiss thair Aunt and uncle every night before they go to bed and wish one for thee. I believe I must close now. With heart felt love I remain thine Catharine. Give my respects to all that I know that thee think are deserveing of such.

Catharine A Peirce Des Moines Iowa Polk County

1. A riot for food (known as the bread riot) occurred in Richmond, Virginia, on April 2. Most of the rioters were women. Similar demonstrations took place soon thereafter in Augusta, Milledgeville, and Columbus, Georgia. Reports from Macon, Georgia, on April 2 indicated that there was a shortage of food there also, but it was due to distribution problems rather than scarcity. Food shortages were reported in Savannah on March 25, and railroads were forbidden to transport food out of the city. A riot did occur in Savannah on April 17, 1864, with women demanding bread. The leaders were jailed.

Des Moines Iowa
April 16 1863
Dear Father

With pleasure I set down to write to thee and let thee know how we all are. I let the baby fall yesterday but I did not hurt him so thee may know that I did not do it perpose. Mrs Smth is here today. Tomorrow mother is going write so that I write to day. I have a new hat Mother bought out of the mony thee sent Mother. Cousin Annie Mary Gibson sent thee her love. So I cant think of much more. I will try fill up the [illegible]. Thy baby is as cross as can be. I want thee to get a ferlough as soon thee can. Mother is going to send me to scholl. I feel glad to get to go for thee knose that I never went. Somebody let uncle mule out of the Sable. He calls it betsy. I made a mistle aboute the mule. I go to Sunday chool. I am a frade that thee will not like it because thee saide thee wold not let one of thy children go to Sunday chool but Aunty thought it best fore me to go to Sunday chool. It is a splended morning. Trees are in bloom but thigs are not so farward as [illegible] right up above the house. I wish thee write me a [illegible]. Frank [scratched?] the lady. Last week the cavelry past here. I must [illegible]. Auntie and uncle sends lov to thee.

    Sarah

    Richmond La April 18 1863[1]
    Dear Catharine

I set down this morning to write a few lines to let you all know what I am doing and that I am well. Our whole army is moveing down this side of the river to Carthage which our troops occupy. There is one continual string of soldiers passing through this place for the purpose of getting below Vicksburg. Our Division is encamped 15 miles below here and about 7 or 8 miles from Carthage. Genl McClernand is still below us and yesterday Genl Hoveys Division passed down[2] with some two or three others which I do not know. The 28th Iowa is in Hoveys Div. I seen some of the boys of Myers company[3] yesterday as they passed down. I am detached from our Regt now with a lot of men to transport provisions to the army from this place in flat boats. How long I will be at it I can not tell but I reckon several Days. Yet I have nothing to do but to command the men and see to the safety of the Stores. I like the work very well. Genl Carr is a fine sociable man and we are used very well and have a good time of it. We live on the fat of the land. I tell you the fair part of rebledom looks black at us yankees when we make them shell out their good things for our benefit. But I do not allow the men to disturb anything but what we want to eat for I do not like to see their things destroyed that is no benefit to us. The country is being laid waste so that there will be nothing raised here this year and what the people is to do for something to eat is more than I can tell. They say that their is not more than two weeks provision here and some of them is being fed by Govt now.

    Truly war is a terrible calamity to any land when it exists and I pray god that it will soon end in our beloved country and that we may once more enjoy the blessings of Peace.

    I do not think we will have any battle at Vicksburg at present. I think from the movements here that our destination is Port Hudson and communicate with Farragut and Banks and the evacuation of

Vicksburg will become a necessity. The gun boats and transports run Blockad night before last withot much injury. I heard there was one boat burnt which was all the loss we sustained and I suppose we will be put aboard the transports at Carthage and run down the river to some other point and I reckon you will not get a letter from me for some time again. I will continue to write and trust to providence to it getting through. I have had no word from home since the 8th of March and am getting hungary for a letter I tell you. But I keep up my spirits by thinking you are all well and happy. I would be happy if I knew that you were all well. Capt Ault is with his company and I understand is going to resign. He left his wife on a commissary boat at the Bend I suppose to wait untill he could get his resignation accepted so that he could go home with her but this is only reported to me. As I do not have any communication with him myself I go to Col Stone for what I want and let Cap Ault attend to himself. If he does not resign as soon as the army stops he will be court martialed again and I think we will get shut of him. There my paper is full and I must quit. Direct to Taylor Peirce Co C. 22nd Iowa Vol Inft: Care of Col Stone Memphis Tennasee. Kiss the children for me and give my love to all.

I remain thy affectionate Husband Taylor Peirce

1. The 22nd Iowa, along with the other regiments in the brigade, left Milliken's Bend on April 12 and reached Richmond that evening.

2. Brigadier General Alvin P. Hovey's Twelfth Division, Thirteenth Corps, reached Richmond on April 16. By April 18 McClernand's corps, including the 22nd Iowa, was bivouacked near Pliney Smith's Pointe Clear plantation about two miles from New Carthage.

3. John Meyer was a Pennsylvania native and Newton resident when appointed captain July 14, 1862. He was promoted to major on March 14, 1863, received a brevet promotion to colonel on March 13, 1865, and a promotion to lieutenant colonel on June 15, 1865. He was mustered out on July 31, 1865.

April 19th 1863
Des Moines, Iowa
Dear Taylor

We are all well but Cyrus he is not well nor I do not think he ever will be. He did talk of going to the mountains but he is not well enought to go. He could not stand to travel two days for he is so weak that he dose not get up to feed the cows in the morning half the time. I receved thine of the seventh with pleasure and am pleased to know that thee is well and so well contented for I would feel badly if thee was a way down there and could not get home and was unhappy and in trouble. Thee nead not be in any anxiety a bout us for we get along finely here. We have all we want or that we realey need but thy presents to make us perfectly happy. I have had one hundred and fifty dollars to do with since thee went away. I have paid seventy seven to Cyrus for our boarding and fifteen and a half to the Doctor for myself and the children when we had the lung fever in the fall. We have been here just eight months yesterday so thee may see how much it will take to keep us while thee is away. I have got the children well clothed but not verey finely and have money enough left to send them to school this summer and get Books for them. Sallie must go any how and Frank may if he wants to for he is to watch all the time at home to keep him at home. For there are so meny boys for him to play with that I think it would be better to pay a little to a school for him than to have him running on the bottom with all the young Irish that can be raked up.

Dear Taylor I am sorry thee has not got my letters regularly for I have made it a sure thing to write every week ever since I got able to last fall only in March when I thought thee would be at home in few days. I wrote the 23rd of March and send thee the Book account of Aults and Mary and Franks picture[1] which I hope thee will get yet. And this day a week ago I sent thee Aults note that thee spoke of wanting.[2] I have directed all my letters for sometime to St Louis in the care of Col Stone for I did not know wether Ault was your Captain or not so I though that I would send them in the care of the Col and they would be safe. I want thee to write as often as thee can for I like to hear of the doings away in Dixie and how thee gets along. Pretty often I have not much to write of for I do not get out to learn any thing of importance so I remain thine afc wife

Catharine A Peirce

1. In her letter of March 22 Catharine states that she has not received the record of Ault's account, nor does she mention sending the pictures. Apparently she wrote the next day, but that letter is missing.

2. See Catharine's letter dated April 12, 1863.

Head Quarters 22 Regt Iowa Volunteers
Suzette Plantation Louisianna April 21st 1863[1]
Dear Wife, Sister, Children, and all the rest,

I received your letters of the 18th and 30th of March[2] yesterday and you can not think how good it made me feel to hear from home once more. It has been more than a month since I received any things from you and I had begun to be anxious about you for I dream of you every night and sometimes my dreams is not of the agreeable kind and then I feel badly for a time over it although I know that it is but the workings of a [illegible] mind yet I can not help it.

I received Aults accpt all right and also the news of Ingersolls anxiety about the stock which does not trouble me much. You can just tell him that he can have the [Hussat] mortgage for the claim he has against the Mill and nothing more and if he wants to sue for it you can make an affadavit that I am in the Service of the United States and that my presence is neccesary for a just and fair trial of the causes and he will have to wait untill I come home to get his money. If he wishes to push it go to T E Brown and employ him to attend to it untill I come home.

I do not want to sell the stock for I feel as if I would be at home in time to put up feed for it this fall. I also received Marys & Franks Picture and was glad to get it for the sight of a favourite Sister and a beloved little Boy is enough to gladden the heart of a Brother and Father in a more peacable and better situation than the one I occupy at present. If I now had the Mother and the little one I would be satisfied for I have never been satisfied with Catharines picture for I do not think it looks like her. And Murray tells me that the little fellow is the brightest looking child he ever seen and so I am beginning to feel as if I would like to see him. Sallies picture is so like her that I am satisfied with it and the one I got yesterday is all right. Mary is as natural as life and Franks countenance shows that he is going to have plenty of back bone in him to make his way through this world. In short I am highly pleased with you all. I wish Cyrus could have his health so that you could all enjoy yourselves once more.

Mary wrote to me in her letter on a subject that she evidently misunderstands my opinions on and I think it due to her as well as myself to set her right. She thinks that I do not like to talk about religious subjects. In this she is mistaken although I have always dispised sectarianism of all kinds and the religion that is founded on a blind belief in the Divine origin of the bible. Yet I have never ceaced to believe in a great and overruling power that controls and Governs all natural and whose laws are as fixed and as imutable as the universe of which he is the Soul and Substance. I also never doubted the immortality of the Soul and its liability to receive future rewards and punishments. Not as is generally believed in corporality but intelligently as the Soul is all intelligence and nothing tangible can operate on it. Corporally the rewards and punishments must be of a nature commensurate in the substance to be operated upon. Therfor as God is intellect Goodness Virtue and love the reward must be a higher degree of all those Godlike qualities and the punishments must be the reverse of these. And what can one imagine a more miserable state than to exist through all eternity divested of all qualities that tend to exalt and elevate the mind of man.

In conclusion I then say that I have an unbounded confidence in the goodness of God and the final ratification of all his rules an laws as laid down in the great book of Nature which should be the Study of all. It is evident that the disobedience of any one of these laws either of a physical nature or of right must be followed by its just punishment and the more frequently they are broken the more severe the punishment and the harder to render atonement, as in the case of the Drunkard or the Human Tyrant. Now if you can understand this you can see what my hopes are in this and a future life and what great inducements are offered to live an honest and virtuous life and do unto others as you would have them do to you. These are my principles and I would like my children taught the same untrammeled by any Sectarian feelings and without one feeling of bigotry or fanatasism. This is all.

The Army is still moveing South. We are now near Carthage 20 miles below Vicksburgh and where we will stop is impossible to tell. Suffice it to say that we are numerous enough to overun the rebellion and put a stop to its further progress if not to utterly anhilate it.

Ap 22nd. This day we moved to Carthage 20 miles below Vicksburg. I can see the camp of the Federal Soldiers as far down the river as the eye can reach. The rebles is fortifying at Grand Gulf[3] some distance below us and it is thought that we will have a fight there. It is the residence and homestead of Jeff Davis[4] and I want to help raze it to the ground and leave his hearthstone as desolate as many of those that has been desolated by his infernal treachary. This is about all I know of the army or its workings. Lt Murray will be tried by a court martial in a day or two for being absent without leave so as to receive his pay in future as he can draw nothing untill he has had his sentance. He will then proceede against Cap Ault and I think will dismiss him from the service. I think Mrs Ault is still at the bend yet liveing on a comissary boat but I am not certain. She got a bad name when she was down here but this is confidential.

If Ingersoll commences suit you must not let him get judgement untill I get home and I will work him. I am going to send some money home by Mr Allender our Chaplain and if he calls on you I wish you to use him well for he has been a good friend to me and has been of use to me in a moral view. I will send $20 or 25 dollars. As soon as we get through I will get a furlough and come home for a time. I am well and I hope this will find you all so.

    Farewell your affty
    Taylor Peirce

[This portion of the letter was undated and unattached to any other letter. Based on its context, it is possible that Taylor added it to the letter above.] One More word with regard to the bible. I believe that the bible eminated from the divine esence of man, for without the godlike qualities of man he would not be able to reason or write on any reasonable subject and of course he would be unable to form any rational theory for any thing that was not permanently brought to his notice by his opperation of some one of the five sences. I therefor come to this conclusion that all the maxims laid down in the bible that are in accordance with the well known laws of nature or as some call it God are good and have came from a true source namely the reasoning power that comes from God. But any maxim or theory laid down in that book that we know are contrary to the fixed and unalterable laws of god are not correct and must have eminated from a diseased mind made so by constantly dwelling on abstract and visionary theorys. But I love to dwell upon the greatness and the beauty of God as it is made manifest to our earthly intellects by the opperation of the senses which are given to us for the purpose of giving us the means to comprehend that we are a part and portion of the same great intelligence that govern and formed us.

I wish this copied off in ink and if I should never return I wish the children to be taught to read all good works. The bible also. But I want them to take it for what it is and not what sectarians say it is and let them read this and judge for themselves.

My love to all kiss the little ones for me
Taylor

1. Peirce may be referring to Somerset Plantation owned by Judge John Perkins. The plantation was about eight miles from New Carthage. The 22nd Iowa would not reach Somerset until April 24.

2. No letter of March 18 was found. Catharine and Sallie wrote on March 8 and again on March 22. Based on this pattern, Catharine also would have written on March 15, but no such letter is in the collection. Catharine wrote on March 29, and that is probably the March 30 letter that Taylor mentions.

3. Confederates began to fortify Grand Gulf, about eighteen miles south of Vicksburg, in early March. By late April it was well defended by infantry and heavy artillery.

4. Briarfield, Jefferson Davis's plantation, was located on the east bank of the Mississippi River almost directly across from Perkins's Somerset Plantation.

Head Quarters 22 Iowa Inftry
Port Gibson Mississippi May 4th 1863
Dear Catharine & all of you,

I have set down to write to you knowing that you would hear of our battle and would be very anxious about me and as soon as I found that I could send a letter I concluded to do so. On the 29th day of April we tried the experiment of bombarding the fort at Grand Gulf with the view of landing our forces at that place but the fort was impregnable being hewn out of the rock and after six hours cannonading it was found impossible to silence their guns.[1] So the Genl concluded to run the blockade with the Transports and as they kept along side of the Steamboats and kept up such a continual roar of cannon that they did not get to injure one of them and there was not a life lost. So we were then marched down the river on the La side three miles below where we encamped for the night.[2] Early the next morning we were then on board. There was 3 divisions one under Genl Carr one under

Genl Hovey and one under Genl Ousterhouse.[3] The whole under Comd of Genl McClernand. The whole number of men amounted to about 20 or 25 thousand men and said to be the finest army that has ever been together. We were taken down the river on the 30th of April about 10 miles to Rodney where after feeling for the rebles and finding none we landed[4] and drew 3 day rations and left about 3 oclock P.M. for this place. We marched out about 6 miles and halted and eat supper. In about an hour we started again. Our brigade being in advance we moved along sloly expecting every minute to hear our advance Guard fire on the reble pickets. About one oclock at night the long expected sound was heard. After some pretty sharp firing we were opened on by the reble battery which they had placed to rake us as we come up a lane but oweing to our caution and silence we had passed our whole brigade along the lane before they were aware of it. As soon as the battery opened on us we halted and laid down untill Harry Griffith come up with his six pieces of cannon. As soon as he got them fixed we were moved on the double quick around behind it into the head of a ravine where we all laid down and at it they went and kept it up untill near daylight when the rebles ceased to fire and we laid and slept on our arms untill sunrise. We were all tired and anxious when the morning came knowing that the rebles would contest the ground to the utmost. Our regiment was ordered to support the battery through the night and of course we lay right where the ball and shell flew and if a man has weak nerves then is the time he will be likely to feel it haveing to stand inactive. And the roar of the guns and this whissing of ball and bursting of shell is terrible but thank fortune I am not of the weak nerved kind and did not suffer from that sickning failing called fear and am very thankfull that I am so constituted that I do not.[5]

Well after about an hours suspence waiting to see where the attack was to come from as the rebles were concealed in the cane breaks and gullies we sent a challange to them in the shape of a shell and imediately they opened on us in earnest the ball for the May party was opened. Our forces was in three divisions. Our regt under Carr with 21 & 23 Iowa the 8th [&] 18 Indianna & 11 Wisconsin formed the right wing of the army.[6] Genl Hovey the centre. I do not know what troops he had. Genl Osterhouse was on the left. I suppose our lines were 3 miles in extent and the rebles under Genl Green Stacy & Bowen all under Genl Baldwin[7] attacked all three of our divisions at once about 7 oclock in the morning and attempted to surround us. The Battle became general abot 9 oclock and continued without intermission untill about 1 pm when our division made charge and the rebles gave way and retreated across the Bayou burning the bridge. That left us at liberty to go in on the Centre which we did and after some pretty hard fighting the rebles broke and run and Osterhaus had got through with his work and by sunset the whole reble army was in full flight and our victory complete.[8] This is said to be the most unfortunate battle of the war for them. They came down in the morning with about 13,000 fresh troops boasting that they would just capture the d—d Yankee and make slaves of them. They retreated in the evening a defeated and dispairing rabble without order leaveing about 3,500 of their men behind them. The slaughter on their side was dreadful for the number engaged although they had the advantage of knowing the ground and kept hid in the cane breaks all the time just standing far enough in to keep out of sight so that they could fire out at us. But our English rifles sent their Leaden messengers in and thinned their ranks as if the plague was amongst them. Harry Griffith with his first Iowa battery tore their ranks from end to end. He is as brave as Ney.[9] All night long we could hear him giving his commands with a clear loud voice and urging his men to give it to them while he sat or moved round amongst the guns on his horse amid a perfect shower of grape canister and shell as though it was but a May shower of rain instead of a shower of iron and seemed as unconcious of danger as when he used to walk the streets of Des Moines. Indeed our Officers all showed a bravery that was sublime. Not one of them but seemed that on his coolness and example before the men depended the fate of the battle.

Our loss is small. Our regiment was more exposed than any other but it come of the best except the 23. Our regt lost 3 killed and 12 wounded. 2 of the wounded are mortally. The rest will all get well. The 23d met the 23d Alabama and after about an hours hard fighting put them to flight. What the loss is in the 23 Iowa I have not learned certain but not much. I suppose 30 killed & wounded will cover the loss. The 23 Alabama left 360 Dead in the field or rather in the cane breaks and I suppose a number that was not discovered. We took some thing over 500 prisoners and been gathering them up ever since. I guess we will not have far short of 7 hundred. I heard we got 12 of their guns but I do not know whether it is correct or not. I do not know what the official report is but you will see it and the comments on it before you get this. We had one man wounded and none killed.[10] Cap Ault showed considerable courage and behaved much better than I expected he would. Our Lts are good men and true and Col Stone showed us what he was as brave as he is good by the way they talk of making him governer of Iowa. Although I do not want to lose him from our regt yet I would like to see him at the head of the affairs of the State for he would give the copperheads hell and I want you to do all you can for him to get him in there. If there is a man in the world deserving it is him. Lt Col Glasgow[11] is another here. Although I was a quarter of a mile from him I could hear him shouting to his men and telling them to give to the damd rebles and well his men obeyed him. Genl McClernand remained on the field all the time of the battle and actually sighted some of the guns himself. Old Grant heard us fighting and come on to the field about 11 oclock and when the victory was complete you ought to have heard the shout that rung out on the evening air. It was enough to pay us for all our fatigue and dangers. I am well and stouter than I have been for years although I had gone 48 hours without sleep and had to eat my meat raw with hard crackers and water and twice a little tea and marched with 40 pounds and my gun and 80 rounds of cartrige. I was able to fight the whole day among the cane breaks and ravines with the thermomater up to 90 without anything to eat. I walked 2 miles for my supper and back again on to the battle field when we lay and you had better believe I slept sound that night. After we got a little breakfast we all started after the retreating rebles but they had burned the bridges. And so we had to stop and make a bridge across bayou peirie [Pierre] when Genl Quinbys brigade started after them at 3 oclock P.M. of the 2 and Osterhaus and Smiths Divisions started at one oclock in the morning.[12]

At 7 oclock we started for Grand Gulf to take the forces there and capture the battery by land but the rebs were to smart for us for they evacuated. And so we are laying now about 2 miles west SW of Port Gibson and 6 miles from Grand Gulf awaiting orders. I understand the rebs will make a stand at willow springs 18 miles from here.[13] But I think they have either been whipped or they have not stopped there or else we would have been ordered up to assist in the fight. If they do not make a stand there they will evacuate Vicksburgh without a fight. I have just learned that the 23d lost 7 men killed and 24 wounded. Smith is safe and all the rest that you are acquainted with. Our forces engaged was abot 7,000. The rebs about 10,000. Our whole force could not get up in time to help us. I must quit as my paper is done.

Your afft Taylor

1. At about 8 A.M., April 29, the Union fleet under Admiral David Dixon Porter began a bombardment of the Confederate positions at Grand Gulf. The objective was to destroy them and then ferry the Union army across the river near there. At about 2:30 P.M. Porter and Grant broke off the engagement. One Union gunboat was disabled, eighteen sailors were killed, and fifty-seven wounded.

2. At 7:45 that evening Porter steamed his fleet past Grand Gulf and anchored near Disharoon's plantation on the Louisiana bank about four miles below Grand Gulf. One Union sailor was killed in the firing when the gunboats passed Grand Gulf. The Union army marched overland and encamped near the plantation.

3. Brigadier General Peter J. Osterhaus commanded the Ninth Division, Thirteenth Corps.

4. On April 30 the Union army, led by Carr's division, was ferried across the Mississippi and landed near Bruinsburg, a few miles north of Rodney.

5. The Army of the Tennessee advanced inland led by the 21st Iowa Infantry. About 1 A.M., May 1, they encountered Confederates near Port Gibson, Mississippi. Captain Harry H. Griffiths's 1st Iowa Artillery went into action against the Confederates. During this night battle the 22nd Iowa was in the second line and did not participate. Griffiths was a Des Moines resident who was appointed captain of the 4th Iowa Infantry on August 8, 1861. He was appointed captain of the 1st Iowa Light Artillery Battery on May 16, 1862, and was mustered out June 12, 1865.

6. The 8th and 18th Indiana were in the First Brigade. The Second Brigade consisted of the 21st, 22nd, and 23rd Iowa and the 11th Wisconsin.

7. Brigadier General Martin E. Green, Brigadier General Edward D. Tracy, and Brigadier General William E. Baldwin commanded Confederate brigades under the overall command of Brigadier General John S. Bowen. Tracy was killed during the battle.

8. At McClernand's direction, Osterhaus deployed his division along the Bruinsburg road against Tracy, and Carr and Hovey were deployed along the Rodney road against Green. At about 6:30 A.M. the Union forces attacked. Baldwin reinforced Green, but the two were driven back by superior numbers. By nightfall the Confederates had retreated through Port Gibson.

9. Michael Ney was a marshal in Napoleon's army. He was known as "the bravest of the brave."

10. The 22nd Iowa had 2 killed and 21 wounded. The 23rd Iowa had 9 killed and 26 wounded. There was no casualty report for the 23rd Alabama, but total Con-

federate losses were 60 killed, 340 wounded, and 387 missing. They also lost four cannon. Total Union losses were 131 killed, 719 wounded, and 25 missing.

11. Lieutenant Colonel Samuel L. Glasgow, 23rd Iowa Infantry, was an Ohio native and resident of Coryden when he was mustered in as a major on September 19, 1862. He was promoted to lieutenant colonel on December 1, 1862, and to colonel on May 19, 1863; he was mustered out on July 26, 1865.

12. Brigadier General Issac F. Quinby commanded the Seventh Division, Seventeenth Corps. He became ill in late April and did not rejoin his division until May 16. In the meantime it was commanded by Brigadier General Marcellus M. Crocker. At 4 P.M. on May 2, after awaiting construction of a bridge over Bayou Pierre, Crocker's (Quinby's) division began to cross. Brigadier General Andrew J. Smith's Tenth Division, Thirteenth Corps, and Osterhaus's Ninth Division entered the town of Port Gibson on May 2.

13. Carr's division, including the 22nd Iowa, garrisoned Port Gibson until May 5, when it joined the other Thirteenth Corps divisions at Willow Springs.

> May 17, 1863
> Des Moines City Iowa
> Dear Taylor

I receved an envelop this week with 20 Dollars in it. I suppose it came from thee as it was endorse in thy hand writing and mailed at knoxville in this state. I conclude thee had sent it by the chaplain and he concluded not to come up here so he sent it up by mail. I have receved no letter this week but I will keep my spirits up untill I do get one for I still trust to the all wise to take care of us both thee and myself and provide for us and watch over us. We are all well here except Cyrus. He has had another spell of the Asthma this week and is quite unwell. Yet the Children are well and full of fun. They talk about thee every day and want to see thee very bad. They and thair Aunt have gone to Vans hill to gather flowers and the baby is asleep so I have a nice time to write if he dose not wake up to soon. Mary wrote thee this day a week ago[1] and I did not. But what she wrote I do not know but I expect she gave thee a ful account of all the doing here. We are haveing the most delightful spring here this year that I ever remember of seeing. The Crops are going in good time and there is a good prospect of a bountiful Crop of all kinds of fruit and every thing is in a florishing condition here. If it was not for this turable war every thing would be well. For from the present accounts they are likely to get the Copperhead pritty much all killed out of Iowa. But accounts differ so that I do not know what to believe for we hear one day of a great Victory and the next that it has been a defeat or something near to it.

Dear Taylor how I would like to be down there with you boys if I had no young child that nead my care at home. It would be a glorious thing to be down thare to adminester to the wants of the poor ignorant freed people there. To teach them to read and to write even as much as to learn them to write their names if I could do nothing more. The baby woke up this morning and nocked my thoughts galley west so that I do not know where to begin again and the Children retumd and one and another came in till it is now dark and the baby is a sleep again and I thought I must try to fill the sheat with something. Mary has been to church to day for the first time in two years and there has been a great amount of spreading done to day by the quality up town after flowers [illegible]. I have no news that I can think of but what thee will be likely to know. If thee has a chance to get the late papers only that Des Moine has shone herself for the Union by the City election the other day.[2]

I will close with true afect Catharine A Peirce

Give my respects to all the boys and tell them I think the soldiers every night thee in particular.

1. This letter was not found.

2. The Des Moines election for mayor and alderman resulted in the election of an "unconditional Union candidate" for mayor and ten Republicans and two Democrats to the city council.

May 24th, 1863
Des Moines City
Dear Taylor

I received thy letter of the 4th yesterday and hasten to write to let thee know that we are all well and glad to hear from thee and that thee is well and all right. We have such sturing news of the doing down there that it makes us feel bad in deed for those dear to us that is ingaged there but glad to hear of your victory so far and hope to god that vic-

tory will go with the strips and stars untill there is not a rebel stronghold left in the whole Country nor a traitor in the land. The republicans seem to be in good heart a bout the death of the copperheads in
Iowa and if you are successful at Vicksburg that the war will soon be
at an end. There is accounts of the takeing of V in this morning paper
but wether it is to be relied on or not is not for me to know which is
the correct way of what they hear. Mrs Slaughter was up here this last
week and give us all the news from the grove. In general Mag Shreck
is maried to John Berry and gone to house keeping on old Clines farm
and Mary and Blanford is maried and still live with the old folks and
Wash farms a part of the home place. Aunt Susie is keeping house for
Mrs Ault while she is away on her spread. Mrs S says Mrs A is known
at Newton all of her doings both at home and a broad. I did not tell
Mrs S what thee had writen to me for she seems to know so much
more than I did that it was not worth my time to talk at all. The last
letter that Juliea Piptren receved from Joe Kuhn[1] he was some where
in Arkanssas belonging to company of cavelry from the mountains.
More than she could not tell of him. The people at the grove are in
better surcomstances now than ever before I guess for they have more
money. Bluford Sumpters[2] wife for one she has more than she ever
had before and a good many more I might name. John Sumpter has
receved a good bit of money from Bolaver and Josh Adamson this
spring with the privelage to lay it out in Stock or some thing that will
pay the interest. I beleive that is about all the particulars from the
grove so I will conclude by telling of the children. They are well and
right good considering. Sallie gos to school and is well pleased with it.
Frank says his lesson to me every day and can spell right well in four
letters.

　　The baby has got to be right well and grows well enough now but
still is verey backward. He is nine mounths old and he cannot sit alone
yet nor has he any teeth but he seems to be bright enough intellectually.

　　　　　I remain thine forever Catharine A Peirce

　　1. See the letter dated June 14, 1863.
　　2. Bluford Sumter was an Indiana native and Des Moines resident. He enlisted
August 12, 1862, in Company I, 39th Iowa Infantry, and was mustered out June 5,
1865.

Camp of 22 Regt Iowa Vol Inft June 7th 1863
Rear of Vicksburgh Mississippi
Dear Catharine and the rest of you

I am once again with the regiment and have regained my health but not my strength. I think we are all haveing our acclimating sickness now. The company has lost verry heavily since we started on this campain. There had been no death in the co since we left home until the charge was made here on the 23 of May in which there was 4 killed Dead on the field and 23 wounded.[1] 3 of them has since died and the ballance is getting along but the most of them is in a condition to be discharged from the service. Our company now only numbers 77 men all told for duty and 80 men in all. We have no commissioned officer now. Murray was forced to resign for cowardice. Mullins was wounded and has gone home on sick leave of absence so our orderly is in command of the Co and I am acting orderly for him. I think Cap Ault will not come back again and if he knows when he is well he will not. When I get home I will give you the whole history of the affair as I hear it from the boys here. I do not know wheather I can send much money home next pay day or not. I had to spend $10 while I was sick for things to eat and they sell things so high here that it takes a good bit to get enough to do a man any good, chickens 50 cts little ones butter 50 ct pr lb dried fruit 25 cts per lb and potatoes $4 per bu buttermilk 20 cts per grist blackberries 20 cts pr qrt. So you see I had to pay out my money for nothing. I could not get things out of the comissary for they had not got them and I had to have something besides hard crackers and sow belly[2] to put in my stomach for you know when I am getting over a spell of sickness I have no stomach for rough victuals. But I think I can send as much as I did before if I meet with no other accident.

Well we have laid a regular siege to this place and are receiving reinforcements every day and this place must fall in the course of a few weeks and the reble army here must surrender at discretion for we have got them tight. James Halpin and Joseph Powell wer both killed at the battle of Blackriver Bridge.[3] Powell had his leg taken off and it mortified and Halpin was killed. I have not seen the 23 since the fight and can not tell wheather Smith is safe or not. All the rest of our acquaintance is safe. Well Kitty War is a strange thing. I am laying within

400 yards of the reble forts and close to our batteries that fire a shot every 5 minutes all the time both day and night and the muskets are all the time fireing and sounds for all the world like a woodchopping. And I have got so used to it that I do not hear them unless I stop to listen for it and sleep as sound as I would at home in bed. The rebs have pretty much quit fireing on us and we have not lost but one man in our lines for a week and that by carelessness. This is all the paper I have and the mail is going out and so I will close. I will write again in a few days. Give my love to all. I received thine of the 26 May and 5 other letters when I got back all at once.

I remain affectionately Thine Taylor Peirce

1. The attack on the Vicksburg fortifications was May 22. The 22nd Iowa lost 27 killed, 118 wounded, and 19 missing, most of whom were captured. (These numbers are included in the *Official Records of the Union and Confederate Armies.* A report submitted by Adjutant Samuel Pryce to the Iowa adjutant general on December 15, 1864, gives different numbers: 42 killed, 128 wounded, 19 captured.) Colonel Stone was wounded, and Lieutenant Colonel Graham was captured.

2. Sowbelly is salted pork.

3. James Halpin, Company G, 23rd Iowa, was a native of Ireland and a resident of Vandalia when he enlisted August 15, 1862. He was killed May 17, 1863. Powell was wounded May 16 at Champion Hill and died nine days later (see March 28, 1863, letter). Champion Hill is approximately twenty miles east of Vicksburg. Big Black River is approximately ten miles east of Vicksburg. Both battles were Union victories that drove the Confederates back into the city.

Head Quarters 22 Regiment
Iowa Vol Near Vicksburg Mississippi
June 13th 1863
Dear Wife and friends and also the little ones

I am here within 3 miles of Vicksburg along with the regiment shooting at the rebles and getting shot at by them. We have been lying in the head of a little ravine that runs out of a hollow with the noon day sun beaming down on us like a furnace for 3 weeks and I do not see much prospect of us getting out of this for the next three weeks to come. However we are doing very well now. We have to go on duty every other night and stay on duty 24 hours. That is one third of the time 4 hours on a relief and the rest of the time we have to ourselves to cook and keep clean. We have to Stay in the hollows for as soon as a man sticks his head above the top of the hill hiss comes a bullet at him and admonishes us to keep out of sight. We have a good safe place to lay just over the brow of the hill about 400 yards from the reble breast works. We have good water for this country all along the lines and the men is beginning to look much healthier than did when I come up to them from Grand Gulf. We are getting good liveing now and have some fruit such as plumbs blackberries Dried Peaches Apples and potatoes and now get good sugar cured hams twice a week and we do much better than we did before we got set down to the Siege.

Well now for a discription of the opporations here. You can look on the map and see the situation of V. You can also see the Black and Yazoo Rivers. You will see that the Yazoo comes in close abov V and the Black some 50 miles by River below. Well we hold all the country between those Rivers as far up as Machanicsville about 40 miles. Our lines are about 14 miles in length Extending from Hains or Walnut Bluffs on the Y clear around V about 3 miles distant untill it reaches the Mississippi 4 miles below that impregnible and far famed city.[1] Our lines are abot 3 regiments deep or if drawn up in line would form a collumn about 6 men deep all along the line and batteries stationed every 200 yards clear round. Our rifle pits are now being extended within 40 or 50 yards of the reble breast works and forts and in some places we are right up against them and have undermined some of their works. We work in the rifle pits at night and then lay in them in the day time and if a reble shows himself we shoot him. We have got so close to them that they can not work their cannon and have not been able to fire more than 50 shots at us from their forts since I come here. But their sharp shooters still lay in their rifle pits and shoot at us if they get a chance but they seldom hit anyone. I think we have had no man hurt within our division for 10 days but one man who lay down right on the top of the hill and went to sleep in open view was shot in the hip. Our artillary keep up a continual roar night and day each battery throwing one ball every five minutes through the day and every 30 minutes through the night. And as soon as it is dark the boats takes it up and throw 3 shell every 15 minutes all night and those bursting in the air keep up about the same sound as it does through the day. Then in the day the men in the rifle pits keep it up so constantly that it sounds just like a chopping frolic where the axes are going continually. You may think this is quite an interesting place at this time but I have got so used to it that I seem lost if the ceases to fire for a half hour or so. We cook eat and sleep under the roar of artilery and are luled to rest by the softer sound of the rifle.

June 16th. Dear Catharine I have been so busy making out our pay rolls and other duties that I have not had time to finish my letter. I will now commence it again. We are having a high old time of it here. These two days we have got so near to the rebles works that they begin to feel uneasy and have opened Some of their inner works on us. But they have not succeeded in doing us any harm yet for as soon as they shoot one of their guns about 6 or 8 of ours lets off at them and makes it so hot that they have to dry up untill they can steal in and give us another sly shot.

Our Pickets stand guard at night within 20 feet of one another and have quite a time conversing with one another. The reble soldiers are all tired of the war and if it was not for their leaders this war would close in a month for they all acknowledge that they can never whip us and would be glad to lay down their arms. They are getting very hungry in Vicksburg and our Pickets give theirs crackes and coffee nearly every night as they seem almost starved.

Gen Pemberton[2] has ordered them to charg on us twice within the last week but they will not do it and he swears that he will keep them there untill he starves them to it. This is their own words.

I do not know what is the program with us. We are doing well now and seem to be getting along finely with the work and I would be satisfied to let the siege drag its slow and tedious length along. For I am not foolhardy enough to want to go into a useless battle or one that could be avoided as well as not but if it becomes nessessary I am ready. I think our Generals are good men and seem very considerate about the safety of their men although there is a continuous firing both of Artilery and musketry both day and night.

June 20th. Dr Catharine I commence again this noon to write. It seems as if I would never get this letter finished. I have so much to see to. We have no commissioned officer with us now. Murray resigned after the

battle of black river. Mullen was wounded and has gone home and
Capt Ault and his duck has gone home and I hope will never return.[3]
I have seen Marion Smith. He come over and stayed with me last
night. He is not very well. In fact all the new regiments are looking
bad I suppose for the effects of acclimating. He made the whole cama-
paine and was in every battle except the charge on Vicksburg May 22
but he was in one at Millikins Bend[4] where 160 of the 23 and 900 Niggers defeated 4,000 Rebles. The 20 was badly cut up loosing nearly
one half of their men. They now only report 150 men fit for duty and
the 22 only 215 for duty. This is awful. Two of the largest and finest
regiments in this army numbering 1,600 effective men exclusive of officers when we crossed the Miss not quite two months since now reduced to less than 400. Of course they will fill up as the men get over
the fatigue and get used to the climate but 400 of them is lying in the
soldiers grave or are rendered unfit for the service from wounds received in the various battles. Well Kitty we have had another high old
time of it to-day. Last night after we had laid down the order come
to fall in at 6½ oclock this morning. So we thought we were good for
one nights rest but in about 15 minutes the order come to get in line
in five minutes and go and lay in the rifle pits all night. So out we went
and when we got to Head Quarters they concluded that we might go
back and sleep if we would be sure to get into the rifle pits by 6½
oclock. So back we went and slept untill morning. At Day break I was
arroused from my sleep by the cannon and soon it become one continual roar. We hurried up and got our breakfast and went into the rifle
pits expecting the rebles would make an effort to break out and then
we lay under the broiling sun, and the cannon balls and shells flying
over us at the rate of 50 pr minute all forenoon and one continual
storm of grape, cannister, & schrapnell, enough to have annihilated all
the rebles on the Southron confederacy. At noon or a little after we
were relieved and I am now trying to finish my letter before we are
called out again. I keep midling well in fact very well except my stomach. You know how it troubles me always after a spell of sickness and
the food and way of living makes it as hard as usual on me. But I am
in much better health than the most of the boys and if I can get my di-
gestion regulated and get some strength in proportion to the flesh. I
think it is on account of the climate. The days are no hotter here than
in Iowa but every day is hot alike. The nights are quite cool and if it

was not so we would be unable to do anything at all. For the heat is so weakning that it seemes impossible for a man or at least one of us to muster up energy enough to cook a little victuals. Boliver was over to see me last week and is as fat and hearty as ever but would like to see the war ended. Smith is sick of it and offers a premium to get out of the service and most of the men who has been through this campain is tired of war but do not seem dishartened at all. I would like to see the war closed but I would not leave the service untill it is peacably and honerably wound up for all the wealth in Iowa. I feel confident of the final success of our government and her ability to take the first place among the nations of the earth surrounded with a halo of glory such as the world has never seen before. I received thy letter of the 8th and was glad to hear that you were all well and such good prospects of plenty in the fair lands of the north. Dr Hunter & his brother is down from Jasper[5] sent by the citizens and supervision to attend the sick and wounded soldiers of the Hawkeye Republic and are doing a great amt of good not only with medicine but of their old and well remembered faces and many comforts that they bring for the boys. Dr Hunter says that land is a fair price now in Iowa and all things are going up. As soon as property gets high enough I want thee to have our property sold for I will not settle again to labour as hard as I have done.

Well this is the third sheet. I have so much to write that I do not think I will ever get done. Cap Ault has completely run out in his company and also in the regiment. He ruined Murray. It was in this way. Murray was somewhat cowardly so much so that he showed it at Port Gibson and at Black River and when they come to make the charge Murray went up to look up the ground to charge over was shot through the fingers. Ault to[ld] Col Stone that he would swear that Murray shot himself and Stone told Murray he must either resign or Stand a court martial for cowardice and so Murray resigned. On the morning of the charge some of the men were so sick that they were not able to go and asked to be excused but Ault swore that no d—d coward should leave the ranks and ordered the Sergeants to bayonet anyone that offered to drop back. They then started on the run and Ault run about 50 yards and him and Major Atherton crept into a gutter and that was the last ever seen of them that day untill after night they crept out.[6] If our company had have had an officer that would stayed with them to have given them any orders they need not have lost more than 3 or 4 men. The company and the whole regiment was left for 8 hours without a commander. Col Stone was wounded in the arm severely early in the fight and Col Graham was taken prisoner in one of the reble forts and Atherton the coward was hiding in the gutter and the men fighting without orders all the day. No better or brave men exist than the 22 & 23 rgts of Iowa Vol. Col Glasgow is a gallant and brave officer and the Capt of Co A Cap Houston now Major is a regular fighter and a good man. I am afraid we will loose Col Stone which would be a sore thing for us now for a better or braver man does not live than he is. We have no field officer in the regiment no with us. Atherton has resigned. Col Graham is a Prisoner of war and Col Stone is wounded and at home so you see that we are nearly out of officers. I have tried for a place but I do not know wheather I will get one or not. I have asked Stone for a recommendation but wheather I will get it or not I cannot tell for I expect he is so busy he will not think of it unless I had some one to remind him of it. Cap Ault had better not return to the company for there is men here that swears they will kill him if he ever shows his face here again and they are men that will not stop at anything. One of the men that he drove into the fight was very slightly wounded a mere scratch but his health had been so poor for a week or so and the heating of the blood in the charge made his system in such a state that his wound inflamed and mortified and killed him. This was J Newell nephew of Hugh Newell. J.R. Kenady[7] was another sacrifice of his evil nature and several others that I could name but you would not know them.

Tell the people of Iowa that Atherton and Ault are not fit to be citizens of the U.S. nor are they suitable persons to receive the protection of Government. They are both cowards and are both perjured. Atherton perjured himself by not proforming what he agreed to do for the country and will perjure himself to resign his commission.

Dear Catharine this is the only place that a man has got walk straight or be caught that I have ever seen. One of these shifters like Ault gets caught every pop but if a man goes Straight through he can get along as well now as any place. Tell the children I send my love to them and want each of them to have two kisses from me. I will try and send $20 when I draw my pay which will be next week I expect and you can give them some presents. I will get 2 months pay $34 and I owe 4 or 5 that I got while I was sick and I must keep some for fear that I can not get things when I get sick again. Tell Sallie to write me a letter and Master Frank to send me some word in they letter. How does the baby look and what is he going to be? Is he Milner or Peirce or both? I do not like his name. If he is going to be any thing you had better change his name for I and my father both had such hard times that I would be afraid he would inherit the ill luck without any of the good qualities of Father and all the bad of mine. However you can do as you please. If you think it all right I am satisfied.

I must now wind up. Write to me soon. I am now looking for a letter from you. I intend to come over as soon as this place is taken.

I remain your affectionately Taylor Peirce

1. Mechanicsburg is about twenty-five miles northeast of Vicksburg between the Yazoo and Big Black Rivers. The town was the site of several clashes, but on June 13 it was occupied by Confederate cavalry. Haynes Bluff was along the Walnut Hills about ten miles northeast of Vicksburg, overlooking the Yazoo River. By June 16 Union troops had occupied defensive positions at Haynes Bluff. The Union siege line around Vicksburg was about twelve miles long.

2. Lieutenant General John C. Pemberton commanded the Confederate forces at Vicksburg.

3. Murray was wounded May 22 and resigned May 27. Mullins was wounded May 22 but remained in the army until mustered out July 25, 1865. Ault resigned August 8. See the letter dated August 20, 1862.

4. In early June the 23rd Iowa reinforced the African Brigade, District of Northeast Louisiana, at Milliken's Bend. On June 7 Confederates attacked those forces along the road to Richmond. The Union forces were driven back until fire from three gunboats halted the Confederate advance. Confederate losses were 44 killed, 130 wounded, and 10 missing. Union losses were 91 killed, 285 wounded, and 266 missing or captured.

5. Dr. Henry E. Hunter was a physician from Newton. In 1858 he was chairman of the Newton Medical Society. On June 3, 1863, the Board of Supervisors appointed him to visit soldiers from Iowa serving near Vicksburg. The name of his brother cannot be determined.

6. There is no record of charges against Lieutenant Murray. Atherton wrote the report of the May 22 assault because Colonel Stone had been wounded and Lieutenant Colonel Graham, who assumed command, had been wounded and captured. Certainly Atherton made no mention of hiding in his report. Reports of the battle indicate that those in the 22nd Iowa who were not captured were forced to use the

available cover, such as ditches, to protect themselves until dark, when they could return to their lines.

7. Jackson F. Newell was a native of Ohio and resident of Newton when he enlisted August 2, 1862, in Company C, 22nd Iowa. He was wounded May 22, 1863, at Vicksburg and died of those wounds on June 1. Josiah R. Kenaday was also an Ohio native and resident of Prairie City when he enlisted September 6, 1862, in Company C, 22nd Iowa. He was killed May 22, 1863, at Vicksburg. Hugh Newell had been elected mayor of Newton in 1857.

June 14 1863
Des Moines City Iowa
Dear Taylor

I and the children are all well this week and Cyrus and Mary are both well. Cyrus is better this week than he had been for a week for some time but whether it will last or not I can not say. He has been trying Ayers Cherry Pectorial[1] for two weeks now and I think that and the warm wether is helping him. We have verey warm days and cold nights with little or no rain. The rivers ar lower now than they were any time last year and no sign of rain to raize them. They say that the crops all are doing well not withstanding the want of more rain. Fred Smith got home yesterday from the mountains and he says that he met with plenty of wet wether after he came into this state and that the crops look fine in the western part of the state and that time are better in the Mountains this spring than for the last two years. Money is plenty and provissions are all a good price but hands are scars there. A good hand will get from 3 to 5 Dollars per day for all most any kind of work. The City of Danver was nearly all distroied by fire this spring and they are building it up again and that makes work plenty there for a time.[2]

Joseph Kuhn was here this last week and looks as well and just like he used to. I can not see that two years delveing in the mountains hase made any change on him at all. I tryed to make him believe he came home to get maried but he sayes that there will be widows enough without him leaving one but there is no telling what he may do by what he says. I do not think he ever made enough to bring him home. While he was at the peak he joined the 3rd Colorado Vollenteers on the first of March and they were just fifty one days in marching into the Mos river. His reg is stationd at Pilot Knob Mo. for the present.

They have never been in a battle yet.[3] Joe liked soldeiring first rait and dose not want to quit untill all the rebels are conqured or killed so thee may know that he is a good Union man if he was Democrat. He brought up word of Joe Powel haveing his leg shot off just below the knee so I suppose he will have to come home before the war is ended. He has all ways writen that he did not intend to come home untill there was not a reble left. Powel as thee know, I suppose was at the fight at Jackson Mis and Vicksburg. At which place he was wounded I do not know.

Dear Taylor I have writen all I can think of but about the baby. He is growing nicely now and can sit alone and is siting on the floor beside me while I finish writing to thee. I think if thee can not get home soon that I will get his and my picture taken before long and send to thee for I would like thee to see him now. He is so fat and every one that see him say that he is pritty and that he looks like thee more than either of the other children and I tell thee that I think he smart for us to have. Sallie gos to school and is trying to learn all she can. I think Frank says his lesson at home ever day and can spell in three and four letter very well and is very mischievious still.

> I remain thy affc wife
> Catharine A Peirce
> I hope this will find thee in good health and spirits
> Dear One

1. Ayer's Cherry Pectoral, made by the J. C. Ayer Company of Lowell, Massachusetts, was advertised to cure "colds, coughs, and all diseases of the throat and lungs." Ayer took the profits from his patent medicines and invested in paper and cotton mills. The town of Ayer, Massachusetts, is named after him.

2. At 1:00 A.M. on April 19 a fire broke out in Denver, causing approximately $350,000 in damage and destroying the central part of the town.

3. Joseph Kuhn lived in Des Moines in 1860. On December 8, 1862, he enlisted at Denver, Colorado Territory, and was mustered in January 13, 1863. Initially he served in Company A, 3rd Colorado Infantry. In February the regiment was assigned to the District of Southeast Missouri and in April marched to Pilot Knob. In October 1863 the regiment was reorganized as the 2nd Colorado Cavalry, and Kuhn was assigned to Company H. He was killed by Indians while he and another soldier were en route from Fort Larned, Kansas, to Fort Zarah, Kansas. His service record indicates that he was killed on May 22, 1865, but the commander at Fort Zarah reported that he was killed May 20. (See the January 25, 1865, letter to Taylor from Mary.)

June 21st 1863
Des Moines City Iowa
Dear Taylor

I received two letters this week and I tell thee I feel good to hear thee has got well again. If thee can only take care of thy self and get home safe. One of the letters was from Grand Gulf and the other from the rear of Vicksburg. Thee wants to know what kind of a boy Frank is. I can hardly tell for he is so very mischievious that it is hard to keep the run of his doings but he mostly minds what is said to him. He is pretty determind in his own way but when he has to give up he is not sulkey like Sallie. He get over it and is as plesant as ever in very short time. The most trouble I have had with him since thee went away was to stop him from going to the river with Finians young one. In the spring when the weather begin to get warm, I gave him to understand at once that he could not go and I have had no more fus with him about going to the river. Sallie thee knows is verry stubborn as well as self willed and I do hope thee will get home safe to help me bring her up. For if we ware taken out of time I do not know what would become of her for she knows to much for a child of her age a bout some things. It was a bad thing we ever had Mrs Wilson about our house for that childs sake, but enough. I will explain it all when thee gets home. I think the little one will be like Frank in disposition and will not be hard to manage. I think he looks like his sister Mary did at his age. He has the same big eyes and wide forehead like she had. I went up town this week to get his picture but did not succede in geting a good one so I will try again in a day or and if thee cannot come home soon to see us I will send it to thee.

I do not know much news but what I expect thee knows by this time. I see in the daily yesterday that Marion Smith was wounded at the Battle at Millikens bend. Whether he is severely hurt or not the account did not say.[1] That was all that I was acquanted with in the list of wounded and also that they have nominated Col Stone for Govneor and Eastman for Lt Govenor.[2] So I suppose that you will have a new Col for your Reg before this get to thee. I do not know how to direct my letter but I will direct as usual and hope thee will get it all right. I would like to know if thee dont think that I can write better than when thee first went away or not. Thee knows that it is a faling with us to not spell well and therefore I hope thee will excuse my spelling. We are all as well as usual but Cyrus he has had another bad spell of the asthma for three days and Sallie has a cold but I do not think it will amount to much. Cyrus has his spells about every two weeks no matter how the weather is. He still talks of leaving home to see if would not get better. I have to stop so often to at tend to the baby that I can not write a sensible letter nor a very long one.

> I remain thy wife Catharine A Peirce
> The children send their love and want thee to come
> home soon.

1. The *Des Moines Register* on June 23, 1862, listed Merion Smith as having been wounded at Milliken's Bend. No records of the 23rd Iowa Infantry, no battle reports, and no lists of Iowa soldiers wounded during the war support this.

2. Enoch Worthen Eastman was born April 15, 1810, in New Hampshire and moved to Oskaloosa, Iowa, in 1847. Originally a Democrat, he became a Republican in 1857 and was nominated for lieutenant governor in 1863. He was elected along with Stone, who ran for governor when Samuel J. Kirkwood decided not to run for a third term. Eastman died January 9, 1885.

> Head Quarters 22nd Regt Iowa Vol
> Vicksburg, Miss July 4th 1863
> Dear Catharine

The Gibralter of America has fallen. It surrendered with all its munitions of war and from 30 to 40,000 prisoners of war.[1] Not a man escaped. The surrender was unconditional and took place this morning at 10 oclock. At the appointed time a white flag was raised on every port and battery along the line as far as the eye could reach. Then went up to heaven one long loud simultaneous cheer from the brave soldiers who for six weeks have worked incessantly amid whissing of bullets and the explosion shell to accomplish the what has just been proformed.

Truly it was a sight and sound to awaken the livliest feelings in the heart of the lover of his country. To us who have been in turmoil and strife of battle day and night for so long a time it seemed as though a weight was lifted from us that well nigh bore us down. I cannot discribe the scenes here on paper but some of them were exciting in the highest degree and some of a truly harrowing nature but it is all over now and the rebles and the Yankees as they call us are conversing exchanging things on the most friendly terms. It seems strang that men can engage in deadly conflict one day and the next mingle freely in social intercourse but such is human nature. Since the 4th day of June I have not passed one 15 minutes but the roar of artilery and the sharp sound of the rifle resounded in my ears untill yesterday mourning abot 9 oclock. All of a sudden it ceaced and on going on to the top of the hill on which our camp stands to learn the cause of this unusual occurrance I seen the men of both parties who were on duty standing on their works without arms and issuing from one of the forts three men in horseback bearing a white flag riding towards our lines. This state of affairs lasted about 3 hours when the flag of truce returned and in one minute all were again in their defences and fireing away again. This state of affairs lasted about two hours more and another flag of truce appeared and the fireing ceaced and was not resumed again. To day no sound occurs to break the stillness. All is quiet and it seems as if all nature felt relieved. The day is sultry and very enervating. Some of our troops have marched in and took possession of the reble works and the prisoners. But we are ordered to prepare to march this evening at six oclock with five days rations and one hundred and ninety rounds of cartridges although our regiment has been in the front and center the whole time of the siege and had hoped that we would be rested. But there is no rest for the brave 22nd. Our regiment is truly in a bad condition. We have no field officer and but few company officers. Our co has none at all and we have to do a great amount of duty which I think we would not have to do if our Col was with us. But if by doing hard service will end this I for one will not complain. Our men is very much out of heart this evening having to pack up and march so soon after accomplishing so much and doing so much labour but I hope in a few days we will be all right again. I just seen the adjutant of the brigade and he says that we are going out 8 miles to guard a pioneer corps to build a bridge on black river and will return here in six or eight days at the furthes so you may expect a long letter from me when I return. But as we march in an hour and I have my comissary to arrange I must now stop. I received thy letter of the 21 of June yesterday and was sorry to hear of Cyruss illness but I hope he will be better after while. I feel in great heart now that we have done the hard fighting. I have got well and feel as good as a man that has found an old knife but I have not got my usual strength but I am gaining finely and have got up to my usual weight again if I did have to eat under the cannons mouth. I hope soon to get a better position but thee knows that I am one of the hopefuls and do not often meet with good fortune so I may never get it. Tell the children that I will try and get home soon to see them and they must be good children and try and learn their lessons. Tell Mary to write to me oftener and Cyrus to for it seems to me that he does not have much to say for I have never received but one letter from him since I came away. I have written my letters for all of you as my time is most always occupied with my duties. When I am able to write I thought you would understand it and did not make much fuss to write to you seperately but it is diferent with you. You all know something different and three letters from three different persons is better than three letters from one person.

I have just seen an officer from the city and he tells me that the number of Prisoners amounts in all to 44,720 forty four thousand seven hundred and twenty about 7,000 of which are sick and wounded soldiers. So you see that we have made a pretty good hall. This is a loss to the reble arms since the 1st day of May when we fought the battle of Port Gibson of about 90,000 men in this department. One more such a campain and the southron confederacy is gone under. If old Hooker[2] can get Lee as tight as we got Pemberton we are all right in sixty days. But I must stop gassing and go to work but you must forgive me for feeling good for this is enough to make one feel good and military and all that. If I only had the whiskey I would feel very valient but it is not here so I must submit.

I remain truly and affecty yours Taylor Peirce

1. Pemberton surrendered 29,491 men.
2. Major General Joseph Hooker was relieved by Major General George G. Meade on June 28, 1863.

Des Moines City July 5th 1863

I sit down to write feeling a little bad again not having had a letter for two weeks but I will try and be patient hopeing thee is well and that I will get one in a few days more. We are all well to day. Cyrus seems to be in a better condition this two weeks than he has been for a long time. I do not know whather it is Ayers medicine that is helping him or not. We have had a very pleasant summer so far with the exception of a few very warm days but our fourth was not near so hot as it was last year I do not think. We had a very nice celebration on the fair ground and a real good addres by a Mr Palmer[1] in favour of the war the Union and the Soldeirs and death to all Copperheads and rebel sympathisers. It was a good thing and just suited my stile. The speaker went on to say that Goverment must be sustained and the soldiers cared for at all hazards but Dear me I can not write half of the good that was spoken in behalf of our Country and our Countrys cause. Mary received a letter from Rachel day before yesterday. R writes they are all well but Aunt Hannah she is no better and there appears very little prospect of her ever being any better. Rachel writes very gloomily of the times. The Rebels have got up into Penn and are doing a great amount of damage.[2] But if thee has a chance to see the Union papers thee will know more about what they are doing than I can write, but it seem as our army in the east has not or can not attane much some how or other. What is the reason I am shour I can not tell. It seemed to me if they let the rebles overrun them there that there is very little hope for our beloved Country. But I still hope and trust there is still a just God in heaven that will set the Nation right one of these days, wheather we live to see it or not Dear Taylor. I can not write to do any good or that will be interesting to thee for the simple reason that I do not know of any thing of interest to write of.

I have not had any news from Jasper Co for a week or more. Mr Vowel and his wife was up here about two weeks ago and gave me the full news. There is nothing of importance except deaths. Preston [C]aloson was killed at the Battle of Black river Bridge and Willis Greens son also[3] but I expect thee has seen the account of the killed before this time. Vowel says that there is no thing doing in Newton this summer to a mount to any thing. He thinks if the railroad should mis it a few miles that it will die a naturel death and that right soon they have got the cars runing to Grenell[4] now and are working on this side. They say thair are going to grade Skunk bottom[5] this fall but it may not be done if the Draft gos on. The baby is siting on the floor by side me and is beginig to fuss and I will have to close.

With love I remain thy wife Catharine

1. Frank W. Palmer was publisher of the *Des Moines Register*. On the fourth of July he spoke to a crowd of about 5,000 people. After the war he published the *Sioux City Journal.*

2. This campaign culminated in the battle of Gettysburg.

3. Andrew P. Callison (listed as Preston Callison in the 1860 census), Company K, 28th Iowa, was a resident of Newton when he enlisted August 14, 1862. He was killed at Champion Hill on May 16, 1863. John L. Green, Company C, 22nd Iowa, a resident of Newton when he enlisted August 2, 1862, was killed at Vicksburg on May 22, 1863.

4. Grinnell is about twenty miles east of Newton.

5. The Skunk River is approximately five miles west of Newton.

> Camp near Jackson Miss
> July 13th 1863
> Dear Catharine

I snatch a little time. We have been fighting for 2½ days[1] and it looks as if we would fight a week longer. I am in midling health nothing but diarhea and that not bad. The hot weather the march and the change of water makes it prevalent. Jo Johnson is here with a strong force and our generals are working things slowly but I think surely we have driven them over a mile and I think we have them out General. I received a letter from Ingersole yesterday[2] in which he stated you were all well. Tell him I will answer it if I get through this fight. As soon as it is over I am going to try and get a furlough as soon as this place is taken. It is so dark that I must quit. Kiss the children for me and give my love to Mary and Cyrus and receive a good share for thyself. When Jackson is ours Mississipp is conquered. We heard that the Eastern troops had gained a victory and that Fort hudson was taken.[3] If it is true the war must end soon.

> I am affty thine
> Taylor Peirce

1. On July 5, 1863, the 22nd Iowa left Vicksburg as part of a three-corps movement under Major General William T. Sherman toward Jackson, Mississippi. The mission was to destroy the Confederate army that had gathered there under General Joseph E. Johnston.

2. This letter was not found.

3. Port Hudson surrendered July 9, 1863. The victory in the east was at Gettysburg, fought July 1–3. The Army of Northern Virginia was forced to retreat from Pennsylvania to Virginia.

Camp in line of battle near Jackson Miss July 15th 1863
Dear Wife Sister, Brother & Children

I take the time while there is a little lull in the conflict to write you again. I wrote you 3 days since hastily. As the time was short I made my letter short and how far this will extend will depend upon circumstance. I am well except the diarhea which prevails here without exception in almost every person. It is weakning but like the ague it is not dangerous. This is the 5th day we have been in line of battle sometimes shooting at the rebles and sometimes building breastworks. We generally have about 3 strikes per day. We all rush for our guns and in two minutes are formed ready to [illegible] the rebs but a few volleys soon send them back again and we are left quiet for two or 3 hours in our front but still the sound of war continues along some portion of the line night and day. Day before yesterday Osterhaus drawed the rebs out and succeeded in getting them to make a charg on him in which he fell back and when they advanced into the trap he let loose on them and defeated them killing and wounding over 1,000 of them.[1] Since that they have not tried a charge in mass but keep up the skirmishing in detached bodies to try our strangth. Truly war is a terrible thing. We have not laid under a roof for 13 days and the most of the time we have been under arms with the artillery roaring around us and the musketry rattling all along the lines are far as we can hear. Our lines are from 10 to 12 miles in length and extend to pearl river on both sides of the Reble forces which completely surrounds them and I heard to-day that we had a force in their rear and had cut of the mobile RR and their supplies. If so we will make a regular Siege of this as we did at V and I hope take the whole army.[2] We have news to day of a great victory at Gettysburg and another in Tennasee by Rosecrans.[3] I think now I can see the end of this war for the Rebellion cannot hold out much longer. Their army must be diminished terribly since the first of May. They have not lost less than 120,000 men in the western department and the news that comes from the east makes their loss there not less than 30,000. So one half of their effective force must be destroyed or at least rendered ineffective while our loss cannot be more than 25,000 in all of this western campain. I know something near the total and of the East I only take the published figures. As you have never had a description of the manner of conducting a battle or at least the details of it I will endeavour to describe the situation of our troops and the way we opperate. We moved up to this place on 3 parralell roads with our whole force which extend some 5 or 6 miles in solid column of 4 men abreast when they could be kept so. But the weather was so warm that they were often in single file and sometimes the men would go to the shade in spite of the officers. We moved only 8 or 10 miles pr day and the Straglers generally got up in the evening or early in the morning. When we got up to where the rebs began to fight us in earnest our forces was streched out to the right and left so as to form a line as long as possible with the front to the enemy leaving about 3 regiments one behind the other for support but all extended with their front to the enemy and these commenced the maneuvering to drive the enemy before us. The Batterys belonging to each brigade was placed in the centre of their line which placed them about 400 yards apart with 6 cannon to the battery. And then commenced the cannonading which would make the rebs fall back when the front regiment would advance 2 or 300 yards and hold the ground untill the artillery was in position again when the whole thing would be enacted over again untill we gained our present location which is about 400 yards from the reble breastworks. Since we have got here we just watch them. How long this will last I cannot tell but I hope not long. We being in the centre and are further advanced than either the right or left we will not be likely to have another engagement untill there is something done on one side or the other of us. I am satisfied that the rebles expect to get whipped here but are going to defend the place as well as they can for this is the last hold in this state for them. Our Brigade consists of the 21, 22, & 23 Iowa and the 11 Wisconsin under Brig Gen Lawler[4] a fat prissy old fellow as big a Cap West and a good officer. We have no field officer with us at present. Major Houston[5] formerly Cap in the 23rd commands us sometimes and is a brave and good officer. I like him very much. Marion Smith is out with the regt but was not wounded as reported. He has been sick and was left behind at Vicksburg.[6] Capt Ault has not returned yet and I hope he will not. We are looking for Col Stone daily now and I hope soon to see his manly form amongst us again although I know he will never take command again yet it will do us good to see him. I tell you that this is a hard life for a man that loves his ease and you ought to hear the shirks grumble. We have to lay on the ground with our rigging on us ready to fall in at the least alarm and our living at such times is hard. We have to eat the most portable kind of food for there is little time to forrage, or hunt things to eat so we eat hard bread and raw ham when we can get it and when we get sow belly and fresh beef we have a cook to cook it and bring it to us in the line where we eat it with our guns by our side and our harness on. You may think we are compelled to do this. It is likely that our Genl would have us stay close about but we stay in line of our own accord and build breastworks without orders. It seems as if every man was determined to whip the rebs and does every thing he can to insure success. We need no orders to form our line for at the least unusual motion in the enemys line we are formed and ready for them before an officer gets on the ground. I tell you that the men here would whip their equal number of any men the world ever produced. Our Co. now has 55 men present and 25 of them are shirking and the ballance are on duty all the time and I believe there is not a man but would rather die than let the rebs whip us and all the rest of the army is in the same condition. The 23rd Regt only has 85 men here but they are looking for the ballance of them up in a day or two. The 22 & 23 now will not muster more than 1000 men in all not much more than one half what they started out with but many of the lost ones may get back of them will be discharged on account of wounds and disability.

I had to stop a while to come out and place the picket Guard. We stand about 200 yards from them and they always shout at us when we go to the posts which are behind trees here where the ground is open. We take advantage of some hollow in the ground to protect ourselves. I post the guard at their places along the line and then have nothing more to do untill it is relieved which is about 3 hours. I then take my guard and fall back sleep 6 hours which brings daylight. I then take my guard and place them single about 10 or 15 yards apart and let them shoot till 9 or 10 in the morning when we are relieved and fall back and support the ones who take our place. This lasts 24 hours when another set comes out and we go back to the lines some 200 yards in the rear. These turns come about 4 days apart so you see if we do not get up a scare I get considerable rest from being under fire. I have got so used to being shot at that it does not excite me any more than the sound of the engine used to. Yet I take care of myself and never expose myself to their open sight unnecessarily. Sometimes the bullets whistle round me like hail but I put my mind on my work

and do not think of danger. There is another feeling that gets possession of a man here. I can not tell what it is but it is something like a
determination to conquer or die on the ground. I never felt it untill I
got into battle. I used to fear that I would be nervous like my mother
when I got in danger but I find I have her fortitude without her timid-
ity when the trial comes and Dear Catharine if I ever live to get home
I fear you will find me sadly altered. I have become unsociable determine and stuborn here and I fear hard hearted for I can see things here
that used to arouse my sympathy that has no more effect on me than
to eat my meals. I will probably alter if I get back into peaceful life but
I can not tell. I have a good many friends here but whather they are
so from feeling or a knowlede that I fear or care for no man is more
than I can tell. This is more than I have ever wrote about myself since
I left home and I hardly dare to think how my nature is changed or
least what the war has brought to light so you may prepare yourselves
for it and be not surprised. So I will quit the subject.

July 17th. I was hurried up from my letter the other day by the rebs
who made a sudden charge on us and so we had to form and fight
them back which we done in fine style leaving a good many of the
Rebs on the field. Well fighting continued yesterday all day. In the
evening the 6th Iowa drove the Rebs out of one of their forts and took
possesion and we supposed today would be the last of the battle here
but the rebles fooled us. For when we sent out our skirmishers this
morning behold the whole reble army had disappeared and we were
left in undisputed posession of the Capitol of Miss.[7] So I think this is
the last battle of the war. I feel now as if I would get home to cut hay
for the cous [cows] this fall and vote for Col Stone. By the way Col
Stone is with us and has taken command of us again[8] and we feel the
effects of it already. The whole brigade is in fine spirits and I believe
if he would tell us we could whip the Southeran confedercy ourselves;
this is gass; but God never made a better man according to my notion.
Cap Ault is on his way here with the sick but he takes care never to
get up in time to fight any. Well Kitty as I feel good to day over our
victory I will try and give you a description of the country and things
in general. First the country. This part of Miss I have seen the land is

about as level as Iowa but the soil is not near so rich. It is a kind of yellow clay mixed with sand and a poor country for corn and grass. I suppose Cotton grows well here althogh I have seen none growing not being any planted this year. Peaches and Blackberries is the fruit that seems to thrive the best with them. Pears and apples do not seem to do well. I see pleanty of figs but they will not be ripe for a long time yet and I hope we will not have to stay here long enough to see them ripen. The water is bad and scarce and I would not exchange my own beautiful Iowa with its refreshing breezes for all the boasted Sunny South.

So much for the country. Now for the people. There are two classes here as different as day from night. One class rich well educated and lazy loving in a kind of bawdy aristocracy not that kind of aristocracy that arises from a cultivated taste but a low born aristocracy that come by wealth. The furniture is costly and of the most extravagant kind but after all it not finished out the most costly and elegant things being put in the shade by being brought in contact with something of a low and vulgar nature showing the bad taste of the owner. They dress in the same manner. You will see woman dresed in the most elegant and costly fashion with the starch all taken out of her elegance by wearing an old pair of shoes and stockings with holes in them or a dirty old handkerchief on her head.

The poor class is as low as the slavs and as ignorant and the d—dst meanest of all white men. The slavs look down on them as much as the masters do on the slavs. Now for the army. It is gradually getting acclimated and the spirit and the moral courage of it was never better than it is at this time. Our men are in town to-day sacking the place. I do not like such scenes and have not accompanied the men to town and have concluded to finish my letter. We lay in lines yet and as soon as we get rested and washed up we will be likely to move again to what point I do not know nor have I any Idea. But if the news from the east is true we have no more to fight in this state and we may possibly go to Montgomery or Mobile in Alabama and may be the Iowa boys will get North but time will tell. I will now close as this is about all I can think of at present. Kiss the children for me and give my love to all our friends. I hope to be in the home of my family soon.

> yours affectionately
> Taylor Peirce

1. Brigadier General Peter J. Osterhaus commanded the Ninth Division, Thirteenth Corps. On July 9 and 10 his division drove Confederates back from Clinton toward Jackson. On July 11 Confederates counterattacked but were defeated. Exact losses were unknown, but the reports that exist indicate considerably fewer than 1,000.

2. The Thirteenth Corps, to which the 22nd Iowa was assigned, occupied the right of the Union line to control and destroy the New Orleans and Jackson Railroad. There was skirmishing during the next few days, but no assaults. During this campaign the regiment suffered seven wounded.

3. The Union Army of the Cumberland under Major General William S. Rosecrans drove Confederates under General Braxton Bragg south of the Tennessee River near Chattanooga. This campaign, known as the Tullahoma Campaign, set the stage for the battle of Chickamauga.

4. Brigadier General Michael K. Lawler had served in the Mexican War and been wounded at Fort Donelson. He replaced Colonel Stone as brigade commander on May 2, 1863.

5. See the letter of February 27, 1863.

6. See the letter of June 21, 1863.

7. Johnston evacuated the city on July 16, and the Union army occupied it the next day.

8. Lawler left on a leave of absence on July 18, and Stone took command of the brigade.

Desmoines July 19th 63

Dear Brother

We Received thy letter with the account of the fall of vixburg yesterday and was pleased to here from you as well as to here of the surrender of the place. We are all as well as usual now. My health is better than it has been for some time. I think it is owing to the warm weathe for I got much better last Sumer. I am doing all I can to get things fixed her So that I can leave this winter and go South or to the mountains one or other if I can get away but it looks doutfull fr I Dont know yet where the means is to come from unles I keep able to work. I have been at work for 3 week and Seem to Stand it fairly well. We have had a very Dry Cool Sumer and the crops Suffring verry much unless it rains Soon. We will have no potatoes hardley and corn will be quite a short crop. The wheat and oats ar a average crop. The wheat is of a first quality if nothing injers it yet. But it is sprinking rain this morning and looks like a wet Spell Setting in and if it dose it will Spiled much of the wheat as it is all in shock purty nearly.

*   *   *

We have a great deel of Sickness here among children and a great maney are dying of various Diseases. Scarlet feiver is bad and Diarea also. We have a purty full crop of copperheads. The two Johnsons are verry noisey and Small the murdrer of his partner the horse theives Some years ago is their choosen chief. If they dont carry party Straight forward they will all get strat one of thees Day. For we are not going to wait for them to rob and murder as when we can prevent it and that that is their design is beond a doubt for they are organizing for some purpose and it cant be for no good one Shur.

I want to get Sold out here if we can get a piece of govement land. If I cant get it at the mountains I intend to try Kansas and Settl Down on a small farm and try to make a living for the remainder of our dayes and quit trying to make money, as my time is Short now. At best mary has her health better this Sumer than ever she had for five or Six years and that is all the reason that I have for not leaving here but she Say that She will go anywhere where I can get well. We hope that the good new is all true and that the Rebellion will Soon be Sat down and you may get home With us again.

We remain your affectinat friend

C Milner and all the rest

Tell Col Stone that we have made up our mind to Ellect him by 15 thousand and the army must make it 30 thousand.

Des Moines City Aug 2nd 1863

Dear Taylor

It is three weeks to day since I have writen thee. C and Mary have both writen in that time and I thought I would not write when they did for I suppose that they can give a fuller account of what is going on than I can for they are out in town and know what is going on better than I do. I do not know much news to write of nether public or private. Things seems to move on in the same old style as they did a year ago since the Democratic convention on the 8 of last month only that they say that thair nominee has declined to run on their ticket it being I suppose a little bit to coppery for him.

The Country is filled with rejoyceing ove the late victorys and the puting down of the riot in NY.[1] It appears to of been a well laid plan of the rebles and thair northern friends to make a desperate strike last Mo. to retreve fellen cause. But I think that old Abe will be to much for them yet and bring the ship of state out of those troubled waters all right and then our enamies will have to acknolegage this one of the greats and best Goverment in the world. But Oh! dreadful to think of the acheing hearts there is through the land and will be before that glorious day can arive to our once happy nation.

Dear Taylor thee must excuse this letter if it is full of blunders for I do not feel verry well to day but I do not think there is any thing more the matter with me more than my old warm weathe weakness and nursing or babe. Hee is verry fat and heavy and is trouble some as he can not creap or stand on his feet any and Sallie has been going to school so she could not help to take care of him. But her school is out now and I think I will not send her any more untill the hot weather is over for her own sake and my own to for there is a good deal of sickness a mang children at this time here and she might get sick. The children have all been so well and healty since thee went away and grown so well that I want to try and take good care of them untill thee can get home to help me and then we can have such a nice family if we all live to be united on earth again. I must say I feel a little gloomy but I will try and shake it off and try to look on with hope for the best and trust that God has orderd it all for our good if we only make good of it. For we must be tryd as in a furnace to make us willing to leave this world when God sees fit to call us off.

Dear one the last I receved from thee was dated the 13th of July and was not so cheering as I would have liked for I was sorry to hear of thee haveing the diarhea and fighting at the same time. I hope if thee has got through the fight thee will try and get home for a little while so thee can get it cured up before thee gets run down with it so that thee will not be able to get home. It is all most a year now since thee went away and I think thee ought to have a furlough to come home for a short time. I have no wish for thee to come home to stay untill the work is all done that thee can do, but I do want to see thee and have thee at home a little while to see to some things of ours. I suppose that it was about the mill that Ingersoll wrote thee. He was to see me about it and tolld him to write to thee and then he would get to know just what thee wanted done with it and then he could do it what ever it was. Mary receved a letter from Aunt Lydia last week in which she says the friends are all well but Aunt Hannah she is no better and Uncle Nathan was thrown from a mule and his foot caught in the stirip and he was drug by it for one quarter of a mile and almost killed or so badly hurt that it will take him some time to get over it. Aunt writes as though Lees raid in to that country had made sad times there. She says that it fritend the Cops—but as soon as they were drove off were just as bad as ever. We are all well.

I remain afc thyne C A Peirce

1. The Union Enrollment Act of March 1863 resulted in riots in New York City July 13–16, 1863. The governor challenged the constitutional authority of the federal government to implement a draft. On July 11 names were drawn and the next day were published in the newspaper. Approximately 50,000 people joined in the riot, which ended only when federal troops arrived. More than 1,000 people were killed or injured.

Des Moins City 2/8 Aug 1863
Dear Father

It is three weeks since I have writen thee any but I did not sent it to thee becuse I did not write it good enough. I want to hear from thee and hear if thee has been in any more battles. Hear if thee has been wounded. If thee will get home pretty soon. School was out Friday. Aunty got letter from aunt lydia. Uncle Nathan fell off the mule broke his ribs. We hav had a nice rain this morning. We have some apples. Uncle is a black berrying. We have good time playing. We are looking fore thee home pretty soon. I did not get the [illegible]. Mary Johnson and Mary Jane [illegible] got it. I did not like it for I give the teacher ten cts fore the picnic and I would not go. I think she aut to give me a card any how. Frank likes her but I do not like her as well as I did at first. I love thee dearly well. I never got one bad mark but I was bad twice but she did not [illegible] a mark. She sent Mother a dres for the Mony. I love my Sunday School. I hav fore the first tim read the Sweet story of old. I think it is pretty story. It tells a great many good storys of the lord Jesus christ. The baby is as fat as any little pig in the world. I seen he is nearly year old and cant walk.

Sarah A Peirce

[undated, but probably August]

[first page missing] oppertunely for I receved thine of the 15th and one from John Sumpter with Aults account and ten Dollars in money. I suppose it is the rest of the hog money. He did not write any thing but what I send to thee. I am truly glad that Ault did not sucsede in geting Murray dismised for I do not want the vile scamp to get the better of decent man for thy self. Thee will have to do the best thee can for I can not help thee any. I suppose thee will know if the account is right or not for I never looked at the books so as to know how it was. Mary has concluded to send her and Franks picture as thee is not comeing home soon and says she will write again before long. Cyrus is quite unwell and feels quite discoraged. He talks of trying go from home some place to see if he will get any better but has not conclud where he will go yet. He would like to go to the Mountain if there was not so many Copheads going to get away from the Draft. He dose not want people to think him one or affraid of going to the war. All he would like would be able to go. I must close for the baby is awake again and is crying like fury.

thine afy
Catharine A. Peirce

Iowa City Iowa Sept 20
Dear Folks

I arrived here last evening and stoped to see Gene Kirkwood but he is in Davenport. I will go on in the morning. You need not be surprised if you did not hear from me for 2 weeks again for I will not write if I go on untill I get to Memphis and it will take a letter one week to get from there home. I am pretty well and feel in good heart. I wish thee to get some one to go down or go thyself to the grove and collect some mony. It is all ready for thee but I could not get to see any of them. When I was there I got $15. Ther will be $21 due from the judgment on Hurst $6 from Jas Parks 12 from Roraberry and 13 from T P Jones 12 from G Fugard and I think thee can get the most of it. I will get 100 as soon as the next pay day comes round and send it home. There is nothing new only I hear our regiment has gone to Texas.[1] I do not care much to go to Texas for I think it will be further from home or at least further from where we can get things and we will not see as good times as we would if we could have stayed in the coast country. I am going to try for a Majorship in the ninth cavalry[2] to-morrow but do not say any thing about untill I see wheather I can get it or not.

They were having a high time in Newton as I come through with Mrs Ault. She has proved herself to be a strumpet of the lowest class and what she and her pimp will do I can not tell. He it was proven knew of it and allowed her to do so for his own benefit.

I tell you they were mighty shy of me. I made a statement to the church about her conduct and they never whimpered. I felt as if I could have eaten him up but I could not catch him. I do not know what to write about more as there is nothing going on here to interest you. When thee goes down I want thee to go and see H Sumpler wheather he sold that hog to Jo Slaughter and if so what he got for him and what he done with the money. I went to see him and he was away from home and so I did not get to know any things about it. John could tell nothing about it. James Parks has the money for thee and I think thee had better go to Prairie City in the Coach and thee can see Jim Butters and Fugard and John Aikens will take thee over to the grov. This is all. Give my love to the children and take the same for yourselves.

> I remain affety yours
> Taylor

1. On September 20 the regiment was encamped at Brashear City, Louisiana, located on Berwick Bay.

2. The 9th Iowa Cavalry was organized by a War Department order dated September 7, 1863, and was mustered into service at Davenport on November 30, 1863. There is no record that Taylor applied for a commission as major in the unit.

Des Moines City Sept 24
Dear Taylor

We are all well but Cyrus. He has had an other bad spell this week and that always makes me feel bad so thee need not expect a very good letter to day. C says that he will go down to the grove for me as soon as he gets over this so he will be well enough to go. If he can get the money there it will be a benefit to him to go and be around a little. I think it will do him good. He is so tyrd of staying home that may be a short journey like that might satisfy him that home is as good a place as he can get to. The Children are all well and they talk of thee fourty times in the day and wish thee was at home again. If we had a home that was our own I might join in the wish, but Will endvour to be contented with what I have untill thee gets back so thee can provide a better one for us. Dear one I do hope that it will not be long untill thee can get home to stay. If the news is true that we are receveing daily now from all parts of the Army it appears as if the Rebs are on thair last legs and thay are in a fair way to have them knocked from under them and then this war must close soon I think. I can not see what will keep them up unless they should gain a small victory or some thing to in courge them on for a short time. But I hope nothing of the kind will take place to give them any thing to hope on. The first news this week we had from the army of the Coumberland was not as good as might of been wished for[1] and the Cops took pains call a meeting of rejoysing on the strength of it but the later accounts are more incouraging and they (the Cops) do not seem so well pleased as they did at first. They are haveing a Cops meeting to day on the fair grounds and they go by Harraing for Jeff Davis and are geting drunk and fighting among themselves just as they did at their [illegible] convention in July. Whether thair doing will amount to anything more than it did at that time will be to be seen in the events of the future. There is one thing they have but a short time to yell and will have to give it up here as well as thair Southern Brothern. Taylor I have no advice to give thee but to take the best possible care of thyself and keep in good heart and think of me and the children as being safe and well and as well off as we can be without thee. I do not want thee to think I want thee to give up untill the war is over unless thee gets sick so thee is not fit for duty. Then I want thee to get home as soon as thee can for my sake and thy own and Uncle Abe allso.

With love I remain Catharine A Peirce

1. On September 20, 1863, Bragg's Confederates defeated Rosecrans's Army of the Cumberland at Chickamauga and drove it back into Chattanooga. Bragg occupied Missionary Ridge and began a siege of the city.

Texas and Louisiana

EDITOR'S NOTE. During October the 22nd Iowa campaigned in southern Louisiana. Between October 2 and November 10 the regiment conducted operations in the vicinity of Brashear City, Berwick, Vermillionville, New Iberia, and Opelousas. The regiment returned to Berwick the night of November 9.

On November 17 the 22nd Iowa, which had received orders to sail to Texas, left Berwick and marched to Algiers. Five companies, including Company C, departed Algiers by steamer on November 20 and landed at Mustang Island near Aransas Pass one week later. The 22nd Iowa was assigned to the Second Brigade, First Division, Thirteenth Army Corps, Department of the Gulf. The department was commanded by Major General Nathaniel P. Banks.

> Sunday Morning Oct 4th 1863 on board the
> Steamer Tecumseh near New Orleans Louisianna
> Dear Wife and friends

I now commence to give you some account of myself and my passage down the Mighty thoroughfare that connects the different portions of country. After two days loitering around davenport to see if I could get a position more congenial to my feelings I found that I could get nothing but a recruiting commission with the promise of a commission if I could raise 25 men for the service. I concluded I would rather soldier as a private than to run the risk and maybe that I could not raise the required number I would loose all my labour and so I left for Cairo and arrived there on the 22 Sep. On the 23 I left for Memphis and arrive there passing Major Houston and Mullins on the White Cloud. On the 25th, after lying at Memphis 2 days I took passage to New Orleans on this boat. I stoped 2 days at Vicksburg and took a view of the old battle field and the works around there. I found some of the Jasper boys there in the 13th regt[1] and had a good time of it. I have better health than I have had since the battle of Port Gibson and I believe better than ever had before. I feel just as well as a man can and the weather has got so cool here now that I think I will be likely to keep well untill this war is over. For on all sides I hear the idea advanced that the rebellion is about crushed out. If Rosencrance only succeeds in defeating Bragg in Georgia[2] the thing is done and the Gov is reinforcing him to a tremendous extent. I never seen the like of troops on their way to join him. The river was full of transports from Cairo to Vicksburg black or rather blue soldiers and I suppose that Ohio and Ill. have sent out 20,000 new troops augments his force to full 150,000 men and if that force will not do we can send him 40,000 more from the Department of Miss. and hold the Miss too. There has been a great many steam boats burned on the river within a few weeks supposed to be the work of an organized band of incendearies for the purpose of destroying the means of transportation so that the govt will be compelled to march the soldiers over land. The morning we got to Vicksburg the steamer Robert Campbell was burned[3] and 40 odd lives lost among them was some woman and children. The thought is horrible the poor little helpless things and their worse than helpless mothers standing on a burning deck with [last page missing].

1. The 13th Iowa Infantry Regiment participated in the siege of Vicksburg. After the surrender the regiment engaged in a campaign against Monroe, Louisiana, then returned to Vicksburg on September 3 and remained there until February 1864.

2. In late September the Union Army of the Cumberland under Major General William S. Rosecrans was defeated at Chickamauga, Georgia, by the Confederate Army of Tennessee under General Braxton Bragg. The Union forces retreated to Chattanooga.

3. The steamer was burned September 28 near Milliken's Bend, Louisiana, by guerrillas. Official reports do not mention casualties.

Des Moines Oct 12/63

Dear Brother

I have a little leisure to day for the first time in many weeks and I concluded to spend it in writing to thee. We are all midling well now. The children have had colds but nothing serious. Sallie goes to school. She received a letter from thee yesterday[1] which elevated here some. She likes to go to school. Frank would like to go to but they divided the school and Catherine did not think it suitable to send Frank alone. Cyrus is his best fasheon now. He has had two verry severe spells since thee left. He still talks of leaveing home before winter sets in if he can raise the meanes. I want him to sell the mare and go. I do not know as he will. We hav five boarders now beside thy family. I have a good girl and get along verry well but am kept buisey all the time but my health is good and work never was any trouble to me when I felt well.

Times are good here now. People who should know think better than ever they ware money is plenty and work also if the war was over. So thee could come home thee could be getting a good start now. I am looking forward to the close of the war with a great deal of anxiety. I long to see the country at peace once more and men at liberty to come home and take care of their familys.

*   *   *

Oh how I wish it [Mary is referring to whiskey] was all in the bottom of the ocean. It carries more trouble in the world than all the disease and other ills humankind are heirs to. If by raising my hand I could annihilate all intoxicating drinks from off the earth how quick it would be done. Lizzie writes that Gardner was a bright Lawyer and good pleader but he is lost to the world and himselfe by the love of strong drink. What a sorrow he must be to his old mother. What a blessing to her had he died in infancy. Gov. Stone has bought a large brick house that Close built south of Frank Aliens and is getting it fitted up for a residence. He is going to live in Des Moines. I expect the town will be crowded this winter when the legislature meets. It is full now people boarding for the want of houses to live in. I am kept so busey that I do not know much news. Things are moveing along much as they did when thee was at home. Reinig is moving his house into town. It leaves a bare looking place on the bottom. Vain has sold his fourty acre field up towards Bells to Crain for sixty dollars per acre. John Smith is going to marry Crains daughter and put it in grapevines. Old Smith has fell out with John because he wants to marry miss Crain. John has moved to Crains so reports says. At any rate he has left home. Farmers are making it pay this fall. Corn is woth new thirty, old corn fifty, potatoes fifty, pork from three to four dol per hundred and other things in por portion.

October the 16th. Dear Brother I commence agen to day to finish. I left off thursday evening to get thy [illegible] fixed. Thought to have finished writing on friday but we have had a hard rain storm since and this is the first day I could get to town. Cyrus was verry unwell but is better to day. The rest are well and getting along well.

We received a letter from Marion Smith[2] to day. He has got his discharge and is comeing to Iowa if he lives till spring. We have got two rooms finished in the third story and Page is plastering them to day. Please write soon and as often as thee can. We feel anxious all the time about thee so far away. Cyrus, Catherine, and the children all send their love to thee. Frank thinks he would like a pony but he thinks Sallie must have one too. I must close.

I remain ever thy affectionate sister Mary

1. This letter was not found.
2. This letter was not found.

Des Moines City Oct 25th/63
Dear Taylor

I sit down to write thee a few lines to day to let thee know how we are. Cyrus is very bad to day and yesterday with the asthma and Mary has no girl so thee will not get much news today for I try to help her all that I can, and do not expect to get time to write much. We are all well (C excepted) and are doing well enough. I have not had time to read any thing this week and therefore I do not know what is going on in the army or any where only that Mary recived a letter yesterday from Lizzie D Haines saying that Jonathan P Cook was dead. That he had died in August sometime and also that W and his wife and Children ware there on a visit and that William was coming home and going to let Mary stay yet longer. L writes as though all the rest of the relations ware well in that part of the country. I have not had a letter from the east since thee went in to the service nor I have not writen any so I expect our communication is at an end unless I write first which I may do or may not. I feel that if they do not care for me I need not care for them for they are all in a better way of geting along than I am. Therefore I suppose it will rest for nobody cares for a poor relation. I suppose if thee had of made fortune here we would of been as great as any of the folks but as that did not happen we must submit to our fate. I for my part am very contented for most part.

I would like to of had a little home of my own if it could of been as well as not but it was not and I have concluded to take things of this life as they come and try to make peace with God and man (if possible) so that I may grow rich in kingdom come. For if one counts the cost of the pleasures of life of this world the cost all ways over runs the profits. Some seem to act as though there was no time or place but this and it seems to me that they forget there is a God an that thair is any thing wrong they do but so it is the world over and I can not help it so I will leave all such to thair way for may be thair are right as well as I. Thee did not say where to direct to in thy letter so I will still send mine to thee by way of Memphis hoping thee may get them soon. The Children are well and I can not write thee half they want me to write. Sallie she wants thee to try to quit swaring before thee comes home again and Frank thinks he will never get drunk if he lives to be a man for he seen Henry Smith drunk the other night so that he could not unharness his horses. F said he would not like it be himself or his papa that was drunk so thee may take the words of thy child as best suits thy concenious. It is supper time and I must close for this time as we have six boarders and no help so I have to pitch in.

I remain thy wife Catharine A Peirce

Head Quarters 23rd Regiment Iowa Vol,
Camp New Iberia, Nov 1st 1863
Dear Catharine and all the rest of you
This morning I again have a chance to send out a letter and gladly embrace the opportunity, for this is the longest time that we have been without mail facilities since I hav been in the service. In the first place I have not received but one letter from you since I left home and am getting anxious to hear from you, but I hope we will soon be so that I will get your letters more regular. I am enjoying first rate health and the weather is so fine that one could not help but feel in good spirits. You will want to know all about things here so I will give you all I know. I arrived at the regiment on the 11th of october at Vermillion hill La and we lay there untill the 23rd when we took up our line of March for Apalousa [Opelousas] 25 miles west of Vermillion where the 19th Army Corps was encamped under Genl Franklin.[1] The 19th was the advance force for the purpose of engaging the rebles under Genl Dick Taylor[2] but after following them to apalousas they found that the rebs would not fight a battle but kept following back and scattering their forces so that we could not do anything but occupy the

country and catch a few gurrillas. As we were only the reserve for the support of the 19th if they should need any help and none being needed we were ordered back. So on the 26 we again started back to Vermillion and after laying there one day we started back here and arrived here on the 29th or day before yesterday.[3] We were mustered for pay yesterday and I understand the paymaster is here paying off the 1st Brigade and I suppose the 22n will be paid in a few days. I do not know what our next orders will be but I hear that we are going back to Brazier City in a few days however. There is nothing for a large army to do here and as Genl Grant only loaned the 13 army Corps to Genl Banks with the understanding that we were not to be used unless his army could not succeed in the expidetion I think it probable that we will not do much for some time yet I have not been able to get any late news from the other Expiditions. I can not tell what will be likely to be the next move but I should not be surprised if we would go back to Brasher City and lay there untill the rebles were all drawn out of Mobile and then take transports and light on that nest of traitors like a hen on a June bug and take it. Brasher City is situated at the head of Berwick Bay about 25 miles from the Gulf and is a very suitable place to rendezvous a force for such an expidition as it could be done so secretly that the rebles would know nothing of it untill the blow was struck. But this is all conjecture and of course not worth any more than my private oppinion.

Genl Ord who was our corps Commander has not been with us for some time. Genl Washburn has taken his place.[4] Genl Lawler is our division Commander and Col Harris of the 11th Wisconsin is in command of the Brigade. Major White is in command of the 22n, Glasgow of the 23, and Col Vannanda of the 21st.[5] Lt Mullins has not reached the regiment yet. He was taken sick with Erysipitas[6] in his leg at Memphis and was there on the 15th but was some better and expected to start to join us in a few days. This is the most beautiful country and has been settled a long time. The country west of Brasher is open Prairie and nearly level. The plantations have trees planted along the lanes and lawns in front of the houses that look as if they might 100 years old. And much of the land has the appearance of being worked out and now lays open having been left in ridges just as it was farmed for cane and is grown up with a kind of grass much like the crab grass of Penna and I think it is the same. Blue Grass nor timothy is not seen here nor do I know whether it will grow or not. There is some white clover along the roads and around the houses but no red clover. I see corn and cane cotton and rice but they say wheat will not grow to do any good. Corn yeilds about 20 bu to the acre. I can not tell the yield of the other products. Peaches and oranges, bannanas, grapes and figs seem to be fruits that are produced here. All kinds of vegitables seem to do well. I see cabbage plants set out in the garden but whether they are for the next years crop or for greens through the winter I can not tell but I intend to inquire as soon as I get a chance. There is some large fields of cane and the sugar making is just beginning. It is a heavy business and occupies many hands to carry it on successfully. In my next letter I will try and give you a more minute description. The orranges are almost all sour and are used for preserves but there is some sweet orranges raised for the table. The sweet potatoes is not so good as those raised in Iowa but they grow large and are very easily cultivated. Hogs do not do much good whether it is the stock that is deficient or whethe the climate will not make pork I do not know. Pork is very high. A hog that will weigh 150 lbs is worth $100 in confederate scrip and what it would be wort in Green Backs I do not know for when we buy we pay in their own money and pay just what we please and sometimes we do not pay at all which is most generally the case. Chickens have become very scarce and the orders are very strict against jayhawking but the Iowa offices are very short sighted and seldom see the boys carrying off any thing that is good to eat which is very annoying to the Eastern troops as they have always been prohibited from enjoying the luxries of the land. Genl Banks and Franklin issued very stringent orders against forageing making the penalty for such conduct death and in one case the penalty was carried into effect in a New York regiment. After a time some of the western boys was caught and a court martial held condernming them to be shot and the time set for the execution of the sentence. But the night before some of the men pined a paper to Franklins tent giving him notice that if the sentance was carried into effect he would suffer the same penalty. The men were not shot nor have I heard any more of shooting since. But the orders against it still remains in force. Genl Washburn caught a fellow the other day carrying up a piece of hog that he had jayhawked. After reprimanding him ordered him to carry it up to his head quarters and leave it which he proceeded to do and give it to the cook and while the cook was taking care of the meat the fellow stole all the warm biscuit he had baked for the Genl supper. On receiving notice of the fact the Genl swore that it was no use for the Iowa boys would live well if they had to go to the Presidents table for the food and seemd to think it a good joke.

We are encamped in a live oak grove near the Bayou Tash [Teche] and from an old Brick Kiln the boys has built themselves little Brick houses and covered them with their gum blankets and have things quite comfortable. We have fresh beef and sweet potatoes and crackes coffee tea and lots of sugar and molasses to eat and the regiment is enjoying better health than it has since it has been out. We have no tents with us and not much of any thing to encumber us on our march. They hall one woollen blanket a piece for us and we carry our gum blankets and one shirt in our knapsack. We confiscated a mule and a cart in which we hall our knapsacks and cooking apparatus and rations so we get along easier now than we ever did before on a March. The weather is so warm that now as I write it is quite uncomfortable and the sweat runs off me as if it was the middle of summer. There has been no frost here of any account yet and things look as green as they did in Iowa when I left. I think I would like to live here if the war was over. Oysters crabs and fresh fish can be got redily very cheap and I think a man could enjoy himself very well and live with little labour. But there is no good water like there is in Iowa. The cisterns have to be built above the ground and the water is always warm. I will write again in a few days and will then send you an account of all things. I have been kept so busy since I come back fixing up the affairs of the co that my time for writing has been very limited but I am now up and will not hav so much to do. Give my love to all and kiss the children for me. I am affty
       Taylor

1. After participating in the battle of Fredericksburg, Major General William B. Franklin was assigned to command the Nineteenth Army Corps on August 15, 1863.

2. Major General Richard Taylor was the son of President Zachary Taylor and the brother of Jefferson Davis's first wife. He commanded the District of West Louisiana.

3. On October 22 the 22nd Iowa and other units of the Thirteenth Corps were ordered to reinforce the Nineteenth Corps. On October 24 Washburne reported that the Confederates were retreating toward Alexandria, Louisiana, and that he was unable to engage them in battle.

4. Major General Edward O. C. Ord replaced McClernand as commander of the Thirteenth Corps on June 18, 1863. On October 12 he reported that he was ill and on October 26 went on sick leave. On October 20 Major General Cadwallader C. Washburne assumed command of the corps. On October 26 Major General Napoleon J. T. Dana took command.

5. Major General Michael K. Lawler took command of the First Division, Thirteenth Corps, on October 19. Colonel Charles L. Harris had commanded the 11th Wisconsin and had also commanded a brigade several times during the Vicksburg campaign. Samuel L. Glasgow was an Ohio native and resident of Corydeon when appointed major on September 10, 1862. He was promoted to lieutenant colonel December 1, 1862, and to colonel May 19, 1863. He was mustered out July 26, 1865, at Harrisburg, Texas. S. G. VanAnda was a Pennsylvania native and resident of Delhi when appointed major on August 2, 1862. He was wounded May 22, 1863, at Vicksburg and promoted to lieutenant colonel the next day. He was mustered out July 15, 1865, at Baton Rouge, Louisiana.

6. Erysipelas is an acute skin infection caused by parasitic bacteria that results in inflammation and fever. Forms of the infection can affect subcutaneous tissue and form abscesses.

Des Moines City Nov 1st

Dear Taylor

We are all well to day. Cyrus is much better than he was this day week and we have got a girl and things are going off better all around except we have had a very bad snow storm this week. The snow fell in the 23th of Oct but is going off to day and appear as though we might have some good weather again yet this fall or I should say this winter. I believe I have nothing new to write of more than I have writen before without. I forgot to tell thee about John Sumpters house being set on fire a few weeks ago. It appears to me to of been set and then put out again for it can not be possible that fire could catch and burn like that did and then go out again. It seem to of a caught on a chest that they had keept the money that the boys had sent home for John to take care of. John and his wife had gone to Newton and Emoline was at school untill about two oclock in the after noon and there was still some fire on the chest and the other was all out and there was nothing in the house or about the place that was disturbed. Who ever it was must of had some knolledge of his having the school money and the boys money but they did not get it for Mrs Sumpter had taken it with her to town. The fire burnd up from the chest to the seeling and about the width of the chest and the lid of chest was burnd in holes and that was all there was of it.

Dear Taylor I tell thee that I do not know much to write to day for I have not had a letter from thee since the one thee wrote at New Oleans but I will indvour to find something to say so thee may know that I think of thee any how. I do not feel that lonesome sadness that I did before thee came home and I hope thee will feel better to of being at home for a little time if it did thee no other good. I can not hear any thing from your Regiment what it is a doing or where it is for some time more than it had gone to Taxas and tharefore I do not know just where to write to. But I shall write hopeing it will find thee safe and all right some time and some place. We was haveing more boarders now than they have ever had since the first winter after they built here. And Cyrus is going to get the house finishd and has give out the notion selling out for the present if it will only last. But he never can be well again no how now I do not think and if he could only be contented he is as well off as he can be in this world. But he seems to act as though thare was some place here on earth that he might get well and it might be if he would go off east to the coast or near to it he might live a little longer than if he staed at home. But it is not often that we see traveling do any one much good that is as far gone as I think he is with that disceas though it might be that he might live a long time yet. Dear one it is nearly night and I must close. The children and all of us send a bushel of love. Hopeing thee well.

I remain thy loving wife

Catharine A Peirce

Des Moines City Nov 6th 1863

Dear Taylor

I sit down to write thee to day just to let thee know how we all are. Not that I have any news for I have not seen or heard any thing this week but the baby and him crying. For the children all have had such bad colds and are so trouble some that I have not done much but attend to them though they are geting better now. We all have had the same kind of a cold and it seems as though every person in the region have the same. It was so cold here this time last week that it froze one through to the core but it has got more pleasent again and has the ap-

perance of haveing better wether for a time at least. Cyrus is as well
as usual to day and is going on to work in the third story to finish
some more rooms up there as soon as he can so as to take some of the
representatives for the town is full of people now. Every one is got
boarders that can accomodate any so there is a good chance to make
some money this winter. Board is from three to five Dollars per week
though other things are high in perporsion. Flour 93, Potatos 60 cts,
corn 60 cts per bush and stock of all kinds have gone up so that times
are better than they have been for the last seven years. Money is plenty
and people will spend it the same as though there was no war going
on. For there has been more goods of all kinds brought to town this
season than ever before and they sell faster to and for the money cash
down. It seems the farmers ought to make something this year for
they are geting good prices for there things and there is a good bit to
sell in the country so they say. At least there are plenty of hogs. They
have slaughter 8,000 head up to the fourth of this month and had 2,000
more in the pens waiting thair fate. So thee may expect plenty of sow
belly next summer if thee still stays in army. I do not think there is any
danger of our army being starved or citizens either for another year
to come for all the frost came early this fall. Corn is more plenty than
it was supposed to be before it was all gathered though I suppose it
is not all gathered yet in some parts of the state. For thee knows how
slow they are about thair fall work commonly and they are worse this
year on account of help being scarce and hard to get. Yet if it should
be as good a winter as last was I do not see but we in the north will
get along quite as well as we did then. I for one have as good a time
as I want only I would rather have thee at home if the war was ended.
But untill that time comes I will make the best of time that I can hoping it will not be long now till thee will be able to get home to stay and
then we can have a good time indeed. I do not want thee to be uneasy
or troubled about us at home for we will get a long all right. But take
the best care of thy self that thee possibly can so when this warfare is
over we can settle down in some little corner of this great republic at
peace with all mankind and enjoy life as it comes along quietly. I belive I have nothing to say to thee, but to keep in good heart for I know
that thee will do thy duty more if need be.

   I remain thy afc wife
   Catharine A Peirce

Head Quarters 22nd Iow Vol
New lbeiria La Nov 7 1863
Dear Catharine

I am in a great hurry today. We have been in line of battle since yesterday morning. About 3 oclock the trumpet sounded and we got up and got breakfast and long before light the brigade moved out to the west of town. We heard the rebs were coming to attack the place. Although the 19th army corps is in advance 25 miles yet we heard that old Price had got in between us and the 19 and were going to take this post where we have all our supplies.[1] We laid about 4 miles west of our Camp when our regt was sent out on picket. We laid untill this morning when we were relieved and apart of the Osterhause brigade took our place and now we have fell back [illegible] our line which is about 3½ miles west of our old camp. We hear that price and Col Dick Taylor has about 2,000 men but we have 35 to 36,000[2] men and we feel confident of a victory if they should attack us but I am of the opinion that they will not dare to attack us. I feel confident that they will never attack us but we may be compelled to attack them in order to clear the country of them. Our troops are all in good spirits and you would have thought yesterday morning that the 22nd was going to a party instead of a fight if you had heard the jokes and laughter accompying them that was continually passing. I do not believe that twice the amt of troops can whip the 13 army corps. They hold the 19th in utter contempt for their weak defense and triffling conflict with the rebs a few days since when the rebs attacked them with 12,000 men and the Feds had about 8,000.[3] And after fighting about 2 hours the rebs fell back and the 19th had not enough of mettle to follow them and let them be reinforced and in turn fell back themselves. And now it is supposed that we will have to lick old Price ourselves or let him advance to this important post. I tell you that the eastern troops have not the sense to fight that our western boys have for the reason that the officers put on to much style and make underlings of the soldiers and break their spirits before they come in contact with the enemy and are then so degraded that they only fight from a sense of submission to the orders of their officers and not from an inate sense of right and manhood. But the principal of the western boys is such that the officers are not above us and we fight from inherant feelings of right and manhood and in a few days we will be likely to show them that we, if we are western solders and badly clothed are able to contend with twice our numbers successfully. While I set to write this I hear that they are fighting 25 miles west of us and we are in momentary expectation of an order to March. As soon as this battle is over I will give you an account of it. I must close for fear that the mail goes out. Give my love to the children and all the folks. I feel no doubt of our final success, for the right must and will prevail.

Mullins and Col Graham has got to the regiment and I am recommended for 1st Lt but wheather I will get the commission is with the future.

> I remain most affectionately your husband Brother
> and Father
> Taylor Peirce

1. On November 3 a Confederate force attacked the Fourth Division, Thirteenth Corps, near Bayou Bourbeau, Louisiana. Burbridge's division lost 26 killed, and more than 500 were taken prisoner. Major General Sterling Price commanded the District of Arkansas in the Confederate Trans-Mississippi Department. The rumor that he was moving to reinforce Confederates in southern Louisiana was false.

2. The Thirteenth Corps had approximately 21,000 troops in the vicinity of New Iberia and Opelousas. Taylor had approximately 13,000 troops present for duty in the District of Western Louisiana.

3. In the battle of November 3 Confederates were estimated at between 2,500 and 6,000. Burbridge had about 1,700 before being reinforced with about 3,000 men from the Third Division, Thirteenth Corps.

> Des Moines City Nov 8th 1863
> Dear Taylor

I sit down to write to day hopeing it will reach thee some time. I have not had a letter from thee since the one from New Orleans dated the 8th of Oct and there fore I do not know where thee is but I will write any how to let thee know how we are. We are all as well as usual this morning. Cyrus is his best at this time and is at work lathing up stairs geting two rooms finished before it get cold so that he can not get it plastered. The house is full of boarders and they could get more if they had house room to take them in. It seems to me that they will do well this winter if times keep as good as they are at present. The town is full of people and runing over. There not an empty house to be had for love or money and all the boarding houses are full of folks waiting for houses to be put up yet before winter sets in. There is more dry goods than there ever was in the place before and they seem to sell faster and at about the highest prices. Callico is from 25 to 30 cts and all goods are in the same ratio. The farmers are geting some of their money back this fall. Potatoes are from 50 to 60 cts per bu and corn from 25 to 50 cts according to the location that it sells in. I believe that they give but 25 at stillhouse but it is 60 along the road between here and the railroad. There is so much halling to be done this winter on that rout that it is thought that corn will be scarce in Jasper Co. I was down there and the farmers all say that the September frost bit the corn so that it will not be more than two thirds of a crop at best.

Dear one I had to brake off writing all at once to attend to the children to give them their dinners and to eat my own so I will endevour to write some thing more. I have eating such a haerty meal that I feel very lazy about it but none of the rest seem inclined to write so I had better try to find something to say. Cyrus is gone out to see Clarks fish [illegible] up the river by the old mill and Mary is reading at the present time. Sallie has gone with Bella Baker to a concert at Capital and Frank put in his time cracking hazelnuts and wallnuts so thee may have some idea how the day is going on at home when thee gets this. It is a most beiutiful day for the time in the year. We have had one snowstorm that fell about six inches but it was all gone in two days an then we had an all days rain on Friday so that I think the ground will get filled with water yet before it frizes up for the winter and according to thy sign or what thee used to say I do not think we will have very much here this winter.

I tell thee now for all thee thinks I have a good time of it here. I am pritty well imploied all the time between attending to the children and sewing for them. The baby has got to creeping and is all over the house in a minute and keeps me all the time looking after him that he dose not get his neck broake. He is well and is doing well. Now he is seting on the floor by me trying to make me stop and take him up so I will have to close for this time. I think if I could get shet of the bother of him I might possible write a letter that would be worth while to read but as I can not I will quit for this time and remain thyne afc wife,

    Catharine A Peirce

Head Quarters 22nd Regt
Brashear City Nov 11th 1863
Dear Catharine

I received thy letter and one from Sallie of Oct 18.[1] The first I have had for a month and I hope in this that you have received mine from Mr. Houston also one I wrote from Orleans. I wrote two others since one on the eve of battle which I expect you will get before you get this and will be anxious untill you get this to let you know of my safety. The battle was severe and lasted nearly all day but our loss was not heavy. About 30 killed 75 wounded and 200 prisoners will cover the whole of our loss. Our boys whiped the rebles bad and buried more dead rebles than we lost altogether beside taking over 200 prisoners. The report is that the reble loss is over 1,500 in killed wounded and missing. Our regiment was not engaged nor any of Gel Lawlers Division. A part of Gel Hoveys Division was in but the loss in the 28th Iowa was very small[2] and I think the troops belonging to the 13th army Corps did not amt to more than 10 or 12 men. The 19th done the fighting before we got up and as soon as the rebs formed the 1[0?]th was going at them. They run and left their dead and wounded behind them. On the next morning we were ordered to March and made 68 miles in 2½ days arriving here yesterday noon where we are resting.[3] I understand that our destination is Point Isabell on the Rio Grand where Genl Herron with a part of our army Corps has affected a landing[4] and I [think] we will form the army of ocupation this winter and probably will not have much hard service. For the rebles have but little force now west of the Mississippi and the Federal army surrounds the territory occupied by them as it were with a wall of armed men and Warlike engines. They never attacht us any more on this side and if they can avoid it they never fight; even when we mov on to them. The battle was brought on the other day by our forage train advancing beyond their lines. When they thought they had a good thing of it and attacked it with their whole force the guard formed and held them until a part of the 19th got up and then fell back. The rebles then followed them thinking they had the whole of our forces whiped. Our troops lay concealed behind a strip of timber that grew along a little stream and as soon as the reble line advanced through the timbers they let into them with canister and grape and the slaughter was tremendous. The rebles fell back and a deserter says that Genl Price come up and reinforced them with 15,000 men and tried to make another stand but our men steadily advanced pouring in the shot and shell with a sprinkling of minie[5] bullets and they once more broke and the battle was over. Once more the Victory is with the stars and stripes and we all feel good about. Even the poor wounded Soldiers is joyful over the event. Oh how long must our country endure such scenes for the crimes of the Slaveholder? It seems sometime that the curse upon us is like that uttered against the egyptians for their oppression of the children of Israel that was that the first born of every family should be brought to die. And it seem to me that for allowing the South to continue their oppression of the poor negro there will be a vacant seat in almost every household. But as every wrong must have it equivalent of right I hope soon the tidings will come that a just and avenging spirit is appeased and [illegible] nature will once more resume her peaceful dominion over our land.

Dear Catharine I have only been with the regiment one month to day. In that time I have marched 200 miles been at one battle and am back here again in better health and better heart than when I first come in the service. I felt very serious the other day when the battle was raging knowing that in a few hours and maybe in a few minutes we might be called on to defend our country and knowing to that the bullets will kill and that the fly thick in action. I thought how soon might many of my brave comrades lay cold in the arms of death and maybe myself along with them. It seemed to me that could I only gather you once more in my arms I could face the danger without tremour but the faces of those I love would come up before my eyes and my throat would fill up in spite of me. But thank the power who gave me life I was not afraid of death amid it all and most thankful am I that my love of country and right is strong enough to enable me face the enemy without murmuring. I do not say without fear for I appreciate the danger to well to say that I fear it not but I acknowledge that I would rather be at home caressing my family than here fighting if the rebellion was over. But not untill the last vestige of it is crushed do I wish to take my ease. What is left of our company now is as well and hearty as they ever were and are anxious to get at the rebles as can be. Mullins has got back to us and things is going on all right with us. I will not get my commission for 1st L as our Co. has got so small we are not allowed 3 commissioned officers but I have the promise of the first

vacancy that occurs and if I do not get it will make but little difference. I will have the conscieousness of having done my duty and fill-
ing the place I occupy with ability and fidelity which is more than a
great many of them have. I want thee to have all your pictures taken
and send to me for I have somehow lost all that I had and I am lonesome without them. Get Marys and one of the childrens togather and
take the rest of you on one plate if you can.

As for money I do not know wheather I will be paid before we
leave here or not but I hope we will for I would like to send it home
from here as I think I will have a better chance to send it from here
than I will have from the Rio Grand. I am glad that thee got money
enough to do thee and help Cyrus some for I was afraid that the cold
weather would come on before I could get you any and you would
suffer for the things before you could get them.

The weather is mild and beautiful her. We have had one or two
Northers here. One day we marched all day facing an ugly cold rain
Storm and had to lay down at night in the wet without shelter without cloths on and if I had been at home I would have expected to have
been sick. But the cold nor wet had no efect on me at all and I felt as
well the next day as I ever did. I have stood the march first rate and
only got tired one day on the whole rout and I went to the hospital
and the Surgeon gave me some old rye and it soon renovated me.

This is a tolerable good country but I think likely it is not healthy
in the hot weather but I can not tell for certain. The people here says
that it is healthy but they do not have the robust appearance that our
men do either from climate or from physical causes. They are more
slightly made and have less muscular energy than the northern men.

Sallie writes that she is going to Miss Putman. You give them my
respects and tell them that their acquaintances Mr. Ely Virgil Hart-
soch old Dr Ely Walter Lee[6] and all the rest that are with us is well and
they wish to be remembered by them. If you see Col Stone give him
my respects and tell him that the 22n regt never knew the worth of
him untill they lost him and would gladly welcome him if he would
make a visit to us. He has many warm friends here many more than
he had when he was with us all the time. I intended to have written a
long letter when I wrote again but I am not in the humour of writing. Today things do not come to me as they do some times. I think
it is becaus there is such a hurrah around one all the time and I have

so much of the co affairs on my mind that I am not in writing spirits. I am glad to hear that Cyrus is better again and hope he will remain so. Tell the children that I want them to be good and mind what their Aunt and Uncle says to them and obey their teacher and be good to their mother and try and act with propriety while at school and not act badly like some children do because they see others do it. But behave well and before they go to amuse themselves think wheather they will infringe on any other persons rights by their actions and if they do not let them take all the pleasure their young hearts wants without injuring themselves. Tell Frank he must try and be a man so that he can help papa and mother when the war is over and we all get togather. And Sallie must learn her lessons and try and be a nice girl so that Pap can be proud of her and she can enjoy herself with pleasure and contentment in the time to come. I must now close. If I get the spirit on me I will write again before I leave here. If not you will not get a letter untill I get to the Rio Grand.

I remain your affectionate
Taylor

1. These letters were not found.

2. Brigadier General George F. McGinnis replaced Brigadier General Alvin P. Hovey in command of the Third Division, Thirteenth Corps, on September 13, 1863. In the battle at Bayou Bourbeau the Fourth Division, Thirteenth Corps, suffered losses of 25 killed, 129 wounded, and 562 missing. The 28th Iowa had 2 wounded. Confederate losses were 22 killed, 103 wounded, and 55 missing.

3. On November 8 the 22nd Iowa and the remainder of the First Division were ordered to Berwick Bay. They arrived on November 9 and 10.

4. On November 2 the Second Division, Thirteenth Corps, commanded by Major General Dana, landed at Brazos Santiago, Texas, at the mouth of the Rio Grande. Major General Francis J. Herron would not take command of those forces until December 24.

5. Designed by Frenchman Claude Minié, this cylindrical, conoidal projectile had a hollow base that expanded to grab the rings and grooves of the barrel when fired. This projectile increased the range and accuracy of rifled weapons.

6. David H. Ely was a New York native and Iowa City resident who enlisted August 13, 1862. He was wounded September 19, 1864, and discharged because of the wound on May 2, 1865. Virgil Hartsock was an Illinois native and resident of Iowa City. He enlisted August 14, 1862, and was mustered out July 25, 1865. John W. Lee was also an Illinois native who enlisted at Iowa City on August 14, 1862. He was promoted to first lieutenant of Company G on July 4, 1865, and was mustered out July 25, 1865. Dr. Ely cannot be identified.

Nov 14, Saturday 1863

Dear Father

I am well and hope these lines will find thee the same. Our unkle is
better than used. He had one of his choking spells last night but he got
beter of it and I bellieve that hes getting well. It wold be a [illegible]
good thing if he wold get [able?].

I got thy letter and could read the most of it with out Mother to
help me. I love the best of all things. I think theres never was better
in the world than thee is. My arm is getting tird. Want to tell thee a
bout what a time we had geting a girl When Mar left us and when we
did get one we got one her name was Sallie Mohnrern. We got to
know oure names apart but at first I could tell who aunty was talking to me or Sallie.

Sarah A Pierce [Sarah spells her last name Pierce in this
letter]

Des Moines City, Nov 22 1863

Dear Taylor

I set down to write thee to day and I do not know what I may find
to write of but I will tell thee that we are all well at this time. Cyrus
is well and we could get along fine if he was not so cross but that spoils
it all. Thee need not say any thing about it for I can get along for I do
not let him trouble me but then thee knows how it is with him and
Mary. I do not know how any man can let his self get to be so discontented. For my part I think I have had enought to make any one
unhappy as far as worldly things is conserned. But I endevour to think
of something be sids my troubles and try to be as happy as circumstances will admit and still hope for better times to come and then if
they never are any better why then I can not help it. But I will tell thee
about thing out from home. We have had the largest Ladies sanatery
convention that has been held in the west[1] but the amount of good it
will do will be for time to show. I did not get to attend myself on
acount of haveing no one to leave the baby with but Mary went two
days and thee cannot guess who she seen that we knew when we were
children, why no less than our old school teacher Edith Rodgers. She
is Maried to a man by the name of Mc Connel and lives in Iowa City
and she told Mary that she had visited the camp of the 22nd when it

lay at the City but she did not recognise thee among the soldiers. So after long years of toil and strife the old and young meet again. It seems a long time to me since we went to school to her at Baillys old house. And hearing of her put me to thinking of the ups and down I have seen since then so that I could not sleep all the next night and so it gos. We know not what will be our lot when we set out in this life for it is all dark before us and we have to grope our way along the best we can. Not that I think that I have had a harder lot than many another but I think mine has been quite as variable as any ones could be. I think I have had a tryel of good and bad fortune up to this time. Let the future bring what it may. I have come to the conclusion not to bother myself before hand. So I get enought to eat and some thing to keep us warm. I will take times as they come and wate to see what will become of us after this war is at an end. I have been so busy sewing since we got a girl that I have not took time even to read the Daily paper so I do not know much of what is going on in the Army. But the talk that I hear seem as though there would not be much more fighting and if that is true I for one will be glad if peace can come the right turmes. And Jeff Daviss and some more of the big ones of the South can be got and hung so that they will be no more trouble after the end is come on that they will not have a chance to do any more mischief in the country. For dear knows that all the attonement they can make will never replace the blood and tears that has been spilt for or by them or thair doing an the wrong they have done to the slave long before the war commenced. As I have nothing new to write I will close.

> I remain thine affe wife
> Catharine A Peirce

I send some of Sallies scribling but I do not expect thee can read it.

> Des Moines Iowa
> December 6 1863
> Dear Father

I am well and hope these lines will fine thee the same. I expect that thee will think my wrighting is black anough. I suppose I right wright better if could but I cant and there is no use of talking any thing about it. I dear never can wright worth any thing as long as I live so I cant I just kow. But as aunty says I must not get get in dispare. I feel as though I fellt disappointed about smething. This is Sunday after supper and the work is all done and Anna Skelly has gone to curch aunty up town to Elisebet today. I read in the fifth reader. I had been wanting a third part of arithMetick. I love to study but if I am what I want to be I will be a good scholar and be a school teacher. I could become one. I will not want to be one but have a good teacher. I like her so well. The baby is not very well. He has a bad cold. He has had a bad cold Monday to afternoon. Aunty was not abel to set up. She had hot fever. I felt all bad about it jeste the [illegible] the last letter. Mr Bakers house bernt yesterday wek and the old folks staed over night Sunday.

Frank is as mischivoeos as can be. I not much more to say to night seeing it is prety neer bed time for this time. Write soon.

Thy affecte daughter Sally Peirce

1. The convention of the Ladies State Sanitary Commission was held in Des Moines November 18–19. Also represented by delegates were the Loyal League and the Soldiers' Christian Commission. Governor Stone gave the introductory address, and Annie Turner Wittenmyer also spoke. The convention voted to organize a state sanitary society with subordinate leagues or societies.

Des Moines City Dec 13 1863
Dear Taylor

We are all well to day and I for one feel very thankful for as good health as I enjoy and that the Children have as good health as thay have when there is so much sickness among others as there has been this summer and fall though there is no much at this time but bad colds. They do not prove fatal although it is very disagrable to have so bad a cold as that which has been going for the last two weeks. The wether has been so changeable all that time there was no chance but to have colds. We have had one of the old cloudy times this week. The sun has not shone out all week though it has not been cold. The snow is all gone off and the ice is gone out of the River but the mud is about as bad as it ever gets to be in Iowa. It has the apprance of snowing again this evening for it is geting colder and I expect it will snow by morning. I see acounts in the papers of the snow falling very deep both east and west of us. I see that on the plains east of Denver that it was so deep as to imped the traines as the ware on there return from the Mo. River. And the coach ware delayd from three to four day so thee may know that we are likely to have a good old cold time of it up here this winter without there is a change for the better pritty soon. Has thee seen the Presidents Message yet? We have it and all of us think well of it and think that Father Abraham is all right on the Nigger as well as all other national affairs.[1]

If I be aloud to have an opinion on the subject which I suppose I can take this far from the seat of government and privately to thee if it will not amount to much to any one. It is a time that I look to the leaders of the nation and the Army to make a bold strike at the rebelion in all possible points so as to anihilate it as soon as possible. For I do not see how on earth the rebles can hold out much longer hemed in as they must be. If the accounts is half true that we see published though they oftimes are very conflicting and unsatisfactory but still some must be true. I see by the same source that Banks expedition in to Taxas had been altogather sucessfull and not likely to have much fighting to do which is a great pleasure to me. For I still thought that going there would be about the worst of all the other points in Dixie. For all the scoundrels have gone to Taxas for the last twenty years and I expected to hear of them being the hardest set of any to conquest. I still hope that Banks has done so well that thy Devision will not be needed to go for it will be so far for letters to go and come. It takes all most a month for one to come here from New Orlanes and that seems a long time for me to wait for to hear from thee. I receved two letters this week one from Orleans and one from Bradshear City. The one Orleans I got first writen when thee was on the eve of departure for the land of Rebles and was glad to hear that thee was so well and in such good sprites. For I think if thee can only keep in good heart thee will get along fine. Though no doubt but you all have a hard enough time of it down there, marching and fighting.

> I remain thyne truly
> Catharine A Peirce
> to Taylor Peirce

1. Catharine is referring to Lincoln's Annual Message to Congress on December 8, 1863. It was printed in the *Des Moines Register* on December 11. Lincoln stated that 100,000 blacks were in the army and that "no such insurrection, or tendency to violence, in any city has marked the measures of Emancipation." He jus-

tified the Emancipation Proclamation by stating that it was enacted to aid suppression of the rebellion. The message also mentioned ratification of a treaty with Great Britain to end the slave trade, as well as other national and international affairs.

>Des Moines City Dec 27, 1863
>Dear Taylor

I have not writen for two weeks to day and I have so much to say that I do not know just where to begin. But first I and the baby ware both so unwell this day a week ago that I could not get to write and all week we have been so busy that it seems I could not get time for we have had twenty Soldiers here this week untill this morning. Twelve of them left for Davanport and we expect that there will be more in a few day so they will keep comeing and going all the time for two months if they keep on Vollenteering as well as they have for the last week or two. I do not think there will be any need of the Draft going on in this State for the news we get now is all as good that I do not see how the war can hold out six months longer though it is not for me to know any thing about what will be done in that length of time. But still if they go on as thay have for the last year it will surely be over by this time next year. For our forces have recovered neerly or quite half or more of the country from the Rebles that they started out with at the commencement of the war. So I think there can not be another year of war unless it is keept up by the officers for the sake of officers or to make political capital of so as to gain their own promotion to some thing still higher.

Dear Taylor We are all well to day and in good sperits. The Children are well and so full of mischief that I can hardly get a chance to write a word so thee must excuse all the blunders in this. We had a good time christmas cooking for the Soldiers. They had the satisfaction of a good dinner on that day if they never get another. Poor fellows they seem to be in good heart at their going out at this time for they seem to think that they will not have to stay very long and I hope they will not to for if they do not I think that thee will get home all the sooner. Though I do not want thee to think I want thee to back out now untill the end unless thee gets sick then I want thee to try to get home as soon as possible so thee may have a better chance to get well again and be of more use to thy family and thy country too. I have not had a letter from thee since I receved the one dated at New Orleans on the day before you embark for Taxes so thee may know that we begin to look quite anxious for one about this time. If I do not get one this week I will begin to feel troubled though I will wait as patiently as I can and think the more of and when I do get it. Mary wants thee to say in thy next if thee got her letter with thy papers in conserning thy furlough as she got them fixt for me and wrotĕ and sent them to New Orleans about the time for thee to get them before thee left for Taxas. Dear One I have had no new from Jasper Co. for two month so I can tell thee nothing of what is going on down there this winter. I do not know if George Bennet[1] has got well or not but if he has he has likely to of gone to rejoin his regiment by this time. There is a great amount of business doing here this winter and I suppose there will be more gasing done after New years is over and the Legislature men all get in town and get in to full blast puffing and blowing. Cyrus did think he would take some of them to board but now he has take a contract of Soldiers that will be here this winter so he will not be able to accomodate such big bugs.

Dear Taylor I had so much to say when I began and have had so many interuptions from the children that I have got it jumbled up at such a rait that I do not expect thee will be able to read it when thee get it. But I will trust to thy good nack of reading and send it any how.

We are haveing a good old time of it this winter with snow and in it has been colder and there has been more snow already than we had all last winter and if it dose not hold up after New year we will be likely to have as much snow as we had that cold winter six years ago. And I feel very sorry to think it is so on account of so many poor people there is in our once happy land that is in a suffering condition. I did not know that there was so much of it untill the Ladys of the Legue[2] went to work to hunt them up about town. They found nineteen Soldiers familys that were realy in a suffering state for food and fuel when they proferd them assistance. Still I feel thankfull that I can be warm and comfortable all the winter if thee is away so I will bid thee by for to day hopeing thee well and that I may hear from thee in a day or two.

   I remain thy afc wife
   Catharine A Peirce

1. George T. Bennett was a New Jersey native and Newton resident when he enlisted in Company C, 22nd Iowa Infantry, on August 2, 1862. He died of disease in New Orleans on May 9, 1864.

2. The Ladies' Union League, also known as the Ladies' Loyal League, was an aid society that sought to assist the families of Union soldiers. Women were not allowed to join the men-only Union League (or Loyal League) but could form auxiliaries of their own (see the letter dated October 17, 1864, for more on the Union or Loyal Leagues). The first meeting was held in New York in May 1863. The organizers of the Ladies' League were emphatic that it was not a "women's rights institution." The Ladies' Loyal League of Des Moines held periodic meetings with guest speakers, some of whom were well-known Iowans serving with the army. A December 1863 report indicated that there were 35,000 members in Iowa.

Dec 27 1863
Dear Father

I am well and hope these few lines will find thee the same. Last Sunday I wrote to my cousin Mary Gibson. Told her that you were well the last time we herd from thee. I got her [illegible].

She wrote fore [illegible]. I not got it yet but intend to get it as soon as Mothe gets her mony. Some Soldiers went away this Morning. We took them in on wensday.

I got a nise book on christmas. We had a nise dinner. We had fifteen soldiers here. I got sum chesnuts a chrismus. One of the soldiers give me a Webster Speling book. My chrismas book is a [illegible] at work. I have a sore mouth I dond know what to write one thing. I do not fell very well today.

I have vacation now. In a week it will be over. Frank grows fat. He is so mischeivous that I cant hardly live. I must begin to close my letter for I have not much to writ this time. So good by Dear Father

Sallie Pierce [spelled Pierce in original letter]

Jan 3d 1864
Des Moines City,
Dear Taylor

It is with pleasure I sit down to write to day. We are all well but Cyrus he is not very well but he has not had a bad spell for six weeks and is not bad now for him to be. The wether is very cold this week quite as cold as ever it get here except those cold winter we had seven and eight years ago. The Mercury was down to 28 deg below zero so thee may know that it was pritty cold. Thare was three persons froze to death on wednesday night in the coach between here and Adell and how many more that we have not heard of. The Dear only knows for I think any porr soul that was caught out that night must sertainly perish. I could not help to be thankfull when I lay down with my children around me that I had a good warm house to stay in if it was not my own. I have about all that I need so thee may be contented as for me. Though if thee could get thy pay so I could let Cyrus have it I think it would be well to let him have it to finish off the rest of the house. For I think they might make a good bit this winter at the rate that the people are flocking to this place. Every place is full and more comeing and boarding is from three to seven Dollars per weeks though every thing is up accordingly. Flour is three Dol per hundred potatos 60 cts per bu and butter 30 cts per lb. Eges is selling at 3 ct a peice and hard to be got at that. Why eges are so scarce I do not see for shurely this is a good country for to keep hens enough to of had a supply of eges on hand in the fall to do through the winter. But I guess it is because the people are from hand to mouth. Any how if the winter last as it has been up to this time in all probability there will be as much stock lost for the want of feed as there was that last cold winter. Corn is plenty and pretty good but the hay is short and scarce. Cyrus paid thirteen Dol for a ton this week and that would do him all winter if he keept no stock but his own. He sold or let Smith have two of the cows early in the fall and I lent him money to pay for young [poultry?] so he has but those to keep and his mare. He did talk of selling her but he has not done it yet. If he was to get what he asks for her and what thee would send home he could fix up since and I think he would get to be about as well as he ever was. And then if he still wanted to take a trot round he could go and leave Mary a good home to stay in at the same time. I for my part I do not know what to try to do untill thee gets home but to remain just as I am. Without I should sell out here then I will do the best I can but I do not much expect that he will get a chance to sell though property is very high at this time and there might come some one that was fool enough to buy if he was to offer it as low as he still has done for the sake of geting away.

Dear one I have nothing new to write of to day. There has been no news of importance since the holy days commenced but I would like to know how thee spent thy holy days and if thee had a good time of it or not. I received two letter this week from thee from Texas and if I feel good to think thee is well and in such good spirits. So I will close with love to thee.

I remain thy aff wife
Catharine A Peirce

Des Moines Jan 10th 1864
Dear Taylor

I sit to write thee a few lines just to let thee know that we are all well and have lots to do. We have 30 soldiers here and six boarders so thee may know that we are all very buissy. But if we can make it pay that is all that any of us will ask. Cyrus is not very well but it is just a cold and if it dose not run in to the asthma he will be able to keep up. I have a few minutes to write while the baby is asleep and thee must excuse this for it is writen with Joe Kuhn old gold pen and it is the worse of the ware so that I can not write much. I have some considerable that I would like to tell thee if I get time to day. In the first place Wash Blanford was up from Jasper this week and they have a baby a month old and they are doing well. He says that there will be no Draft in that district. There was one man Drafted here in the fifth according to the law but they let him off and the Drafting is postponed untill the fifteenth of next month and I think by that time there well be no need of a Draft for Volunteers are pouring in from all direction[1] and it is almost as it did at the time thee went out. There is so many soldiers around but I do hope that they will not have to stay in the service very long. For I would be glad if the war would be over by the first of June and then they would reelect old uncle Abe and let him have four years to fix up in. For I think that he will bring things out about right if he lives to be able to get the chance. There is a good bit of talk of runing Lincoln again but is only talk as yet of coare. For the time is not yet to set on that question.

Taylor, I and the Children are doing fine. We have all that we are in need of so thee need not be any in trouble about us. But if thee could get thy pay to send home for to let C have it to work on and then he will get all fix here so if he still wants to go any where off from this. I do not want to werry thee about the money only to let thee know that Cyrus wants to try to pay the taxs this winter. And if we get that and what he will make off soldiers that will pay it all up and give me all I shall want to get things for me and the children too. I will try write a little every week to let thee know how we are but when thee will get it I cannot tell for it is so cold and so much snow that that mail is very uncertain at this time. It is as cold as it was that winter we lived in newton and has the apperance of holding on as yet. The baby is awake and it is dinner time so I must close. Mary says she will write as soon as this rush is over and she has time to think. I am writeing without taking time to think of what I write so thee must keep in good heart untill I have a better chance.

    Thine

    Catharine

    1. On October 17, 1863, Lincoln called for 300,000 volunteers. If that quota was not met, a draft would be initiated on January 5, 1864. The draft was postponed, and a call for 200,000 additional volunteers was made on February 1, 1864. A draft to make up the difference between requirements and volunteers was to begin March 10.

    Head Quarter 22nd Regt Iowa Infn

    Indianola Texas Jany 18th 1864

    Dear Catharine & the rest

I commence to write to you this morning being the first time there has been a chance to send out a letter for 2 weeks. The one I wrote before did not go out for some time after it was written so I concluded not to write again untill there was some prospect of it going out.

    Well we are now at Indianola. It is situated on Lavacca Bay about 15 miles NW of Dr Crows Point. We came here on the 4th of this month[1] and went in to quarters in the vacant houses in town. This has been a nice place and there has been considerable business done here. At one time there was about 500 families here but when we came the rebles army forced about 200 families out of the place with the intention of burning the town by the order of Genl McGruder.[2] But the rest of the citizens who were mostly Germans resisted and our troops arrived before they were forced to yield and run the rebles off and save the place. This is naturally a very strong place the town being built on the Bay Shore which is several feet higher than the water with a deep and narrow bay or slough running in the rear of town about ¼ of a mile the whole way from one mile below this place up to a mile abov Old Indianola which is about 4 miles abov this place. This Town is called Newtown as being built since the old town for the purpose of getting the advantage of the landing which is much better here than at old town. One part of our brigade is stationed at Old Town. The 23 Iowa came up from Fort Espiranza last night and we will go with them to old town to-day and will probably stay there for sometime, untill the army is concentrated.

The rebles have made two attacks on our pickets since we come here. The first time they had quite a skirmish. We were on dress parade when the scout came in and brought the News. We were imediately put in motion but before we arrived at the scene of action the rebs drew off. In a few days they again advanced in considerable force. The whole division was out on drill where they were discovered advancing in line of battle threatning to attack in three collumns. The 11 Wisconsin was stationed at old town and the rebs made a move to cut them off but we were a little to quick for them. We double quicked up to them and joined them before the rebs could get to the bridge that crosses the bayou that I spoke of running in the rear of town. The rebs seeing us join the 11th halted at that point while their right wing advanced at a quick trot to attack this place. When they got within about 300 yards the 6th Michigan battery which had just came up the night before from the Point opened on them with shell and so well directed was the fire they did not wait to see what was the matter but the whole line broke and retreated at full speed. We had 2 guns with us and as soon as we could get them in position we opened on those who were in front of us and one round done them and we were left in quiet posession of the field and we have seen nor herard no more of them since. While We had no artillery with us they continually hovered around our lines but we taught them a lesson that day that I do not think they will forget for a time to come.[3] Our division is commanded by Genl Benton[4] who reviewd the troops on Saturday. The whole army was out and a finer body men I never seen. In point of members it is not equal to the army that Grant crossed the Mississippi with but they are the veterans that remain of that host and at this time are in splendid health well clothed and armed and without exception are physically and constitutionally the best body of men now in the service. You may judge of the superior health of the men when I tell you that our brigade amounting to 2,000 men present there is only 10 men reported on the sick list and those are not in a bad condition. They have colds or rheumatism or something of that nature. Our Co has no one sick at all. There is one man with sprained back but that is all. I never seen the troops in as good heart as they are now. Col Stone told me last spring that he never seen an army in as good heart and condition as Grants was when he crossed the Miss but tell him if you see him that the troops are in better spirits and in better health now than they were then. There is one reason for this. The feint harted and the weakly ones are all weeded out and what is here thinks that as they have never been defeated even by the best troops in the confederacy that they can just eat up these texian renegades. I must tell you though it is a little Bragadocia about what occurred the other day when the news come that the rebs were moving on us. We were standing in line. Graham was putting us through the manual on dress parade when the scout arrived and galloped up to him and told him. He imediately put up his sword and announced the news and sent an orderly for his horse. Such a yell as went up from the 22 you never heard. There is always a few men who do not go out on parade being to lazy to get ready untill after it is too late. On that evening there was about 100 laying in camp. But as soon as the shout arose and the news was spread every man run for his gun and was in line before the Cols horse come. When he mounted and commanded right face Quick March the men seemed wild with enthusiasm. You know I not very excitable nor anxious to face danger if I can help it but I actuly felt as if I could chew up a half dozen texian rebles and when the rebles run I as well as the rest felt disappointed in not getting to give them a good drubbing and the march back was not near so joyful as the march forward. I do not know when I will get a chance to send out another letter but you need not get alarmed if you should not hear from me for some time as the line of communication is very uncertain. But I will write as often as I can get a letter out. When we leave here we will have to leave our tents and everything that we can possibly do without as our transportation is very limited and the nature of the Service such that if we have a great train with us it is in danger of being cut off as the enemy are all mounted in this country. So we are only allowed one team to the regiments and of course the march will be fatiguing and if the weather is bad it will be hard on us but any thing to whip these rebles. I think the Govt ought to furnish us a body of cavalry to protect our flanks as the movement of cavalry is necessarely much quicker than that of Inftry. They anoy us very much although a body of Inftr can always defeat a body of cavalry in a close fight. Yet they are unable to follow up their victory with advantage. I think that we will move from here to Lavacca which is 18 miles up the bay and from there we will march on Vittoria [Victoria] where we hear the rebles are going to make a stand. The citizens have word here this morning that a party of McGrudders force has laid down their arms but what authority they have for it I do not know. But they seem highly pleased at the news for they do not want to fight and I believe the state will not hold out long. Whatever may be the end of it I hope we will get at it before a great while. There is a mail in and I expect a letter. I have not had one since the 1st of the month. Paper is scarce and I must close. I am in good health and spirits. Kiss the little ones for me and give Col Stone my respects and that the 22 loves him better to day than they did a year ago. They begin to understand his worth now when they have officers to command them that does not care a bit for their comfort. We are in hopes that he will come to see us this winter. If he does he will receive the most heart felt welcome that any man ever received since Washington took leave of his troops. I must stop. Give my love to all my friends.

I remain yours affectionately
Taylor Peirce

1. On November 17 the 22nd Iowa was ordered to move from Berwick to Brashear City, where it boarded a train for Algiers. It arrived there on November 18. The next day five companies, including Taylor and Company C, embarked on the steamer *Thomas A. Scott* for the mouth of the Rio Grande. On November 27 the companies disembarked on Mustang Island because a storm prevented a landing at Brazos Santiago. The regiment advanced against Fort Esperanza on December 1, but the Confederates had abandoned it on November 29. The next day the regiment was ferried across Pass Cavallo and encamped at DeCros' Point on Matagorda Island. On December 2 the remainder of the regiment arrived from New Orleans. On January 4 the regiment was ferried to Indianola, where it went into winter quarters.

2. Major General John B. Magruder, a West Point graduate who joined his home

state of Virginia at the outbreak of war, had been ordered to take command of Confederate forces in Texas on October 10, 1862.

3. On January 12 Confederates approached Indianola and were met by the 11th Wisconsin Infantry and the 7th (not 6th) Michigan Battery, also known as Battery G. The attackers were driven off.

4. Brigadier General William P. Benton had commanded a brigade under Grant during the Vicksburg campaign.

Jany 27

Dear folks

I again set down this evening to write you a few lines to fill up the time. Our mail has not gone out yet but I think it will tomorrow. I have not received any thing from home for one month. The last letter I got was dated the 8th of December.[1] Since that I have written some 5 or 4 letters so that you might get word from me if I do not get any from you. Well I think we are booked here for the rest of our term of service for the way things look now. I think we will not have any more fighting. Our fellows took a prisoner the other night who deserted the rebles at Galveston who says that there is only 5,000 troops there and none at Houston[2] except the home guard and they are entirely composed of old men and little boys who are anxious for our army to come there so that they can surrender themselves and receive protection. He says also that the squd that took our men on the Guadaloup as soon as they found we were here imediately moved their camp to Victoria which is about 65 miles from here and he says that the citizens would gladly welcome our army at Galveston. For the army there takes whatever they want from them and makes them take their money which is only worth 10 cents on the dollar or at least was only worth that before our troops come here and it will not buy anything since we come and made it so that they could get what they wanted for what they had to sell. Greenbacks go as well here now as they do in Iowa and they are glad to get them for whatever they have to sell.

The men who were gobled up while we were out at Opaloosas La got back on Sunday[3] and they corroberate the principle part of what the prisoner says. They also say that the talk was in the army that they would lay down their arms if we invaded the State. They say they do not want their State used up as Miss and Louisianna is. 4 of our men who were left back at New Orleans Sick came up yesterday say that there was an election held in the Parrishes around New Orleans and in the City on New years day and the vote was almost unanimous for the State to come into the Union without slavery.[4] They also took 1,500 convalescents from there and went to take possesion of Mobile as all the troops were taken from them to reinforce bragg and at the same time the Gun boat fleet went round into Mobile bay to cooperate with them.[5] But it is to soon for us to hear anything from the expedition so from all I can learn from the different parts of the country the war is over.

Our Pay rolls have gone to the pay master to be fixed up and I expect we will be paid in a few days which will relieve my mind very much for I am begining to fear that you will be short of means before it can get to you. But as soon as you get this you may begin to look for the money at the express office for I will express it by the paymaster and you will get it sooner than I can get it to you by any other means. If you do not need to use it for any purpose to live on or Cyrus does not need it to fix up some of his things you can keep it by you so that if I should get home this spring I can have some thing to commence with. But if Cyrus can make use of it I want him to have it. My wages will now be more than it has been and I will have more to send at a time hereafter and my health is so much better than I ever was before that I do not need to buy any thing to live on but make the rations do me and they more than do it. I have some clothing allowance due me from last year yet and as this year is half over I think I can save all my next years clothing allowance which will be 45 dollar which will make my wages amount to nearly $300 and I think that with my bounty and what little I can scrape togather at home will start me again pretty well. And if Old Col Stone does as he promised I will get something better before I get out of the employ of Government.

Well I must stop writing. I believe I have given you all the news and I think we will not move from here this winter so we are looking for a good time of it. Write to me often. Give my love to all and kiss the little ones for me.

Affty yours
Taylor

1. This letter was not found.

2. Union forces at Galveston numbered less than 1,000 men. Galveston and Houston remained in Confederate hands until the end of the war.

3. On January 4, 1864, representatives from Major General Banks and Major General Taylor agreed on terms for the exchange of prisoners captured in western Louisiana.

4. On September 22, 1862, Lincoln had proclaimed that any state represented in Congress on January 1, 1863, would no longer be considered as being in rebellion. On December 2, 1862, an election was held in the thirteen parishes near New Orleans that were occupied by Union troops. Two congressmen were elected and, after a contentious debate in the House of Representatives, were allowed to take their seats on February 17. On January 11 Major General Banks ordered that statewide elections in parishes controlled by the Union be held on February 22 to elect a governor and members of the legislature. One dominant issue in New Orleans during December 1863 and January 1864 was black suffrage. There were many Unionists in Louisiana who objected to extending the right to vote to blacks. The other dominant issue was the registration of at least 10 percent of the number of voters who had registered in 1860. The newspapers were full of the debate over these issues, and this may have led to confusion among the returning men as to the date of the elections and their significance.

5. In November a brigade commanded by Brigadier General William A. Quarles had been ordered from Mobile to reinforce Bragg at Chattanooga. In January rumors of an impending attack on Mobile by Banks caused the Confederates to order the brigades of Quarles and William E. Baldwin to reinforce that city. Sherman was to move his army to Meridian and asked the navy to maneuver near Mobile to prevent Confederate forces from being withdrawn from there to attack him. In early February naval forces under Rear Admiral David Farragut began to bombard forts that protected Mobile.

> Des Moines City Jan 31st /64
> Dear Taylor

I sit down to write to thee this evening and I feel very much as if I had the Blues though I am as well as common and all the rest of the family and things are right. For all that I am lonesome for it is a dull day and has set in to snow again. I feel affraid we will have more cold weather. It had got warm enough to take off nearly all the snow and brake up the ice in the river so that it would of all went out in another day or two and I was in hope we ware about done with such severe cold as it has got to be this evening again. But that is the way the winter gos so we will have to make the best of it and be satisfied with what comes. We are haveing a good time working for soldiers all this cold time. There has been some here now for five weeks and some times as high as thirty and forty. We have thirty one here to night and six others boarders besides so thee may know we have to step around for we have but one girll and that is Anna Kelly. She was here when thee come home in the summer and I must say that we get along very well. I must tell thee what a trick Sallies cow playd off on us. Cyrus keept scolding about her not giveing as much milk as he thought she ought to so one morning Anna milkd her and got quite a lot of milk and before ten oclock she brought forth a fine bull calf and then C was beat for he said she would not be in again before late in the summer. I was well pleased for I think she will be the very cow for us to have for then we will not get out of milk for Frank will live on bread and milk if he only can get it. Dear Taylor I do not know much to tell thee about to night for I realy do believe I do not know much only of the children. They are in bed and asleep and are all well and hearty and full of life in the day. Sallie got to school all the time when it is not to stormy or cold and if she has to stay at home a day I have to scold her to make her quit her fusing about haveing to stay. She is so well pleased with her teacher and school that it is a punishment for her to be out of it a single day. She gos to Mrs Denison that thee saw here in the summer. Taylor I expect thee thinks my letters are very poor ones but thee must not look for much from me for I have not got the chance to write much if I could. For Ellis is still as trouble some as he was when he was younger and I do not know wheather he will ever be any better or not. I get all most out of heart some times with him for he is surely the crossest child that ever was yet he seems to be well now and is fat enought for any child to be. Well I must close for he is about to wake up and then I cannot write. I have not had a letter this week but I hope there is one close at hand for me for the last one I got was dated the 21st of Dec[1] and I would like to have a later one. I remain thy wife

        Catharine Peirce

    1. This letter was not found.

        Head Quarters 22nd Regiment
        Iowa Vol Infantry Feby 3 1864
        Dear Catharine and the rest of the friends
I set myself down again this Evening to write to you as I have got my work almost done for the end of the year so that I have some Spare

time. I concluded to take all the paper I could find and write it full. Well in the first place I am well in health and I received 3 letters from home this week which has made my mind feel in a very happy state. I am pleased to hear that the hawk Eye Boys still have their patriotism up to boiling heat. But I am sorry that there is no way to compell the cowards and Secish Sympathisers to come to war but maybe it is all for the best for if they do not help us to Save our country we will not feel like treating them with any great amount of benevolence or consideration when we get home which I hope will be eer long. Well now as to what we are doing or what we are going to do here. I am entirely ignorant of the latter but of the first I can tell you in a few words.

We come up her 2 weeks ago[1] and we have got our tents piched on the beach about 100 yards from the Bay shore or waters Edge. We have drilled about 3 hours every day and the rest of the time is spent in keeping ourselves clean and keeping our arms and accoutrement in good order and Eating. We have pleanty of every thing to eat that is good and we have ours well cooked. In the first place I have roast beef and onions for breakfast in with boiled rice and sugar and corn mush and sometimes I vary it to a dish of hash made of cold roast beef and potatoes. Then for dinner I have baked pork and beans with boiled potatoes dried apples stued and light bread and gravy. Then for supper I have steued beef and fried potatoes and the coffee 3 times per day. This is the general rotine unless I wish to have some dainties. Then I get just what I want fried mush and molasses being the easiest to come at. That is generally the dish. Sometimes it consists of fried crackers and sugar and just whatever I take a fancy to. My duty consists in getting up when the bugle blows and call the roll and then getting breakfast. Then I take the men who are detailed from the company up to head Quarters to mount guard. After that is over I go back to the quarters and make out my morning report and take it to the adjutant and then I fix up our Company business for an hour. I then take the co and drill an hour or go out with them and be drilled an hour. Then come in, prepare dinner, rest till 2 oclock go out and drill 2 hours and come in rest ½ hour then go on dress parade. Then come in and get supper and the rest of the evening I straighten up the books or do something of that sort untill tattoo beats. Then I call the roll and set and talk awhile and then go to bed. I have that to go through with every day with very little variation. If I wish to rest a day I get leave and go out some place and walk round. I do not suppose there is a man in the whole army that is as well fixed as I am. I do just as I please and have just as much liberty as I ever had. I feel and do just as I did when I hired out to work. I always done what I was hired to do. I have contracted to serve the government and I do it and when that is done they ask nothing more of me. I can not see for the life of me what people find such fault with the army for. There is some of them always finding fault with every body and every thing and never proform one half of what they contracted to do and yet they curse their officers for trying to get what little they can get out of them. When if they had justice they would get no pay and half rations. Me and my officers all get along fine and the company and we get along well and are much better satisfied than when Ault was in command. We have a good Col although the men now think if they had Stone back again they would never make a complaint again. The majority of them says that they did not know how to appreciate him untill they lost him. How is he getting along as chief executive of the State? Does he seem to take hold of things as if he meant to do something? I hope he will for I have a very friendly feeling for him for the many kindnesses received from him while I served under him. If you see him tell him the 22nd remembers him and would be happy to receive something from him to show them that he has not forgoten them. Something in the way of a letter or a little address. There is many a poor fellow whose heart would be warmed if he knew their old Colonel still remembered them with kindly feelings. All I am sorry for is that some of the officers that received the most favours from him did the most against him at the time of the Election. I could have kicked them if I dare do it but I had to let it go. However we done pretty well for him only 36 against him and 276 for him beside a great many that voted for him that was in the Hospitals and absent on detached service. Well I need say no more about him now but go on with something Else. Our regiment is in fine health and spirits they have laid up so long that they are beginning to get restless and are spoiling for a fight although I do not wish to get into a fight if it can be helped. Yet I feel as if I would like to be at the rebles while the weather is cool if we are going to have any more of it to do. The weathe has been fine for the last three weeks and things looks as if spring was coming. The grass is beginning to grow and the buds is swelling but the wind is disagreeable at times. Yet it is more like the month of May in Iowa. There is some talk of us going in a few days to take Port Lavecca.[2] It is about 12 miles from here and is said to have a fine harbour and there is a passage for small craft from it to Galveston. We can see them passing out every day. It is said that the inhabitants are leaving it and it is supposed they intend to burn the place and I think the intention of our commander to save the town and I would not be surprised to hear the bugle blow the assembly this night to fall in and march and it may be some days first. Yet I am ready at all times to go at a minutes notice as all Soldiers ought to be. This is one of the things that I do not like in the military service. We never know what we are going to do an hour before hand when it seems to me that we might as well know it as not so that we could prepare a little for it. But I suppose if we were used to being told before hand we would not always be ready as we are now. I thought when I commence this letter I would try to make it interesting to you but I somehow have got so that I cannot write a letter worth anything. Wheather I am harder to satisfy with my own writing or wheather it is that my mind is occupied with other things to the exclusion of letter writing or wheather I have not as much Sence as I used to have I do not know. But something is the matter for my letters are of very little effect and the subject is so disconnected that you will learn but little from them. I like the weather or the climate here but I do not like the land. Yet I think a man could live easy. There is plenty of oysters in the bay and we can get them easily if we try but we have become used to them so that they have ceased to be a luxury. Corn does not grow well here nor does wheat and oats but rice and fruit seem to do pretty well. That is peaches and oranges but apples do not grow here. They raise vegitables and cattle but the cattle do not look like the northern cattle. Wheather they will do as well in this climate as they will further north or not. There is thousands of them roaming over the plains and deer and other game in abundance. There is also the Large Rabit or hare. We see them in the mornings playing around. They look almost as large as a fawn and are very good eating. I am about out of anything to write about and guess I will have to stop. Oh yes I have the itch and am just going to put some red percipit on it. I caught it from Cap.[3] I expect he got it while he was running about home and he and I have slept togather ever since he come back and of course I got it but if I keep it long it will be becaus it cannot be cured.

I have a little journal almost full which I am going to send home in a few days and I want you to preserve it for future reference.[4] I have put down all the transactions as they occur and many of my thoughts during my spare moment and if there is anything in it that will be beneficial to the children or anybody else you can let them see it. I have written it with pencil as I could not always have ink to write with so I kept it with me and recorded the things as they occurred. I intend to write Sallie and Frank both a letter and send out with this and you must tell Frank that he must learn to write next summer so that he can send me a letter. I am very much delighted in getting Sallies Epistles. She seems to understand the art of putting her ideas on paper which is more than many do that is older.

It is getting late and I think I will go to bed and as I will not be very busy to morrow if we do not go out to fight I can finish it then and if we go out I can finish it when I come back and the news will be so much the fresher. By the way I expect to get my money in a few days as the pay Rolls have been sent off to the pay masters to have them counted up and we are looking to have him here now every day. And as soon as I get it you may begin to look for it at the express office and I want Cyrus to have it and make what ever use he can get of it so as to help him out and get him fixed up. I am glad to hear that he is better this winter and hope he will not suffer so much hereafter. I will have nearly $200 due me but I do not expect to receive more than 140 now and the ballanc will be paid about the first or 5th of next month so you can have enough to do something with. Well I must stop for this time as it is midnight.

Friday night Feby 5th 1864. I thought I would finish my letter to night. I have not much more to write. Things is still going on much the same. The first brigade of our division went up to Lavaca this morning and we expect have run the rebs out or else we would have been sent for before this time. It is only about 15 miles and they went out early and of course if there had been any fight we could have heard the firing as there is nothing between them and us to Stop the sound. So I think we will have no fight. I heard from on old Woman who is a doctor this morning that our forces was giving the rebles gass at Galveston. She had a son in the army and she said he was taken prisoner and she was glad of it. She says that the messenger told her that Genl McGruder could not get his men to fight and was keeping about one half of his men to guard the other half. If this is a fact Galveston must fall. I also seen an old man who come up from Brownsville with Genl Dana who says that they have formed a whole regt of refugees there since our forces went there and the citizens will soon raise enough to protect themselves if we will only protect them untill they can get organised and armed. This is all good news but on the back of this I hear bad news from the tache Country in Louisiana. I hear that the 19th army corps has been driven from New Iberia[5] and the rebles come in and hung several of the Citizens who showed our men favours. The hanging of the men I care very little about for if they had shown the man they would not have been there to have been caught. If they will carry water on both shoulders let them suffer the penalty of hippocracy. But I do not like to hear of our men giving back an inch and if the Iowa boys were there they could not have driven them. But the more I See of the milk and water troops[6] from the east the more I dont like them although one cannot lay the blame to on native born americans. For the most of the nineteenth Army Corps is Irishmen and the lower of all the eastern Yankees and of cours they lack the energy of the western pioneers. I do not want you to think that I am gassing about the Iowa troops but I do think whatever can be done they will do and do it quick too. There is an other thing that looks me in the face. Many of the officers of the east are superanuated politicians and Editors or something of that kind. Men who in the matters of Dollars and cents are good enough but when it comes to managing an army where it takes courage an energy they are not the men. And I hope to See such men Superseded by men who have the sand in their gizzard to carry out the neccesary plans to crush this Southron Oligarchy. Old Abe has his proclimation offering a free pardon to the private Soldiers[7] and Genl Dana is having copies of it and some orders of his own issued and published throughout this State as far as he is able to get them distributed. And the men that can get to us is taking the oath of allegiance keeping the Provost Marshall busy from Morning untill night administering the milk of kindness prepared for them by Doctor Lincoln.

Well I have about run out and I guess I will send you a little song or some dogeral to fill up as the tattoo has beat and all are laid down but me and time is not so precious as it was. I mybe can write something to amuse the Children if it is not fit for any thing else. So here goes. Remember we are on the Sea Shore and after a hard day work I go down to the shore to rest and get clear of the noise of camp.

> At night by the beach as I wandered a while
> To rest me an hour e'er my head pressed the pillow
> And escape for a time the noise and turmoil
> And look at the dark rolling billow
> Me thought I could see, on its rough changing breast;
> Some resemblence, to the years thats passed o'er me;
> And I wonder, if ever, again, Ill have rest,
> In the days that are yet, still before me
> My thoughts answers no: rests not of this earth.
> For that is found only in heaven
> But toil is a debt contracted at birth
> And life is the recompence given
> And when death comes at last and cancels the debt
> Thus ending all human sorrow
> Then lifes gloomy night giving way to the light
> Brings a glorious; Eternal to-morrow

I think you will not be able to bare more at this time and as paper is scarce I will close. Kiss the children and give my love to all.

> Affectionately thine
> Taylor

1. Initially the 22nd Iowa encamped at "New Town" Indianola but on January 19 was ordered to move to "Old Town" Indianola.

2. The regiment would not move to Port Lavaca but would remain near Indianola.

3. Red Precipitate Ointment was used primarily for eye inflammation. Such ailments were often attributed to sun glare and sand particles, and soldiers in the Department of the Gulf were particularly susceptible to such irritations. "Cap" is Captain Lafayette Mullins, who took command of Company C on August 9, 1863, when Captain Adam Ault resigned. Mullins's oath of office, however, is dated November 11.

4. This journal was not found.

5. On November 17 the Nineteenth Corps had gone into winter quarters at New Iberia. On January 6, however, the corps moved to Franklin because Major Gen-

eral William Franklin believed that the New Iberia position was too exposed to Confederate attack.

6. "Milk and water" was a derogatory term that meant weak, dull, or lifeless.

7. On December 8, 1863, Lincoln offered a pardon to persons who had participated in the rebellion, with exceptions for senior military officers, former U.S. military officers, former members of Congress, and several other categories. Those seeking a pardon had to swear an oath of allegiance.

>   Des Moines Feb 7th
>   Dear Taylor

I sit down to write this morning to let thee know that I received thy letter of severel dates and that I feel very glad to hear from thee but I am sorry to learn that thy hearing is getting so bad.[1] If it is no better by the time thee gets this thee had better try to get home. For a man that is deaf would be better than none atall and then I think if thee was to get home thee could be doctered up in a little while so that thee could reenlist or be of use in some other place where thy hearing would not be of so great use as it is as a private soldier. And still thee could be of as much service to thy country and may be more to thy family. How ever thee must do just what thee thinks is best about it for it is not for me to know what is the best. Only I think if thee is likely to be in any more danger on account of deafness thee had better try to get home.

I am as well as common this week. I have had my old winter cough for a bout four weeks and the ulcer on my left lung has come off and I feel much better for it. The soreness and pain has all left and I think I can go on again untill another forms or some thing else comes. I have not been sick this time like I was last winter all though some days my side and breast hurt me quite bad. We have had so much to do that there was no time to think of pain or aches for there has been soldiers here scince Christmas more or less all the time and we have been busy cooking for them. I see by the paper that thare has been a call made for five hundred thousand more troops and Gov Stone reply was there will be no Draft in Iowa.[2] We are comeing Father Abraham with our five hundred thousand more. But I am afraid that Gov will be disappointd about the draf and I would not care if he was. If the draft would only take the Cops out of the community and place them in the front or some place where they would have to fight for the old flag.

I do not know what the legislature is doing for there is none of us get time to read the daily doing of the house though what I do see they are doing things up about right. I hear that Capt Ault is trying to get up another company in Jasper but of the truth of it I can not say. For if it is so and he gets the men I shall think the race of fools has not ran out yet. I have not seen any person from Jasper for a long time and therefore I do not know what is done in that county towards raising the amount due from there. But if they turn out as they have else where your Reg will be filled up to its first amount and more for the next call. I had to quit to help get dinner and now I sit down to write some more. I see by to days paper that Gov Stone has give out a presing invitation to the people of Iowa to answer to the call with out haveing to be Draftd.

Sallie she commencd to write to thee and did not do much so I will try to make some amend for her. She gets all my pens so that I can not keep one that I can write with to do much good. But thee will have to excuse us. The children are well and hearty and are growing fine but they are very trouble some because of it is sunday and it is so mudy that they cannot get out of the house and every little noise they make is heard by all. It seems to me that I would be glad if thee was to get home for to help me with the children for I fear I will not be able to make any thing of them my self for they seem to get more and more mischievious every week they live. Or it may be because I feel it more than I did in the summer when they were out at play.

Dear Taylor thee must excuse me for not writening more for the baby is so cross that I will have to quit. I guess Mary got a letter from Rachel the other day and they are all well and would like a letter from thee if thee could find time to write them. She dose not give much news only that J P Cooks widow has removed to Oxford and that William and his family was at her house and she can not see much change in them for 12 years in Iowa.

> I remain thy afc wife
> Catharine A Peirce

1. The letter in which Taylor mentions a hearing loss was not found.

2. On February 1, 1864, Lincoln ordered a draft for 500,000 men to take place on March 10. The men would serve for three years or for the remainder of the war. Iowa's quota was 6,000 men, but Stone declared, "There must be no draft in Iowa."

Sunday the 7th 1864

Dear Father

I am well and hope that when these lins reach thee thay will find thee the Same. I feel glad that Henry Smith gave me five cts. [Ian?] and I bought five sheets of paper for my self and I am drawing a map of the united states for the last day of school. If I had the mony I would buy five cents of paint to paint it for me and then it wold look nice. I was a visiting yesterday to Mr Mensons Motherinlaws.

I wrote a letter to my cousin Annie Mary Gibson and I intend to write another as soon as aunty writs agan.

I dont think of eny thing more.

I still remin yor efectionate daughter

Sallie A Pierce to her Father [spelled Pierce in original letter]

March 15/64

Des Moines City

Dear Taylor

We are all well to night and I have got the little ones to bed and I thought I would improve the time by writing to thee. We are have-ing a little spare time just now as there is no soldeirs here but two that was left here sick with the lung fever because Cyrus was taken with one of his old spells last week and was very sick. Indeed so that we did not think that he could get through alive but he has get up and around again and is right well. He did not have the asthma this time. He has not had that since in November to amount to much so that he had gaind in flesh and in health so that it did not get him so weak as the asthma usually did and I think he was doing a little to much for his ability to bare up. For it is no use for him to try to work much any more. While there was so many here he had to be going all the time to get things to cook and that was to much for him to do. But he thinks he will make some money if he did get sick and likely he would of been sick any how and so it might of been worse if he had of set in the house all the time through the cold weather. The weather has got to be very nice for this time in the spring and has the appearance of a nice spring. It would be a very good thing to have an early season this year so that the farmers could get some of thair spring work done before all the men has to go to war. For I see by to days paper that there is another call for 200,000 men and that the Draft will be put in force on first of April[1] with out a doubt. And I hope it will try the Cops and find where they are so that some of them will have to husel out or pay out their green backs which will hurt them almost as bad as to go. For most cowards love money better than any thing else. It seems from the election that there has 140 of the Union men left town for the war this spring so that they got a Copperhead Mayor. But all the rest of the City oficers had a good Union magority. So take all in all they did not make much for they are loseing foot hold all the time so that there will not be many left by the time the war is over and the boys get home. It will not be hard to kill them all off. But I must stop gassing and tell thee that Mary got receved a letter from Rachel last week[2] in which she says that Aunt Leidia Hanes daughter Lizzie was married to a man by the name of Abe Lincoln from Maryland. She has done well if he should turn out to be as good as old Uncle Abe in principal though I expect he must be about right or he could not come in at all. She all so says their boys have left home to work. Ellis has gone to learn the saddle buiseness and Henry is in Washington working for 30$ per month and Aunt Hannah is no better or never will be. She R feels very much discouraged on acount there of for she says She can-not see how they can keep Aunt much longer for it is as much as they can do to get a long themselves. They ware all well when she wrote. She said that she would like a letter from thee if thee could get time to write for she has writen to thee twice and has never had but one from thee and that thee sent when thee was at home last summer. So I think thee ought to write to her if thee can get time for she has her share of trouble along with the rest of us. I think sometimes that I have more than my share by giveing consent for thee to join the Army before I had a home of our own and means to take care of the children with out being dependant on thee for it during the time thee is away. But I have got along very well all things considered though I will not com-plain of my lot for it is all for the best. If thee can get home when thy time is out we can fix up very nice and I think that we will be likely to set more valieu on a home than we have ever done before. For we never have had a permanant home on this earth to gather and if we never have I hope we will live so that we can enjoy our rest after this life is done. It is times that trys mens souls to the utmost and I think if I bare my share with patiance that maybe I may get my reward. God knows I have all ways tryed to do my duty as far as I have had health to carry me and if I have commited any great sin it has been through ignorance not knowing right from wrong.

March 16th. Dear Taylor I did not finish all last night that I had to say so I will tell some news from Jasper. I hear that Henry Sumpter has taken old man Johnson's wife and left for parts unknown. His wife died in September and they ware very thick so much so how ever that Johnson made a fuss about it and he divided his property with Mary and he has gone to his daughters Mrs Jordans. I suppose that H and Mary should of left last week taken all their things with them. The rest of the folks are geting along about the same. Garland Edwards got a discharg[3] and come home this winter but I can not find out wheather John Akins[4] ever has gone back to his Reg or not nor how his family gets along this winter. It seems as I have writen about all that I can think of at this time. Will quit. Ah. yes this is my birth day. I am thirty six years old to day and thee will find an old greay headed woman when thee gets home in place of the girl thee Marred some eighteen years ago though my heart feels as warm towards thee as it did the day we ware first togather and I hope the time will come yet that we will be as happy as then. I am happy to know that thee is so well off in thy situation for if thee was unhappy I should feel bad for thee. It makes it go off a heep better to know that thee is geting along well when I know that I could do nothing for thee if thee was not doing well.

Taylor I have writen all that I can find any since in and may be a good bit more so I will close. I remain thy affe wife.

Catharine A Peirce

The Children all send a kiss and a wish for papa.

1. On March 14 Lincoln directed that 200,000 men be drafted. The order established the date of April 15 for voluntary enlistments, after which unfilled quotas would be filled by a draft.

2. This letter was not found.

3. Garland Edwards, Company E, 40th Iowa Infantry Regiment, was a Kentucky native and Newton resident. He enlisted August 15, 1862, and was discharged for disease October 23, 1863, at Mound City, Illinois.

4. John Aikins, Company K, 28th Iowa Infantry Regiment, was an Ohio native

and Prairie City resident. He enlisted August 7, 1862, was transferred to the Invalid Corps February 15, 1864, and was discharged March 11, 1864.

> Metagordo Island Head Quarters
> 22n Iowa Inftry March 17 1864
> Dear Catharine & all the rest

I have but a few moments to write and will have to cut it short. We have moved back onto the Island again and have commenced to fortify on an extensive scale.[1] What we have moved back for is more than I can tell for we have seen no signs of rebles for some time and we continually hear of them leaving for the north and attempting to cross the miss to reinforce the Rebles east of that stream. It is the belief among the best informed that we will lay here all summer and hold this place so that if the texians will not come in we will have a place to commence from and this is the key to the state. There has been considerable change here since I wrote last. The 33 Illinois has gone into the veteran[2] and the 11th Wis and the 18th Indianna and also the 8 Ia all of which belonged to our division but of both brigades. So they have consolidated the 2 Brigades and we are now the first Brigade of the 1st Division of the 13 AC[3] under Genl Warran Brig Comdr and Genl Dana Division Commander and the whole commanded by Genl John A McClernand[4] our old Commander and we are all well satisfied with the change. We are having a good time of it and I do not care if we serve out our time here. I am in good health and in good Spirits and have things just as much my own way as I wish. I am busy the most of the time but I think I will have more leisure soon. I have not had a letter for three weeks and I hear that we will only get mail hereafter once a month and you will not be surprised if you do not get a letter oftener. I will write once a week so that if there is a chance to send out I can send it. We have had a very cold spell for the last 4 days but it is a little warmer now. The grass has started and the leave has been puffing out for the last 3 weeks but every thing comes on slow here and they are not as large as they would be in Iowa in 5 days after starting. We get no news here and I can not tell thee anything about what is going on. Write to me and give me all the particulars of everything. Excuse this short letter and badly written for I have no place to write only on the ground as we only got here yesterday. Kiss the children for me. Farewell.

      Taylor

1. On March 13 the regiment moved from Indianola to Matagorda Island. It was put to work strengthening the island's defenses.

2. War Department General Orders Number 191, June 25, 1863, allowed individual soldiers to reenlist "for three years or during the war." The reenlistees would be designated "veteran volunteers" and would receive a bonus of $402. Under General Orders Number 85, April 2, 1863, each soldier who reenlisted would also be entitled to a thirty-day furlough. By General Orders Number 216, July 14, 1863, a regiment "shall bear the title of 'veteran'" if one-half its members were "veteran volunteers." General Orders Number 376 declared that if three-fourths of a regiment reenlisted, the regiment would "be furloughed in a body." Those who did not reenlist would be assigned to other companies or regiments.

3. The First Division, Thirteenth Army Corps, was reorganized March 10, 1864. Prior to the reorganization, the 22nd Iowa was in the Second Brigade with the 11th Wisconsin and the 21st and 23rd Iowa. The new organization assigned the 22nd Iowa to the First Brigade, which consisted of the 33rd and 99th Illinois, the 8th and 18th Indiana, the 11th Wisconsin, and the 21st and 23rd Iowa.

4. Brigadier General Fitz-Henry Warren had been assigned to the Department of the Gulf in September 1863 after participating in the battle of Gettysburg. Major General Napoleon J. T. Dana was replaced as commander of the Thirteenth Corps by Major General John A. McClernand on March 10 and reassigned as commander of the First Division.

      Head Quarters 22n Iowa Info
      Matagorda Island Texas April 18, 64
      My Dear little Franky

I am going to write a long letter to him so that he can have something to look at and read when he gets old enough to understand what it means and can give some Idea of what his Papa has seen and how he felt at having to be away from his dear littl children and their mother to fight for the country in the war of the rebellion.

It is now going on two years Since I first enlisted to serve in defence of the Government. Before I done so I had a long talk with your mother about the propriety of going and leaving her with the little ones all alone without any protection or any one to help her get along. Your mother felt like I did myself about it. She was very loth to let me go but she thought it was the duty for every one to defend the country that was able and she looked around and seen others that had gone and left their families in as bad a condition as we were and she thought she would not have it said that her selfishness kept her husband from his post. And as all people then was convinced that the rebellion could not be put down without the government got more help I finished up some sawing I had to do and two days afterwards I was on the muster Rolls. My Dear little fellow it fellt as if I was tearing the last chain of affection from my heart when the day come to leave you all. I hope that none of you will ever have to go through the same trial. But I did not let your mother know any thing about how hard it was for me to part from you and helped her to bear up as well as I could and things all went off very well. But when I started from Newton to go to Iowa City I could hardly keep my throat from choking right up and I determined as soon as I could get to I would set to work diligently at my duties as a soldier and not let my mind dwell too much upon home. I also knew that the mind has a great deal more to do with the health than any thing else. So as soon as we got to the rendesvous I was called on to help makeing out the proper papers for the Organizing the Company although it was not properly my duty to do it. Yet I was nearly the only one who was capable of doing it and as I was well qualified for the business I went into it with all my might and worked night and day untill I got things ready to be mustered in to the united States Service. By this time the homesick feeling left me to some extent and I began to take an interest in preparring myself for the arduous duties that alwas belongs to the Soldiers life. After I had been in Camp about 2 weeks I got leave to go home on a visit which I would not have done if you had all been well for I knew that the parting would be hard again and as it was over I did not like to go through the trial again. But I got along with it very well and got back to the regiment and went to work again as hard as I could to keep up my Spirits. And by the time we had orders to march I had got the better of my feelings and begun to feel quite cheerful.

I write this description of what one may do for himself when any circumstances occur when it becomes his duty to act contrary to his feelings and what I conceive to be the right principle to go on. When once we are convinced that it is our duty to do anything We ought to do it if takes the last hair and do it too with all our might.

Well I thought that the war would be over any how in one year and that there would not be much fighting and I went into the study of tactics and everything that I thought would be of use to me and I got along fine and had many friends in the regiment. I was very much interested in the events of the war for with the love of country which I wished to see at peace again I felt a reluctance to having to participate in a battle for several reasons. Probably the greatest reason or the one that I will be sure to get the most credit for was fear of being killed. However to tell the truth I could hardly say what was the greatest motive. I was always troubled to see my fellow beings suffer and I thought I could never bear to see the dead and wounded on the field of battle. And another thing was I was sprung of a race that was nervous to pitifull degree and although I had never felt it myself yet I feard it might show itself in time of eminent danger and I would be called a coward. I believe this was a scource of the most trouble to me of anything else. However things went along very well. After we got in to camp at Rolla missouri I had quite an easy time of it thanks to my education. I could do any thing of a business nature required and I was relieved from many of the rough jobs for the purpose of being Employed in making out the nescessary Reports of the Company and was for good conduct given command of a squad and sent to guard the town and keep it quiet. While there we had a fine easy time of it. At length the news come that Sherman was defeated at Vicksburg and we were ordered to leave Rolla and go to West Plains. During the march I hardly know how I did get along. The roads was rough and muddy and we had not learned enough about soldering to take advantage of circumstances and besides that we had all our cloths and accoutrements to carry not having disposed of any that we drew at Camp Pope. The Clothing consisted of two full suits and weighed about 50 lbs. That with our arms amounted to about 90 lbs and the load and the journey was very hard on me as I would not ask to ride and shrik out as some of them did. Well I made the march but I caught cold and was very near having to give out but I got along untill we got to Thomasville where we run out of provisions. There Col Stone got an old mill and set me to grinding corn. I worked at that 2 days and 3 nights without resting or sleeping and when I got enough ground to feed the brigade I got halled for two days and got along untill we reached the Mississippi River where we rested 3 weeks and I got well as ever. We then entered into the campaign of Mississippi and I was with the army untill after the Battle of Port Gibson. I had been healthy untill the day of the Battle. I had been marching with 10 days rations and my clothes what I had of them for I [sent?] my winter cloths home. As I said I had been marching with ten days provision on my back and 100 rounds of cartridge all day and untill about 1 o clock in the night when the advanced guard run into the reble pickets and soon after they opened on us with cannon and I was in the Battle which I had dreaded so long.

Although it was the first cannon that I had heard that I knew to be intended for us I think the sound of it did not make my pulse beat a bit faster and I do not recollect now that I felt any different from what I have done hundred of times when starting up the old Saw Mill. I was anxious to see morning come so that we could see how to get at them and whip them. After they had shelled us for 3 hours and not being able to run us out of the place we had got into they quit and I lay down and went to sleep and when I woke up it was sun up. I then for the first time began to feel something like fear for I knew that the rebles had come to try and keep us from advancing into the State and all expected a desperate fight. And if we were whiped there I knew we could never get away and I did not like the idea of being a prisoner. An oppressive silence reigned around for two hours. Not a sound was heard and the suspence was awful to me but at length Harry Griffith opened the ball with his battery and instantly the rebles sent back a shower of grap shot and canister and the bullets were flying amongst us like bees with pretty much the same noise. The suspence was over. We knew where the rebles were and could see what we had to do. From that time untill the battle was over I never thought of hunger or fatigue or danger as anything to hinder me from helping to whip the rebles. But the next day after we found that the rebs had left and there was no more fighting to be done I began to sink and the heat and the fatigue had put my system so out of fix that I had to be sent to the hospital. I was there untill a day or two after the assault on Vicksburg when I got permission to join the regiment. I was then employed everyday for 40 days in the Siege of that place and from first to last nor up to the present time have I ever felt as if I was afraid of a fight. Although I do not wish ever to see another one if It can be got along without. Now I will explain why I have written so much about my first Soldering and the impressins that it forced upon my mind. I wish to impress upon the mind that there is two stages of life although they are all so blended togather that you can not discover wher one stops and the other begins. Yet the controling power of the two are intirely different. The feelings and the impulses of the boy are entirely different and different motives actuates the boy in his movements than does the man. The boy just let loose from the controll of his mothers love full of generous impulses and without experience in the ways of the world is just in the situation to become the dupe of every designing individual he meets and only when it is too late does he find that all is not gold that glitters. Or in other words the people he has to do with has not his mothers affection for him and all will fleece him if they can. On the other hand when he becomes an experienced man in the ways of the world he will be actuated by different motives. He will not act from impulse but from principle or from selfishness (which last I consider the most unprincipled motive that a man can have). For instance if he is asked for a favour while young the impulse of the human heart will be to grant it without enquiring wheather it is right or not. When the same individual comes to mans estate he will be very likely to stop to consider wheathe it would be right to grant the favour before he done it and the more advanced in age he is the longer he will be in makeing up his mind wheathe it would be right to grant it or not. There is an entirely dfferent set of feelings and incentives to action when the boy becomes a man, is matured in Intelect and body from what there is in the boy inexperienced and full of Generous impulses. The stream rippling and foaming on its mossy bed or gliding smoothly among flours and grassy banks,—the young sapling waving its slight branches in a boastful defiance of the Storms with which it has yet to contend—the glorious morning sunlight streaming in all its freshness on dewy greens [warming] in the wood—all are emblems of our boyhood. It is reckless and turbulent or calmly joyous like the Stream. It is proud and aspiring like the sapling—and it is bright and resplendent like the early sunshine. But the stream gradually deepens and its flow becomes more full and more strong. The sapling grows into the majestic oak no more ambitious but resting securely on its own strength. And the sun attaining its maridean pours down a more widely diffused light and stronger heat. And thus boyhood growes depens and brightens into perfect manhood.

But what great change is this? Does the boy differ from the man only in external appearances or is the inner temple of a different construction? Yes! It is the mind which makes the mighty difference. The boy is often more fully developed than is the man with respect to his physical powers but his mental powers are generally in a far lower degree of maturity. The mind sometimes comes to maturity before the body, and the body sometimes before the mind. The first is the case with undergrown men. The latter the case with overgrown boys. The fires on the boyish alters is the sacrifice of reason and the devotee is passion. The flame of manly hearts is the reverse. In youth it burns with a fitful, yet splendid glow. In the man it is moer equal but less dazzling. Let us examine a few characters of each age.

The prevailing characteristic of the mind of the young may be said to be passion the first born of the mind. The wild flowers that spring up in every uncultivated mental path. And of these the chief is Ambition. The young have nothing to look back upon. All their objects of mental view are future. And with them, ambition is the flattering oracle which presides over the yet to come. How fresh is the steed bounding into the course panting for the race. How impatiently the warrior, whose ill fortune has detained him from the battle rushes forward to the glorious field, when so many are plucking laurels, in the harvest of death. In the race of existance, in the battle of life the young ambitionified heart sees many bright names who have reached the goal, who have nobly triumphed. Why shall he not surpass them? Self confidence boldly declares his ability. Hope gently acquieses. And from every noble deed and manly effort of boyhood goes forth the proud determination, "I will be renowned." There was once a Napoleon, a task dreading School Boy, and a few years later there was a Napoleon who sat on the throne of France, I might say, of Europe. Had the mighty torment of the mans success no bubling fount in the boys ambition? It must have been so; and thus he who held in his power nearly one half of the civilized world could call his conquests merely by the fullfillment of boyish aspirations.

If the characteristics of the boy is ambition that of the man is reason. The one acts from impulse: the other from principle. The steed is halfway to the goal. The warrior his impatience at length appeased in the thickest of the fight. Hopes and wishes now are useless; action is required. The ardent temper of the boy learns this after a few rough experiences and passion conscious of her inferiority give place to reason and cool judgment. When with passion for its guide the soul is melted to unnervedness by an affecting scene; or transported to rapture by a beautiful one, or lost in admiration of a great or heroic one. How much less likely will it be to guard itself against deception and the allurements of error, than when reason warns it from the labyrinths of the emotions? But which would be the more acceptable offering, that of passion at reasons alter, or the reverse? To be cheated is not often agreeable. But when our own emotions are the involuntary instruments the vexation seem diminished. The boy feels more deeply than the man; and this is the cause of his frequent failures in judgment.

There are many men who seems to have utterly forgotten their boyish days, and have "put away childish things" so far, that they seem to have lost from recollection that that they ever had them to put away. Such men as these become, perhaps eminent for their devotion to business, their sagacity and other very commendable qualities. But are they ever celebrated for the display of the finer qualities which adorn humanity, that appreciation of the beautifull that feeling for the sorrows of others, that admiration for the heroic the virtuous and the noble which togather with these qualities go to make up the perfect whole — a man? If then with these boyish feelings and emotions is joined enough of manly judgment to counteract the influences of passion, we have at once the picture of a true man.

It was never designed that as we grow old in years we should make an entire change in our mental habits and give the inner temple of our hearts a new occupant entirely. The feelings of the boy are not to be cast out as unworthy by the man. Manly sentiments are to be grafted on the slight trunk of boyish passions, that thus both acting in concert may bear the golden fruit of manhood. Such were the feelings of the poet when he sung:

My heart leaps up when I behold
A rainbow in the sky;
So was it when my life begun;
So is it now when I am a man;
So be it when I shall grow old,

or let me die!
The child is father to the man;
And I could wish my days to be
Bound each to each by natural piety.[1]

What can be more descriptive of the aspirations of the sensitive man?

Fired with lofty aspirations and buoyed up by self reliance the youth enters the arena of manly life.

Now is the time when his ambitions hopes are to be realized he would say and with eager confidence he engages in the struggle. But to what a low degree has he estimated the strength of his opponents? There are others in the arena who likewise have lofty projects in their mind and not lightly will they allow another to win the gladiatorial prize.

Strugling in the thickest of the battle and aroused by mortified pried to increased efforts the youths neglecting too the counsels of reason instead of those of passion finds himself encompassed on every side by hosts of competitors striving for the mastery. Like the wayside but beneath the rush of the avalanch he is swept down. Onward rush the mighty host and through the clouds of conflict the youth sees their number continually lessning untill one is left alone. The conquerer in the struggle of life!

The Storm is over and a calm, more tranquil from contrast with the fury that preceded it, descends on the troubled mind. Baffled ambition, weary of its efforts gives place to peace and contentment.

The striver for fame, humbled beneath a more favorite devotee of the goddess, gazes with unensying eyes at his success, and then, looking higher, praises the Hand which has restrained him for glory.

Reaching forward no longer in vain efforts for renown, and his further aspirations taking their shape from hope rather than ambition he passes through the remainder of the vale of tears. Better pleased with the humble flowers which grow by his path than with the haughty exotics which deck the heights above.

The full flow of the stream is loosing itself in the unmoved expanse of ocean. The mighty oak, leafless and bare is totering to its fall. The sun, sinking behind western hills breathes a gently deepening shade over the earth. And man having fought the conflicts of life, is laid to his final rest, by hands all forgetful of his human faults and remembering with thankfulness his joyesness of boyhood, his noble struggling of manhood and end of peace and faith.

Now my little Frank I have passed through these different scenes in life and myself have experienced all their different feelings and now at nearly 45 years of age I have neer fully realized any one of my youthful ambitions. And I have come to this conclusion—that to be honored a man must live within himself never trusting to the world at large for his enjoyments or pleasures. For the pleasures that are derived from that source are valueless and will end in sorrow. But the pleasure that will be derived from well chosen pursuits and well centered affection will last through life. Then cultivate a sincere attachment for home and all its comforts and try to attain a good friend of useful and entertaining knowledge and when old age and sorrow comes as it surely will you can have that within yourself that will not fail in the hour of trial. Amongst all my troubles and they have been many, I still had the affections of home to fall back on. And it was no odds how dark and gloomy the world seem without. There was always a warm heart and a smile at home for me that dispelled all forbodings. You are too young yet to understand this but you must read this untill you know it all and impress it on the mind and in time you will understand it.

I must now stop writing for I am going to leave here tomorrow morning. Our Regiment is going out on a scout for five days and when I return I will write mother or Auntie a letter. I have not had a letter for 3 weeks and am very anxious to hear how uncle is and how you are all getting along. I will try and send you home some curiousities by Mr Thatcher[2] when he goes home. He is going to be discharged for sore eyes. I am in good health and good heart only. We have heard here that General Banks let a part of the 13th A.C. get whiped up on Red River last week and General McClernand has taken the 2nd Brigade under old Lawler and gone to New Orleans to reinforce Banks[3] and left us here under General Warran to hold this post for which I am both thankful and sorry. Thankful that we will not have to undergo the hard ships of the campaign and sorry that we will not be allowed to share in the work of whipping the rebles. There is no rebles now near here all having gone to help McGrudder to fight Banks and if Banks and McClernand succeede in defeating the rebles I think we will be done in Texas.

I will send you another likeness for you to send to Aunt Rachel and when you write to her tell her that I have written to her and I want her to answer it. I will also send you some books the next chance I have. I want to know if get the money I sent you. I sent 100 dollars and have another hundred coming to me which I will get in about a month or less. If uncle can use it to make him and you comfortable and happy I want him to have it. If he does not want it you can lay it up untill I come home and I can use it myself. I sent home some of my old cloths with Mr James T Daily[4] who went home on furlough. He was going to leave them with Edward Quick and he will take them to you. There was 1 linnin coat one Blouse and a pair of linnin pants. I suppose you will get them and have them as they are as good as new.

The army is in good health. We have no sickness at all. There is abot 3,000 troops here now and I have not heard of a single death since we come here. Give my love to Auntie Uncle and all and tell Mother and Sallie to write and I want the rest to write to me too, for I am lonesome sometimes and it does me so much good to hear from home. I think I will get home this summer for I think the war will be over. But if it is not and you all keep well I will not try to get another furlough. It makes so much trouble and is not much satisfaction. The weather is fine and we are living fine now. Only the sand is troublesome.

I must close. I want you all to be good children and try to learn your lessons.

> My love to all and a kiss for all
> I am you afft father Taylor Peirce

This is the 20th day of April. Your last letter was dated the 16th of March.

1. "My Heart Leaps Up," by William Wordsworth, was written in 1807.

2. Joseph M. Thatcher was an Ohio native and resident of Vandalia when he enlisted July 25, 1862. He was wounded at Vicksburg on May 22, 1863, and was discharged for disability on June 23, 1864, at Baton Rouge, Louisiana.

3. On April 8 Banks was defeated at Mansfield, Louisiana, by Confederates under Richard Taylor. The next day at Pleasant Hill, Louisiana, Banks repulsed Taylor's attack but withdrew to Alexandria. McClernand, with a portion of the 13th Corps, reinforced him there.

4. James T. Dailey was a Pennsylvania native and resident of Vandalia when he enlisted July 28, 1862. He was captured at Winchester, Virginia, on September 19, 1864, and died of disease May 31, 1865, at Davenport.

Head Quarters 22nd Iowa Inftry
Matagorda Island, Texas April 27/63 [1864]
Dear Catharine and all the rest,

I again set down to write agreeable to promise made in my last letter when I was starting off on the expidition to port Lavacca. Well we made the trip all safe. We did not loose a man. We had but little fighting. There was a small detachment of reble cavalry at Lavacca and we sent out 3 companies to give them a fight but they concluded that they would rather fight some other time and so they ran away and left us alone in our glory. After getting some 15 or 20 prisoners and as many deserters and about 20,000 feet of lumber we left and returned to Indianola when we stoped and took about 100 men and women on board. We left for home where we arrived all safe the evening of the 4th day.[1] Port Lavacca is a most beautiful place and has been one of the most business places in Texas before the war here. Is a great many Yankees settled there and there is some Union feeling but a great deal of Rebleious feelings mixed up with it. When we were getting ready a circumstance occured that has made me feel bad ever since. We had had a norther the night before and the wind was blowing very hard from the north. When we were about ready to embark some one set fire to a large empty building and all the town being wooden building soon two of the best blocks were in flames. Then occured a scene that I shall never get used to if I am in the army the rest of my life. Several of the houses were inhabited and as soon as the fire was discovered General Warran like true philanthropist as he is ordered every man in the expedition to assist in saving the property of the citizens. And with an energy took hold himself and made every effort to save the effects and suppress the flames which he eventually did though not till after the 2 best blocks in town was entirely destroyed. The most of the men done all they could but there is some bad men in all ranks of life and our command is not exempt. Even while the brave and good were fighting the flames these fiends in human shape took advantage of the tumult and rifled every dwelling they could get to of any thing they seen that they wanted or fancied they wanted. But thanks to the Generals vigilence few of them got away with the spoils of robery. Oh! dear ones these things are too terrible to think of. I am not made for a warrior. I can stand and fight when I am opposed and make every effort to conquer but when a scene like this is witnessed it frees up all my energys and I think that it is worse than useless to spend blood and treasure to save our institution to protect such a set of demons as many of our solders are. But then they are not all so and I hope by far the greater portion of them will be able to appreciate the many benefits they may receive by restoring the reign of civil authority.

This is the last letter I shall write from this place as we are now under marching orders and the right wing of our regiment has already gone to New Orleans and we are only awaiting transportation. I expect to take this to New Orleans myself and when there to finish it and mail it. I think our destination for the present is Port Hudson. From the best information I can gain General Banks has allowed the Rebles to whip him and I think we will be called on to retrieve the fortunes of the Union cause in Louisiana. At all Events Genl McClernand has taken the field and the 13th A.C. is being concentrated at diferint points on the Mississippi from Baton Rough to Natches and I think his intention is to hurl the whole force of the department of the Gulf against the rebles and defeat them in one decisive battle which will be fought in May. I have heard nothing certain about the battle at Moss Hill except that Banks allowed his advance which consisted of 2 divisions of the 13 A.C. to be attacked by an overwhelming force of Rebles and whip them a brigade at a time and take 18 pieces of artilery and 130 Wagons having his train so situated that he could make his retreat with his cannon. And of course had to leave them, his reinforcement being 16 miles in the rear he could not protect or reinforce his advance untill they were completely routed.[2] My oppinion that Banks is no General is confirmed. I have thought so ever since I come into the department and my convictions are strengthened by the last movments made. Instead of doing any one thing or trying to do he has allowed 5 months to pass in inactivity when the men could have stood more hardships than they can now and had a more effictive force than he can have after this defeat. I will close until I get to New Orleans as I expect we will go to night or tomorrow.

May 2st. Well friends I am in New Orleans again this morning.[3] We arrived here about sunset last night and lay on the boat untill this morning when we were marched off the boat and quartered in the Virginia Cotton Press along with the 20th Regt. I have been so busy that I have not got out in town yet having our monthly returns to make out and our pay rolls to prepare so that it has kept me very busy. It is now about 7 oclock and I concluded to finish my letter before I run about any. Another thing is our company is all out but myself and one corporal and 2 men. And as the rules does not allow the company to be without at least one commissioned officer with them I have to stay and act Captain while he takes a little run. For the Lieuts is not worth a d—n and are gone all the time.[4] So if I did not stay the Cap would not get out at all. However I will get out this evening in time enough to see all I want to. There is a rumour here that we start for Red River in the morning but what truth there is in it I am unable to say. There is also another rumour that Genl Grant has ordered that expedition to be abandoned and to merely defend the river communication un-till the eastern army does something. This looks to me to be the most sensible and I suppose is really the movment that will be made. I just received Catharine's & Sallies letter of the 17th of April and was very glad to hear from you all before this time. I recon you have my letter and your money. I do not know wheather we will get paid off here or not. I understand we leave here to morrow Evening for Alexandria when I will write again. All is in such hurry that I have but little chance to write. I have given you all the news that I have myself and I expect it will all be old to you.

There is some prospect of our going to some post on the River to Garrison. I hope this will not be the case for the sickness attending the river encampments are more fatal to life than reble bullets. I am going to try and get my likeness taken here so that you can send it to Rachel. I have not had a letter from her yet and maybe the mails do not carry as sure in that direction as they do up the river. I received a letter from Jo Kuhn a day or two since he is in Missouri and is well.[5] I am going to write him as soon as I get time. I will have to stop writing now and go to something else. Give my love to all the friends and kiss the little ones for me. Tell them I dream of them nearly every night. I remain yours

      Affectionately

      Taylor Peirce

1. On April 21 the regiment steamed to Port Lavaca, arriving the next day. It returned to Matagorda Island on April 24.

2. Taylor is referring to the battle of Mansfield.

3. The 22nd Iowa departed Matagorda Island on April 29.

4. Company officers were Captain Lafayette Mullins, First Lieutenant Robert W. Davis, and Second Lieutenant Samuel C. Fugard.

5. This letter was not found. In April 1863 Joseph Kuhn and the 3rd Colorado Infantry were at Pilot Knob, Missouri.

Des Moines May 1st 1864

Dear Taylor

It is a beautiful Sunday morning and we are all in good health and things go on in good style. Cyrus and Mary is doing well boarding Soldiers and are geting the house finished off with the Idea of haveing a nice home of their own in thair old days. Cyrus is a great deal better this spring than he has been for a long time and seems to be better contented too. I think it owing in part to the chance he has to do something that pays. For he is so organised that he must work and when he is making money he can get a long every well.

I for my part get along fine. I am as well off as I could be in this world any where with out thee so therefore I have no right to complain nor do I think I have to a mount to much. What makes thee think that we think thee done wrong in going to the war? I can not see for I surely have writen to thee that I was well off and contented and for thee to take care of thy self and be as happy as thee could and as easy about us as possible to be and be away from us too. I think that contentment is a great coarce of health and I also think if it had not been for my contented disposion I would of been dead long ago. For thee knows I have went through enough sickness to kill a half dozen others that ware healthy in comparison to what I ever was. I have nothing to do now but to take care of myself and the children past my own will and that is only enough to keep me in good health and in good heart. I have feelt a little discouraged this winter on account of the baby. He is so very troublesome and all ways has been that I sometimes do get out of heart with him. But maybe by the time he is three or four years old he will get over his fretfulness so that I can take more comfort in life. He is now about like a child ten mounths old generally is. He is not as forward as Frank was at that age for he can not walk yet nor is he so large as F was though he seems to be as healthy now as any of our children ware at his age. Thee wants to know how the children are getting a long with thair leaning. Sallie has learned very fast this winter and is geting along fine with her studies and Frank is learning very well since he commence to go to school for he likes to go better than any of us expected he would for it seems as though he thought it would be a turable thing for him to stay away from his Aunt and I all day at school amongst strangers. But he has got to like to say his lessons and to play with the little boys so that I do not antisapate any more trouble with him but to keep him on the right track. For he learns very quick and he remmembers all he hears or sees so well that I have great hope if thee gets home soon we will have no trouble to make a good scholar of him. Mary wrote to thee this day a week ago and I expect she gave thee a full account of all that is going on better than I can.[1] For the little ones occupy my mind so that I can not write as well as might with out thair bother but I will try to write something that thee will take to time to read at any reait. In the first place we receved thy letters of various daits mailed New Orleans April 9th one for Sallie and one for my self with thy likeness in and also the money and book by express on Friday 29th so thee may see that they come strait along all right. I wrote thee I was out of money the last time I wrote I believe and that I had writen to Sumpter for some of but I have gave Cyrus seventy $ of what thee sent home and think that thirty $ will do me to get all I and the children will want this spring for things are so very high that I will do with as little as I can. I will send thee a bit of all the dresses that I have had since thee was home just to let thee see what goods are at Des Moines this season. The callico was twenty five cts per yard and the other the same price owing to it being an old peice of goods that had been on hand for four or five years. New goods of the same quality sell for forty or fifty ct per yd and all things in the same ratio. As to thy letter being good I do not know that I would be considered fit to judge for I recive so much pleasure from them that I could not tell wheather any one but myself could find the same amount of interst in them or not. But not likely that any one else would be as much of an admirer of thy letter or thy likeness as I would be. I think the picture makes thee look at least ten years younger than thee did when thee went away from home or that much younger than the one thee sent from

St Louis. Thee want our likeness. I have thought offtimes that I ought
to send them but the children have had sore mouths, or Ellis has been
afflicted with sores on his face or something been in the way that I
have neglected it up to the present time. I will try to get all things
ready soon and have them taken and send them to thee for I do not
doubt that thee is oftimes lonesome and the sight of our ugly faces
might drive it off or perhaps they might make thee forget for the time
the distance that intervene between us or some pleasent things. For
Dear Taylor I do think we have had about much pleasure togather as
the most folks do in our station in life or that is common to fall to the
lot of mortals.

We have had no letters from the east since I wrote before and I have
not taken time to read the news much so I do not know much what
is going on. I see that there is another call for men[2] and Gov Stone has
pledged 10,000 of them from Iowa. They are to garrison the post
along the border of the states for one hundred days while the vetre-
ans go fourth into field during the spring campaign[3] and it appears as
though there will be no trouble to get the men. I guess I will quit as
Sallie wants to write some and write gain in few day. I have began to
ween the baby and he is a little extra troublesome to day unless Sally
has him out of door all the time. So Good By this time.

Catharine A Peirce

1. This letter was not found.

2. Lincoln called for 200,000 additional volunteers on March 14, 1864. If state
quotas were not filled, the additional requirements would be filled by a draft to
begin April 15, 1864. Iowa's quota was 6,439 men.

3. On April 25 Governor Stone issued a proclamation that President Lincoln had
agreed to accept ten regiments for 100 days "for the purpose of enabling the veteran troops to be pushed forward and achieve decisive results over the enemy in the
approaching campaign." Lincoln's rationale was that experienced troops should
be relieved from garrison duties so that they could participate in the upcoming campaign season. Stone directed that 10,000 men be recruited, and four regiments and
one battalion (4,159 men) were raised as a result of the call. The regiments guarded
railroads in Tennessee, and one garrisoned Helena, Arkansas; the 48th Battalion
guarded Confederate prisoners at Rock Island, Illinois. These troops were in addition to a similar call by Stone on October 8, 1862, for four battalions to protect
the border with Missouri.

May the first 1864
Dear Father

I am well and hope thee the same. I do not know what to write. I love you very much. I go to school to the public school the same as in the winter. My teacher is Miss Rasburn. I do not like her as well as I did Mrs Denison. We got thy letter and thy picture. I just wish I could see them pretty little birds that thee speeks about in his letter. I wish that this war was over so thee could get home. Franks out playing with tony Lindy. He is real mea. I do not want him to play with tony at tall. I cant think of one thing more. O yes. I was so glad to get your picture and a letter from you. I get letters from my cousin every time Aunty gets one from her. Mother is going to get me a new Dress. It is going to be a pink one to. She is put in a peace of her Dress we hav of the cavelry mess. I cant think of eny thing more so I guess I will quit. So good by.

Sallie A Peirce to her Father Taylor Peirce

Head Quarters 22nd Iowa Inft
New Orleans La May 4th 1864
Dear Catharine

We are now ready to march on to the boats and will leav at 5 oclock this Evening. Where we are going is unknown to the troops but it is supposed that we go to reinforce Banks on Red River.[1] The battles fought there has proved more advantageous to us than to the rebles and their loss is as much more as ours. I expect ere you receive this there will have been another battle fought. I will keep you posted as to the movements as well as I can.

We were all ready to be paid and the paymaster paid the 23d but the order came to move at 5 and there was not time to pay us. We are under command of Major White[2] now and he is so inattentive to the wants of the regiment that we do not get our rights untill after all the rest have got and then we often come in at the tail end.

I send my likeness and want you to send it to Rachel and give my love to her and her little children and tell her when this war is over I will either go to see her or she must come and See me. I am well and in good heart and feel as if we could whip all the rebles in the western department in about 2 hours if we could get them to stand a fight. Give my love to the children and kiss them all for me and tell Cyrus and Mary that I would like to hear from them once and a while for I get no letters except what thee writes and they seem so few. I have had an easy time of it and I hope I will have a better time this year than I had last. The Captain has agreed to hall my knapsack and blankets for me so that I will not have such a load to labour under as I had through the miss campaign. I send also a likeness of Capt Mullins and Genl Grant and I wish you to retain them as the three likeness are all from great men especiely self you know.

> I am affectionately Thine
> Taylor

1. For this movement the regiment was divided into a left wing and a right wing. Company C embarked with the right wing on the evening of May 4 on the *New Kentucky,* but the boat was forced to land because of a mechanical problem. The regiment reembarked on the *St. Mary* and proceeded to Red River on May 7.

2. Ephraim G. White was a Pennsylvania native and resident of Agency City when appointed first lieutenant August 15, 1862. He was promoted to captain on January 30, 1863, to major on June 9, 1863, and to lieutenant colonel on May 6, 1864. He was wounded September 19, 1864, at Winchester, Virginia, and was mustered out July 25, 1865, at Savannah, Georgia.

> Mouth of the Red River
> May 11th 1864
> Dear Catharine

I am well and we have just arrived from a trip up red River. I wrote to you at Orlean but I do not know wheather the letter ever got off or not. Things have go so jumbled up in this department. Well we started up to Alexandria to report to Genl Banks. On the 4th We left in company with the 23rd and Genl Warran in command. He was with us (and the 23 follows in sight) under the escort of 3 Gun Boats. We proceeded up red Riv about 100 miles when we were compelled to stop on account of the rebles having got behind Banks and planted a Battery of 16 guns on the Riv and rendered it impossible to pass with the transports or the musquito fleet.[1] We lay there 3 days all the time exposed to the attacks of the Rebles. But they did not succeed in getting any of our boats or capturing any of us.[2] This has been one of the most disastrous campaigns of the war. For Why? In the first place there was nothing to be gained by the occupation of the country gained. Then the expense of fitting out the expedition and the way that it was managed is enough to d—d Banks in the eyes of all reflecting people to the end of eternity. There is one thing I wish to mention. It is with regard to the coloured troops. On the second day of the fight at Grand Echore the Reble Genl Taylor son of old Zach sent in a flag of truce to Banks and told him if he did not take out the Negro Brigade which was about 2,000 strong he would not take any prisoners but put all to death that he could get his hands on. Banks like a pucilanimus coward as he is instead of sending him back word that two could play at the same game at once ordered the negro Brigade to the rear and weakened his force thereby.[3] May God damn him—If the army of the United States has got so low that the enemy can dictate the manner in which we must fight we had as well desert and let the Union go—This is the first time since I have been in the service I have felt out of heart. When such men is placed in command and for the sake of a few Bales of Cotton sacrifice the lifes of so many I think we had better give up the government.[4] Banks like all the leaders of the republican party is so d—d selfish that he does not care for the welfare of others. If he make money and saves himself he does not care. This war could be put down in 3 months if there was such men as old Abe and Grant in all the departments but such men are scarce. I have but a little time to write. The mail is going out soon and I must cut it short. I will write in a few days again. Give my love to the children and a kiss for all. The Right wing of our regiment is not with us being left helping at new orleans and have never come up. We lost a man this morning by being jerked overboard while he was drawing water to wash himself and although he was a good swimmer he got frightened and drowned before we could save him. He was a good soldier and we all mourn his loss. His name was Charles L Mc Donald.[5] I will have to write to his folks and it will be with a heavy heart that I will fulfill my task. I do not know wheather you can read this or not but it is the best I can do and you must do the best you can. I am looking for a letter by the mail. Pleas answer and tell me if you got the 100 dols and the pictures.

     I remaiy affty
     Taylor

1. "Mosquito fleet" was a derisive term applied to small, lightly armed vessels.

2. Confederates had placed two howitzers and two ten-pound Parrotts along the river below Alexandria and inflicted heavy damage on Union boats attempting to reach the Mississippi. The guns and Confederate soldiers blocked the passage of the 22nd Iowa to Alexandria.

3. This is not true. The Corps d'Afrique was assigned to guard the army's supply train and was not involved in the battles of the campaign.

4. Thousands of bales of cotton were believed to be stored in western Louisiana. Speculation was that if Banks could seize it and sell it to New England textile mills, the owners might be motivated to support him politically.

5. Charles L. McDonald was an Ohio native and Newton resident when he enlisted August 2, 1862. He drowned May 11, 1864, in the Red River.

Des Moines May 29th 1864
Dear Brother

We received a letter from thee written at the mouth of red river. I need not tell thee that we war pleased to hear from thee but I was surprised that thee has not got my letters. I have not written as often as I would like to have done but still I have written.

Catherine and the children are well. Sallie and Franky go to school and appear to be learning. Frank has learnd to talk and cand spell off the book. He does not like to go as well as Sallie but I think he larns as fast. Little Ellis has got to walking and he has such a short neck and is so short he looks so cute. He knows every thing that is said to him. He come to the bed side every day while I was sick to kiss me and still he has not taken the measles. He is petted to badly. We all have a share in that. His Uncle thinks he must do just as he pleases. Catherine got all their likeness taken and sent them to thee. I will get mine taken when I get better if I ever do. I am nothing but skin and bone now. I took sick on the fifth of this month with measles. I had them bad. I lay eight days wihout eating anything or drinking any thing but cold watter. I took a little medicine but did not keep it down. The measles broke out as thick as could be and I think I done fine. I still have a bad cough and not much appatite but feel as if I would be better soon. Catherine and Cyrus took good care of me and Sallie excelled herself in kindness to me all the time.

We had fourty three men when I took sick but Mrs Finan come in and took my place at the work and they got along verry well. We have but two solgers now. They ware sick when they left. We have three boarders besid. It seems so good and quiet after five months of uproar and hard toiling. Cyrus is better than he has been since he left for the mountains the first time. We have got a new roof and a small garden. The place begins to look like some one lived here. Cyrus is working at the house getting it ready to plaster. He has one half of the upper story ready and the other well on. We have the two cows which makes us plenty of butter. [illegible] has a catt. We have about seventy chickens and I think we are all getting along as comfortable as people can at least I feel so. If we could know every knight when we lay down that thee was well and happy I think we would have but little trouble. I do not think their is a man in the army who has left more loveing harts at home. Catherine and the children seem to live for thee and I seldom lay down at knigh with out offering a prayer to the throne of Grace that thee may be kept from sin sorrow and dangers of all kinds and be restored to thy little family. I fear thee will think this a dull letter but I have not been out of the house to get any neiws since I was sick.

*   *   *

I suppose thee will hear before this reaches thee of Grants victory and steady march to Richmond. Yesterdays paper stated that Grant had a shorter road to Richmond than Lee. It will be a tight race which reaches there first. I must close. My eyes are weak yet. Please write often and mention wheather thee gets any letters from me. I shall continue to write any how.

Thee must excuse the spelling. I remain thy affectionate sister Mary

Catherine and the children sent their love to thee. The children wants thee to write every day so they can know thee is well. Frank wanted to send thee a pie plait pie. He thinks they are so good. Cyrus sends his love and wants thee to look out for southern locations. He still thinks of moving some where.

Mary

Head Quarters 22n Iowa Infty
Morganza Bend La May 31st/64
Dear Catharine & all the rest

I once more set down to write you and let you know what is going on here and how I get along.

I am well though not as well as I was while I was in Texas. We have been having a pretty hard time of it for the last month and the weather is so hot that it is beginning to tell on the system.

Our living is very rough. We have nothing but sowbelly and hard tack[1] and that with the heat and exposure is creating a great amount of Diarrhea. I have had a spell of it but I have got over it. If I can keep my diet right I think I will have no more of it. I have had the acclimating fever but It only lasted two days and so I think I am in a pretty fair way to stand another years service without sickness. We are encamped on the Bank of the Great Miss. at Morganza Bend about 35 miles abov Port Hudson.[2] There is about 12,000 troops here. I do not know wheather we will stay here or not but I hope not. We are now laying in between the River and levee as thick as 3 in a bed and the weather is so hot that it almost suffacates one. The Rebles have a force on the land between us and the Atchafalaya but what their numbers is I am unable to say. Genl Lawler went out yesterday morning with about 11,000 troop to give them battle but I do not think he succeeded in getting them into a fight. They have been so badly punished in the last few weeks that it is very hard to get them to stand. They have a large amount of cavalry and they hover around our lines and pick up any poor devil who is unlucky enough to get out of the protection of our guard but that is all the damage they do us. There is news here this morning that the 19th A.C. is ordered East and that we are going to New Orleans to man the defences there. I do not vouch for the truth of this for one can hear any thing in a camp that he wishes. This is the place when the 19th Regt of Iowa Inftry was taken prisoners last winter[3] and is the place of great importance to us on account of the navigation of the River it being the narrowest place in the Miss below Vicksburg. And oweing to course of the River a single Battery placed in the curve of the River can command the channell for 3 or 4 miles each way so that it is almost impossible to pass with boats if a battery is allowed to be placed there. I think there will be a sufficient force kept here to hold this place and the rest of us will be sent to Port

Hudson, Baton Rough, New Orleans, and Brashear City and will lay at those points untill the hot weather is over and then I think we will have another campaign if Grant does not throttle the rebellion before that time. We still have good news from Grant and I hope he will suc- ceed in cleaning out that nest of rebles.

I have had no letter from home since Marys letter which was dated 22n of April[4] more than a month ago. I tell you I am getting anxious for one.

Why we do not get our letters more regular I can not see for there was some of our men arrived last night who had been home on fur- lough that was only to day, coming from Iowa City and does seem to me that 5 weeks for the mail to come through is a little to long. We are looking for the pay master now. I hope he will come for I will have another hundred to send and I would like you to have it so that you could use it in fixing up your house and makeing yourselves not only comfortable but easy. Now Thee thinks thee would like to have a house to thyself and live alone. I am of the oppinion that unless you cannot agree that there is no place that thee will be so comfortable or so well taken care of as thee will be in the place thee is in while I am away. Surely no one can have the interest of thy welfare and that of our children so much at heart as my sister and thy Brother. I judge from my own feelings towards them. They have alwas felt as near to me as myself and their troubles have given me as much trouble as my own has and I think it very likely their feeling are of the same kind towards me and mine. It would be well enough if the children were old enough to help thee. If thee was to get so thee could not do for thyself but just think for a minute if thee is unable to get round what thee would do all alone.

Now my oppinion is that the best thing that you can for the bene- fit of all concerned will be to just be contented. Try to make your- selves comfortable and send the children to school and try and pre- pare them for the battle of life so that when they arrive at an age when they will have to go forth in the world they will not go without being capable of contending with the trials that await them. I think that Cyrus might use some mony to advantage in some easy little business that would be beneficial to his health and advantage to him in a fi- nancial way and if so let him use it. I will be getting more wages and will be able to send you more money hereafter than I have and with my little help if it is carfully managed you can do a great deal. But I leave all to your own consideration as I do not pretend to dictate. I only suggest and whatever you think best will do me. I hear that our mail has come so I will stop untill it is distributed. Well the mail is in and I got thy letter of May 1st with the calico in it. I am glad to hear you are so well and in such good heart. Sallie is learning to write very fast I think and if she is progressing as fast with her other studies as with her writing she will do.

Tell Frank he must only play with good little boys and he finds little boys who try to pursuade him to do what he is told not to do not to go with them any more. Tell him that I want him to be good and mind what is Said to him. Kiss all the children for me and give all my love to my friends. I must quit now and will write again in a few days.

I remain affty
thine Taylor

1. Hardtack is a cracker made of flour and water.

2. Unable to reach Alexandria, the 22nd Iowa encamped at the mouth of the Red River until May 16, when it was transported to Simmesport, Louisiana, on the Atchafalaya River. The retreating Union forces joined the 22nd Iowa there, and the army marched to Morganza on the Mississippi River. The regiment reached Morganza on May 22.

3. On September 29, 1863, the 4th Iowa Infantry had 210 men captured at the battle of Stirling's Plantation near Morganza.

4. This letter was not found.

Head Qurs 22n Iowa Inft
Morganza Bend La June 5th /64
Dear Catharine and all the rest,

Sitting under the verticle rays of a boiling sun with nothing to do I concluded to occupy the time by letting you know on paper what I and my comrades are doing in this land of rebles and Aligators, languishing females and aristocratic paupers. We are still encamped on the Bank of the mighty River at Morganza Bend. There has been no alteration in the state of affairs here since I wrote before. News came up from Orleans Yesterday that Fitz Henry Warren was ordered to take command of the post of Baton Rough and an order for us and the 23rd Iowa to report to him at that place[1] which I hope is so for Baton Rough is a nice place and I would like to get to do Garrison duty for a while at least untill the weather began to turn cool in the fall. I do not know what is going on at the seat of War in the East. The last news that I seen was up to the 24 of May and things seemd to be progressing very well then. I have seen that Sherman has defeated Johnson in Gorgia and is driving him. I hope he will not let him stop this side of hell.[2]

This department is not doing any thing worth speaking about. Old Lawler took 8,000 men on Monday morning and started out to hunt up some rebles that were said to be concentrating their force about 8 miles from here. They hunted 4 days and seen abut 50 or 60 bush whackers, killed 2 men and took 20 prisoners and we had one man killed and 4 wounded by being fired on while marching through a thick wood in the night by about 40 Guerillas who lay behind a levee along the side of the road. Our men as usual was not loaded and when they were fired into they loaded as quick as possible but the rebs had plenty of time to get out of the reach before our men was ready to fire. The men killed and wounded was members of the 24th Regt of Iowa Vols. The man killed was a captain from the western part of the State. The rebles afterwards moved a little further along and got behind another Bank and fired into the 19th A.C. as they come along. They were all loaded and returned the fire. Next morning when they went to look over the ground they found one dead reble and marks of several who had been wounded.[3] The one killed had been to the General the morning and claimed to be a good Union man and got a guard to protect his property from the soldiers who would be stragling about. I suppose that he concluded he had got union men to guard his property he would go out and shoot one or two for past time but his time was extremely limited and his shooting done him little good. I think there will be a different policy pursued towards the citizens here soon if they do not alter their course. It will be the best in the long run. It will cost less life than the way things is going on now. I mean to clean out the country men woman and children. If they are not union enough to leave and go into the union settlements send them to their long homes. And we will soon get shet of Bush Whackers. They are a mean cowardly set of skulking dogs. They have not enough of courage to go into the Reble army nor honour enough to avow openly their enmity to the union so they lay behind logs and ditches and shoot some solitary solders who has got seperated from his comrades and murder them in cold blood. I hope some measures will be taken to sweep them from the face of the earth.

The 28th Iowa is encamped within a few rods of us. There is a good many of my old acquaintances here and upon the whole I have a pretty good time of it.

I am acting Sergeant Major for this part of the regiment and have no duty of any kind to do only to notify the Co Commanders what orders has to be attended to and make out our reports to the Comdg General. This is quite easy and I am doing fine. Our living is very hard now. Vegitables can not be got and we are compelled to live on Hard Tack and Sow Belly and coffee and the weather being so hot the food is too strong and many of the men are unwell with diarrhea. I have been troubled with it myself but I am better now and have been for several days. But I had nothing to eat but some Baked beans for dinner and I am afraid it will return again. I am going to get some fine hominy and flour this evening and boil the hominy untill it goes to mush and then mix some flour with it and bake it into a mush cake and see if I can not get along better with that than I can with hard tack. I have the piles some but on the whole I am in pretty good health. I have not been under a tent for 6 weeks nor do I know when we will see shelter again. We have had a fine rain yesterday and the weather is not so deathly hot to day as it has been for some days past. The water we get out of the River to use and as it is quite full the water is right good. I think it much better than the well watter here and much healthier. I had hoped to have been paid off before this but the regiment being divided and our pay Rolls being with the other wing the paymaster could not pay us when he was up and so we have to do without our pay. I have $130 due me now and if I could get it to send you now it would be a great help to you in getting fixed up.

Capt Mullins only Brothe is dead and he talks of resigning now soon as his mother is entirely dependent on him for her support and he is not sound in his foot and he thinks it better for himself and the govt that he should quit the service. I will be very sorry when he leaves for he is a very good officer and the company has flourished under his mangement. He will call on you when he arrives at home and will give you an account of things generally. I will finish to morrow.

June 10th. It is 5 days since I commenced to write this letter and I have just concluded to finish it as the mail goes out in 2 hours.

I received Thy letter of the 22n of May[4] with the childrens likenesses but I have not received theirs yet. I suppose that it is with the other part of the Regiment and we are expecting to get with them soon and they have retained our mail untill that shall occur. I was very sorry to hear that Mary had been sick although thee does not say how bad she has been or what was the matter with her. The likeness of the children is correct enough in the features but the artist has made a poor picture. They look as if they were a milk and water pair without animation or life in them. He forgot to put the eyes in them. They are not half as good ones as the others were that I had the misfortune to loose. But it is still their pictures and they awaken all the tender feelings of the parent to look at them. Oh that I could be with them to watch over and direct their tender years and guide them in the paths of virtue and give them the benefit of my experience such as it is. For I believe I know what is right if I have not always done it. I am in good health and in good heart and am beginning to feel as if my term of service would not last always. I have not heard from Grant for some time. The latest news we had was up to the 24th of may. What he has been doing since I have not heard. I do not know what we are going to do in this department. There has been orders issued to prepare for an active campaign, but such orders are so common that I do not know what this one will amount. We are not strong enough to make an advance into the enemys country with success and hold the Miss River too, and I think it likely that our movments will be confined to raids along the River and attacks on the weaker posts of the rebs untill the result of Grants movements are known. We have had another death in the Regiment. George Bennett[5] died in the hospital of Disintery at New Orleans on the 9th of May after a few days illness brought on mainly by exposure and carelessness of Eating. We also heard that Daily who was at home was missing from the Steam Boat in which he was coming to the regiment and it is supposed that he fell overboard and was drowned although no one knows anything certain about it. My oppinion is that he was afraid to stay on the boat while it run past the Reble Battery at Greenvile, Ark. and as the boat stoped a few miles above to put off some citizens he slipped off and is laying along the River some place and will either run off or will be sent to his regt under guard for he was the only real coward we had in the Company.[6] Mary wishes to know wheather I am going to reinlist. Now that I just what I want to know about. When my 3 years is out I will have done as much as I think was my share and if there is men enough to fight it out I feel as if my duty was done. But I find disinterested Patriotism is scarce and wheather there will be enough of it found after the term of those now serving has expired to keep up the Army if the war lasts is more than I can tell and what I ought to do is not apparant to my mind. Selfishness says do not reinlist. Patriotism says reinlist. My judgment tells me to wait and see what is best to do when the time comes. Now I want you all to just say what you think about. Jist speak out plainly what you think and how you feel about it for I think you have a right to direct my future course concerning this war. All good men and woman can judge of the necessities of the country and can tell near what will be right under the circumstances. So when you write just put it in and let me know exactly what you all think. I am truly glad that Cyrus did not go into the 100 day service for with his health and the fatigues that a soldier has to endure I am certain he could not last two months and I think that one of us is enough to battle for the country in the field. Let him stay at home and use his voice for the cause where it will be of more effect than his assistance could be in the field. I can feel for him for I know he would like to bear his part but he is physicly unable to do it and he must try and be satisfied. Well I must close for the mail is waiting. I send you some of thoughts and you can comprehend the what I mean I reckon for I am not very inteligable this morning writing in such a hurry. I am still acting Sergeant Major and am pretty busy although it is not hard yet it is confining. It has rained every night and day in this month and we are beginning to get tired of it. The showers come on and after discharging a perfect deluge of rain the sun breaks out and is just as hot as it can get. While I write the sweat pours off me. Oh I forgot. Some one stole my pants out from under my head the other night and took my purse and the last thing I had in it. I only had 90 cents and some stamps so they will not get rich off of me. I lost some papers that will be a loss but I suppose they will have to go. There has been a great deal of stealing in this army since we got along with the 19th A.C. They are from the eastern Citys and are the lowest of the low many of them gamblers and pickpockets and have not quit their tricks here. Give my love to all and tell Mary and Cyrus to write. Kiss the children for me and make that young scion of the old stock go to walking. Tell him that I say he must hurry and catch up with Frank. So farewell.

    I remain affect thine

    Taylor

1. Warren was assigned to command the District of Baton Rouge on May 30, 1864. The regiment was divided into two wings. One wing reached Baton Rouge on June 10 and the other on June 13.

2. On May 7 Union forces under Major General William T. Sherman began an advance against Confederates in northern Georgia and by May 24 had driven them back to New Hope Church, about twenty-five miles northwest of Atlanta.

3. On May 30 Lawler led a combined infantry, artillery, and cavalry (from the 19th Corps) force from Morganza to prevent Confederates from crossing the Atchafalaya. Several skirmishes resulted, and Captain Benjamin G. Paul, Company K, 24th Iowa Infantry, was killed. The skirmish with the cavalry resulted in the death of Lieutenant James R. Leavy and three enlisted men from Colonel George T. Madison's 3rd Regiment, Arizona Brigade (Confederate).

4. This letter was not found.

5. George T. Bennett was a New Jersey native and resident of Newton when he enlisted August 2, 1862. He died of disease May 9, 1864, at New Orleans.

6. See the letter dated April 18, 1864.

[This letter was probably written between June 10 and July 4. In it Taylor mentions Rachel Gibson (his sister) leaving Little Britain—a reference to her letter of May 8 (not included in this book). He also mentions some of the men going to town, which is possibly a reference to Baton Rouge.]

[text missing] to write to her to-day and see what I receive in return. When I do I shall post you as to our correspondence. I shall come the highfalutin on her and as she is smart I expect something good from her. She is very much liked in Iowa City and the Col says is one of the best wives and mothers he ever seen and a perfect amazon in the way of a Union War Quaker. I shall also write to Rachel in a few days and try to encourage her some. I shall not advise her to leave little Britain although I am satisfied that her and her children would do much better in the west for she tells me that Ellis could not stand it to work at his trade and Henry has gone out to work with his Grandfather.

Whereas if they could come west they could keep their little ones at home untill they were grown up and could direct their course in virtues paths untill their characters were formed. If I was once more settled in life I would try and pursuad them to sell out and settle near us So that we might end our days in the same neighbourhood. But as it is things are so uncertain that I shall say nothing that will tend to alter the course of others. Well I am now about out of any thing to write about and if I cant think of something more I will have to stop.

Well I will try to finish my letter. The boys have all been down to town with the ostinsible purpos of going to church but they have got back and I thnk from the signs they have been in the lager saloons more than the church. Appropos, I have got so that I can neither drink lager or wine or any other strong drink. The last I have taken was on the 20th of Nov/63 and since that I have lost all Idea of How it tastes. This climite will not do for me to use any thing stronger than tea or coffee. Coffee is to strong to drink during the hot weater. Our army rations is to strong for us, and the Sanitary good are Scarce and hard to obtain. I got a pound of butter this morning for 50 cents and a lb of cheese for 40. This is all I have bought for food since January always having had enough to do me untill now from the Government. But since it become so hot I have quit eating the pork and feel like eating something more light nourishing. I am studying Grammar and Plane & Spherical Trigenomitry over again and am getting along quite well with it. It keeps my mind occupied and will if I live be of some benefit to me in instructing the children. I have quite a collection of scientific works collected around me and my time is fully occupied with something useful. I seldom leave camp. I have not been in town since we came here although I could go at any time. Yet I have no arrand there and so I stay where my duty requires me. I get along fine with my officers both Co and Regimental and am well contented. I hope before this reaches you Mary will have got well and you will all be enjoying yourselves. How I would like to spend the 4th of July with you this year. We heard bad news from Grant yesterday that he had been defeated with heavy loss but extras have come in claiming a great Victory.[1] Which is true I do not know but God I hope will end this rebellion in the right way before long for it is dreadful to think of the slain and wounded that lay on those fields. I must close. Give the children my love and all a kiss. Bid them be obedient and good and then they will always be respected and be loved. Give my love to all my friends and take my warmest feeling for thyself.

I remain affectionately thine

Taylor

1. This probably refers to the battle of Cold Harbor, Virginia, that was fought between Grant and Confederate General Robert E. Lee on June 3, 1864. The Union Army of the Potomac sustained about 7,000 casualties. The two armies remained facing each other until June 12.

Head Quarters 22 n Iowa
Baton Rouge[1] July 4 18[6]4
Dear Catharine and the rest

I received Thine of the 9th of June[2] and was glad to hear from you for I had been two weeks without a letter and the time runs slow without some news from the lovd ones at home. This is a very hot day. The weather is, and has been very warm, I think hotter than it was at Vicksburg last summer or at least I think I feel it more. It may be that I am not so used to being out in the sun as I was then that it seems hotter to me when I do go out. We are having a good time of it here now. We are not doing any thing but one hours drill in the morning and dress parade in the evening and enough of fatigue duty to do our own work such as halling rations wood and cane to make fresh shade with to keep ourselves comfortable. I am well and in good heart and things seem to be going on well in every respect. Our Captain talks of resigning but I think he will not do it for I will protest against as we all get along fine and I have a good time under him. One reason for which is that he does not know much and has to depend on me for his accounts and business being kep straight. I will get a commission if any vacancy occurs. At least Col Graham told me so but I am afraid that I will not be capable and will be sorry to leave the place I hold to take one of more responsibility. And if it was not for your benefit I would refuse anything of the sort for I have the name of being a good soldier where I am and I would be very sorry to take a position and not be able to fill it with honour and ability.

With regard to the Mortgage on the old Mill I think there is nothing of it, and I do not wish thee to pay one cent out for any debt or to any man untill I get home. Now I will tell thee what I think. When I purchased from McMullin there had been a tax sale when Gaston held the property but as Gaston had no title the sale was not valid as against the property. Gray frequently told me that he held a claim against the mill and as McMullin had warranteed to me I went back on Mc but he would not pay it because the law would not compell him to do it. Now I have no right neither according to law or justice to pay it and I will not do it nor I will not allow thee to do it. If Mr. Granston wishes to take advantage of a soldiers wife while her husband is absent defending that that he has not the courage to defend himself just tell him to go to hell. He knows there is no mortgage on the mill nor any claim that is lawful or just that I am bound for and I think it dammd small for such a man as him to try and draw fifty dollars out of a woman who has a family of little children and no certainty of her husband ever being again with her. And if he is he may be in such a situation that he will be a scource of expense to her rather than a help. I want thee to just keep what money I send thee or give it to Cyrus for if I get home I will have to have something to commence work on. For although a man may have done much for his country and sacrificed his pecuniary means for the nations benefit yet when he comes to want the almighty dollar swallows up all other considerations, and thee and me will be left to our own rescources and all we will have to fall back on will be our love and the concienciousness of having done right will be all that we can expect to have. But true to the words of the Poet, man wants but little here below nor wants that little long.[3] Well this is the 4 of July and the officers are alowing the boys to have a good time and I have a time keeping them straight so this letter will not be much of a letter. I have the piles and do not feel as good as I would if I was all right but still I am in good health. I wish thee to let me know wheather you get the letter I wrote Frank.[4] And I would like you to always mention the letters you receive from me for I then can tell what you have had from me.

Well, I expressed some money to you on the 25th and yesterday the agent came round and notified us that all the moneys expressed that day had been stolen and he returned it to us. Theirs was over one Thousand dollars expressed from Co. C and it was all refunded. I think I will not express a gain untill I am paid which will be in about

8 or 10 days when I can express the whole of it. There is no war news as I have heard and I am without anything to send you this morning. Things are very high in this place. I would like to buy some things here but they are so high that I have to live on Sow belly and hard tack although the weather is hot and I would feel much better if I could have vegetables to eat but I cant have them so let it go. Fresh meat is 40 to 50 cts pr lb and onions is 10 cts per lb potatoes 8 and beets about 5. We do not get beef here from the govt for I think the men in office speculates on it and the soldiers have to do without it. It is very tempting for some of our officers to have a chance to make a little money if they do not do what is right to take the advantages of the soldiers and sell them rations when they can make a large sum out of them. Well I must stop writing. Give my love to all the folks and kiss the children for me. This is the poorest letter I have written for everything is in an uproar and I can not write worth any thing at all. So farewell.

> I remain Thine afft
> Taylor Peirce

PS I have looked over it that is the letter and find that I can hardly read it myself. Let me know when you receive it.

1. On June 9 the 22nd Iowa was ordered to Baton Rouge and arrived there the following day.

2. This letter was not found.

3. From "Night Thoughts" by Edward Young.

4. This is probably the letter of April 18, 1864, from Taylor to Frank.

> Head Qurs 22n Regt Iowa,
> New Orleans July 9th 1864
> Dear Catharine and all the rest

I have a little time this morning to drop you a few lines to let you know that the 22nd is still on the move and that I am with it and am well.

I wrote you on the 4th but was in such a hurry that I think you will be good schollars if you can read it so I will recapitulate a little and give you some additional news that will be interesting to you. On the 6th Just as we began to think we were going to remain at Baton Rouge the rest of the season We were notified to pack up our camp and be ready to moved in fifteen minutes on board a boat for New Orleans.

So at it we went and were Steaming down the river in about 10 hours and landed here on the Evening of the 7th and went into camp. There is about 20,000 troops here and are evidently bound for some point to opperate against the Rebles but where that point is I am just as much in the dark about as you or any one else. But I think the chances are that we go to Genl Grant and you need not be supprised to receive my next letter from Fortress Monroe department of the East instead of department of the Gulf. There is a total dismemberment of the 13 A.C.[1] and we are now in the 2nd Brigade 2nd Div 19th Army Corps Commanded by General Reynolds and General Grover Div Comder and our Brigade is comded by a New York Col[2] with fine Hair and wears paper collars and dont speak to privates. Well maybe his own men will fight for him but I am afraid that he will not get along well with the Western men if he does not pursue a little different course.

We hear middling good news from Grant and Sherman and I think if they will send 20,000 more men round to Grant the Southern Confederacy is gone up for if the 22nd rgts after them they must fall sure. Well I am not spoiling for a fight but if it is nescessary for us to go into it again I would like to go and help take Richmond and Capture Lee. It may be possible that we will be ordered against Mobile but that is not the general oppinion here and I feel certain that we will be in at the fall of Richmond as we were at Vicksburg.

I expressed you some of my clothes. I had accumulated too many to carry on the march and as goods are very high I thought I would send all that could be used to clothe the children and also all my good ones so that when I get home I will not have to buy any for 3 or 4 years. I send the receipt along with this letter. I expressed my orderleys coat one Great coat one Blouse 2 pr pant 2 Shirts 1 kickory shirt 3 pr drawer and I sent home by Daily one complete suit which he left at Cap Mullins Mothers and Ed Quick promised to send them to Des Moines. But he may forget it so you had better drop a few lines to Edward Quick at Vandalia about them for it will stand us in need to save all we can to commence on again when my time is out or the war is over.

My humble oppinion is that the war is nigh about played out. There will be some hard fighting done yet but the Government has got in earnest now and the confedercy must nescessarily yield to the overwhelming force that is arrayed against it. I see from their own manifesto that they are begining to whine but avoid saying anything about what their great principals are that they are contending for or what rights has ever been invaded only that they wish to be left alone which would be a grand doctrine for horse thieves and pickpockets. After stealing all they could and breaking all laws of society just fall back and luxuriate on their ill gotten gains and bid defiance to those who has been despoiled and be let alone. Truly a fine theory. I think we will be paid off in 2 or 3 days and I will try my luck again in expressing my money. I will send 100 dollars and some more clothing as I can get it for my clothing allowance and get it much cheaper from the government than I will be likely to ever get it from other scources at least for several years and I wish to be in such a fix that I will not have to spend money for clothes when I am ready to go into business again. I intend to write to the Children again soon and want Sallie to write to me every time thee writes so that she may not only give me the satisfaction of hearing from her but also improv herself in composition which is one of the most essential things in a good education. Tell Frank that he must learn to write so that he can send me a letter too. Kiss the little folks for me and remind them that their good behavior is a great comfort to me in my absence from them. I would buy them some presents if I could get time to get out but if I do not you can take some of the money and buy something for them and it will do them as much good as if I would do it.

The weather is very hot now but the army is in good health and buoyant with the hope that their term of service will soon expire when they can return to their homes. Alas how few of all that have left will return to gladden the hearts of those they left behind. But the sins of the nation must be atoned for in the lives of her citizens and the curse of slavery washed out with the best blood of the land and hardly a home but will have a vacant seat by the fireside.

Well I must close. I will write a line again before I leave here and if possible give you some Idea where you will next hear from me. But where ever I am you may know that I am just as eager to put down the rebellion as ever although I would like to be at home once more. I will not get home this summer on furlough unless something occurs that I do not know of now. Give my love to all and receive a share for thyself.

> I remain thine affectionately
> Taylor

1. The Thirteenth Corps was disbanded on June 11, 1864.

2. Major General Joseph J. Reynolds had commanded the defenses of New Orleans since January 1864. He then took command of the Nineteenth Corps. Brigadier General Cuvier Grover fought in the Peninsula Campaign and at Second Manassas before being transferred to the Department of the Gulf. He took command of the Second Division on December 30, 1862. Colonel Edward L. Molineux commanded the 159th New York Infantry before becoming brigade commander.

Des Moines Iowa July 10 64
Dear Taylor

It is sunday again and I sit down to write to thee all that I know that has taken place for the last week. Well we have been well as could be. We all have been very busy cleaning up after plastering and are not quite done yet. But if nothing happens to prevent it we will be all done by the middle of the week comeing and then they (C and M) will have a nice house of their own and if they only will try and be contented they have nothing to trouble them very much. Of cource me and my children disturb them Some but they put up with us quite patiently considering they have none of thair own and maby better than if they had some of thair own for maby they would not have us here at all if they had. I do not want thee to think I write so to complain for I have nothing to complain if at all. Only I know that the children are a trouble but not any more than other peoples that I see in my accquiantances. Therefore I will endevour to be contented untill the time comes that thee can get home to provide for us thyself. Thee asks to know my mind about reenlisting now. I wrote thee last spring on that subject but if thee has not received that I will just say that if I think it will be time enough to reenlist when thy time of service is out and then if thee is ancous to go forth to fight for the country then I will say as I did at first. Do but I shall expect thee to come home and see how things are geting along and see what can be done for the best for the children. For I feell it a great responsibility on me to take care of them and train them up in an others house all though I do not have to work as hard as I would have if I was by my self. Yet it is very different and more difficult to watch and see after all thair mischiefs that they do. For children are not men or women and we can not look for them to be such untill they have age on their heads to make them so. I suppose that I look at my children with a mothers eye so that I can not see the faults in them that others can and that makes all the difference in the world with children. For all parents (or neerly all) think their own children the best though I think that when mine do wrong I know it as well as any other person if I do not make as much fuss as many others would under the same circumstances.

The children are done going to school now and I endevour to hear them say their lessons every day so that they will not for get what thay have learned. Sallie has learned verry fast and is I think a going to make a good schoolar if she has a fair chance and seems to understand why it is best for her to study so she will be of use in the world. Frank also learns fast and I think has a better memory than Sallie and it will not be so heard for him to study. And if when he gets old enough to go to his books in a proper manner to learn right along he will soon get up to what Sallie has now. And I think too if he lives to be a man he will be a verry good one or right the revirce a verry bad one.

Taylor Dear me how time does go on. This is thy birthday eighteen years since we ware maried and just to think of the changes we have seen in that time. It makes me begin to feel old and that I had all most spent my life in vain for I have nothing to show for all I have done and I begin to fear that this war is going last so long that thee will either be killed or worn out in the servise so that I will have no chance to make a mends in the time to come. For with out thee I can do nothing yet as I always have done. I will hope for the best and meet the worst that comes with a calm and stern look that will drive all fear and doubt away. For I have great faith in the Almighty power of God and I will look to him for help in the time of need and I also think I will not be cast off to perrish. Well perhaps I will seem to write a doleful letter if I keep on in this way. I therefore will stop and try to think of some thing not of the doleful kind. Well we are all well and doing well. We have had nice rains last week to and the corn is growing just the nicest kind and the wheat is being harvested. But they say that the chinch bug hurt the spring wheat a good bit in some sections of the State. Though as a general thing there will be enough to do all of us at home and I hope when the time comes for threashing out the grain that it may turn out better than it was expected too. Well the children

have come in from takeing a walk and I will have to stop for this time.
I will sign my self thy own

>Catharine

>Ellis can say some words but not enough to make out
>>much at talking.

>Cat Peirce

>Head Quarters 22nd Iowa Inftr
>Algiers La July 14th 1864
>Dear Catharine and all friends

I again set down to write you a few lines to inform you what I am
doing and what our prospects are for the future. In the first place I am
well except I have eat so much fruit that it has soured on my stomach and and has given me the diarrhea but I think it will get well of
itself as I feel much better of it this morning.

Well Kitty we are bound for Virginia. We are waiting here for transportation. A part of our Division Embarked yesterday and I think it
likely we will have a vessle for us in a day or two. We will see it all I
gues before we get home. I think that the western Boys will show the
Rebs a different method of fighting from what they have been seeing
down there if they do not come to the conclusion to quit and let Old
Abe take charge of them. I think we will take Richmond and will
eventually take the whole Southron confederacy but it will be some
time yet before we are through with the war so that we can come
home. For my part I expect to serve out my 3 years and some more
and will be well content to give my country my time if we can only
obtain an unconditional victory over those who hold the pernicious
doctrine of Secession and Negroe slavery. I will write you a gain as
soon as we set foot on the shore and you will probably get it as soon
as if I would write it here for we will not be over 5 days on the Voyage and then We will be that much nearer New York the way that our
mail has been going nearly ever since we come here. You need not stop
writing but just direct your letters as you have done until you get notice from me to direct them otherwis. They will find the regiment. Let
them go where they will. I received my pay a few days since and sent
the $100 by express. I had loaned out $30 to one of the Officers and
he has not paid me yet but I reckon he will soon and I will send it

home. Or maybe I will not send any more home untill next payday when I will be able to make it up to $75 and can send it all togather. Now I do not want thee to pay out any of the money I send thee for any of the old debts for the most of them are paid. And if they find out that thee will pay them thee would be likely to have to pay them that had been paid or that had no real claim against me. So just inform all that bothers thee for money that if they will present themselves to me on the battlefields of Virginia with their accounts properly adjudicated I will settle them and if they do not chose to do that they may wait untill I get home. But do not bother thyself about any of them. Keep all thee can get and get all thee can for if anything should happen to me so that thee would be deprived of my assastance as small as it is thee would be hard set to get along with that little family. I wish them to receive a good education and that will be more than I had to start on and I think if thee have no more thee can make a living. I send the Express bills and wish thee to inform me when thee gets the things. I sent the first time 2 pr pants 1 blouse 1 dress coat and a lot of old shirts and drawers and 1 great Coat. Thee can write me if they all come through safe. I sent thee one Hundred Dollars the day before yesterday. Please let me know when thee receives it. Well I must quit writing more for we are expecting to be ordered to embark any hour and I have a good many things to attend to to insure comfort during the trip through to Fortress Monroe. Kiss the Children for me and tell them to be good and learn their lessons well and when papa comes home they can all be so happy togather if they are good.

I have been looking for Mary to send me a letter for some time but I do not get it yet. I think her or Cyrus might write once in 6 months at least. It may be that they do not find time so long on their hands as I do and forget that I have nothing to take the thoughts of home and home scenes off my mind but what I can gather up arround Camp and that is not always profitable and I keep away from it as much as possible. For I think it better not have any enjoyment than to have that that would injure me. So I do not have much except my work and therefore I would like you all to write often. Well I must now quit and bid you all Farewell.

    Affectly Yours
    Taylor Peirce

Head Quarters 22nd Iowa Inftr
Algiers La July 16th 1864
Dear Catharine and all the rest

I concluded to write you a few line as I have nothing to do and the weather is so hot that I can not stir out with any comfort! We are still laying here awaiting transportation. How soon we will get away I am unable at this time to say. But I think it will not be more that three of four days. I will keep this letter open and as soon as I find out when we are to start I will finish it and tell you where to direct your next letters too. We have heard of the sinking of the Alabama by the Kearsearge off the Coast of France[1] and it has caused quite a sensation here. The loyal people are rejoicing over the prospect of the future safety of our shipping interest and the Sympatizers of the Confedercy look gloomy as anothe prop is knocked from under their totering Structure. We have no news from Grant for some time and but little from Shearman and can give but little Idea of what is occurring at the different seats of war. But one thing I feel confident of that Grant will drive the Rebles from the line they now occupy or take their army. I think Lee will certainly be too sharp to allow his Army to be captured and so allow the Government to close the thing up all their own way without another Struggle which in all probability he can make if he can retreat to anothe line. But even if he could do that it would only prolong the war and increas the loss of life without giving him any prospect of success in the end. For the North can hurl enough of men against the Confederate forces to swallow up the entire south and completely Yankeeize it. The Territory that is now under the protection of the Govt is fast assuming the peculiarities and feelings of the Eastern portion of the United States and a few years will completely change the feelings and views of the Southern States and the whole. When the Slavery Question is once Settled will become blended in one vast community of free labourers with all the Elements within themselves to lead to prosperity and happiness. That such a revolution will take place is just as certain as that water runs down hill.

For Why? The Southren States Settled with an indolent race of poor whites who have become degraded and Idle by comeing in contact with slave labour, and the better class never having had to use any of their own exertion to procure their livelyhood have become enervated to such a degree, that the whole must succumb to the enterprise and superior Energy of the free and labourious men of the north, whose Education has been both of the mind and body and who have no such word as back out in their vocabulary. I am just as well satisfied as that I live that if there were not another battle fought the confedercy must go under. But under the present state of things I fear that much blood will be shed before the final adjustment of the difficulty.

I suppose that it is right that the nation must pay in Sorrow and blood for the blood and suffering of the poor African.[2] And as it rains on the just and the unjust, the inocent must suffer for the guilty. I may not live to see the end of this struggle but I am just as well convinced that it will all end right as that I am contending for the right to-day. I have just seen an account of another raid into Maryland and Pa but to what extent the newspaper does not state.[3] I hope the party will be met as they were last year and be captured before they get back again. I am sending the children some verses[4] to amuse them and if in after years they may find anything in them worth reading they will at least know the kind of feelings their Father had while enduring the life of a Soldier. Although they are not fit for the public eye I wish the children to preserve them so that If I get home I and they to can have something to carry the mind back to these trying times and scenes.

I have been waiting anxiously for Marys letter and likeness and am in hopes that I will receive it before I leave here for the mail will not be likely to reach us soon after we once get started. I want you to write me how you all get along and wheather Mary gets entirely over the Measles and how the little fellows get along. I wish to know wheather Ellis is likely to be as intelligent as the rest of the children and wheather his constitution is improving as he grows older and how master Frank is making it and if he gives his uncle any trouble and if Sallie will be able to comprehend Mathematics of the rest of her Studies. I have no doubt of her ability to master them. I am convinced that Frank can learn figures and use them but what else he will be able to learn I was not with him long enough to form an opinion. Tell Sallie that she must now write to me once a week and take pains to spell her words and do the best she can to form her letters neatly so that she may become a good writer. For her old Pap would be very glad to get a letter from her once a week and oftener if he could for he is very lonesome these long days. Col Graham and Capt Mullins both promised me a furlough after this Campaign is over without my asking it and if I should get one I shall accept it although I had not intended to apply for one untill my time of service expired. Well I will stop now and finish when we get orders to move.

Sunday 17th Dear Catharine I received thine and Sallies of the 3 today[5] and it was a scource of happiness to receive it. Tell Mary to write soon. The next letter you write direct to the Department of the Potomac. We are embarking this Evening. I will write again as soon as we land.[6]

> Affty yours Taylor
> I am in good health and fine spirit. Tell C. Van to stick to old Abe through this Presidential Campaign and his Election Closes the War.

1. On June 19, 1864, the Union ship *Kearsarge* sank the Confederate commerce raider *Alabama* off the coast of France. The *Alabama* had seized or sunk sixty-five ships since being launched May 15, 1862.

2. Taylor's comment is strikingly similar to a statement by Lincoln in his Second Inaugural Address, March 4, 1865: "If God wills that it continue until all the wealth piled by the bondsman's 250 years of unrequited toil shall be sunk, and until every drop of blood drawn with the lash shall be paid by another drawn with the sword."

3. On July 5 Confederates commanded by Major General Jubal Early crossed the Potomac River to threaten Baltimore and Washington. The latter city had been reinforced, and Early recrossed the Potomac on July 14.

4. Several pages of poems were among this collection of letters and are reproduced below. Because the poems were not dated, it cannot be determined whether these are the specific "verses" referred to by Taylor.

5. This letter was not found.

6. The 22nd Iowa embarked on the steamer *Cahawba* on July 17 and departed New Orleans the next day.

Poem I

The maiden too whose plighted faith
Was given to him now cold in death
Whose heart was warm and brave
Will in the anguish of her soul
Pour fourth her grief without control
Oer his untimely grave
The day has closed and ends the strife

In which the waste of human life
Was awful to behold
The dimly seen by the stars pale light
In courses all bloody and stiff and white
A fearfully appalling Sight
A dreadfull close for a dawn so bright
Now friends my tale is told
A closing both dark and cold

He hoped to see that aid advance
But not a collumn met his glance
It shames me to relate
For when the battles near they hear
Their coward souls is blackened with fear
They leave him to his fate

He turns again amid the strife
Resolved to win or yield his life
Amid his comrades brave
Hid by the shares of coming night
As others did by speedy flight
He scorned himself to save

At length with numbers overbourn
With hardship and with hunger worn
They are compelled to yield
Now oer that land of Iowa braves
The hated reble banner waves

They force them from the field.
Oer all that field throughout the day
The hawk eye Boys in ambush lay
And wage the bloody strife
For not a reble shows his head
But then by messengers is sped
To take his hated life

Now the day is almost gone
Field is neither lost or won
But on that bloody plain

Lie many whose Star of life was bright
When dawned that mornings rosy light
Now low in everlasting night
They slip among the Slain

Oh War what dreadfull scenes are thine
The bursting shell the exploding mine
The Streams of human gore
The whistling ball, the furious shout
The dead, and wounded, strewn about
Their life tide, slowly oozing out
They'll heed thy din no more
The wife and mother oft shall weep
While by her side her children sleep
Unconscious of their loss
And in her lonly widowhood
Kneel down in mournfull solitude

And meekly take the cross.
And Sitting round their winter fire
The little ones prattling of their sire
The tale she oft will tell
How he in Vicksburgs bloody fight
Stood for his country and the right
And bravely fighting fell

Poem II
Champion Hill

1. Twas morning of a sultry day,
The sky was clear the wind was still
And nature with the robes of May
Had Clothed the woods of Champion Hill
As marched in slowly over the plain
Mid wayside flowers and sprouting grain
All nature seemed at rest to day.
The wild birds carrolled in their mirth
It seemd that everything of earth
Was keeping holyday

2. And can it be I asked my soul
As glancing oer that armed array
That wars terrific thunder roll
Will burst upon our ears this day
But ere another hour had past
Was heard the bugles martial blast
And sound of musketrys sharp rattle
And quickly on the army rolled
Which to the anxious mind fortold
Of an approaching battle

3. Hark to the turmoil and the shout,
The war cry and the cannons boom
The stubborn conflict and the rout,
Tells death has to the harvest come.
Where Hovey charged with deadly force,
The ground lies strewn with many corps.
Still heaves the battle like an ocean
And Hawk Eye brave and Hoosier stout
Yield up their spirit with a shout,
Amid its fierce commotion
High oer the din of battle rolls,
The fiery Logans charging yell
It strikes the rebles guilty souls,
Like echoes of their funeral knell.
Our gallant men hard pressed the fight,
For Victory e'er day closed in night
The boasting southron chivalry
Was hurrying from the field this lost,
Close followed by a gallant host,
Of Northern cavalry.

Like an avenging angel, hard,
Brave Osterhaus pressed their retreat,
The fiery Germans headlong charge,
Rendered our victory complete,
The sun is down night closing in.
The cannons soar and battles din
Is heard at distant intervals.

These sounds at length has died away,
And silence again resumes her sway
Along these gloomy dells.

Poem III
"The Charge of the 22nd Iowa Infantry on the 22 day of may 1863
on the reble works in war of Vicksburg Mississippi led by Cols
Stone and Graham"

The night has settled sun in gloom
And all is Silent as the tomb
Save where Some Sentinel
Along the lines kept watch while they,
The Hawk Eye Soldiers Sleeping lay
Within the Silent dell

What Sound is that? a low command
And soon amazed that Gallant band
In line of battle Stand
Forward: and onward side by side
They move to where the hill will hide
Then rest them on the sand
The weary night is almost gone
The eastern sky proclaims the dawn,
The Morrows welcome light
And looming darkly in the west
Is Seen a hills unbroken crest
The Vicksburgs famous height

Ah; Well we know what work's to do
And when tis done alas; how few
may live its pints to share
Far as the eye can see along
Are breast works high and fortress strong
And many a reble there.

Our leader then with cautious care
Bade that the colors feel the air
Brav Hartly[1] then unfurled,
That Flag for which our fathers bled

And which in triumph of had bid
Defianc to the world.

With lines now formed that gallant bands
In Silent expection Stand,
Each man resolved and Stern!
Each man resolved and Stern:
Each man has fixed his bayonet bright
And with what courage hawk Eyes fight.
The rebles soon will learn.

Now with the warriors air of pride
Stand Stone and Graham Side by side
And wonder how their Men will bide
The approaching battles shock.
The doubts dispelled for even now
Is Stern resolve wrote on each brow
As firm as granite rock

Forward Stone Shouts and up the hill
Each man and muscle strains untill
They stand in open view
And then first breaks upon their sight
The ground oer which they'll have to fight
And what they have to do

A moments pause and down they rush
Oer ravine deep and tangled brush
With yells upon the foe
Oh God it was a gallant sight
To see these men charge in the fight
For Justice liberty and right
And deal the avenging blow
With nerves of steel and courage high
The twenty Second onward fly
They surely cannot fail.
But like the thunder crash of heaven
When all the elements are risen
Forth from the cannons mouth is driven
A Storm of Iron hail

Now Iowa thy happy homes
Will echo with the widows moans.
For the loyal brave and tried
Must fall before that deadly blast
Then only the annals of the past
Can tell you how they died
Wounded at length, Stone's vioce no more
Is heard amid the battles soar
They bear him from the field
Next Hartley falls the flag is down
But Norris[2] caught it from the ground
And raided it high while all around
Is heard the sells destructin sound
That Flag he'll never yield

Brave Robinson[3] wholed his men
Though Wounded forward rushed again
Come on brave boys he cries
But ever the words were fully Said
The fatal messinger had sped
He sinks no more to rise
And many more there might name
But on Young Iowa page of fame
Their names will proudly stand
Engraved in characters of light
A record Sorrowful yet bright
Of those who file amid the fight
To Save this Glorious Land

The Gallant Graham where is he
Look towards you fort and you can see
Him ware his sword on high
See now he scales the outer moat
Soon from the walls his flag shall float
See: See the rebles flag

The foe soon mark their numbers few
And rallying now the fight renew
Oh wheres his promised aid

Then well may Grahams Eys flash fine
His gallant bosom swell with ire
As he field surveyed

1. Thomas Harper, a native of Ireland, enlisted at Iowa City on August 6, 1862. He was wounded at Port Gibson and was wounded and taken prisoner at Vicksburg on May 22. He died of those wounds on June 8.

2. Edward M. Norris was an Ohio native and resident of Vandalia when he enlisted July 25, 1862. He was wounded at Vicksburg on May 22 and received a disability discharge on December 29, 1863.

3. Captain James Robertson was a Pennsylvania native and Iowa City resident. He commanded Company I and was killed at Vicksburg on May 22.

> Des Moines July 17th 1864
> Dear Taylor

I sit down to write this morning not knowing just what I will find to write. We are all in good health and in good heart. The children have gone to Sabbath school and Ellis is a sleep so I thought I would try and find some thing to say to thee. If I did not know anything that would be interesting it seemd as if I do not get a chance to know any thing worth writing in one week for I go no place and I do not get much chance to read for the baby so that I can not write much. Cyrus is quite well this summer and has been working very hard for the last six weeks to at his house. He done all the carpenter work himself and tended the plasterer and is still well which is rather a wonder for him to keep well that long without working at the same time. We have got the house all cleaned up and it is nice. If they had the furniture for it movd they would be fixed and I suppose they will get their money from Government in a week or two more and then they can get all they want. I believe I told thee they had earned a thousand by boarding the seventh Cavelry.[1] Well they have not got that yet but C thinks he will get it yet this month and if I get what thee spoke of in thy last letter we will be as nice as you pleas. For I shall not want to use much of it for myself or the children for we have all we will want untill winter. Then we will have to get some warm cloths and they will cost a good bit for goods have got up to such a pitch. Calico is 40 cts per yard and cotton flanen to seventy five cts and woolin flannen is one dollar per yard. So thee may see that if I want much it will take some money to buy with. I have not receved that money from Dixon yet but Sumpter toll me that Dixon had kept it out of the payment to Hurst so that he intends to pay it to me and I suppose I will get it this fall. Thee wanted to know if it was so about Henry Sumpter. It is all true and more to for him and Mary have got a young son that must of been on hand about the time that Henry's wife died from the time that it made its appearance into the world. So I will leave thee to guess at the rest of their doings. Mr Jonhson is farming for Robert McConnels widow this summer and he divided all he had with Mary so I think he done more than he had any right too from all that I can hear. But as I am not given to spread scandle I will not write what I have heard. Joe Slaughter and his wife was here the other day and told all a bout these things. Of course I did not say any thing to John when here about it. Slaughter was here to see Ingersol about a suit that Ingersol had against Joe for dammage for the Injoinment of that money that Joe had from Ingersol and Inham they sued Joe for fifty dollars damage. But wheather they will make him pay it or not tell. Well I guess I must stop for the children are comeing. I have had no letter this week and I feel lonesome without one but I hope thee is well and that I will get one tomorrow. I close with love to thee.

Catharine A Peirce

1. The 7th Iowa Cavalry was organized between November 1, 1862, and July 25, 1863. It was assigned to protect settlements on the northern and western frontiers from attacks by hostile Indians.

Des Moines July 24/64
Dear Taylor

We are all well to day and are doing just the same to day that we do every sunday with very little varity. Mary and I went to hear some old quakers preach on last sunday evening. That was some change to the common things of the day and to day William Johnson and wife is here. I would like to write thee some thing that would be worth reading but it is very doubtful if I will be able to write any thing at all. It seems that thee get the news as soon as I do so that it is not worth my while to write thee the war news and an other. I do not get time to read the new un till every else has read it. There is one good piece of news and that is the sinking of the Alabama by the steam ship Kearsage but I expect thee will have seen the account of it before this reaches thee so that I will not make any remarks about it. I do not know what I will fill up this with for between the talk and the children there is not much chance to write.

Well Taylor it evening and there is quite a calm in the house. The visitors have gone and is got cooler and the children have gone out to play so I can write better. Well thee wants to know if I got Franks letter.[1] I got it all right and I think that I mentioned it at the time but may be I might of not. I think I all ways say what letters I get for I write every weekend and when I do not get one I feel bad so that I am sure that I would be glad to get one that I would have to tell of it. I did not get any last week and this week I recieved two to make up. My head is troubled with the bother of the children that I can not think of much. I had got them started out to play and thought I was going to have a good time writing when here they come back with Ellis hurt and crying not hurt bad but just enough to stop me right off. Well I will be gin again and see what will come next. Mary wants to know if thee got a letter from her dated about the last of may for thee has never mentiond it and she thinks if thee dose not get her letters it is not worth her while to write any more.[2] I do not think Cyrus will take time to write untill he gets all his work done which will be some time yet. For he under took to build a house for a war widow yesterday that will take him about a month and he talks of takeing soldiers to board if there is any raise on this new call of 500,000[3] and I suppose there will be. For Iowa has always been along and a little ahead of all the calls for troops before and I think she will not behind this time. Thee must forgive this poor letter this time for I will try and do better next.

I remain thy ever afect wife
Catharine

1. This is Catharine's response to Taylor's question in his July 4 letter.
2. This is Mary's letter dated May 29, 1864.
3. On July 18 Lincoln called for 500,000 additional troops, but the number required could be reduced by credits for men who had entered service previously in several categories.

Virginia

EDITOR'S NOTE. After the Thirteenth Corps was disbanded, the 22nd Iowa was reassigned to the Nineteenth Corps. At 8 P.M. on July 17 the 22nd Iowa embarked on the steamer *Cahawba* at New Orleans and headed for Virginia. The regiment arrived at Fortress Monroe on July 24 and disembarked at Bermuda Hundred, farther up the James River. After a short stay they were transported to Washington on board the *Wenona* and arrived there on August 1. From there they marched to the Shenandoah Valley to participate in the campaign against the Confederates under Lieutenant General Jubal Early. Throughout the valley campaign the regiment was assigned to the Second Brigade, Second Division, Nineteenth Corps.

The 22nd Iowa participated in several battles while in the Shenandoah Valley. On August 18 the regiment joined Major General Philip Sheridan's forces near Winchester. The Union force fought Early's men on September 3, September 19, and September 22. Several other engagements followed in October and November. In early December the regiment went into winter quarters, and military activities were limited to guarding buildings and escorting wagon trains.

> Head Quarters 22n Iowa
> Bermuda Hundred Virginia
> July 26th 1864
> Dear Catharine

We have arrived in Virginia after a vouage of 9 days. We embarked on board the Steam transport Cahawba on Sunday the 17th and arrived here last night. We had very pleasant weather but the boat was so crowded that we were not very comfortable although we made out to get along with it. We had the 131st New York 159th NY and our Regt the whole amounts being 1,700 men so you may know that the boat was crowded. There was 2 men died on the passage. Both of them had been sick a long time and the crowded state of the vessle and the want of attention was too much for them.[1] I am glad I do not belong to an eastern Regt. The Soldiers get no better treatment than brutes. Their officers are generally pimps and Saloon keepers who have had some little political influence and have obtained their commissions through this means and are the lowest of the low and the old adage of Beggar on Horseback will apply in their case.[2] They had one of our men up for some trifling offence the 1st morning after we went on board and as the Iowa boys were not used to that kind of treatment we turned in and compelled them to release him and gave them to understand that the first man that they tied up again would be cut down and the man or men tying him should go overboard. So they have been quite civil to us ever since and when they see any of the Iowa boys coming they stand aside and let us pass.

Well we are in Bermuda Hundred within sound of Grants Artillery at Petersburg and Butlers at Ft. Darling. The Cannonading from Butler does not sound so plain as that at Petersburg. I therefore infer that it is further off and Butler is nearer Richmond than Grant. Our destination is Ft. Darling. We report to Genl Butler. I suppose we will be in the front to-morrow or next day.[3] I can not tell you much about the way matters are going here. We heard that Sherman had defeated the Rebles at Kenesaw Mountain and that the Raiders into Maryland had mostly been captured. Also that our Gen Lee had been attacked near Washington by a force of Rebles and taken Prisoner but his troops whiped the Rebs and recaptured him.[4] It was stated here last night that the Reb Pickets told our Pickets night before last that Sherman had taken Atlanta.[5] This is all the news of Importance. Our work will be the reduction of Ft. Darling and the capture of Richmond. I thought when Vicksburg surrendered that if I could help take Richmond I would be satisfied with what I had done for the Union. But I did not dream that the 22nd would ever be called to take part in its capture. But here we are full of life health and vigor and I will say as much Patriotism is exists in any Regt in the service. What our future Record will be remains hidden from human observation but I hope it may be as successfull as the past has been glorious. I sent you some money $100 from Orleans. I wish you to notify me when you receive it also the clothes. I wish you to save all the clothes I Send home for I feel like this thing would come to a close some time and then I will need them. I am in good health. The trip round done me good and the fresh northern air as infused a vigor into my frame that I have not felt for nearly 2 years. No person would believe the difference in the feel of the air between this place and the low bottoms of the Miss. The temprature is not so different but the air of Louisiana as an enervating influence on the system that all the efforts of the mind can not counteract. On the other hand the atmosphere here seems to diffuse an elasticity to the frame and that gives a corresponding action to the mind which is truly invigorating to one who has endured the deadning influence of the extreme south. Well I will have to close up my letter soon as we will be very busy soon and I must be ready to see to my part of the programme. While I set here and write I can distinctly hear the Roar of the Artillery Both at Ft. Darling and Petersburg. We are about 2 miles above City Point encamped on a nice old Virginia farm that the war has laid waste. The passage up the James River from Ft. Monroe was very pleasant. The country presents a most beautiful appearance consisting of farms interspersed with woods like it used to look in Penna and the farmers here have evidently been very wealthy and have lived in luxury and splendor but pride and avarice has done their business for them. The James River up to the mouth of the Appomatix is from 3 to one mile wide. That is it is 3 or 4 miles wide at the mouth and one mile at its confluence with the Appomattix. Above that it becomes very narrow not much wider than the Des Moines. The land along the River is undulating and has the appearance of having been very fertile but looks much impoverished from over tillage. This is about all I think of now. You must direct your letters to the 22n Iowa at Bermuda Hundred Virginia. Give my love to all my Friends and kiss the little fellows for me and keep up good heart for god must prosper the right and I feel as if the future was full of promise for me and peace for thee and thine. Tell Mary and Cyrus to write often to me for while I am here I will not have much to amuse me except the roar of artillery and the crack of the Rifle if that can be called amusement which makes a man shudder when he thinks of the effects of it. You must all write and I will post you once a week of the state of afairs. So farewell.

> I remain affectionately thine
> Taylor

1. A letter from another member of the 22nd Iowa states that the two men who died were from the 159th New York. They were probably Private Peter R. Conklin, Company K, who died on July 21, and Private John A. Klinsing, Company D, who died on July 22.

2. "Set the beggar on horseback and he'll outride the devil." This is a German proverb, but there is a variation in *King Henry the VI* by Shakespeare and in *Anatomy of Melancholy* by Robert Burton.

3. The Union Army of the James under Major General Benjamin Butler had cap-

tured City Point on May 4, 1864. By June 15 the Army of the Potomac, accompanied by Grant, had joined Butler to invest Petersburg. Fort Darling was part of the Confederate defenses at Drewry's Bluff on the James River between Petersburg and Richmond. The regiment did not move to Fort Darling but occupied trenches between the James and Appomattox Rivers. The 22nd Iowa, 131st New York, and 159th New York were temporarily attached to the First Division, Tenth Corps.

4. Perhaps Taylor is referring to the capture of Colonel Horace C. Lee, 27th Massachusetts Infantry, at Drewry's Bluff on May 16, 1864. He was exchanged on September 12, 1864, and received a brevet promotion to brigadier general on March 13, 1865.

5. Sherman's frontal assault at Kennesaw Mountain on June 27 failed to dislodge the Confederates. He then resorted to maneuver and forced them to abandon the position. In early July a Confederate corps commanded by Lieutenant General Jubal Early crossed into Maryland and by July 11 had reached the outskirts of Washington. Arriving Union troops forced him to withdraw, and he crossed back into Virginia on July 14. Confederates would not abandon Atlanta until September 1.

Hd Qrs 22n Iowa Inft
4 miles N.W. of Washington
Aug 2n 1864
Dear Catharine Cyrus Mary & little ones

I again set down again to write you. We lay at the front of our lines at Bermuda Hundred until 3 oclock on Sunday morning when orders came for us to be ready to March in an hour. We accordingly got ready and marched 7 miles back to the landing and embarked on the Steamer Winona for Washington D.C. where we arrived last Evening. We landed and marched up to the capitol and from there to the Barracks where we halted Stacked arms and partook of a cooked supper at the Soldiers Rest, the first supper we have had prepared for us since we came into the service.[1] We lay there all night. The Bugle sounded the assembly and we file in and marched on the Tauney town Road and encamped where we now lay while I write this. There is a rumour that 48,000 rebles are at Rockvill 10 miles from here intending to attack Washington but for the truth of it I can not vouch.[2] There seems to be no apprehensions here that there is any danger and I think myself that the number of rebs would not be permitted to remain long in this vicinity if they should be so bold as to come. I suppose they have burned Chambersburg but the force that done that was a small party of Cavalry and skedaddled as soon as they committed their depredations.[3] Grant had a hard fight at Petersburg on saturday and after blowing up one Fort and taking two lines of the Rebb works had to fall back to his original lines with a loss of 200 killed and 100 wounded. This was oweing to his reinforcements not comeing up in time to keep the rebles from massing their force on him and he was compelled to get behind his breast works to protect his men. Burnsides corps was the only one engaged and was on the extreme left. I suppose the attack was made more for the purpose of ascertaining the situation of the Rebs than with an expectation of forcing their lines or else the attack would have been made along the whole lines at once.[4] But I guess Grant knows what he is about and I think you will soon hear of another Flank movement for the purpose of compelling the Reb Army to fall Back so as he can invest the whole army at the same time. He lay seige to Richmond. He got about 400 prisoners on Friday and Saturday. We can take care of the rebles now north of Richmond and I think they will do well. If they ever get back again I expect we will have a hard time of it. For the Genl has ordered every thing to be left that is not actually nescessary and officers and men have left every thing behind but a change of clothes and their Havarsacks. We lay on the ground without tents or cover and have one days rations with us at a time. I am in good health and feel as if I could march 30 miles per day if we could catch the rebbs by so doing. I have not time to give you a description of things here but I will try to do it as soon as I get to a place where I can write. The weather is quite hot but we have good water and the air is fresh so that we do not suffer so much with the heat as we did on Red River. The Springs here are delightfull and to get to drink out of one seems like old times. Kiss the little ones for me and receive all my love for yourselves. I hope the war will come to a close where I can once more clasp you all in the embrace of affection. I have had no letter from you for 2 weeks and feel as if I would like one. So farewell.

yours affty

Taylor

1. Taylor is possibly referring to the Soldiers Home that had been opened by Amy Bradley of Maine. The home usually provided tea, coffee, chocolate, music, and magazines to soldiers in Washington.

2. On the morning of July 31 the 22nd Iowa was ordered to sail for Washing-

ton and arrived there at noon, August 1. The next day it encamped at Tennallytown in the Georgetown area of Washington. The rumor of Confederates in Rockville was false.

3. On July 30 approximately 2,800 Confederate cavalrymen under the command of Brigadier General John McCausland looted and then burned the center part of Chambersburg.

4. On July 30 a division from Major General Ambrose Burnside's corps attacked after a mine had been exploded under the Confederate line. In the battle of the Crater, the Union army sustained 3,798 casualties and the Confederates about 1,500. The Union forces had to withdraw after the botched attack.

> Head Quarters 23d Iowa Infty
> Camp near Tamelly Town. Md. Aug 7th 64
> Dear Catharine and all the rest

This pleasant Sabbath I again set down to write you a few lines about myself and the news in general.

1st then I am in good health and in good heart. We are Encamped about 4 miles from Washington on the Frederick Road and have been ever since we come up from Bermuda Hundred. The 2n Division of the 19th Army Corps is all encamped here awaiting the movements of the Rebles in the Shanandoah Valley and the Valley of the Cumberland. We do not know much of the movements of the Rebs. It was reported yesterday that they had taken Hagarstown and that the forageing parties had raised the Black Flag and again this morning we hear that they have evacuated Hagarstown and are in full retreat up the Potomac towards Harpers Ferry. I do not know wheather any of these reports are true but I suppose there is some grounds for a part of them at least.[1] I do not know what we are going to do but I think we will not do much of anything but call up Govt Rations and draw our pay. For it seems to me that the only thought of the majority of our commanders who are not imediately under the control of Grant is to do just as little as they can and blow in proportion to make it up. We have 25,000 men now in this Corps who might have made a hasty advance towards Frederick and either captured the rebles or have driven them out of Md. and Pa.[2] But instead of that we marched out here and sat down and have done nothing since but eat and sleep and put on style. I think I can discover the reason why the army of the Potomac has been so ineficient or so much less sucessfull than the western army. It is this. The Army itself is made up of the most doless and worthless part of the Population and the officers are men of the fine haired milk and water kind either out of some law office where they had been setting for two or three years trying to get hold of an Idea, or else some clerk from behind a dry goods counter whose only thought was to oil their mustache and show their silly selves to some sillier young lady. And not succeeding in any of these, they have succeeded through the influence of friends in getting just what they ought not to have—commissions in the army. And instead of doing any good for their country they are positively a great disadvantage to it generally being too effeminate to endure the fatigues of camp and too cowardly to engage in the bloody conflict where it takes both muscle and nerve for a man to succeede. On the other hand the western Armys are drawn from the bone and sinue of the Population and the officers generally chosen for their ability are both able and willing to endure the fatigues and discomforts of a camp life to win for themselves a name and for their country a victory. Since we have come into this department I can See through it all and I tell you whatever of benefit the government will obtain by war she will have to look to her western army for it. Our Regt and the Eastern Regts do not associate togather at all and if any disturbance would get up among the men the fight would become general with both Officers and men. We are ordered to be ready to march with 2 days cooked rations and have stored our mess boxes and tents in Washington and are lying out here without anything to sleep under or to cook with excep what we can carry with us and are not trying to do one d—d bit of good. It makes me mad. If we were on the march and did not wish to be encumbered with a train I would not say a word but Grant allowed us more to do with while we were taking Vicksburg and the men at the Front now are better fixed than we are although they are liable to fight at any minute. While we lay 4 miles from the seat of government not doing anything must do without our comforts because an old spooney of Batchelor General wills it so. We wonder he never got a wife and if the Government wishes to save her men she had better dismiss him for such men could not keep an army together to make a fight if they had all the men in the union.[3] However I think it will be a good thing for me that we have got under him for I will not see any fighting while he commands us and I am smart enough to keep myself comfortable and so I think I will not complain for fear I may have something to do. But let others do what they have too and do as little as I can get along with while I am under such officers.

Now I want you to write. I have not had a letter for 3 weeks and am getting anxious about you when I know that I ought to get an answer from you in 7 days. I want to know if you got the cloths and the $100 I sent from Orleans. The cloths were sent from Baton Rouge. I wish Cyrus to get me a tin Box made to carry my rations in as we have no chest with us any more and I like to have my things in some kind of order. I will give a draft of the box and the way I wish it made on another piece of paper and when the box is done I want you to fill it with good fresh butter and send it to me by express and some more good things if you have them for I feel as if I would like to have a good meals victuals once more. Our govt fare is too strong for me and as I sent all my money home except $10 and things are so high that I can not afford to buy anything and feel hungry. I wrote to Rachel a few days since and am looking for an answer from her soon. I want to know how you are all getting along and how the children are and what you are going to do with them this winter. I think you had better not send them to school through the cold weather but keep them at home and let them learn their lessons over well. For it is better to know a little well than a great deal half well. I must stop. Kiss them for me and tell them to be good children. I will write in a few days again.

> I am affty thine
> Taylor

1. In early July Confederates had demanded $20,000 from the citizens of Hagerstown or the town would be burned. They received the money and moved on. No southern soldiers were there in early August. By the date of this letter Early was south of the Potomac near Bunker Hill.

2. At the end of August 1864 the Nineteenth Corps had 14,645 men present for duty.

3. Brigadier General Cuvier Grover commanded the Second Division, Nineteenth Army Corps. In August 1864 he was a bachelor, but he married on August 1, 1865. After the death of his first wife, he remarried on January 28, 1875. He was brevetted major general for service at Winchester and Fisher's Hill and at the end of the war commanded the District of Savannah. He remained in the army after the war.

[Probably an August 7, 1864, enclosure to Cyrus]
Cyrus

I want the Box about the size of this piece of Paper Rounded off at the upper corners and 2½ thick the lid closing and forming one of the sides. The compartments I want made in number and for the purposes as designated in the draft. The size you can determine when you measure the size of the box and can then divide it to suit. The compartments I should not think ought to be more than 3 by 2½ and as high as they will make when divided in two tiers after one inch is taken off the top for the knife and fork spoon.

[Diagram: boxes drawn for pepper, salt, tea, sugar, coffee, rice, flour]

Now I want a tight box with a good tight lid to fit into Each of these compartments so that there will be no possibility for the things to be come mixed. The pepper and salt box can be made with a partition in the box and can be the same size of the coffee Box and will fit one compartment. I want the main lid to shut over the box and a catch to fasten it with so that it will not come open among my clothes. The little Boxes ought to have a wire ring in the side of each to lift them out. Cy I want the lids put on the little boxes so that when the main box sits on its bottom the lids will be on top as that will be the position I will have to carry it in. I also wan two turn loops put on the bottom so that I can run straps through and if I have to leave my knapsack I can strap it on my back and go it the small box to put the meat in. You can put the lid on either the side or on one edge. If it is tight it will make no difference.

I wish the main lock to fasten at the bottom with wire hinges so that it will not be comeing off as it would if only fit on without being fastened with hinges. You know as well as I can tell you how it ought to be made all but the size and that I have stated, about the size of ½ a sheet of foolscap paper. When you go to express it if you can Send it in a box of saw dust and can fill it with butter and some other little things. I would like it very much as we do not get much here but Hard tack and sowbelly and I am tired of them. Write to me soon and I will keep you posted. I am going to be at home this winter or when ever this campaign is over. So farewell.

Your Taylor

Direct your letter to 22n Iowa Inft

1 Brigd 2 Div 19 A C

Washington D.C.

Express the same way. I suppose the agent can tell you more than I can about it.

Head Quarters 22n Iowa

Washington D.C. Aug 13/64

Dear Catharine

I set down to write a few lines this evening as we are under marching orders and will move by daylight to-morrow morning. Our destination is the Shanandoah Valley.[1] I received 2 letters from home yesterday the latest July 19th.[2] I was glad to hear from home but I am disappointed that I have no news from home. By the northern rout most of the boys have letters from home in 6 days and I wrote to you 3 weeks since notifying you that I would be in Virginia and have written 3 letters since. I hope however I will get one yet before we leave here.

I do not know what we are going to do in the Valley but I reckon we will help Sheridan clear out the vally. I understand we are to report to Monocacy Junction when I will write again. I wish you to let me know wheather you have got the money I sent to you from Orleans and the clothes from Baton Rouge. It seems that clothes are so high at the stores that it will take a great deal of money to buy what thee wants this fall so I think I will try and send thee enough of old clothes home to cloth the boys and make undercloths for thee and Sallie. Of course you will have to buy shoes and calico and will be compelled to pay the price for them but you can get along without buying so much if I can send you some although somewhat worn. Yet it will be almost as good as new.

I am glad that thee is teaching the children for I think that by so doing thee can not only learn them but improve thyself and the little things will not see so much vice and ill behavior as they would at a public school.[3] And I wish them to kept as clear of such scenes while they are young as they can be. I think that if they can be taught to the benefit of virtue now in their youth their natural good sence will protect them as they come to a mature age. I am truly glad that Cyrus is getting fixed up so well and I wish thee to let him have all the money thee can spare to assist him. I will have about $10 the next payday and I think that you can get yourselves nicely fixed up for winter. I intend to pay you a visit this winter if the rebles will give me time and I want to have a good time of it. I want Mary to write me. I have been waiting a long time for her letter but still it does not come. I got a letter from Edith McConnell yesterday.[4] She wrote me a very nice letter and reminded me of the years that have gone down the vale of past very forcibly. She seems to have had troubles too. She has lost the most of her little ones and feels sorry for their loss.

If Cyrus gets in the notion of traveling he can come down to Washington this fall and see me. I would be so glad to see him. Well I must close. When you direct your letters send them to 22n Iowa 2 Brigade 2 Division 19 A.C. Washington. If you Express anything to me you had better ask the Express agent how to direct it and then send to the care of Cap Mullins. Kiss the little ones for me and give my love to all.

Affty thine

Taylor

1. On August 14 the 22nd Iowa began its march to join the forces of Major General Philip A. Sheridan in the Shenandoah Valley. It met Sheridan's men near Charleston on August 18 and went into camp about seven miles from that town. After two days the regiment moved to Halltown.

2. This is probably Catharine's letter of July 17.

3. Ladies' magazines in the mid-nineteenth century stressed women's importance in three areas: child rearing, spiritual teaching, and domestic pursuits. Women were to be the "protector and teacher of the young and . . . the guardian of society's morals" and, as such, were performing a valuable function. Home schooling was often required because the demand for teachers exceeded the supply, and schools were often closed during the war. In many cases teaching was left to the family, particularly to the mother. The extent of Catharine's education is unknown, but it was not uncommon for mothers to have as much education as the children they were teaching. Taylor obviously believed that Catharine would have the best moral influence on their children and that she could impart the essentials of education to them. His comment about improving herself may indicate that she did not have much formal education.

4. This letter was not found.

Des Moines Aug 21 1864

Dear Brother

It is some time since I have written to thee. I have had a verry buisey summer and feel weak and feeble this summer. I wrote a long letter to thee after I got better from haveing the measles. If thee ever got it thee never mentioned it in any of thy letters. Catherine and the children are well and going visiting to Clarks to day. The children do not go to school now. Their mother thought it best to keep them at home during the warm weather. Sallie and Ellis had the chicken pox this summer. That is all the sickess they have had. They all grow verry fast. Ellis runs every whare. He is a short little thing but knows every thing that is said to him and can say nearly everything. In his way he has a violent temper but it is soon over. Sallie and Frank are good children, generly obey all I say to them and I try to learn them good behaveyour and good principals. I never want to see them grow up so uncouth and ill mannerd as the Milner children used to be. I think that Frank is inteligent and if he is trained up with good principals he will make a good man. If not he will make a verry bad one. Sallie is a very effectionate child to me. Always seems anxious that I should feel well and I hope to see her a good virtuous woman and that will be better than riches. For riches is but a bubble which may burst at any time and vanish but virtue will render the possesser happy here and hereafter.

Cyrus is better this summer than he has been in a great while. He had a spell of asthma some time ago but did not last so long as it used to do. He is building a house for a war widdow by the name of Hobbs below Vans house. He expects to raise it next week. We have got our house all finished except the bannesters to the stairs and the cornish [cornice] on the outside. We have been secureing the bank this summer and I think the river will never incroach on us any more. It may come in the first story but we have got the house banked up higher than the watter ever raised since we come here. I am better contented now than I have been since I left Mount Airy. I think see a chance to live and pay our debts I suppose.

*   *   *

Thee will see quite a change in Des Moines when thee comes back between Old faces and niew buildings. We have nine men at this time and so thee must understand that I have a plenty to do with no help but Ann. But her sister come on last thursday from England and I am going to keep her awhile till I get rested and see if I will not feel better. I got my likeness taken yesterday. I have been waiting till I would get a little more fleshy but now my face has all come out now and so it is a poor looking thing. But I thought if I waited for my hair to grow thee would be at home. At least I hope thee will.

Catherine wished me to say that she has got that [horse?] all right. She says she wrote thee last sunday all about money matters so I will not repeat today. I had a letter from Anne Mary Gibson yesterday.[1] She wrote that John Taylor and John Morris both had been shot by the rebles and John Taylors boddy had been taken by the rebbels.

*   *   *

Rachel wrote[2] that they had received fourty dollars from the meeting. If I had money of my own I would send it to her but Cyrus always has so much to say bout my relations robbing him that I do not like to send her money. It is a great trouble to me to think that she is in want after a life of industry and toil. She had an unfortunate disposition but she could not help that. She had many virtues. Rachel writes that Thomas and Gardner Furniss have become perfect sotts. The gass works are on second street and is full view from this place. They say the cost of the consern will be over fifty thousand dollars. Rollins is building a large paper mill down towards the fair ground. Given is building a plough shop on his lot near his old blacksmith shop.

I want thee to write me a good long letter. Thee has been in the army two years and has never written me yet. I always see Catherines letters but I want one of my own, a good long letter. I must close. Please write soon. We feel anxious now since thee has gone to Virginia. Catherine and the children sends their love. I remain as ever affectionate sister

Mary

1. This letter was not found.
2. This letter was not found.

Des Moines Aug 28th 1864
Dear Taylor
I sit down to write this beautiful afternoon to say we are all well and in good heart. Nothing to interrupt our happyness but thy being so far

away from us and not hearing from thee this week. But we will wait in hopes that we will get a letter in few days and it will be good news of thee being well and all right. Mary wrote to thee last sunday and I went a visiting to Mrs Clarks and had a nice time. And I expect that M gave thee a better letter than I could and her likeness with it. We have thy box made and ready to send all but the butter. It is hard to get a bit of good butter at this time as we do not make any ourselves. We have but two Cows this summer and they do not make much not half what the family takes. They have 8 boarders and two girls besides me and the children so thee may think there is a pritty good family of in all. Olever White and his brother in law Isaca Paxson is here now but they will leave in a week or two as they have rented Squir Youngs house and are looking for their family's on here in a short time and we will have some old acquatances near to us. But Dear Taylor I feel so lone some with out thee that it do not seem to make much differance who comes or gos. If I am in my room with our children and them good I am as well off as I want to be untill thee gets home. Taylor I can not think of any thing new to say to day and I do not know what I will fill up the sheet with. For I must confess that I do not know much that would be worth writing to thee for the war news are not of the kind that I want to hear for I want hear of some great victory and have it done with. And as to Politics there is nothing of the kind that amounts to anything. The Cops are trying to get a candidate but whether they will get one or it is not known yet. Some thinks there will be warm times at election time this fall but I think that Governor Stone has taken precausion in time to prevent any disturbance or any that will amount to any thing. For his late proclamation forbids any of the refugees from Mo comeing in to this state to work up strife by pretending to be Union men and are nothing but Cops at last and would come here to get away from their just deserts in Mosurri. I will not say home for that they have forfited when they first raised the hand of treason. Well I have got this sheet all most full and I will stop and see what Sallie will have to say Monday. Well I wated to see what Sallie had to say so will have to explain about Ellis. His face and head has been sore the most of the time for the last six months and we are geting afraid that it is something of Scrofula[1] but we do not say positively that it is. And about thy box. I will get it filled to day and have it ready to send out to morrow morning. We are all in good health and heart and doing well. If thee dose get the chance to get away from the army thee might as well go to see Rachel as come home for it would not be so far and thee would be as well off with the exception of seeing us. But that would hardly pay to come so far for all the time thee could stay. So farewell at present. I remain forever thine.

> Catharine

1. Scrofula is a swelling in the neck glands.

> Des Moines City Aug 28 1864
> Dear Father

It is with greate pleasure that I take my pen in hand to let thee know that we are all well. I have been to Sunday School to day. The last time I wrote thee I would send thee one of Sunday school papers. I will send it in the tin box. Bless his Dear old soul. Anns sister has com over from England. Ann sister works here and Ann too. Skatie Slow is Heere today. We have been having a fine time of it. We have six borders now. We did have eight but tow left. It is five o clock. Aunty has gone down to get super. I have been haveing a fine time with [Hartly?] thiss afternoon. The tin box that we got for thee cot five dollars. I want thee to Send me some poetry the next leters thee sends me. It has been a very warm affter noon but it is cool now. It seems like evry body was out thiss affternoon. Skatie is geting in a Hurry to go home but She is wating for me to go a peice with her. Ellis is got the scarfula under chin and back of his ear. I have got a new trunk and a new doll head. Frank is as he ever the ever was. Isaac Pacson and oliver white bords here. I have but three lines moore so I must close. I am youre affectionate daughter.

> Sallie A Peirce

> Head Quarters 22n Iowa Inft
> Charleston Va Aug 30/64
> Dear Catharine and the rest

I set down to write a few lines as things are somewhat more quiet than they have been for a week past. I am well and in good heart for the cause of the Union. On last Sunday night week the rebles made an advance on our division. They had been fighting all day on our right the sixth corps and the cavalry being engaged the 8th Corps and the 19th being held in reserv or at least not being engaged.[1] About 12 o clock we were ordered to retreat towards Harpers Ferry which we did travelling all night. We arived at Bolivar Heights and formed our line of battle about daylight. In a few minutes the Rebs advanced their line through Charleston and formed their line about 2½ mils from ours and there stoped and we lay confronting each other in line of battle untill Wednesday. Our Regiment was sent out on the front and about noon some more of our Brigade was sent out to attack them. After a sharp little fight the rebs run and we fell back into our Breast works. On Friday another attack was made to feel them in which we suceeded in running them again and captured their picket line. All this time Gen Custar was fighting their force that rested on the Potomac.[2] And on Saturday we prepared to make a final and simultaneous attack on them all along the lines but on moving our forces out to the Front we found the rebles had left in the night. So there was no fight that day. On Saturday Sheridan sent out scouts to find them and on Sunday morning we started after them and the cavalry fought them on Sunday. And yesterday they tried to bring on a Genl engagement but the rebs smelt a mice and would not advance on us. On sunday the Cavalry drove the rebs to Bruce Town about 10 miles from Bolivar in a South west course. On yesterday the tried to get them to follow them up as they fell back on our main line which we had formed about 2 miles south of Charleston our left resting on the Shenandoah and the right extending about 7 or 8 miles over towards Martinsburg. But as soon as our Brigade of Inft advanced to attack them they fell back and since that time there has been no fighting.[3] Nor do I think the rebles have ever stoped although it is not safe to advance the army without knowing where they are as they have a very large force and if they were to get us at a disadvantage they might make us pay for it. We fortify as we go and will give them fits if we can get a fight out of them. We are living fine. We have fresh beef and all the fruit and green corn that we want but we are enduring a good bit of fatigue and exposure. After marching all night on sunday night we went to work and throwed up 7 miles of breast works and was in them by noon. And since we stoped here night before last we have another line of equal length nearly paralell to the first and about 6 miles from it. We have no tents nor cooking utensils with us. We roast our meat on the coals and make coffee in our tin cups. Our Books papers and all Equipage are left behind so you may know that we mean fight. The 24 & 28 Iowa are here and I see some of my friends every day. I have had no letter since the date of Aug 2[4] but I got 2 by the way of Orleans since I wrote. I find you do not wish me to reinlist so I will not do it. You gave me up to do what I conceived to be my duty and I will try to gratify you the rest of my life. I hope that we will spend many happy years togather yet and I am certain if spared the evening of life will be like the close of the summer day. Marys letter. I received one from her I think at Baton Rouge and think I spoke of it at the time. I want her to write any how. My love to all. Kiss the little ones for me.

> Taylor
> I will write the children a letter as soon as this campaign is over.

1. The Eighth Corps was also known as the Army of West Virginia and the West Virginia Corps. It was commanded by Major General George Crook.

2. Brigadier General George Armstrong Custer commanded the First Brigade, First Cavalry Division. He graduated from West Point in 1861 and would be killed at the battle of Little Big Horn on June 25, 1876.

3. In mid-August Early moved north in the Shenandoah Valley to threaten the Baltimore and Ohio Railroad, which ran south to the Potomac River. On August 21 Early attacked Sheridan near Charleston. Neither the Eighth nor the Nineteenth Corps was involved. Sheridan retreated a few miles to Halltown. On August 25, Union cavalry encountered a Confederate division near Shepherdstown. During the battle, Custer's cavalry brigade was forced to retreat across the Potomac River. Early fell back to Bunker Hill, and the 22nd Iowa returned to the vicinity of Charleston. Skirmishing continued for the next several days.

4. This letter was not found.

Des Moines Sep 1st 1864
Dear Taylor

It is with sprites revived in deed that I sit down to write to thee this evening for I receved two letters to day. And we are all well was in good heart and times are good for C and Mary. Isaac Paxson and Oliver Whites familys are here and the house is full from the top to the bottom and we are haveing a good time. That thee may depend on.

I have nothing new to write of only that the Cops have nominated G B McClellan for the presidency[1] and are going to try it on a war man. But I hope they will come out like they did in Iowa last fall with thair war man for Gov.[2] Thee seems to want to know about the children. Well I have writen thee all about them very often and why thee do not get the letters is strange. I write for I have not mist a week this summer only last and then Mary wrote and sent her likeness and gave thee a full acount of all thee doing at home. Or at least I expect she did or she said she was going to. Ellis has got so he can talk some and the children kep him talking every day saying papa and calling thee to come home and all such words. Frank is learning very fast now and can read some and spells very well for a child of his age. I think he will make a life top speller or at least better than ever any of my family was. Sallie learns well too. She is good at geograpy and is geting on with her Arithmatic and read I think very well. I think she get along slower with her writeing than any thing else. Well Taylor I have sent a Box to thee by the way of Washington and in the care of Col Graham with Agent. Director it to the 22d Reg Iowa Vol 2 Brag 2d Div of the 19th AC so thee may get it through Col Graham. I suppose the Agent thought it would be best to send in care of some officer that would have power to get it and so I left it to him to direct. Well I must stop for the house is full of children and we can hardly hear themselves think. I have three and Isaac Paxson has three and Oliver has four though one of thairs is twentyone years old and I ought not say she was a child on at least one that makes a noise. All that I want to make me supremely happy for thee to be here at the present time. Well Ellis wants to go to bed and I will have to say good by for this time. I remain forever thine.

    Catharine A Peirce

   1. The Democrats nominated Union general George B. McClellan to oppose Lincoln in the 1864 presidential election. McClellan was nominated on a platform that called for an armistice and negotiations to end the war. His views, though, were ambivalent, for he also proclaimed the need for a military victory.

   2. The election for Iowa governor was between Republican William M. Stone and Democrat James M. Tuttle, whom Republicans claimed was a Copperhead. Stone won with 60.5 percent of the popular vote.

Head Quarters 22n Iowa Inft
Camp in the Field Near Charleston Va Sep 2 64
My Dear Sister

I received thy letter and likeness 2 days since and as all is quit along the lines this morning I concluded to spend the day writing thee a letter.

I am well and in good spirits. We are encamped about 1½ miles south west of Charleston Louden Country Virginia. This is the place where John Brown was living.[1] We came out here and formed in line of battle expecting a fight on last sunday but the rbles retreated and we have been occupied in throwing up breast works and fortifications ever since we come here. On monday the cavalry went out and had a fight with the Jonies and tried to draw them on and we thought for a while that they would follow up untill we would get a fight out of them. But as soon as our infantry advanced on them they fell back and we have heard nothing from them ever since. I seen by the paper last night that Lee has ordered Gen Early Back to Richmond[2] and if so there is no chance for a fight in the Valley. But there is no telling what will turn up. One thing Genl Sheridan has a large army here and it is in the best condition of any army I have seen since Grants army crossed the Miss to take Vicksburg. I should think that there was 50 or 60,000 troops here from the length of lines.[3] Our Left rests on the Shanandoah and our Right extends away across the country 7 or 8 miles towards Martinsburg. Gen Averill is at the place or was and is now said to be advansing towards Winchester, where I think we will go.[4] This army is now preparing for one months campaign, but where it is to operate I can not tell. But you will be likely to see it in the papers when we move, and also where we are going. We are well fed, and well clothed, but we have had a hard time of it, not having any tents but what we carry. And the warm weather, and our load fatigued us very much, but I have stood it very well. Our boys shoots all the fresh pork they want and there is plenty of fruit in the valley so we live pretty well on fresh pork stewed apples and boiled corn.

I went out to the hill in rear of our line last Evening to take a look at the country. The sun was getting low and all things seemed to be at rest. I thought that I never seen so beautiful a country. On the South stands the Blue Ridge rearing its peaks far above the Valley. And Streaching away off towards the North East is lost to view towards Carlisle Pa. on the North is seen the Spurs of the Alleghany. While laying like the land of rest is the beautifull valley of Virginia with its Villages and farms with all the appliances of wealth and luxury. The scene reminded me of the old lines of Gronger [Grongar] Hill.[5]

The fountain falls The River is flow
The woody valleys warm and low
The windy summit wild and high
Roughly rushing on the sky,
The pleasant seat the tower wind
The naked Rock the shady bower
The town and village dome and farm
Each gives each a double charm

It is certainly a very just description of the country we are now in. The land has been heavily timbered and has been cleared out for the farmes, leaving the whole face of the country covered with skirts of timber, and many of the farms have been fitted up in a style of luxury and comfort that I have seen no where in the south. The villages are scattered over the country 2 or 3 miles apart and the most of them have a church spire rising above the surrounding trees which gives the landscape a most beautiful appearance. Add to this the encampments of the different brigades and regiments, with their millitary arrangements. It was a sight that was well worth seeing and one which I never expect to see the like of again. The army lays in two lines about 200 yards apart. Their little tents and their banners, and flags shining in the sun makes the lover of his country feel indeed as if this was a nation and a country worth risking his life for. Dear Sister I have now been soldering over two years and have endured many privations but I would willingly endure them over again and serve 2 years longer if by so doing I could bring peace to this unhappy country and establish a government that would protect the rights of my children. I have always felt that the rebellion could be crushed if the proper means was used and the people of the north would unite in the effort but it seems to me that selfishness has taken the place of Patriotism in the heart of many men in the north. Cowardice and averice is the leading principles with such men and I am sorry to see so many of our people so given up to two of the most degrading feeling that can centre in the breast of man.

Sep 10th. Dear Sister I was taken off the other night very unexpectedly. When it got so dark that I had to quit writing all was quiet, and things seemed to look as if we would not move for some days. But about midnight I was awakened by the quick rattle of the drum, beating the call for the orderlys to repair to head Quarters to receive orders. On arriving there I got orders to have every thing packed up and have the Co in line at 3 oclock with 3 days rations in our haversacks. We got in line and took up our line of march about daybreak. We marched untill afternoon and stoped hear Berryvill about 12 miles from Winchester. That Evening the Rebles movd down from Winchester to take possession of Snickers gap not knowing that we had got between them and that place. While our army was preparing to encamp for the night their advance guard came up to our pickets and supposing that it was only a small detachment they attacked them at once and drove our pickets in. As soon as the lines could be formed the 8th corps advanced and attacked the rebs with such fury that they had to give away leaving some 470 prisoners in our hands and some 300 dead on the field. By this time the night had set in and the fighting cesed. In the morning we fell back ½ mile and threw up works expecting the rebs to attack us, but as soon as they had buried their dead they retreated and we have had no fighting here since. The regiment went out to Opoquon [Opequon] River the other day but had no engagement. However they found the Rebs there in force and then came back to camp and we are now laying behind our breast works not doing much of anything.[6]

The 8th Corps movd from our left over to our right yesterday and now while I write we hear artillery firing off in that direction. I suppose that they have run across some of the Jonies and are trying a few of Old Abes compliments on them. I do not think there will be any General Engagement soon. Genl Averile attacked Imboden[7] on the 7th and whiped him and cut him with a considerabl force off from his main body and it may be that it is their forces that are engaged to day. For from the sound it is nothing more than a Skirmish or reconoisance. Our Train was brought up to us this morning and we have got some paper and a wagon sheet to stretch up to shelter us and feel quite at home. It is Saturday and there is nothing doing but cleaning up and I have seized this quiet to finish up this letter. I am afraid that it will not be much of a letter for the roar of Artillery and the confusion of a camp is not calculated to give flow to a mans ideas, but I will try to write something that will be new to thee. If not new at least readable. I received a letter from Catharine and Sallie yesterday and am looking for another one soon. I am glad to hear that Cyrus has his health so well this summer and that you are getting along so well. I hope after all the vicissitudes of life you will have a comfortable home to end your days in and may yet feel the contentment that a life of industry is sure to bring at the close. For my part I have made no calculations for fear the future feeling certain that if I do right and what I know to be my duty I will be cared for by him who attends to all. I feel it to be my first duty to help put down the Rebellion that whatever I or my children may have we may be protected in the enjoyment of it. If I get through these trials safe I can begin the world again as easily as I have done it before. Although I am beginning to get up in years yet I feel as fresh and vigorous as I did at 20. And I believe my health is better. It seems as if my children were going to be good and will be a scource of great comfort and will be a help to me in the future.

When I look back and see what I have passed through it seem to me that the catelogue of ill fortune must be well nigh spent and I look forward with hope to a brighter and better future. I have lived to learn that Dollars and cents will make no man happy or virtuous but is very likely to destroy both. I think that industry and economy is both right and necessary and by a just observance of both a man can easily have a competency. I am of the opinion that there is nothing so condusive to happiness and usefullness as a good education. I have never felt the insufficiency of my own education so much as I have since I came into the army and if I live I will try to remedy the thing by giving my children an education if they have intellect enough to receive one.

We have notice of the fall of Atlanta. The Soldiers is in high glee and if a man would come here withe the proposition of peace as advocated by the Chicago platform[8] he would have to get out of camp. All good soldiers are in for Lincoln and a peace on honorable terms but have no notion of voting for a platform that ignores the great principles for which they have contended for 3 years. We have no Mc-Cllelland men in our company and but few in the Regt. All the Mc men are the Irish and are the poorest soldiers we have. No good soldier will be found in the Democratic ranks. I want you to write me how the victory at Atlanta is received by the Cops in Iowa and what the feeling is then for peace. I hope our friends will not advocate a peace merely for the sake of those in the army who may be dear to them, and only propose such terms as may preserve the whole Union and the extinction of slavery. For I tell you no Soldier wishes peace on any other terms. If we are to accept peace on the Chicago Platform there is no soldier that could ever be honoured for any thing he had done. But for all time he and his would be looked upon as abettors and aiders in an unholy war and would be branded with the appellation of Robber and murderer. So far too as the principle is concerned. If we acknowledge the seperate sovereignty of the States we at once break up the Government for so soon will the west secede from the East and the different interests will cause disputes and the whole thing will be come one vast field of anarchy. I had not intended to have made a political letter out of this but I fell into it and have taken up nearly a whole sheet with it. My mind dwells on what it is most interested in. I hardly know what to write about to fill up this sheet. Sallie wished me to write her some poetry. I suppose the dear little thing thinks because I have made some doggeral rymes and sent home for their gratification that I can write poetry. I wish thee to try and explain to her the differance between ryme and poetry and make her understand the principles of poetical Ideas. Many things that are written in prose have more poetry in them than what is wrote in ryme. I have thought that if she once could reason and see what great difference there was in the way that different writers have of expressing themselves that she had Ideality enough to appreciate it, and may be would learn to express her self with approporateness and maybe with elegance. I have often noticed her admiring certain passages in any thing she was reading that was really beautifull and have hoped that her mind might be led on to partake of the same notion. I doubt very much whether her reading anything I would write would be any benefit to her except in the way of advice and satisfy her afection for me. Tell her I will try and write her something but the Military Camp is not much of a place to write anything very smart or very good. The Dear little things I long to see them and indeed I long to see you all for it seems to me that all of earth is centred arround your household.

My affections seems to be cut loose from all the rest of the human family and have fastened themselves on you. I have lost all care for any others worldly success but Cyrus's and thine and Catharine and my children. Often when I lay awake in the night my mind wanders back to the days that are past. All the Shadows that rise take the same shape and yours are the shapes that continually pass before my mind. Oh that this war was at an end that I might once more be with you. I think I would try to make it more pleasant than I ever knew how to make it before.

I have seen much of life, of its joys and sorrows. Which has predominated I can hardly say. I have been unfortunate and rendered unhappy in my worldly affairs but I have been verry happy in the affections of a home. And whatever I have suffered has been counterballanced by the knowledge that there were those that had an affection for me that poverty or misfortune could not chill.

I am well in health although cross somewhat with the fatigues of the Summers campaign (which has been one of incessant activity since the 1st of May,) and am not so fleshy as I usually am, and am very thankfull that you approve of my course during this struggle. For if I knew that my conduct was not approved at home it would render the trials much harder to bear. As it is I feel cheerful and as contented as could be expected.

I have been traveling round some in the last few day taking a look at the country. This is truly a place to awaken thought of times past. The grand old woods, the mountains in the distance with their rocks and rugged peaks carrys one back to the times when the red man walked through the groves and traversed the mountains the owner of all he could see. The Eagle wheeling o'er his head Proclaimed that all around was free. But alas, the mind will imediately come from the thought of perfect freedom to the State of Slavery that has existed here between that period and the present. And it at once becomes oppressed with the conviction that the nation is now paying out in blood for the sins it has permitted to lay and fester around this most beautifule part of Gods earth. When I come to think and reflect that the nation has permitted and assisted in that most iniquitous institution I do not wonder at the Rivers of blood that has been shed and the lives destroyed to make a just attonement for its crimes. For it is a law of nature that every convulsion must have it corresponding revulsion and I hardly see when the great sin will be washed away.

Well I must quit moralizing and close my letter. I want thee and Cyrus to both write. It is not because I have not thought of either of you that I have not written you seperate letters but because I wrote to Catharine every week. And when I wrote I wrote for the information of you all and I always wrote all I knew so that it seemed as if I would not be able to write anything more without putting something in that would be of no account. I wrote Catharine last Wednes and she will get it before you get this and it will tell you more about our fight so I will not repeat it. Give each of the Children a kiss for me and tell me when you write about Elliss's scrofula or what ever else it is. I feel very gratefull to both Cyrus and thee for the care and trouble you take with them to try and make them respectable and virtuous and to render them comfortable while so many brave soldiers familys are not so well taken care of that are doing their duty as well as I am and under far more trying circumstances. Receive my sincere affection. And give my love to all my friends.

> I remain thy ever afft Brother
> Taylor

1. After the attack at Harpers Ferry, Brown was incarcerated in the Charles Town jail. He was subsequently tried and executed in Charles Town, the county seat of Jefferson, not Loudoun, County.

2. Early did not return to Richmond, but one division, that of Major General Joseph B. Kershaw, began to return to Petersburg.

3. Sheridan had approximately 37,000 men available.

4. Brigadier General William W. Averell commanded a cavalry division in the Army of the Shenandoah. He defeated Early's cavalry on September 2 near Bunker Hill.

5. British poet John Dyer is the author of "Grongar Hill," which describes the landscape viewed from the hill.

6. At midnight on September 3 the 22nd Iowa, along with Sheridan's Sixth and Nineteenth Corps, was ordered to Berryville. That evening Early unexpectedly encountered the Union forces and, after a brief fight, retired to Winchester. Sheridan described casualties on both sides as "severe." The two armies remained near Berryville and Winchester until September 18.

7. Brigadier General John Imboden commanded a cavalry brigade under Early. A skirmish occurred with Averill's cavalry on September 7, but there are no official reports of casualties.

8. On August 29, 1864, the Democrats' national convention convened in Chicago. It passed a platform known variously as the "Peace Platform" and the "Chicago Surrender," which called for "cessation of hostilities . . . at the earliest possible moment." The convention nominated former Union general George McClellan for president. He then disavowed this plank.

Head Quarters 22 Iowa Inftry in the field near Berryville,
Va Sept 7th, 1864
Dear Catharine and all the rest

I have a little time to-day to write and take the opportunity of doing so for fear I will not have a chance for some time again. I am well but am pretty well worded out. I received Marys likeness in her letter on the 3rd of the month I believe[1] and was very glad to look on her lovd countenance once more if it was but a shadow. Her letter was very acceptable for the others have not reached me as regularly as they ought to owing to their having been directed to Bermuda Hundred. They have went down there and have been sent back. I got the one Catharine wrote since I got Marys. I commenced to write a long letter to Mary and got it about half done when it come night and I had to quit and thought I would finish it the next morning. But after I had got to sleep I suppose about 12 oclock I was roused by the drum beating the orderlys call and on repairing to Head Qtrs I received orders to pack up everything but what we could carry with 3 days rations in our Havarsacks and be ready to March at 3 oclock. So we packed up our things and loaded them on the wagons and sent them to Harpers Ferry and at daylight the whole army moved out of our camp near Charleston and took the direction of Winchester marching in 3 columns. Our Corps moved on the Berryvile pike the 8th corps on our left up the Shenandoah River and the 6th Corps to our right on the dirt road to Winchester. This was on Saturday morning. We met with no resistance untill we stoped for the night. The 8 corp arrived at Berryvile and are encamped and we encamped about 2 miles back and to the right and had got our supper. Was preparing to encamp for the night when all at once the Artillery of the 8th corps opened and the rattle of musketry told us the rebles was on us. It seem that the encountre was unexpected to both sides. The rebles was sending a Division of Inftry and some cavalry with 2 Batterys to occupy Snickers Gap and Berryville and knew nothing of our being there till they come up to our picket line which they thought was a detachment that they could drive back. But they did not drive very well.

The rebles charged and the Pickets fell back on the main line and then our boys turned on them and captured abot 450 persons 20 wagons and a lot of Small arms. We then moved out our Corps and attacked them but the night was so dark and the rebles fell back so that we had to Stop fighting for the night. But the rebles shelled us till after 9 oclock but done but little damage. I heard of one man being wounded. After 9 oclock all got quiet and we lay down in the rain with our arms under us to keep them dry untill morning. We expected a heavy battle with the coming day but the Rebee did not seem to wish to attack us. And as soon as the army was in position we commenced to throw up breast works and before noon we were so strongly entrenched that the rebles got scared out and began to retreat. They left a skirmish line and on Monday the 1st Division went out and drove them off. Since that time we have heard nothing more of them. Our loss in the whole fight will not exceede 200 in killed wounded and missing. The greater part of the loss was sustained by 3 companies of the 4th Virginia getting seperated from the main force in the dark and a great many of them were captured. The loss in killed and wounded will not exceed 100. The Reble loss is estimated 300 killed and wounded and 470 Prisoners in our hands.[2] This was near as I can learn the true state of the case. You will likely see some very different account of in the papers. Our Regiment is out to-day on a rconnoisance. I was going to go east with them but Col Graham seen I was tired out and would not let me go and so I am resting. This is the most fatiguing campaign that we have had since the Siege of Vicksburg. We have been up at 4 oclock every morning for 4 weeks and sometimes all night. We have no shelter but our little tents which are not so large as a sheet nor no thicker nor we have no cooking utencils with us but some little tin buckets to make coffee in and one or two little frying pans. So you see we are going it on a saving plan. We draw 3 days rations and have to make it do us 4. But we forage hogs apples and corn so that we live well enough. We have built 40 miles of breast works and have had 3 battles since we come into this vally. Our Regiment has been very fortunate. It has never been wher the brunt of the fighting was done and we have not lost a Man unless they loose some to-day. It is reported that Early is retreating towards Richmond. If this is true this campaign will soon close. The officers here say that as soon as this campaign is over we are to be sent back to the Mississippi. I do not know wheather there is any grounds for this surmise or not. I know that the Head Quarters of the 19th corps and 2 Divisions of it are still in Orleans and I also know that the 13 AC was only temporarily discontinued and I am of the oppinion that the 13th will be reorganized again as soon as the new levies are in the field. Well Atlanta is taken in spite of the carpings of the Cops and Peace party and Richmond will follow as sure as the sun shines and I think the Copperheads and McClelland will wilt in the November frost. I hope so at least. I think the confederacy is now in its last agonys and a few more doses of Doctor Lincoln pills will send it body and soul to where it ought to have been long since. I would write to you all a letter a piece but I have neither paper pen or ink nor the time to compose one worth anything at present if I had so. I do not want you to quit writing on that account. I think Cyrus might spare time to write a line once and a while for you have no idea how this marching fighting and working wears on the mind as well as the body and a few lines from the loved ones at home does a great deal to cheer me up and render me contented. Oh how I wish this thing was ended so that I could once more be with you and feel that the rights of the future generations was preserved and peace secured for all time. I will be at home sometime in November or December if nothing unusual occurs to prevent. The Officers all offer me a furlough and I have concluded to accept it although it will cost me a month ½ wages to come. Yet it may do me and you that much good.

I send my love to all and will write to Mary in answer to hers as soon as our things comes up to us. Kiss the little ones for me and tell them I am very happy to hear they are such good children and wish they may always remain so. This is a poor letter but it is the best I can do to-day.

I remain affty
Your Taylor

1. In her letter of August 21 Mary states that she had her likeness taken. This may be the letter to which Taylor is referring. No letter of September 3 was found, and it is doubtful that it could have reached Taylor by September 7.

2. See footnote 6, letter of September 2.

Head Quarters 22 Iowa Inft
Camp near Berryvile Va Sep 14th 1864
Dear Catharine,

I received thy letter of the 1st on the 12th and was glad to hear that thee was so happy and that you were all getting along so finely. I hope you will now have some society that you can mingle in without contaminating yourselves with so much of the trash and useless conversation so much used in the uninformed circles of the west. I mean no disparagement when I speak of the western society. But I mean this that the society in the west is made up on the basis of Dollars and cents and not in moral worth or intelect or General information. Hence it follows that at most of the social circles there is not often introduced subjects that tend to instruct or improve the minds. And I know that Pheobe White at one time was not only well informed but her mind was full of the beatics of literature and She appreciated highly the fine productions of the old writers. Wheather her age has interfered with her intelect I do not know but if it has not you can enjoy some intellectual treats with her on the beauties of Goldsmith Pope[1] and many other writers with which she was familiar. I only speak of this as my recollection of enjoying her Company so much when a boy. How the rest of them are I do not know.

I hope however thee will enjoy thyself much more pleasantly during my absence than thee has done before and not give up to dispondency even if I am in the army and in some danger of getting a Reble bullet through me which I hope will not be the case.

Well Kitty we are giving the Rebs the devil in the Shanandoah Valley. We have a fight with them nearly every day and we always manage to get the best of it. Our Cavalry went out yesterday and met the enemy at Berryvile crossing. The first they came to was about 40 cavalry which they succeeded in capturing. From these they learned that the 8 South Carolina Inft was on Picket not far from them. So they found out where they were and formed a line of battle and charged them capturing the whole Regiment and all its officers. Our loss was one man wounded.[2] About the same time the 8th Corps that has been out on our right had a fight with a detachment that was moving from Winchester to Bunker Hill and captured their artillery and about 600 prisoners. Their whole loss yesterday was about 1,000. Ours is very light. Not over 50 in all. I only heard of 3 killed.[3] The Rebs have lost in Killed wounded and prisoners since we come into the valley not less than 6,000 men.[4] If they keep on at this rate a few weeks their army in this valley will whittled down to the little end of Nothing and I do not care how soon. I think we will make a grand move on Winchester in a few days when you will likely hear of another victory if the Rebs does not retreat on our advance.

We have received some reinforcements from New Recruits and about 2,000 convalescents and Straglers came up on Saturday. This Army is in good condition and in fine Spirits and since the news of the fall of Atlanta their enthusiasm is great and if there is a general engagement in this valley you will see the fur fly sure. The news is churning from all parts now and from the depression in the Gold market I think the public is becoming convinced that Old Abe and Grant intends to keep the Stars and Stripes floating in spite of democracy and their brothers the Southern traitors. I am well in health but am pretty well tired out and if this campaign last two months longer I will have to ask leave to quit for awhile untill I recruit up. Though now that the weather is getting cool I may stand it better for the heat and my load is all that worried me.

The officers is very kind to me. The other day the Col came along and I was marching at the head of the Company. I think he seen I was tired but said nothing to me only inquired if I had got some letters by that mail. I seen him ride up to the Surgeon and speak to him who imediately stoped and gave me an order to ride the rest of the day in the ambulence which I gladly accepted and I got into camp feeling quite well and was ready for a fight that we had that night before we got to sleep. Col Graham is a good man and the friends of those who are serving under him ought to be very thankful to him for his untiring exertion for their comfort and Safety. I shall always remmember him with feelings of gratitude. Like myself he has a wife and a family to long for his return and from his conduct I think he loves them as dearly as I do mine. They are neighbours of Edith McConnell's. She Speaks of them very highly. By the way did I tell you that I received a letter from her?[5] A very good one and it done me a great deal of good to get it. She is union to the Hub. I received a letter from William Cook yesterday.[6] They were all well and I guess are making some money. But I think he will never go to war. I wrote Mary a long letter the other day giving her an account of the times and the country around the town of Charleston. So you will know as much about that place of iniquity as I can tell you. I have got this sheet near full and have written nothing that is either interesting or instructive and I have a notion to quit it until I can think. I have so much to think about that I do not think of any thing to any purpose. I think by to morrow if we do not get into another fight I can write something better and something that will be more instructive. I sent for the Box to-day. Thee did not say wheather thee paid the freight on it or not. I have no money and if the man has not the money I will not get it I reckon. But I will see how it comes out and if it is not paid I will try and borrow enough to get it.

Sep 18th. I have not had time to write any more and we will advance towards Winchester to night and I will send this out as I may not have a chance to send for several days again.

I am in good health. Give thy love to all and Kiss the children for me.
I remain thy affectionate husband
Taylor

1. Oliver Goldsmith (1730–1774) was an Irish poet, and Alexander Pope (1688–1774) was a British poet.

2. On September 13 a Union cavalry brigade commanded by Brigadier General John B. McIntosh captured 16 officers and 127 enlisted men primarily from the 8th South Carolina Infantry Regiment.

3. No battle of this magnitude occurred between September 3 and 14. Taylor may be referring to the battle on September 3 when the Eighth Corps engaged Confederates near Berryville. The Eighth Corps had 23 killed, 124 wounded, and 19 missing. Confederate casualties are unknown.

4. On August 31 Early reported 10,910 men present. On September 30 he reported 8,564 present.

5. This letter was not found.

6. Cook's letter, dated September 4, 1864, is not included in this book.

Des Moines Sept 18th/64
Dear Brother
We received 2 letters from thee yesterday and was pleased to here of your getting along so well. We are all well and tolerable Comfortable. Money is right plenty but Everything is high. My health is much better than I ever Expected it to be. We have had no Sickness Since Mary had the measels. I have had one Spell of Asthmath this sumer and it verry light. We ware glad to hear from thee for we Se by the papers acount of any particular ones that is killed or woounded and it leaves us in

Suspence. But we Still hope that you will Survive the Strugle and have the comforts of life to End thy Days. If Everything works right here we can make a good living for all and Something to lay up. The towne of Desmoine is improving verry fast and permanent. We will have gass lights in our Streets in a few weeks and our Rail Road prospects are Brightning. Our farmers are making lots of money and that is what will make this Country. We are right in to a nothe pollitcal campain. The Knowing ones Say old Abes Ellection is certain. The Copps ar verry Sore from Some Cause and I suppose it is Because that they know Defeat awaits them with the young napoleon and mister peace platform. He ought to have tried his peace arangement with Jeff when he was before richmond and See if he would not Suckseeded bette. For I doe think if he had any Backbone in him he could have marched right into Richmond with out any troubl after the Batte of Williams Burg. But the Idea of Retreating at right after whipping the Rebs by Day is truly Rediculas. But he faild to take Richmond and acomplished nothing and I wished in my hart that he might bee Succesful all the time he was their but the thing is differant now. I wish to Se him Defeatted on this campain. It would be a lasting Disgrace to this nattion to hav a man that could not take the Rebble Capitol to take ours and hold the white house for four years.[1] We have a failure in wild fruit this year. Apples appear to be plenty and we can get allong much Better than usual. Potatoes are Scarce and Sell at one Dol per Bushell By the load. Sweet Potatoes I Dont here of any in the Country. Onions are Scarce. Wood is worth 8 Dols per cord and hay from 8 to 10 Dol per ton. Stock of all kinds are high. Sheep ar getting quite plenty and we get some verry nice mutton. Hogs are Scarce and going to be verry high. No End to the Demand for lard to ship. Every kind of meat is high. Catharine Say thee said for me to ware the close thee Sent home but I think that I cant doe it without taking off the straps or they might arrest me for Deserting and that would be a terrible affair. For if old abe has no men in his army thee will turn tale. Till I doe he is cirtain to whip the Rebs and Cops to. Thee talks some of coming home this fall. If thee Does and can I may go back with thee for if I see a chance to leave the family comfortabl I will go East and Se it once more. Take good care of thy Self but be the Death of all the rebbels thee can. We all send our love to thee with our prayer for thy Safty.

> your
> C Milner

1. Cyrus is referring to Major General George Brinton McClellan, who commanded the Army of the Potomac in an attempt to seize Richmond by landing near Fort Monroe, Virginia. The failed campaign lasted from March through July 1862. McClellan was known as the "young Napoleon" and was the Democratic candidate for president in 1864. A rally for him was held in Des Moines on September 3, 1864.

> September 18th 1864
>
> Dear Father

It is with greate pleasure that I take my pen in hande to let thee know that we are all well and hopeing these few lines will finde the same. I am so glad that you are comeing home thiss winter. Maybe thee had better go around by Aunt Raichel so as to see if cousin Anna will come out with because I wrote to her for to come out here when thee comes. I told her that I would tell her when thee was coming home so she could come when thee did.

Day before yesterday we went a hazelnuting and we got a greate many fruits. I said I will stop. I am thy affectionate daughter. 18

> Sarah A Peirce

PS Dear Father I am allmost gone craysy thiss evening. Please to exuse me for puting 18 on there instead of my name.

> from Sarah

> [This letter was probably written September 26, 1864, from Harrisonburg, Virginia.]

It come on night and we went into camp. Early in the morning of the 25 Sunday we were after them again. 23 of their wagons fell into our hands this day and a good many prisoners but the major army travelled all night and having no train we took to the by roads and we did not overtake them during the day. We arrived at this place which is the county seat of Rockingham Co. about 3 o clock yesterday and are now laying and resting ourselves. I think we have done as good a weeks work as has ever been done for the Govt since the commencement of the war. We have whipped them in 2 fair fights on ground of their own choosing[1] and their army is scattered in all directions. One half of them have thrown away their arms and the other half are scared to death. The citizens although they do not like to acknowledge it says that it is the worst whiped army that has ever been in Virginia. I hope these Victorys will put a quietus on the Coperheads and Peace Democrats and give the timid more courage so that they will turn an help us sustain the war to an honerable conclusion. The people in this State is getting very tired of War and one or two more defeats like them will put a stop to it for all time. I have stood the fatigue of theses marches and battles admirably better than most of the men. For on the morning of the 23d when we halted to breakfast and rest I was one of 6 that was there to stack guns the rest having all give out. I expect the excitement of the great victory kept me up but so as I done it no differance how it was done. I carry no load with me and sleep on the ground with an oil cloth blanket over me so that I can just lay down and sleep and get up and go at any time. The nights are getting cold and if I do not get a wool Blanket before long I will suffer for sleep for I can not sleep cold. The days are deliciously cool and I am gaining strength every day. We have plenty to eat and getting along fine for the work we have to do. This is a nice country here and has the appearance of wealth but the boys are cleaning it up now and if we retreat no army can subsist in this vally again for another year at least.

I do not know when I will I have a chance to write again but if you should not get a letter for a month you need not be uneasy. For as we advance the facilities for writing and transmitting letters comes more difficult. And you will probably not get them for some time even if I get a chance to write which is doubtful as I have no paper with me and have to depend on forrageing for what I write on.

I do not know when I Will have a chance to send this out but I will have it wrote and when the mail starts out it will be ready. I will have to quit writing for I see things beginning to move and I must be ready to move too. Tell W.P. Cole that I am well and Gov Stones brother is all right. These are all that I know of any one being interested in your parts. Kiss the children for me and tell them that if we can whip the Rebs 2 or 3 times more I will get home the sooner.

I think we will either threaten or cut the Lynchburg Rail Road before we stop and when we get away down there it will be hard to get a letter either from you or to you. I got thy letter of the 9th[2] on the 21st and expect one to come in the first mail that comes up. I do not expect that we will have any more battles untill we get to Lynchburg if we do then. For if old Grant keeps them busy at Richmond there will be no army to fight us and we will do as we please with that road.

I would write you a description of our battles if I had time and will do it some time soon.

This sheet has been scribbled over but you can read the writing and let the scribbling go. I hope the war is now assuming an aspect that will soon put an end to it. Oh how I wish I could see you once more and rest in your society in peace and security without the fear of insurection and disturbances and when all the citizens of this country can enjoy the rights God has intended for them.

Well I must close.

Give my love to all and be assure that my affections remain unchanged and are a great stay to me in the discharge of my arduous duties. For your present and future welfare is my only solicitude.

> Affty yours
> Taylor

I have not got the box yet and may not get it untill after this campaign is over.

1. On September 19 the army began a march toward Winchester. That day the two armies fought a major battle near Winchester in which Sheridan sustained 5,018 casualties and Early lost 12,150. Early withdrew to Fisher's Hill near Strasburg, and Sheridan attacked him there on September 22. The 22nd Iowa was deployed primarily as skirmishers during the battle. Confederate losses were 3,921, and the Union army had 528 casualties. By September 25 the Confederates had retreated to Brown's Gap, east of Port Republic. On April 28, 1881, the Pension Office of the Department of the Interior inquired of the surgeon general whether there was a record of Taylor Peirce having been wounded in the right hand and spine at Opequan (Winchester) on September 19. The surgeon general replied that there were no records for the 22nd Iowa on file. This is the only mention of the possibility that Taylor was wounded during this battle.

2. This letter was not found.

> Des Moines Oct 1st 1864
> Dear Taylor

We are all in good health I would feel all right if I only could hear right away from thee and know that thy life was still spaird to me and thy country. We hear so much good news of victories and all things are working well. Yet there is a sadness over it at last for there is so many wives and mothers left to mourn the loss of some brave son or husband in our late battles and I do not know but I am one of the number that may have to mourn for thee at this very time if I knew it. Yet I Will hope for the best and trust to God for help to bare my load of trouble in this my hour of trial and wate patiential untill I know how it is with thee. I think I must write to thee any how and if thee is among the wounded or the sick it will reach thee. So it will maybe be a comfort to know that my most anxious thoughts are for thy welfare and if I only had the power how soon I would be down there and know the worst and I might be able to do some good to some of the poor brave that would be glad of a femaile hand to administer to their want. Dear one I can not help but feel sad but I will try and shake it off hopeing I will hear from thee in a few days and thee will be all right. I have not seen any account of the killed or wounded only what was in a letter from Washington in to days paper. It stated that there were 40 to 60 killd and wounded in thy Reg[1] but there were no names so I do not know who they are and I will therefore not grieve thee lost untill I can not help it. But I will try and change my tone of writeing and tell thee of the children. They are all in good health. Sallie and Frank go to school to a new brick house that was put up this summer on our side of the river and they like to go very well and I hope they will learn fast. For I have got them a nice lot of new books and fixt this up nice and I tell them if they do not study now that thee will not have them as thy children when thee gets home.

Sunday 2d. It is raining and dull so there is no company here to day and I ought to write a good letter but I do not know any Public new but what thee will be likely to see before this reaches thee. And our own affairs go on just the same one day with another so there nothing new in family. Except Catharine Kelly Ana's sister is here sick with the typhoid fever and feel as if it would about the last of her. She seems like a good kind of a girl and that is the kind to be taken early from life. Little Ellis up set my ink and that stopd me for a time. Now it is night and he is asleep so I will write on sallies sheet some more and then stop.

Des Moins Oct 2 1864
Dear Father

I love thee very much. It is a very chill and cloudy day. The children and Mother are in the next room. That is their room. I sleep in Aunts room now. I wish thee would come home pretty soon becuse I am lonesome with out thee. Uncle is well. He has not had but one or two sick speel this Summer. I go to school now. I have the Practical arithmatic and the Fourth part of geography and prymery grammar.

Frank is as mischeiveous as ever. Ellis is getting to be a better boy than he was. I have not much to say? Dosnt thee remember the time thee got of the leigh and let Sarah Paxton in? Her name is now Sarah White. She told Mother recellet thee of the time and Mother did not write to day and so I tought I would myself. It is raining dredful hard. I wanted to go a visiting to day and it is well that Mother did not let me becase I would have Been caught in a rain.

Cathern Kelly has come that is Anns sister. She has been here a month and is so sick with tiphoid feaver She has been very low this past week. I go to Mrs Willcot Mrs Denisons sister. I do wish that thee would write oftener to me than thee dose. I love to cherish the letters up that thee sends me. Dose thee think it is woth while to cut this Peice of paper off?

From thy effetinate daughter Sarah A Peirce to
her Father

Sallie has tryd to tell thee about an old thing that hapend in Pa. It was this way. Thee was comeing home from the Lycum at Eastland[2] and overtook Miss Sarah Paxson and my brother Nate he on horse back and she was walking (near to John Harlins). And thee gave them thy buggy and took Nate horse to ride home. I do not think I ever heard of it while we were in that county but perhaps thee will remember of it. I suppose If thee can thee Will know Mrs White from that circumstance. Well Sallie and I have filled the two sheets and with it all. It will not amount much only to let thee know we are well and hope thee is same and that thee will get home soon.

Thy ever affet wife Catharine
C and Mary send their love an respects to thee hopeing to hear soon.

1. At Winchester and Fisher's Hill the 22nd Iowa had eleven killed, sixty-seven wounded, and thirty-one missing.

2. The Lyceum was a public hall where lectures and discussions were held. Eastland was in the eastern part of Little Britain Township, Lancaster County.

Head Quarters 22nd Iowa
Harrisonburg Va Oct 2nd 1864
Dear Catharine, & Friends

I have a few moments to write before the mail goes out and I concluded to add a little to what I wrote the fore part of the week so as to let you know the latest news that we have here. I am well and we have not heard the sound of a cannon for 8 days which is the first time it has been silent for 24 hours at a time since we came into the valley on the 17th of August. I believe I have told you all in the accompanying letter about the battles[1] that I think worth mentioning. The wounded are all doing well and many of them are already back to their command. Of cours there will be Some who will be disabled but the permanent loss to the army will not be 1,000. We received news from Genl Grant last night that Birneys Corps and Ords Corps had made sucessfull advance on the Enemy at the defences of Richmond on the James River[2] and I think now is the time to strike when we have got the thing going. We Received 8,000 troops as a reinforcement last night and 3,000 3 days since which augments our army to near 50,000 men[3] all in good health and in the best of Spirits. I think our next move will be to Charlottsville. That is where the Alexandria R Road and the Richmond & Staunton R Road Crosses. And if you will look at the map you can see that by holding Charlottsvile we can open up the Alexa Road and get our supplies from there by Rail as near as we now get it from Harpers Ferry by team and will be in a position to move either on Richmond or Lynchburg as circumstances may require. However this is only surmise with me as no one knows the intention of the Comdg Officer. You may bet that Sheridan will not let them rest while he has such an army as is now concentrated here. He is now destroying every thing that the reble army could subsist on in this valley between here and Staunton[4] and has torn up the Road from that place to Charlotsville. There was one Brigad of Infty and 6,000 cavalry sent out to occupy and hold the pass through the Blue Ridge between here and Charlottsvile yesterday and I think as soon as we get our Rations we will move. We have been up to Mt Crawford this week and come Back here friday and have been waiting for our Supplies to come up. We have been 3 days without rations but we have been allowed to forrage and we have lived better than we would if we had govt Rations. I have had some good old apple sauce the first since I left Pa. It tasted like old times. We grate corn and bake slap jacks and have sundry chickens turkeys and young hog so you see we live. I have nothing to cover me at night but I manage to sleep in my cloths untill I get cold and then get up to the fire till I get warm and go it again. I gave my Blanket to a wounded soldier and have not been able to get one since the Battle at W. I do not know what I will do if it gets very cold but I will manage some how. I am now Sergeant Major of the Regt and have turned over my Gun so I do not have that to carry any more and will get along much eisier than I have heretofore and will not have to go into Battle unless I wish to again. But I reckon when I see my comrades going in I will not be able to forbear but I will try and take as good care of my self for your sake as is consistant with my honor and duty and will not do anything that my conscience will check me for here after. For I never want you to have to blush for my actions.

I received Cyrus and Sallies letter of the 18th this morning. I was glad to know that Cyrus still thought of me and was glad to learn of his continued good health and I hope he will live to enjoy happiness yet. For he and I have had a good bit of trouble but there is always a reward for those who ar faithful to the end.

I will have another $100 to send you before long and you can make yourselves comfortabl on it. I think things looks as if this state of affairs would come to a close soon and I will be enabled to join you and enjoy ourselves togather once more.

I must close now. Give my love to all and tell them that the 22n Iowa is going to come home with untarnished honor to reap the reward of its trials in peace. Not the peace of the Cop but the peac conqued by the Patriots. Kiss the children for me. I remain affectionately yours

      Taylor

1. This letter was not found.

2. On September 29 Major General David Birney's Tenth Corps and Major General Edward Ord's Eighteenth Corps drove the Confederates out of Fort Harrison, which was part of the Richmond defenses.

3. At the end of September Sheridan's army totaled 56,754 men present for duty. At the end of October he had 61,867 men present for duty.

4. On September 26 Sheridan began a ten-day campaign to lay waste crops, burn barns, seize livestock, and destroy the railroad in the Port Republic–Staunton–Waynesborough region. The 22nd Iowa remained in the vicinity of Harrisonburg.

Des Moines Oct 8th

Dear Taylor

This is election day and a very stormy one at that in this region of the world and I would like to know if is as bad in old Virginia about this time. Well every body has turned out to the election and some of the Cops got drunk but I have heard of no fuss yet. It is six O clock and I reckon there will be none. I received thy letter to day of the 22d[1] and 26th and I am much pleased to learn that thee is well and in good heart and no worse hurt than what thee writes of. And I think thee and I have good cause to be thankful to our creation for the meny blessings we enjoy (but I suppose thee may think that Gray Backs[2] is not much of a blessing but we must have a few of them to mix with the rest of the good things of this life). For we see others that is so much worse off than we. One in stance is an old man that came here this evening to get boarding. His wife, second wife has gone off and left him and his little girl to get along the best they can do. Thee wants to know what we are doing. I was very busy writing when the supper bell rang and I have done better since. If thee only could of had share of our light Biscuit I would of been glad. Sallie says if she could send her share she would go with out for one night but as that is impossible she eats them and is glad to have plenty to eat and a good warm house to stay in this cold weather. Thee wants to know if the children grows. They are as healthy as there is to be found and quite as mischievious though I do not know wheather are any worse than other peoples or not. But I do know that they are as bad as I want to have the care of. They go to school all the time but were not there to day. Thee says Boliver had got home. I have not seen him nor heard from him since his time was out but supposed he had got home safe. I have not heard from Aunt for three months so I do not know much of what they are doing. I am writing with Ellis on my lap and I will have to quit.

Catharine

1. This letter was not found.
2. Lice.

Strawsburg Va Ha 22n Iowa Oct 10/64
Dear Catharine and Friends

Paper is scarce and all other writing materials. So you will have to put up with a short letter untill I get where I can get more. I am well and in good heart about the end of this war. We have driven the Rebles out of the Valley and destroyed their supplys. That is the main Army was driven out but after we began to fall back from Staunton they follow us up with a small force of Cavalry I suppose to harrass our retreat and capture the straglers. Yesterday after we had fallen back from Harrisburg to this place Our cavalry halted on Fishers Hill the scene of our battle of the 22n and concluded to rest a while. And as their cavalry was quite impudent Genl Sheridan ordered out some of the troops to give them a brush. So our forces advanced a mile or two towards Woodstock and attacked their forces. After a pretty hard fight of two hours we succeeded in defeating them capturing 11 pieces of Artillery 42 wagons 9 ambulances and 350 prisoners and routed and run the rest of their force for 12 miles. We got all their train and all their artillery and as we have destroyed all the Subsistance in the Vally they will be compelled to leave it for this fall and winter. We are now laying on the Battle ground of Fishers Hill in Camp.[1] Where we will go next I am entirely unable to tell but I think it likely we will cross the Blue Ridge to Warrinton on the Alexandria and Charlotsville R Road. We can make that our base of supplies and opporate Either against Richmond direct or make a flank movment towards Lynchburg. Although I do not know any thing of the intentions of the military authorities yet this is the most feasable looking movment to me. I think there will be no more battles North of Richmond and if Grant is successfull there the war will be removed to Georgia or Peace will be declared before Christmas. I have received no letter since I got Cyruses but I Expect one the next mail. I have got my Box from the

Express office but it has not come up to the Regt yet. I expect it to-morrow. I have got a quilt from the Sanitary Dept and sleep quite comfortable. We made 2 hard days march last week making 25 miles pr day and carrying all our traps but I made it better than many of the younger men. I feel Bully. The Cool weather has set me up. I am still Sergeant Major and I Expect I will be untill this war is ended. I must close. Excuse the dirty paper for I am dirty all over. I have had no chance to wash my cloths for a month. Kiss the children for me.

     I am thine as Ever.

     Taylor

1. On 6 October Sheridan began to move north down the valley. On October 9 Brigadier General Alfred Torbert's cavalry attacked and defeated the pursuing Confederate cavalry commanded by Brigadier General Thomas L. Rosser. The Confederates lost about 50 killed, 350 prisoners, 11 artillery pieces, and numerous wagons and ambulances. The next day the Union army encamped near Cedar Creek.

     Des Moines Oct 17th

     Dear Taylor

We have had a great old time of it here this week looking for bush-whackers here but as they have not come yet I will give they up for now. The Loyal Legue[1] made quite a demonstration yesterday prad-ing through town and scouting round but they could not find an enemy. Well the way of it is that there came a dispach that the Rebs had burnt the little town of Albia about one hundred mills South East of this and were makeing for the Capital[2] and were likely to take all the horses and goods that they could get their hands on. But I do not apprehend much danger for Gov Stone is on the eleart and will watch they so close that they will not get here. For he had about eight hun-dred of the state fencibles calld out and eight cannon of Henry Grif-fith Battry so thee may see that he was pritty well prepard for the rebs. If they were to try to reach here he could have from three to five hun-dred more Loyal leguers in two hours notice. Well may be I had not better write more on the defences of this place least it might be coun-traband in those times. Well Taylor We are all in good health and in good heart for we think that the rebelion is in it death throes at this very time and that as soon as the November election is over it will kick its last (for there is no question how the election will go). For they the rebs are just trying to grasp the last morsol that they expect to get this side of the place they go to after Old Abe is elected again. They think they have fared hard enough this term but it is likely they will fare worse next (If I might be called a judge). I have had no letter from thee since the one writen the 26th of last month. And as thee sayd thee might not have a good chanc to write I will try and be patiant for one untill it comes. I do not know what to fill up the sheet with for we have been so buisy this week that I have not had time to think. Kate is still sick and it takes Anne all the time to attend to her. Mary got another girl but she had a boil come on her arm so she could not stay but one week so Mary and I have to hump our selves to get the work done. For they have nine boarders besides me and the children and thee must make all due alounce for my poor letter. Things are going on in good style here. Starr has got his gass works all most up and there is so much improvements going on that thee will not hardly know the place when thee gets home. I do not [know] wheather I told thee where the gass works are. They are on the south end of second street and cover a whole lot and are three storys high so thee may think it is some of a building for Des Moines.

I will close for I do not know of anything more that would be interesting to thee.

With love

I remain Catharine

1. The Union League, also known as the Loyal League, consisted of secret patriotic clubs first organized in Philadelphia in November 1862, although its roots can be traced to Connecticut in March 1860. Originally known as the Union Club, one such group first met in Iowa in February 1862. On March 20, 1863, several clubs joined to form the Union League. Republicans claimed that the league was necessary to counter the influence of the Knights of the Golden Circle. The league raised money, distributed literature, and engaged in political activities. It supported Lincoln in 1864.

2. Albia was not attacked or burned. On October 12, however, twelve men dressed in Union uniforms raided houses in Davis County, which is immediately southeast of Monroe County and the town of Albia. They killed three residents before escaping.

Des Moins Iowa oct 16th 1864
Dear Fathe.
It is a pleasate Sunday after noon. It is very sill and quiet and warm.
I wish thee was at home and down at the old place. I still long fore the
woods. Oh do come home bye a place in the woods and do as we have
done. I dear Papie I am so lonesome with out thee. I wish this war was
over so everybody was could get home so that ther mothers and
borthers and sisters and Fathers and wives and children would have
nothing to morn. For oh I am so tirde of liveing here. I am just scolded
all the if not by mother or aunt by the theacer at scool. Oh do come
home and take me away from here. Uncle is well. He has had but one
sickspell this sumer. We hav ten borders now. I cannot think of eny
more so I will stop. Goodby from thy effetinate daughter sallie Peirce
to our Father

Sallie has tryd to write some but she dose not seem to improve in her
writing as fast as I could wish. But maybe she will take a cange for the
better after a time. The other children are all well and full of life. Ellis
can talk quite plain and Frank is the same old boy he uset to be.
Catharine A Peirce

Des Moines Oct 22d/64
Dear Taylor
It is the sabbeth day and stillness prevails in the house for Katie Kelly
is so low that we think she can not live untill night and I let the children be out on in the bar room so they will not disturb her with thier
play and noise. We are all well and in good heart hopeing thee is safe
and well. I recved two letters this week one of the 10th and another of
various daits. But it makes but little differance how many I get I am
just as anxious for another one. For I learn by the papers of all the battles that thy Reg are in before I get thy letters telling of them so I can
not help being some what anxious all the time. But I will try and have
faith and put my trust in him who can take care of us all whether to
gather or far a part. For he is able to save if we were in a firey furnace
and I am all most ready to think from thy letter that it must of been almost as hot as one with thee in those engagements thee speaks of. I can

not give up the thought but that thee will get through this dreadful war all right and we will have meny happy days to gather yet. For I almost feel surtain that this fall will wind up the war. It seemed as though that if every man must put his shoulder to the wheele and then the load would move on with ease, and any that do not come forward on the right side now at this great crisis they are not deserving the chance of American citizen ship an a place on the face of Gods earth. For it is my humble opinion that he formed this earth for the good and breave and if this war do not exterminate all cowards and cops that he will send another flood or some thing else in its place. But I have great faith in the Nov elections frost, holeing up all kinds of reptiles that are inclined to wag thier venimous tongues in trying to destroy this glorious Union. Well Taylor I will quit gasing and tell thee of our friends. They are all well as far as I know. We have had but few letters of late on acount of not haveing writen much. Mary got one a few days ago from A M Gibson saying the folks were all well but Aunt Hannah she is still the same. But I suppose thee gets letters from Rachel and Knows more about them perhaps than we do. We were set out to have a good time this fall Mary and I but Kate got sick and they can not get another girl to stay as yet and we have to lick in to the work a little more than is a greeable. For they are doing a better business than they have ever done. They have all the boarders they can accomodate and get four $ per week and get as many more if they had room for them. So thee may know they are doing something whether they make anything ore not. Thee must excuse this as it is writen in great haste so as to be ready to go to cooking again. I will close with love and with the respects of all.

    Catharine

    Head Quarters 22nd Iowa Inftry
    Cedar Creek Va Oct 23rd 1864
    Dear Catharine & Friends

Before this reaches you, you will have heard of another Battle and Victory in the Shanadoah Valley, and of course you will be anxious to know of my condition, and also of the details of the Engagement. So I will try and give it as well as I can. In the first place I am in good health and good spirits, and I will try to inform you in regard to all the transactions of this army since my last letter.

On the 11th the army fell back to where we are now encamped. On the 13th the Enemy followed us up and made an attack on our lines which we repulsed without much loss.[1] And after laying in line of battle all night we returned to camp and nothing more than the ordinary transaction of an army in the field occurred untill the 18th inst. Before Going into the details, I will give you a description of the situation of the Union Army and its disposition.

The Valley of Virginia is here divided by the ridge of Mountains called the Massanuten spur. It raises near the confluence of the North and South branches of the Shanandoah River and extends up the Valley to Harrisonburg dividing it into two Valleys the one on the East side called the Luray Valley and the one on the west is the Valley of Virginia or main Valley. Both coming togather at or near Harrisonburg where the mountain disappears altogather. There is also another valley runs off west into what is called the north mountain down which flows Cedar Creek which crosses the main valley and emptys into the North fork of the Shanandoah above its junction with the South fork. I will here state that the mountain Rises abruptly from the River to about the same Elevation as the surrounding mountain and the River runs close to the base on both sides. Cedar Creek comes down from the North mountain and crosses the Valley and emptys into the Shanandoah near the North point of the Massanuten Ridge. Our army had taken its position on the North Bank of Cedar creek which is confined in its channels by abrupt hills and limestone cliffs and had thrown up breast works and fortifications on the crest of the hills for a considerable distance. The disposition of the army was as follows. The 8th Corps on the Extreme left, Extending from the point of the mountain across the Valley on the Banks of Cedar Creek to the Turnpike which runs from Winchester to Strawsburg. The 19th Corps joining the right of the 8th and extending along the Banks of the Creek and connecting with the 6th Corps which extended the line nearly across the Valley. The flanks of the Army were both protected by the Cavalry. These different organizations were commanded first the 8th Corps by Genl Crook, Second the 19th corps by Genl Emory, Third the 6th Corps by Genl Wright, Fouth the Cavalry by Genl Torbert, one division under Custer and the other under Merritt.[2] On the 16th inst Genl Sheridan left the Army to Washington, leaving Genl Wright in command of the whole.[3] On the Evening of the 18th our Division which is the 2n Div of the 19th was ordered to be ready to mov at 5 [illegible] o clock on the morning of the 19th on a reconoisance towards Strausburg which is about 3 miles from our lines and about 1½ from the main lines of the Enemy. He having taken his old position at Fishers Hill which I described in my former letter and where the Battle of the 22 Sep was fought.

At 5 oclock the 2n Division was up and had their breakfast and were ready to march, and were momentarily Expecting orders to Move. The Eastern sky had just begun to show signs of approaching day. The men all ready and awaiting around their camp fires for orders to fall in no one apprehending any difficulty when all at once as if from every hill and every valley there arose such a rattle of Musketry as I have rarely heard. This proved to be an assault of the enemy on the left of the 8th Corps who were yet asleep in their camp and were taken by surprise and after a short resistance were forced to abandon their works and retreat from their camp in disorder. A Portion of the Enemy had crossed the Massanewton Mountain in the night and come down the Luray and at the same time that at the attack was made on the left flank and front of the 8th Corps made an attack on and turned the rear of the 8th & 19th corps and took possession of the Pike and the town of Middleburg which was occupied by a detachment of men from the 22n Iowa as provost Guard in charge of Capt Morseman of Co. I.[4] At the time that the 8th corps were compelled to retreat the 2n Brigade of the 19 corps composed of the 159th, 131st N.Y. the 11 Ind and the 3 Mass and 2 Iowa was ordered to move to their support. The 22n and the 3 Mass movd out imediately to their support and the other 3 regts remained to protect the front of our own line. On arriving in the rear of the position occupied by the 8th Corps our lines here thrown into some confusion by the men of the 8th breaking through but the regiments formed as well as they could but were subjected to such a murderous fire that they were compelled to retreat and oweing to the darkness the commands become confused and considerable disorder ensued. After falling back for a short distance the 22n Rallied and made a stand when they forced the Enemy to halt and succeeded in inflicting considerable damage on their advance line. But after a few minutes the rebbs advanced in such force in front and the flanks having been previously forced back the gallant 22n were again forced to fall back. During the time that the 22n confronted the enemy the lines were so close that the fire from the rebles guns scorched the faces and clothes of our boys. But they succeeded in falling back without much serious loss, although there was many wounded and taken prisoners.

At this time the Rebs having attacked us on both flanks and charged the front of the 8 corps which they carried, the whole of the 8th & 19th and a portion of the 6th corps was compelled to make a hasty retreat leaving all our Camp Equipage and the most of our rations. It seemed as if the day was lost and a disasterous defeat was inevitable. The whole army seemed to me to be flying in disordre, and such confusion as existed for a short time among the camp followers and those in charge of the train is never seen except in the case of a defeat. The train containing the ammunition also the Quarter Masters train and the ambulances were flying in every directions across the country towards Winchester regardless of roads, fences or anything else but to get out of the way. These followed by the Artillery and the Soldiers who were vieing each other in their efforts to get beyond the reach of the Rebles. The roar of the Reble artillery the rattle of musketry which reverberated amongst the hills and mountains redoubling the already terriffic roar of Battle, accompanied by the charging yell of the Rebbs—composed a scene that beggars description.[5] [next pages missing]

1. This was a larger battle than Taylor describes. Without orders, a Confederate battery began to fire on the First Division, Army of West Virginia, commanded by Colonel Joseph Thoburn. Two Union brigades advanced but were thrown back by the Confederate division of Major General Joseph Kershaw, which had recently returned to the valley. Southern losses were 22 killed and 110 wounded. The Union army lost 22 killed and 77 captured.

2. Major General William Emory, Major General Horatio Wright, Brigadier General Wesley Merritt.

3. Late on October 15 Sheridan departed for Washington to meet with Secretary of War Edwin Stanton and Chief of Staff Major General Henry Halleck.

4. Westel W. Morsman was an Ohio native and Iowa City resident when he was appointed second lieutenant on August 18, 1862. He was promoted to captain on May 23, 1863, and was captured at Cedar Creek. He was mustered out July 25, 1865.

5. The 22nd Iowa had been awakened at about 3 A.M. in preparation for a reconnaissance to locate the Confederate positions. At approximately 5 A.M. Kershaw's Confederate division surprised and routed the Union First Division, Eighth Corps, commanded by Colonel Joseph Thoburn. Kershaw had not crossed the Massanutten Mountain but had quietly moved to a position where he could out-

flank the Union left. By 5:30 A.M. the Nineteenth Corps was heavily engaged at both its front and its right flank. The 22nd Iowa and 3rd Massachusetts were ordered to support an artillery battery but were soon overwhelmed by Confederate fire and were forced to withdraw as the Nineteenth Corps collapsed. The units fell back about three-quarters of a mile, where they rallied. At 10:30 A.M. Sheridan arrived and ordered his army to prepare for a counterattack, which got under way in midafternoon. By nightfall the Confederates had been driven back to their original positions. In the battle the 22nd Iowa had one killed, forty-nine wounded, and twenty-three missing. The regimental casualty reports list Taylor as having been slightly wounded in this battle. One report states that he was wounded in the right arm, and another says the right hand.

> Head Quarters 22n Iowa
> Cedar Creek Va Oct 26 1864
> Dear Catharine & Friends

When I wrote the 24th I expected we could be on the march before this but things have taken a change and our things are all ordered up to the front. So I suppose that we will once more get to see some cloths that is clean and get some tents to live in. I tell you this has been one of the Campaigns. We have been in this Valley now since the 17th of august and we have not been out of artillery more than 8 days during the whole time. It has been quit since the 18th or at least since the morning of the 20. The Cavalry followed the retreating army to Woodstock and shelled them all the way taking 8 Guns and 2,000 prisoners[1] which was the last cannonading I have heard. I think the fighting is done in this Valley for this winter. The rebbs made a most desperate effort for Victory on the 19 and lost and I am of the oppinion that they are not in a situation to attempt it again. All the Subsistance is destroyed as far up the Vally as Staunton and it is too far from Richmond for them to bring supplies and it takes too much force to protect their train.[2] So I think this campaign is over. I am glad of it. I think now if these Eastern troops would buckle to it that Richmond would fall before the Election. I used to think that it was all gammon about the West producing better troops to fight than the East but I know now that it is so. Every fight that we have been in the regiments in our brigade and also in the 4th brigade who are from the east has given way and left us to bear the brunt of the fight. On the 18 the 3d Massacusetts who were sent with the 22 to support the 8th corps broke and run before they got into line leaving the 22n alone to defend the position who stood and fought the rebs till the fire from their guns scorched their clothes.[3] And the eastern Regt in the 4th Brigade run and left the 24 & 28th Iowa and the 8 & 18 Indanna to stand it. After the reorganizing of the army began Genl Grover Commanding our division was ordered to take the advance and hold the rebles in check. He imediately took all the Western troops togather and gave them to honour of being the first to advance and also to lead the charge which was done most gallantly. You ought to have heard the Western boys yell. The line was about a mile in length and consisted of the 22, 24, & 28 Iowa the 11, 8, & 18th Indianna. When they charged across the open ground the whole line fired Simultaneously and gave one of the most deafening yells I ever heard.[4] One Brigade of the 6th corp who was about 200 yds in the rear lying down in a piece of woods thinking the rebles had charged jumped up and skedaddled but after running about a quarter and finding nothing coming they turned round and come up and helped us to fight it out. Well I must quit bragging but it seems to me that We ought to be allowed to brag some for our months work.

I do not know wheather I will try to get home or not this winter. I have a good place now and I only have 10 months more to serve and it would take 2 months wages to bear my expenses so I am on a study wheather for your benefit I had better not stay untill my time is out. For mony will do you more good than my presence for all the time I could stay with you and the enjoyment would be lessened by the knowledge that I would have to come back. Tell the children to be good and learn their lessons well and I will try and get time to write each of them a letter Soon. I have been writing this whole day and am to tired that I can hardly hold the pen and as it is getting dark I will close up. I hear that Bolivar has got home. Have you seen him and how does he look? Is he going to the war again or has his Patriotism burnt out? The Election will be over before I can get an answer from this but write me how the glorious young State casts her vote. Penna has gone all right.[5] I see by the last paper from Iowa that the copperheads have been kicking up in Poweshiek Co.[6] I wish they would let the 22n out on the Prairies of Iowa. The Coperheads would either leave or the State would Smell worse of Carrion than ever Hell did of brimstone. Oh how I would like to clean them out. I feel as if our little Regt could clean out all the d—d democrats between the Miss

and Missouri Rivers from their junction to their scource. I mean cop-
erhead democrats not such men as Logan[7] Sheridan and a host of others that are as sound as the Granite Rock for the Union. Write me
what you are all doing and how you are getting along and how the
children are growing and if they are good. Kiss the little things for me
and tell them that I think of them at the dead hour of the night when
the greybacks arouse me from my slumber and the fleas dance a horn-
pipe over my emaciated body. Then do I in my imigination think of
and see clean beds where there is no creeping thing to go creshie creshie
in the night time. When lice cease from troubling and weary get to rest.

     I am yours tiredly

     Taylor

If the Editor does not wish to publish my letter he need not do it.[8] For
I am not anxious to see myself in print. I only wrote for the friends of
the soldier.

---

1. Early retreated to New Market and was pursued by Union cavalry to Mount
Jackson, south of Woodstock. Confederate losses at the battle of Cedar Creek are
estimated at 24 artillery pieces, 1,200 prisoners, and 1,860 killed and wounded. This
amounted to about 18 percent of the force.

2. The Shenandoah Valley had been a major source of subsistence for the Confederacy prior to this time. During the campaign Sheridan systematically destroyed
farms and crops and seized livestock that previously had met much of the Confederate armies' food requirements.

3. The 3rd Massachusetts Cavalry (Dismounted) was assigned to the Second
Brigade, Second Division, Nineteenth Corps, with the 22nd Iowa. Both regiments
were employed to attempt to stem the Confederate advance, and both were forced
to withdraw under heavy fire. In the battle the Massachusetts regiment suffered sev-
enty-six casualties to the Iowans' seventy-three.

4. The Fourth Brigade, Second Division, consisted of only the two Indiana and
two Iowa regiments. The brigade was overwhelmed by a Confederate division and
fell back and joined the remnants of the Second Brigade to form a defensive position. At about 3:30 P.M. the Union army advanced and drove the Confederates from
the field.

5. It is unclear to what Taylor is referring. The presidential election was held November 8, and Pennsylvania did, indeed, cast a majority of its votes for Lincoln,
although McClellan won a sizable minority.

6. In 1861 the sheriff of Poweshiek County was called to a Democratic caucus
because of a fight between peace and war opponents. In July 1863 rifles destined
for draft resisters in the county were seized in Davenport. On September 30, 1864,
two U.S. deputy marshals were murdered when they were sent to arrest draft re-

sisters in the county, and two militia units had to be called in to maintain order. Republicans charged that the murders were the result of Democratic propaganda.

7. Union Major General John A. Logan was an Illinois Democrat who fought well during the war. He switched to the Republican Party and in 1884 ran as the vice presidential nominee.

8. There is no record of a letter from Taylor being published in either the Newton or the Des Moines newspaper.

> Des Moines Oct 30th 1864
> Dear Taylor

I am so glad that I can sit down and write thee a scratch that thee may be able to read. If it is not of the best it will let thee know how we are geting a long. We are all well but Kate she is about the same or at least very little change. Since this day a week ago she has lain for two weeks just about the one thing as I can see though the Docter thinks she will get well again now. But I think it is very doubtfull. I would really like her to get well again on Anne account for she has been one faithful sister to Kate and tended her with all the tenderness that a sister could. Well as to things in general. They go on as usual. Cyrus is fixing up for winter with the expectation of doing a good business and the prospect bids fair for doing well. They have fourteen boarders besides a good many stopers and the money comes in all the time though provision is very high. Flour is six Dollars per hundred potatos one Dollar per bu and butter fourty cts per lb and all things in the same propation. But money is plenty and the people do not feel the high prices as much as they did the prices two years ago. Boarding has gone up to with the rest. It is from four to twelve Dol per week in town. The very poors is four Dolars and at the Des Moines and Savary house it is from ten to twelve $ per week. Cyrus is chargeing from five to five and a half in accordance with what they want and the amount of waiting on that they have to have.

Well Taylor I have had no letter this week but I will trust and wait for one untill it comes knowing thee has writen if thee has had a chance. I see by the papers that you keep on puting it to the rebs in good style on in the way that I like to hear of. But I must confess that I can not help but be some what anxous for thee and if I was to have a letter every day I would not be more than satisfied. But I must trust in the Lord and he will provide and take care of thee and me too and

I hope thee will get through this dreadful war safe and then we will know the value of our lives and be more faithful to our trust than we have ever been before though I believe we have all ways tryed to do right. But Oh how often I find in looking back that I have not done as I ought. But I hope that I will be forgiven and I will be able to do better in the future. When I think how I have lived up to the present time I wonder why it is so for there has been so many more healthy persons taken out of time and I am left. I suppose it is for some purpose unknown to me. Perhaps there will come a time that I will have some thing to do and I will be able to do it all at the right time. It is right and I must close with love. I remain thy own

Catharine

The Children all send a kiss and a wish for thee to come home soon.

Des Moines Nov, 64
Dear Taylor

I do not have much to write of to day but to let thee know that we are all well and doing as well as we can with out thee. Well Taylor, Kate died on tuesday and buryied on wednesday so Anne is just as she was before Kate came here. Only she has seen Kate and knows that she realy did have a sister and it dose seem hard that she is called on to give her up just in the prime of life. And so stout and health a girl as she to be taken and such delicate creatures as I be left. Seemes quere but we do not know the ways nor the will of the lord and therefore must abide our time.

Dear Taylor my mind is confused that I do not expect to write a very satisfactory letter. The two older Children are out and Ellis standing on a chair beside me at mischief and prattling so that it is a task to get a word or sentance on paper and thee must make some alounce for me in this case. I would like to write thee something that would be interesing if I only could. But it is me pen mama every minute or some such thing so I can not write and I am almost inclined to stop. But I know that thee will be looking for one of some kind by the time this ought to be there for I do get to want a letter very bad if I do not get one every week. And it has been two weeks since I have recevied the last and it was dated the 10th of last month and you have been fighting at the same old rait down in the valley so that I can not help but be a little anxious for thy safety. But I will hope for the best at all times. Mary recevied a letter from Rachel yesterday saying the friends were all well in that part of the world.[1] Aunt Hannah is still in the same situation that she has been for the last year with out any prospect of a change for the better or any other way. Rachel must indeed have her hands full raiseing her own family and Aunt on her hands too. I think I have enough to do to get along with three children. I do not know indeed if I had six but I suppose there would be a way and maby a better than at present for then I think thee would never of got to go to war. Not that I want to complain of what is done at all. But I think things would of had to have been different if our children all had of lived. Well my little sheet is almost full and I must stop for it is all I have because I neglected to get any paper yesterday and Sallie is writing some so thee must excuse us. Mary says she will write soon. With love an afft I remain

    Catharine A Peirce

   1. This letter was not found.

    Head Quarters 22n Iowa Inftr
    Cedar Creek Va Nov 2n 1864
    Dear Catharine and friends

I sit down this morning to write you once more to let you know what the army of the Shanandoah is doing and particularly what your humble servant is at. When I wrote you last we were all in commotion expecting to go to Stanton. Well that day the rebs made an attack on some of our forces out at Front Royal. Some of our division was sent out there to assist those already there. So they all went into the Johnies and give them another thrashing and they run so far that we have heard nothing from them since.[1] So we have just laid here waiting to see if they could raise another army to fight us in the Valley. I see in the papers that old Early has made a great speece to his army and gives them gass for stopping to pilfer our camps and strip the dead before their victory was complete and promises to lead them to victory if they will submit to strict discipline and fight like they used to under Jackson. That was Stonewall.[2] But I can tell him that they have a different kind of troops to fight now from what has ever been in the Valley before and all that I hope is that if we have to fight any more that they will attack us here so that we will not have to march after them. I also see by the papers that the Union troops are Victorious in every part of the country and that the Legislature of Alabama has refused to grant any more assistance to the confederacy and Georgia is in the same fix.[3] Grant too has advanced his lines around Petersburg and Richmond and is gradually tightening his grasp on the throat of the Rebellion and taking all things togather I think I see certain signs of the confederacy getting weak in the knees. My oppinion now is that the War will be endend in three months but maybe I reckon to fast. We are in camp here in shelter tents and the weather is getting cold. Many of us have but little clothing and suffer by the inclemency of the weather. A great many of the men had worn out their shoes and at the time of the fights lost almost all their clothing so that the army was in a very bad condition for the want of cloths. But we are now midling well shod and cloths are coming up as fast as they can get them and I think in the course of a week or so we will be in a good fix as regards clothing. But we will have to endure the cold as well as we can for I do not think we will get into Winter quarters this winter. I think the Government intends to put an end to the war and I for one am willing to undergo all the fiatigue and hardships of a winter campaign if we can only have peace in the spring. I am midling well clothed. I have got a pair of new Boots and an overcoat and new pants but I have no warm coat yet to wear arround the camp but I think maybe I will draw one to day as their was a lot of clothing comeing in last night. We were paid off for the months of July & August Yesterday and I will send thee some money by express the first chance I have. Well I must close as the mail is starting. Kiss the children. I will write more soon.

> thine affty
> Taylor

1. The 22nd Iowa participated in the pursuit of the Confederate army toward Strasburg after the battle of Cedar Creek. The regiment captured several prisoners and returned to its camp at Cedar Creek on October 23. There is no record of an attack at Front Royal.

2. Lieutenant General Thomas J. Jackson earned the nickname "Stonewall" at the first battle of Bull Run, July 1861. One brigade of Early's command fought under Jackson during the Shenandoah Valley campaign of 1862, during which they defeated three separate Union forces.

3. Relations between Governor Joseph E. Brown of Georgia and the central Confederate government in Richmond were strained throughout the war, primarily over the issue of states' rights. In August 1864 Brown refused to provide Georgia troops to the central government and cited the need for local defense as a reason. The debate continued until the end of the war. Governor Thomas H. Watts of Alabama had complained to the Confederate government since his inauguration in December 1863 about impressment of pork, work oxen, and iron; control of blockade running; and conscription. In October 1864 the Alabama House refused to allow the militia to be absorbed by the Confederate army.

>Des Moines Iowa Nov 6, 1864
>Dear Father.

It is with the greatest of pleasure that I seat myself to let thee know that we are all alive and well but poor kate, she died on wednesday last so now poor ann is left alone.

Frank went to church to day with Mother and I and he acted up so bad. Dear Fathe I do Wish that thee would write every time that thee has nothing to do. For thee dose not know how much good it dose me to get a letter. Oh papa write thee write thy opinion about me goin out and be a nurse girl for somebody and stay there till thee comes back. When thee reads this do not laugh for I can ern something for my self. Do pleas do say yes for then I can do some thing for my self and thee besides that I can save. What I do not use I can save and get clothing for Frank and Ellis and mother so I can do a good eal for myself and mother and little brothers. Oh do let me. Wont thee let me? I implore of thee to let me so I will have the satisfaction knowing wether I can work or not. Dear papa dos not thee think that I can do something or other for my self? Do tell me. It is most time to close my letter. I go to school now. I study the third part of Arethmatick and fourth part of geography and fifth reader and if they had it in the school I would study first part of grammer.
I must close my letter.

>From thy affectonate daughter Sarah A Peirce to her father.

>Des Moines Nov 13th /64
>Dear Taylor

I sit down to write but I do not know what it will be for I have nothing new to write of. We are all well and geting along in the same old

way. Cyrus is puting every Dollar he gets his hands on in improvements on the house. He is building a nice brick kitchen on at the East
end and has bought the small lot between the new stable and the
bridge and has it all levied up above high water from the bridge an up
the river to the edge of his lot west of the house so that he thinks he
has the house safe now. And they are doing a good business and must
be makeing money or he could not do all he has done this summer. As
for Cyrus his health has been as good this summer and fall so far as I
ever knew him to be for a great many years. He has had no bad spell
since the first of March though he is some what under the weather
since the storm. By way we have had a real old fashioned Iowa snow
storm. It commenced on the 8th and snowd and raind togather for
two days and now the sleighing is as good as could be for wishing for.
I do hope that C will get over the change in weather without haveing
the asthma or being laid up with his cold for he has been better contented for the last six months than I ever knew him to be since we
came to Iowa. Yet he wants to sell out and go to Maryland now that
she has come out a free state.[1] He thinks he would like the climate better there than here but it may all end in talk. So thee will have to wait to
see what time will bring forth for none of us can tell anything about what
he will do and therefore I listen to him and then let it go as the wind.

Well thee wants to know if the children grow well. I think they
have all had good health all the time since thee was at home so I do
not see any thing to prevent them from growing. Ellis is standing by
me on a chair and the first thing he said when I got the paper and pen
to write was Papa come home and he has learned to talk of thee every
day or when he sees a letter or a likeness they are all papa with him. I
think thee would think he was doing well if thee could just see him
at mischief and he is just as fat as a child could well be. The other children are well and go to school and I think are learning very well. But
I guess that they learn a good bit of meanness as well as thier lessons
for they are full of life and mischief and it is as much as I want to do
to keep them straight. And it is more than I can do at all times though
they do nothing really bad or wicked and I think that Frank for a boy
is right good for he nether swars or seems ill natured with his play-
mates. And that is quite an item for one of our family to hav a boy
six years old that did not sware and strike his mother. I do not know
of any but Jane [Hank?] that ever had one but did them kind of things

to the full extent of their will. Well Ellis has stood and spit all over the letter and made a pretty looking muss of it but I am so near done I guess I will send it any how and let thee see what thy baby can do. With love

       I remain forever thine
       Catharine

I receved 10$ from Ingersoll of the hundred this week and he wants to know if thee ever pays any tax on that Green County land and if so where are the recepts as we cannot find any among thy papers.

1. In the November 1864 elections Maryland voted for a state constitutional amendment to abolish slavery.

       Head Quarters 22 Iowa Inft
       Camp in the Field Near Opequon Creek
       Virginia Nov 13th 1864
       Dear Catharine

I received thy letter of Nov 1st yesterday and am very glad to hear that Cyrus is getting along so well and hope yet that he may be able to enjoy the closing hours of life with the comforts around him that he has waited so long for.

    Well we are again in Camp About 11 miles west or rather South west of Winchester on the North Bank of the Opequon Creek. We had been laying on the same ground that we fought the Battle of the 19th on for Some time. The day after the Election we were ordered to fall Back to this place which is about 10 miles from the Cedar Creek Battle Field.[1] The Rebles had been advancing on the Road from New Market and the Report was in Camp that Fitz Hugh Lees cavalry was coming down from Richmond on the East side of the Blue Ridge with the intention of crossing through Ashby gap or Snickers gap to attack our army in the rear. But wheather any of this true I am unable to say but I rather think not.[2] However We fell back here and have thrown up Strong breast works. The rebles followed us up promptly and we all expected an attack day before yesterday but after laying on line of Battle all day and all night we were ordered to go into camp again and we put up our tents and settled down in the usual way. About 2 hours after sunrise the Rebles come up and attacked our skirmishes and firing was kept up at intervals until about 2 o'clock when it ceased and the fight seemed as if about to die away. But Sheridan concluded he would give them a little brush any how and see what force they had. So he ordered out about 2,000 cavalry and one division of Infantry and about dark they made an attack on the Rebles and defeated them taking 200 prisoners 2 pieces of artillery and drove them 14 miles back to Fishers Hill. Our troops then returned and today we are all quiet again and I am of the opinion that we will not fight any more battles this fall in this Valley but I may be mistaken.[3] Things are progressing finely. Old Abe is again our chief Executive for another 4 years and if he does not succeed in saving the Union now it will not be because he has not time or power to do it. For I think that the people of the north are more determined to crush the Confederacy than ever before. The weather to day is quite cold so much so that I can hardly write and if I had have written last sunday I would not write. But I know you are anxious for my welfare and so I will do the best I can. I am well and in the best kind of spirit. I think now there is some prospect of the war closing. We are encamped in a fine open Plain. Our Regiment occupies a high piece of ground and we have a splendid view of the surrounding Country and the army as it Streaches off on either side of us for miles. And when it is warm enough I enjoy myself very much walking around to see the opperations of the Army and surrounding country. I have been in hopes that we were nearly through this campaign and that we would get into Winter Quarters soon as the weather is getting so cold that we will suffer if we do not get some more tents and clothing. But I reckon if the Reble Army can Stand it in their poorly arranged camps without any shoes we can stand it if we are clothed as well as we have been heretofore. And it is said that the Government is better provided with cloths than ever before so I suppose we will be clothed as soon as they can be brought in. I am still acting Sergeant Major and have been very busy with the Reports for the different departments at the War office but have got pretty well up now. And if we have no more battles I will not have so much to do as I have had for some time. I have had to work from daylight till 9 o'clock at night ever since I have occupied the position untill we movd and as we have been expecting a fight ever since we come here I have not been doing much. I think I will be at home this winter. I can get leave and I am almost inclined to accept it and pay you a visit and take a little rest. I have a good place and I would like to keep it as long as I can. Our Sergt Major was wounded at Fisher Hill[4] and has gone home and it is not likely he will be back before Spring and I will have to fill his place so I dont want to loose it. And before I conclude to come home I will see how it will affect my interests here. It is much easier to write and give orders than it is to carry a musket with 80 rounds of ammunition and all my traps. So I intend to try and play sharp and not do quite as much hard service from here out as I have done.

I have a good name and I intend keep it so. And if any thing should turn up that there is a vacancy I am sure to get it and if there does not I am well satisfied with what I have got. I am not exposed to near as much danger now as I was unless I chose to be. And I think for the benefit of my family I will not expose myself more than is needful for the benefit of the service.

Well it is so cold and I am bothered so with orders that I will close. If we get fixed up any I will write you a better letter this week. Kiss the children for me and give my love to all. I have $40 I intend to send home as soon as it is safe to send it. We have two months more pay due us and I hope we will get it soon so that I can send it all home at once. When thee writes to me again I want thee to write to me how thee manages about cloths for the children. Everything is so high that I am afraid that my wages will not keep you and if it does not I must make some exertion to make some more some way or other for I do not want thee to be an expense on Cyrus while I am away. I had hoped that what money I could make would more than pay your way and be of some advantage to Cyrus besides. But if it does not I must make it up some way. Write soon and let me know all about things Generally.

> I remain thine affectionately
> Taylor

1. The 22nd Iowa encamped on the Cedar Creek battlefield until November 9, when the Union army withdrew to the vicinity of Kernstown near Winchester and went into winter quarters.

2. Major General Fitzhugh Lee was Robert E. Lee's nephew. He had been seriously wounded at Winchester and did not return to the army until January 1865. What Taylor relates is a false rumor.

3. On November 10 Early's cavalry followed the Union army and two days later met the Union Second Cavalry Division commanded by Brigadier General William H. Powell near Middletown. The Confederates were defeated, with losses of 2 ar-

tillery pieces, 20 killed, 35 wounded, and 161 captured. Union losses were 2 killed and 15 wounded.

4. Sergeant Major David Higbee was an Ohio native and Iowa City resident when he enlisted August 22, 1862. He was promoted to sergeant major September 21, 1864, and was severely wounded the next day. He returned and was promoted to captain March 14, 1865. He was mustered out July 25, 1865.

Des Moines City
Nov 20th 1864
Dear Taylor

It is sunday again and I sit down to write and it Will be the same old thing over again for I know nothing new but what thee will be likely to know by the time this goes to thee. The best of all is that old Abe is reelected with an unheard of majority of the Northern States and with the Soilders Vote[1] it dose make the poor Cops about this town hang their heads very low and keep their mouth mighty close. It will be likely to convince them that it no use talking for the people are bound to have their way and it seems to me that the way that things will be done up in the next four years will be a caushion to Copperheads and Rebles or at least I feel in hope that by the time that old Abe's time is out there will not be one of ether sort to be found in those US.

Well Taylor I have had my dinner and if thee could only of had share of it I would of been glad. I never sit down to a good meals vitels but I think of thee and wonder in my own mind if thee has any thing to eat or any that thee can eat and how thee gets along at this present time and if thee only was with me. Though I do not let myself think of thee untill I get meloncoly if I can help it. For I still think there is surely better times for us yet in this world and that thee will get home to me and the children and then Oh then we Will for get all the troubles and trials we have had and settle down in our old days and be happy with our little ones to grow up to bless us in the decline of life. And we can say we have done our duty to our Country and to our selves and our children as well. As like in our power wheather we have served God in a proper maner or not of that he will have to be the judge in his own good time. But I hope that we will be not cast off entirely for the meny little wrongs done in the mortal life but be excepted into the life immortal for the few good deeds done to our fellow mortals. Dear

Taylor I have had to stop a bout fourty times in writeing thus far and I can not tell how many times more I may have. And I beg pardon for not having written something of more importance than I have. Yet it is a task to me at least to try to write and have to stop and give this child a drink and do some thing for another but that is a mothers work and if it well done it may be pays in time to come. I begin to see the reward of my work on Sallie now for I think we have one of as smart little girls as common to find blonging to such as we. And with the chance she has I will not trouble thee with a catalouge of her doing but suffice to say that she is in all the large classes in the school that she goes to. She is not only in those classes but she keeps up with them in all her studies and is as far advanced as many that come that is fourteen years of age. And thee better think she feels good when talks of it to me and says how glad she is that I taught her so well before she ever went to school. I must say I feel rather good myself to see her get along so well. Not takeing the credit to myself but knowing that I have done all that lay in my power to do for her. Frank is growing very fast and I think is learning some but the school is to large for the teacher to do justice to the little one and then for they will not learn so fast as if the teacher could tend to them better. And there is so much to do here that I can not learn Frank right so I thought he might learn what he could this winter as he has time enough yet to grow and learn too before he is a man. And if he is inclined to study he will be likely to know enough for he can learn fast enough for one of his age. Now as for master Ellis he is healthy as need be now and as full of mischief as I want to attend to and he goes over the house and make all the rest stand about if he takes in his head. For he is a perfect fight a bust and so hard to controle. He has such a temper. It just like fire and tow but I live in hope that he will improve when he gets older. If he does not wo unto him and all concerned.

Boliver was here this week. He has got home with out a scare or a scratch and I tell thee he is a good Lincoln man. But he dose not think he will go back this winter. He says that Doke Cole was taken prisoner in Georgia near Atlanta.[2] I stopd for Sallie to write some and she dose not know of any thing to write so I will close this up and try to write again soon. With love

    I remain thy own
    Catharine

1. Lincoln received 55 percent of the popular vote and 212 electoral votes to Mc-Clellan's 45 percent and 21 electoral votes. The voting among Iowa soldiers was 17,252 for Lincoln and 1,920 for McClellan.

2. No one by the name of Doke Cole served in an Iowa regiment. Samuel D. Cole, Company I, 39th Iowa Infantry, was captured at Allatoona, Georgia, on October 5, 1864. He was a resident of Des Moines and might be the soldier to whom Catharine is referring.

> Head Quarter 22n Iowa Infy
> Camp Ruple Nov 23d 1864
> Dear Catharine

I have not written as I have been in the habit of doing for the reason that I have been occupied all the time that it was warm Enough to write in fixing up the Regimental Business. Well the Campaign in the Shenandoah Valley is Over. We have fought the Rebles 5 General Engagements and any number of partial ones and whipped them every time and at last they have concluded to leave the Valley and I have just drawn one long dilicious breath of relief.

We fell Back to this place two weeks ago today. At that time the remnent of Earlys Army with some reinforcments had been several days at Woodstock and Sheridan had been trying to draw him out for some days without success. So when we fell back Early thinking that Sheridan was going to leave the Valley to reinforce Grant followed us up. Sheridan let him get up to within two miles of the main army and then made preperations to give him another thrashing. He then Sent the Cavalry out to commence the fight who pitched into them and Captured 2 guns and about 250 pirisoners and drew the cavalry up the Luray Vally. The Infantry then movd out to attack their main body but they could not be made to Stand so they had to leave in double Quick. The last we heard of them they were at Staunton about 80 miles up the Valley. Since then we have had breathing time. This took place last Sunday week.

We are now encamped on the Opequan Creek 4 miles from Winchester and 2 from Newton. Orders has just been issued to go into winter Quarters So we will have no more fighting or hard marching this Winter. The weather has been very cold. The men having nothing but Shelter tents and many of them not even them and also poody clad have suffered with the cold. We lost nearly all our camp Equipage on the 19 of October and although it was recaptured yet it was in such a heterogenious muss that we could not identify the articles and but little of it was recovered by the real owners. I have made out to get myself a new pair of boots and an overcoat and keep midling comfortable. Not having any duty to do I fare better than many of the poor fellows. I tell you this thing of soldering in the cold stormes is pretty hard exercise. The Mountains on either side of us is covered with snow and the wind blows off them with a keenness hardly excelled by the cutting blast of Iowa. The War news is not important and I suppose that you hear it as soon as I do anyhow. So I leave it. I received a letter from thee and Sallie on Sunday and will write to Sallie as soon as I can get time. I had intended to have written to thee before this but I could not get time.

I am well and feel now as if this war was about over. I think when Sherman is next heard from he will have cut the Rebellion in two again. And I think from appearances that Grant will give Richmond another turn soon. I am still acting Sergt Major and have been employed for over a week in writing the Millitary history of the Regt. So when it is published you will have a chance to see some of you humble Servants qualities as a Historian among the other things that he has done. I get along fine as far as my dutys is concerned with my Officers and have never yet had a harsh word from any one. They all treat me with much respect and kindness and will always have my warmest regards.

My arm has got almost well again. It pains me sometimes when the weather is damp and cold, but I think it will be all right in a week or so. I forgot to tell you what good eating I had out of my box and what a handy thing it is. I am much obliged to you all for your trouble and will try and repay it. If not in money in sincere affection. I have heard nothing from Rachel Since I came into the Valley and wheather they have written or wheather the letters have miscarried I can not tell. I think of nothing more at present and as the mail is waiting I must close and go to Supper.

I had $40 which I intended to send home but owing to the danger of sending any thing of the kind I did not get a chance that I thought was a safe one. So on Sunday when the fight was about to come off I loaned it to an officer to be returned in 20 days. So when that time comes I will send it to you. I think we will be paid off and I can send

$50 more. With love I must close. Kiss the little ones for me and give my love to all.

I am thine as ever
Taylor

Des Moines Nov 27th 1864
Dear Brother

I have not written to thee for some time. It is not because I do not think of thee but because I have so many cares that I cannot get time. Their is never a day goes past without something being said about the dear absent one.

We are all well at this time accept slight colds. Cyruss healt is better than it has been in a long time. Catherine and the children are well. Frank looks pale but seems well. Ellis is as fat as he can be. Every one is surprised to see him come out such a fine healthy boy. He can say every thing in his way. He calls Frank mank. When Frank does any thing that offends him he says dog on Mank as plane as any one. He is badly petted and spoild. We all help to that. No one can blame the others. Sallie and Frank go to school. I have not herd Sallie recite since Kate Kelly took sick but I think Frank learns. They are good children. Thy have their faults. Who of us have not. Their Uncle thinks they are better than any children that comes here visiting.

We have fifteen steady boarders. We charge four and a half a week but every thing is so high that we do not make any more than we used to at two dollars. We have every comfort. We never sit down to meal but what their is something good on the table that we wish we could share with thee. I hope to see the time when the war will be over and we can all meet around a plentiful table without haveing to regrett thy absence accompanied wiht the painful thought that perhaps thee is liveing on hard tack fat pork and not enough of that. Still my heart rises in thankfulness to our heavenly Father that thy life has been spared. It is my nightly prayer that thee may live to come home and live to raise these little ones. I do not want thee to think I am tired of them or trying to make them comfortable.

Franky and I ware up to Elizabeth Smiths yesterday visiting. She sent her best respects to thee. I suppose Catherine told thee all about

Kate Kelly comeing over and dieing here. She lay nearly six weeks and I had no girl but Amanda Sprague.

Olliver White has two girls by his first wife Rebecca Alexander. Their names are Clara and Addy. Addy looks like Elizabet Paxson and Clara looks some like her mother. Has the handsomest hair I ever seen. It is dark brown and hangs in curls. And they are good as well as pretty. They are not proud nor lazy. They come and set up with Kate and helped me out or I would most certainly have stalled. Phebe White spent the day with us since she come out. It looked so natural to see her old quaker bonnets and cap and book muslin handkerchief. She sent her love to thee. The election went off very peaseable at this place and Abraham is realected. That suits me exactly. I have not herd from Rachel for some time. She was well the last time she wote. This is a poor letter but my eyes have been sore ever since I had the measles and when I sit down to read or write they get a scum over them so I can not see to follow the lines. I have got some drops that I think is helping them now. Please write to me often. We did not get a letter last week. It is a long week that brings no letter from thee. If thee can get off go and see Rachel. She wishes in every letter that thee would come. I hope my eyes will better soon and then I can write more next time. Cyrus send his love. He has wached the post office very closely since thee has been in the Shanendoah vally. I remain as ever

> thy affectionate sister
> Mary

Des Moines Nov 27th 1864
Dear Taylor
We are all well to day and I hope thee is too but we have some sickness amonge the boarders. There is one man has the typhoid fever and a lady boarder has the lung fever here. So thee may know that we still have enough to do there is sixteen boarders in all besides me and the children and two of them sick. So thee better think we have an interesting time with sick folks. But I can not help but be thankful that it is not any of us. I mean myself on the children or Cyrus or Mary. C had a very bad cold last week but he got over it with out a bad spell of the Asthma and that of its self was a good thing. I do not believe

that the house has been clear of sickness six weeks at a time since I came to it two years ago and more. There seems to be some out sick here nearly all the time and there has been two deaths in the last year. One a Soldier died of inflamation of the lungs after haveing the measles in may and Kate Kelly of typhoid fever about a month a go.[1] And now if those folks that are sick are to keep the sickness going. It is much better for me than if it was some of us though. I tell thee it keeps the house in a state of trouble to have someone sick all the time as it is here. I might as well be keeping house to my self for all the time I get past helping in the house and taken care of the children. But I feel so glad that I am well all the time so I can do some thing that I will not dare to complain but try to do all I can to help Mary and take good care of our babys and keep them well if it is possible untill thee gets home to help me take care of them. Little Ellis talks of thee everyday now by hearing the others talking. He can talk so plain for his age more so than ether of the others could when they were no older than he. And he is so fat and healthy thee would not know him I know. If thee dose not come home this winter I think I will have to send thee another likeness of him for he has changed so since I had that one taken that thee has. The dear little thing he has got to be so good and so loveing though he has a very firery temper. But I think with a little training with the intulect that he has that he will not be any worse than thyself or I. He seems to be more like our oldest child than ether of the others with the exception of his quick temper and blue eyes. Well Taylor I have run on writeing and have writen an thing yet that amounts to much. So I will ask a few questions. In the first place how did the Johnies like the reelection of old Abe in that part of the world? And next did any of the contribution for thank given dinner reach you? For there has been a deal gathered up and sent to the soldiers in the way of turkeys and other good thing. And I would like to know if your Reg got any of it and if so how the boys enjoyed thanksgiven. All the truly loyal in town shut up their shops and kept the day in acordance with the proclamation of the Govern and President and the Cops were so badly used up by the election that they had to keep quiet on that day as well as for all time here after.

Evening. I haveing writen one sheet full in the morning I thought I would see if Sallie would write but she is on the fly up so that she has not taken time to write any and as Mary is sending a letter I

though that it would do. We have not had a letter from thee this week but we will wait with patience for a few more days hopeing to get a good one when it dose come. I bleive I have not much more to write of at presant only hopeing thee is well and in good heart and get along with thy work what ever it may be without any trouble to thyself or those that is a bove thee in the service. And thee may be assured that we at home think of thee often and wonder how thee get a long just at this particular time and how we would like to have thee at home and all this if it was so that we could have all we want. Well I have all most run out for I have not been out of the house since the snow that fell on the 8th of the month so thee cannot expect me to know much. We have had one old Iowa winter so far. The snow lasted a week or ten days. Good sleighing and then it rained and now the mud is so deep that it is impossible for a woman to get out side the house without being stuck fast. So I gues I will close for this time
with love

          I remain thy ever efec wife
          Catharine A Peirce

    1. Typhoid fever was particularly prevalent in the armies because of the presence of contaminated food and water, and it was often fatal. It spread among the civilian population as soldiers traveled through the larger cities, and a boarding house was an extremely likely place for the disease to be passed.

          Head Quarters 22n Iowa
          Camp Ruple Va Nov 28/64
          Dear Catharine

I Received thy letter to day and was glad to hear from you and also to hear of the children. The little things I know that they feel as if they would like to have me at home but as the war is not over it is impossible to tell when I will get to see you. I feel as if it is hardly worth while for me to spend 2 months pay to come home to stay 30 days when in the course of 8 months more I will be with you for good if I live. If I should not the money will be needed for the use of thee and the little ones and if I should live and get home I will stand in need of all I can get to start on again for I expect I will have to commence the world again. But I feel equal to the task. I am in good health and in good spirits and feel that if Sherman is successfull in his march through Georgia that this war will end again Spring.

Well we are now laying just where we were when I wrote thee last. We have had nothing to change the routine of Camp life since the Sunday after we come down here.

We had some of the Poultry that there has been such blowing about in the NY papers but the Turkeys all turned into Ducks and geese when they arrived at our camp. And our Company consisting of 27 men only got one old Muss corn Duck and one goose for our Thanksgiving Dinner. But the boys eat it and seemed thankful for it. I gave them my share as I thought it would do them more good than it would me. So I made my Thanksgiving Dinner on hard tack and sow belly. We were yesterday ordered to prepare to go into winter Quarters and as soon as the regiment returns we will go to work to put up huts and make ourselves comfortable.

I had forgot to say the Regt had gone to Martinsburg as guard for subsistance train and I have been left in charge of convalescents and the camp until it returns. The government has repaired the Rail Road from Harpers Ferry to the Opequan Creek within about 4 miles of Winchester and they are about transferring our base of Supplies to the End of the road. And I suppose when the Regt gets back we will not have any more long marches this winter. I suppose that we will have to do our share in guarding the road, but that will be a small job in comparison to what we have had to do. I will be relieved from the duties of Sergeant Major as soon as the Col get back as our Sergeant Major has got back and is again able to do his duty. The weather is now quite mild and we are getting along more comfortable than we have for several weeks. This is a poor pen and if you can read this letter you will do well.

Well Kitty I am going to try for a commission now. I do not know wheather I will have enough influence in the Regiment to obtain it or not and want you folks at home to assist me some if you can.

I will tell you how it is. Our adjutant has been promoted to Captain and the young man who was Recommended to take his place whose name was Oscar. B. Lee was wounded the same day that I was and has since died[1] so that the thing is now open for me to pitch in. I do not know wheather Col Graham will feel so bound to his Johnson County friends[2] that he will pass over me or not but I can get a recommendation from all the rest of the officers in the regiment and I know that Col Graham would like for me to have it. But wheather he will be able to withstand the importunity of the Johnson County friends I know not. The Rule that has been adopted is that the Cols recommendation was all that was required and in the absence of that no Commission was issued. So you see that if his name is not on my recommendation my chance is slim. But I think in this case if the thing was explained to Stone he knowing how things is I think he would not feel obliged to stand Strictly to the rule.[3]

They all say that I am the best qualified for the position of any man in the Regiment and that I ought to have it. Also Col Stone when he left the Regiment told Col Graham that he wished him to give me a position if any vacancy occurred. And I think that if some of you at home would present the case for me that he would give me the commission as it is the first thing of the kind I have ever asked and I have been as good a friend to him as ever he had in the service. I have written to Frank Allen to see if he will use his influence for me and I wish Cyrus to see if I have any show and write to me. I know that I have a right to the position and I Know that I can and will if commissioned attend to with honor and fidelity. And I know also that I have had to preform the duties for which other men got paid because they were not qualified to fill the places they held and I want this place so that I can receive some compensation for what I preform. I am not out of conceit of being a private soldier for I have received the highest praise from many for being the best Orderly in the Regt and I feel proud that I have done my duty and have served my country with honor. And if I should not get any thing more I will feel under no obligations to any one for favors. So I will be contented any how but I would feel much better if I could feel that the Governor would do me justice. For he knows that I had to do Aults business for him and he also knows this Captain Mullins Education was so limited that I had to do that and amongst all I had to leave my company and preform the duties of Sergt Major and Regimental Clerk. And all that I ask now is that I may receive some mark of honor from my country. You need not fear to ask Col Stone personally for if he feels that he can not promote me he will treat you kindly and I am certain that there will be some good reason for refusing you. Now I wish you to write to me imediately about this for the sooner you do whatever you conclude to do the better. If I could get something of that kind it would probably be some advantage to you if I was to get Killed or die. For the pension would be larger and might help materially in educating the children and raising them. This is all recollect. Procrastination is the thief of time. I was over to see the 28th Iowa to day. The boys are all well that are alive. Bill Iliff is cooking for Capt Atwood and I got a good dinner. Wright Wilson has received his commis for Adgt of the 28th Iowa and Major Myers is well.[4] I must quit for the mail goes out. Kiss the little ones for me and tell Sally that I love her very much for the progress she makes at School. As soon as I am relieved from this I will write her a long letter. Give my love to all and receive my warmest affection for thy care and instruction to the children and also for thy fortitude that thee has from my absence through this trying time.

> I am thine affectionately
> Taylor

1. Samuel B. Pryce was a Pennsylvania native and Iowa City resident when he enlisted June 18, 1862. He was promoted to sergeant major May 1, 1863, to adjutant January 11, 1864, and to captain October 1, 1864. He then took command of Company A. Oscar B. Lee was an Indiana native and Iowa City resident when he enlisted August 22, 1862. He was promoted to second lieutenant May 11, 1864, and to adjutant October 1, 1864. He was wounded at Cedar Creek on October 19 and died as a result of those wounds on October 31.

2. Harvey Graham was a resident of Iowa City, which is in Johnson County.

3. On December 3, 1864, thirteen officers of the regiment submitted a recommendation to Governor Stone that Peirce be promoted to first lieutenant and assigned to the position of adjutant. On December 10 Colonel Harvey Graham, regimental commander, forwarded his own recommendation for Peirce to Brigadier General Baker. Major John Meyer, commander of the 28th Iowa Infantry, added his recommendation to Governor Stone on December 11.

4. William J. Iliff was an Indiana native and resident of Newton when he enlisted August 4, 1862. He was mustered out July 31, 1865. Merritt W. Atwood was a Connecticut native and Newton resident when appointed first lieutenant on August 4, 1862. He was promoted to captain April 14, 1863, and was mustered out July 31, 1865. For J. Wright Wilson, see the letter dated March 28, 1863. For John Meyer, see the letter dated April 18, 1863.

> Des Moines City Nov 29h
> Dear Taylor

We are all well today except Sallie has a bad cold and is not very well because of it but I hope it will not last long. We are having about as cold wether as ever I have seen this time in the year. The snow is six inches deep and the river is frozen over so that persons can cross on the ice on foot and that is more than they could do all last winter. It seems as though we are going to have a very hard winter this year if it keeps on the way that it has set in. But I hope that it will not be so cold after New years as it is now. If it is I shall wish my self in Dixie with thee for thee knows that I like warm wether so much the best although it is not so healthy for me. I have as good health this winter as I ever had in all my life I believe. And if thee was at home and fit up to keep house I could do about as much as I ever could. Not that I want to work as hard as I have done some of the time since we have been in Iowa. But then I want to let thee know how well I am so thee need not be uneasy on acount of my health. I have some bad news to write to day that took place yesterday. Turners tall house at the end of the coon Bridge took fire between three and four O clock and burned down to the ground and Mr Baker lost nearly all of his things with it. He and the old Lady are staying here to day and the children are at Dr Mathers in East Des Moines and likely will remain so untill they can get fixt up again. It is a hard matter to get a house in town now. Every place that can hold a person is full and I do not know what they will do. But I suppose there will be some way provided for I neve seen any one get in to a snap but what they got out of it in some way or other. The way may not seem as pleasant as they could wish but be for the best after all. It seems as though no one knows how it the house took fire. The first that was seen of it the [illegible] they used for a kitchen was all in a blase so that they could not put out the fire.

Dear Taylor I had to stop short in the midst of writing to attend to the baby so I will have to begin in a fresh place and I do not know what to write. Only that I received thy letter of the first of the month[1] this last week and was very glad to hear from thee and that thee is well and in good spirits and that there is a prospect of not haveing much fighting to down there. We are haveing good news from all the departments East and the news is to day that Charleston has been on fire for Sixty hours and Gillmores Shells do not put it out at all.[2] So I hope that December will be a mounth that will be equal to july last and then we will have peace pritty soon. I was right well please to hear of that fellow matching the Gen, so well that with his biscute and his pork for I think he had as much right to it as the Genl had. For it is considered as bad to use stolen things as to steal but enough. It is not for me to Judge of those things so I will close. The children are carring on so that I can not write to do much good and their are so noisey that I can not hear my self think. With love I remain thy afec wife

Catharine A Peirce

1. This probably refers to his letter of November 2.
2. Union troops landed on Morris Island in Charleston Harbor in July 1863 and completed their occupation of the island in September. In August guns on the island began a bombardment of the city that would last until February 1865. Fires from bursting shells occurred almost daily, and the lower part of the city was completely destroyed by the shelling. Major General Quincy A. Gillmore commanded the Union Department of the South that was besieging Charleston. He was transferred to Fort Monroe during the summer of 1864 but returned to command the department in January 1865.

Head Quarters 22n Iowa
Camp Russl [Russell] Va Dec 19th 1864
Dear Catharine & Friends.

I set down to night to give you some information concerning things in the Shenandoah Valley and the news from the other Military Departments within the Dominions of Uncle Samuel.

We have got fixed up here and are more comfortable than we have ever been since we have been in the Service. Our Camp is built in regular order of logs and the huts are about 10 feet by 12 and 5 feet high and covered with our shelter tents with a fire place built of stone in one corner and a chimney run up like the Iowa Stick chimneys and are large enough to contain 4 men. The Streets are about 15 feet wide and the companies are encamped on Each side of the Street. Our Co. has 4 tents on Each side and the Captain and I have our tent about 20 yards from the mens quarters at the head of the Street and about half way to the Head quarter tents. We have plenty to eat and have got well clad. The Regiment look as well as it ever did but the number present is not so large as it was one year ago. When we were on Matagorda Island the aggregate number belonging to the Regiment was 666. About 475 of them were present. Now the aggregate is only 570. The number present is only about 345. I have just finished the history of the Regiment and find that we have had one Thousand & Eight men mustered in to the Service. Of those 53 have been Killed in battle, 54 Died of wounds, 101 Died of Disease, 36 deserted, 36 Transferred, 142 discharged, and 54 officer resigned. So you See that the Effective force is continually dwindling away. 208 of the poor fellows now fill gravs in a Southron land far from their sorrowing friends. And many of those who are discharged have their constitutions shattered So that their future will have but little enjoyment. I often feel thankful that I have been so highly favoured as to have escaped thus far without any material injury. We are enjoying ourselves pretty well now since we got our huts up. I have been so busy that I have had no time to look round untill to-day. I finished up my report to the Adjutant Genl of Iowa and the History of Regiment last night and to-day we all took a spree. We had as much ale and Porter as we could drink and had a good time generally. After resting all day I concluded I would try and write this letter but I am afraid it will not be much of a one for I feel wore out in my mind after such incessent Study for over a month. And it seem to me as if the figures and letters were passing continually before my Eyes. Not that it has been difficult but it has been very bothesome to hunt up and State what has become of 437 men for the last 2 years. And tell where they have all gone is a more troublesome job than I ever wish to undertake again. The 28th Iowa and the 24th is encamped in sight of us and scarcely a day passes but I see some of my acquaintainces. They are the only Iowa troops besides our Regt that is in this department and as the western troops do not like the Eastern Irish we keep pretty sociable among the troops from our own state. The News from Genl Thomas, he having defeated Hood, and the News from Sherman at Savanna, is so cheering, that we begin to feel that we can smell our own firesides and see the loveing smiles that are Saved to greet us when we arrive at home.[1] Oh that the time would come. As I set here listning to the cold north wind roaring down from Loudons Snow Capt Mountains and whistling round our wide Solder huts my mind wanders away over hill and plain across the mighty Mississippi to your fireside. Fancy shows a warm room with clean beds, and the little ones dancing around your loved forms. It makes me feel as if all else was naught. Oh how I wish I could once more be With you. With the land in peac and prosperity I think I could be content to wear out the remainder of my life in your company without any other wish. But I am afraid the end is not yet and months I fear must roll over our heads before the time will come that I will be with you.

I hope I will never be called upon to take part in another battle, but if it has to be I will try and do my duty as here heretofore. After the excitement of conflict is over it sikens me to see the effects of war. While my blood is up, I do not mind it, and can see men torn to pieces by my side without feeling for them. But when all is quiet, and the re-action takes place, a man must be made of stone if he can view the dead and mangled forms of his comrades without Shuderings.

But I will not dwell on this. Our Country needs me. It is in dan-ger or at least the liberties of her citizens are endangered, and I feel as if I must help her out. And I would rather fill an honorable grave than come home to you a dishonered Soldier. And I know you would rather I would never come if I can not come with honor. My trust is in him who rules all things. I have just had some stewed beef and hard tack and feel better. Our cook has been stewing some beef for break-fast and dinner tomorrow, and as we have had no supper or rather we have been having dinner and Supper togather about 4 oclock, I felt hungry and Cap and I went into his stew and Eat it up. So we will have short allowance tomorrow, but enough for the present is our mottoe. And we have rarely suffered for our improvidence.

I think when I wrote you last I told you of the snow. Well we have been having a taste of Eastern Winter Since. 3 days of snow and cold, 3 days of Rain, and slush, and now the wind is howling down from the mountains as cold as the heart of a Coquette, and I think by to-morrow the whole country will be frose up. I feel for the soldiers in the field. The 8th Corps left here this morning it is said for Washing-ton, thence to Petersburg and of cours will have to encamp on the wet ground with nothing but their Shelter tent and a blanket on them, and it makes me shiver to think of their situation. There is no troops left here now, but the 19th Corps and Some Cavalry.[2] And I am afraid that we will have to pull up and leave here soon. I would like to stay here now. We have got so well fixed, but I suppose there is no use in tak-ing trouble about it; for when we are needed, we must go. I received two letters from you last week and am now looking for another. I wish to inform you of one thing that I suppose you do not think of. You write your letters on Sunday and put them in the office on Monday. The consequence is they are not mailed untill Tuesday. It is then too late to get through that week, and in laying over on Sunday, they are not distributed at the distributing office and I do not get them untill Thursday or Friday some 10 or 12 days after they are written. Now if you would put them in so that they would come out in the monday mornings mail, I would get them on the Saturday of the same week, and maybe on Friday. The letter that Catharine wrote me on the 9th[3] I received on the 14. So you see when they get a good start they get here fresh, and I feel nearer home then when I get one that has been written 2 weeks. Mary wished me to let her know how our thanksgiving Dinner went off. Well for my part I did not have any. I think I wrote you before that the share we received was two old Ganders, and as there was 28 hearty men to eat them without me, I gave my share to the rest of them. But I tell you it was all a damned humbug. The idea of sending a few old geese out to the army in the field to cook in an old Iron Mess Pan, without any seasoning, is to ridiculous for any but fools to think of. Boiled Goose. Great God. It puts me in mind of the nigger whose master boiled two Eggs in a pint of water and give him the broth.

The thing does well enough to put in the Newspapers to blow about and the men who gets such a thing up are a set of cowards who are afraid to come out and help us fight so they must do something to have to brag about. And as it costs as little to blow old goose as any thing else they go to work and make a mamoth enterprise of it and publish their magnificent munificence to the world. I have no doubt but many who read the papers was amazed at the gigantic efforts put forth to feed the poor Soldiers. But just think of it. 28 men with 4 iron Stew pans with 4 hard tack per day to the man and ¾ of a lb of Pork or one lb of fresh beef making up a large thanksgiving dinner with 2 geese. And the ridiculousness of the thing will occur to you at once. I tell you that the best food for the soldiers in the field is just what Government supplies him with. If he can get a little fruit to prevent the scurvy he will enjoy better health and prepare it with less trouble than he could with all the viands you could send him. In the Hospitals it would be different. There they have fires and utensils to cook with and the sanitary commission[4] furnishes things that they might cook a goose or Turkey with and enjoy it. But the damned drunken, thieving, doctors and their pimps, leave but little for the sick except the Govt rations and generly the sick in the hospital fares worse than they do in the field. If I was at the head of things I would have the majority of the Surgeons dismissed from the service and would cover the face of the earth thicker with their dishonered carcuses than ever Hell was With Fidlers. The sanitary commission too is so corrupt that I fear that much of the comforts placed in their hands find their way into the pockets of the managers, instead of the stomachs of the sick and wounded. For instance, I have known the celebrated Anne Whitemyer[5] Send one Shoulder Strap gentleman a whole basket of Champaign to gorge himself and friends with when the Solders had to go without. When if they could have had a couple of spoonfuls to put in some panada it might have been a great benefit to them. But I suppose she thought an officer could speak more in her favour than a private, and self interest is the ruling principle. I hope the Devil will have Hell heated up and ready for such. I have just heard the most cheering news. Genl Sheridan just received a dispatch from Genl Grant stating that he had a reliable news from Richmond than Jeff Davis had twice tried to poison himself and that yesterday morning his life was despaired of.[6] It also stated that the success of the campaign in Georgia was the cause of the depression of spirits that caused him to take this step. If this is so (and I hope his soul has left his infernal body) we will be at home in time yet to put in our spring grain. Well the hour is late and I am getting cold so I think I will stop writing untill morning.

Dec 20th I begin again. The weather is very cold to day. We had a regular north blow last night and the ground is as hard as a rock. The field and Staff are erecting huts and I think we will get to occupy our quarters some time yet. I had forgotten my Commission. How is it? Has Govonor Stone come to Washington and had he left before my recommendation got there? If so I suppose it will have to lay untill he gets back. The Col is very anxious for it to come as our old adjutant has received his commiss and has been mustered leaving the Regiment without an adjutant. And I am now acting without any other authority than by order of the Col. It is possible that you had better send my recommendation to Genl Baker[7] if Stone does not get home before the last of this month. However I am pretty certain to get it when the time comes round as the Col has refused to recommend any other one so I do not feel in any way uneasy about it. I am having a very comfortable time for one in the Field and am very thankfull to our officers for it. I am truly glad that Sallie is making such progress with her studies. As for Frank I do not care wheather he does much at it or not. For I am of the oppinion that it is not right to tax the mind while too young, and I feel confident that unless he alters there will be little trouble in instructing him. Sallie will require an effort to make herself a good scholar but from that very fact it shows that she has the will to study and where there is a will there is always success and many a slow scholar makes the brightest men and woman. Tell her if she is able to tell me the principles of the right angle Triangle when I get home I will give her a new dress. I hardly know what to write about. I suppose the little one is all right. You say that he has some temper. I am glad of it for people without temper is a poor stick in this world unless they are fools and I do not believe our children are such. I have all your pictures before me and all that I see wrong about him is that he does not show enough of activity but he may come of that when he gets in motion. I glad that you are comfortable and I hope you will all be contented for I find that one spot of cool fresh air suits me better than the damp frozen atmosphere of the Shenandoah Valley. Although this is a beautiful country to look upon yet the cold damp winds strikes me to the heart. I doubt very much if I will enjoy as good health here as I have done heretofore in the West and south. I am having the first real old cold that I have had since I left Penna and feel just like I used to then. But I think I will get over it without much trouble as it has broke up and I have been getting better for some days. I guess I must stop for the mail will go out soon. Kiss the little ones and recive my tenderest regards.

     Farewell

     Taylor

1. On November 30 Union forces under Major General John M. Schofield defeated Confederates commanded by General John Bell Hood at Franklin, Tennessee. On December 15 and 16 Thomas inflicted such a decisive defeat on Hood at Nashville that the Confederate Army of Tennessee was virtually ineffective for the remainder of the war. Sherman departed Atlanta on November 15 and reached Savannah on December 10. On December 21 the Confederate army abandoned the city, and Sherman occupied it.

2. On December 9, 1864, the Sixth Corps was recalled to Petersburg. The First Division, Army of West Virginia (also referred to as the Eighth Corps), departed the Shenandoah Valley December 19. The Second Division would move to Cumberland, Maryland, on December 30.

3. This letter was not found.

4. The U.S. Sanitary Commission was created on June 13, 1861, to fulfill functions the government could not meet, such as raising hygiene standards, caring for the sick and wounded, and arranging for food and other supplies to be sent to the armies. The commission also applied political pressure to erect hospitals and evaluate surgeons. Several of Taylor's letters are written on stationery provided by the Sanitary Commission. Soldiers often complained, though, that the commission deferred too much to officers at the expense of enlisted men.

5. Annie Turner Wittenmyer moved to Keokuk, Iowa, from Ohio with her husband, William, in 1850. She became concerned about the food served to hospitalized soldiers when she visited her brother, who was sick with typhoid fever and dysentery, in a military hospital in Sedalia, Missouri. She established what became known as Diet Kitchens to provide the sickest soldiers in military hospitals with meals that resembled, as closely as possible, those they had at home. She soon became the superintendent of Army Diet Kitchens and wrote a manual on feeding the sick. By the end of the war the Diet Kitchens were serving 2 million rations each month in military hospitals. She became friends with Julia Grant, and after the war the Grant administration provided her with a pension of $50 a month. She then became active in the Anti-Saloon League. On April 12, 1863, she was at Milliken's Bend, and it is possible that Taylor met her during that visit.

6. In December there were many rumors that Confederate President Jefferson Davis was ill, dead, or dying. In fact, he was ill and did much of his work from his home.

7. Nathaniel B. Baker was adjutant general of Iowa. He was a Democrat who strongly supported the war. Previously he had studied law in the office of Franklin Pierce, had twice been Speaker of the U.S. House of Representatives, and had been governor of New Hampshire.

[No date, but refers to the photographs mentioned in Taylor's December 25 letter]

Dear Kate

I have a few little things for the children in the shape of Photographs that I will send and taking them for my text I will write thee some for thyself and the little ones. In the first place I look upon the art of taking the form of people and scenes as being a gift that few have and even those few have frequently not had their gift cultivated. It shows to me that those who have it are persons of fine sensibility and impressible natures who when they see a thing either beautiful or ludicrous makes such vivid impressions on the mind that they are enabled to transfer it to paper, or to give it form in some other way. Hence the reason why so many of the gifted become unhappy. It is not because of their gift, but because there is so few that can appreciate them, or enter into their feelings. And as man is of a sociable nature and need companions he becomes morbid by not having companions who can comprehend his feelings. I like to contemplate many of these subjects.

The first that I shall consider is the little one at the preserves. Her countenance betrays nothing but there appears to be no thought of doing wrong. It shows to me a countenance wher kindness and virtue has held the sway over it. That look could not be place on the face of a child that had been subject to harshness or cruelty, but the look would have partaken of the crafty and cowardly. Further the sin would have been measured by the punishment not the punishment by the sin. How few parents understand the true Principle of governing. The rod or the fist are the first thing that many bring into use and as all children have or ought to have a will of this they soon learn to use craft against force and become the reckless sneaking coward that their parents makes them. I would rather have my children not know what wrong was than to have them desist from it through force.[1]

The dear little thing what great harm could there be in her hand being in the preserves when older peopl would most likely taste them without leave and as they were made to eat. I think she was mine and she should eat them. I would rather she should do it again than to cause her to desist through fear of physical punishment. The next one is all Quiet on the Potomoc. What an Idea it conveys. The moon just rising and the rays of light stealing through the woods and shining on the straws no armed foe no charging horseman but all seems hushed in the repose of nature. This is a far different scene than I have had the pleasure of witnessing much on the Potomac.

The next one Is the Inconvenience of Single life. Just look at the poor Devil sitting there trying to thread his needle. His very countenance shows that his soul could go through the needle if the thread can not. To Small to marry for fear his wife would cost him Something. He worries along with life and knows nothing but avarice. Such men certainly can not have the same kind of souls as other men. But as whatever is right I suppose it is all right that he is not making a hell for some woman on earth.

The next and last one I shall notice is the Convenience of Married life. I do not just like the picture for it brings to my mind certain occasions when I acted as is represented in the Picture. Just take a look at the old rep holding out his wrist to have a sleeve button sewed on and see what an affectionate and longing look his wife gives him. As much as to say it is not very bad and asks for a kind look or a caress in return but the Old bull dog stands just like a hog and does not deign to notice her appeal for an affectionate adjustment of the difficulty. Just as I have done with you many a time. I have often though of my stubborn acts of unkindness to you without any greater provocation the one in the pictures and my heart smote me many a time for it. Dear Kate I know that your whole heart is mine. And I have fully given you all my own but it is a hard one and I know that I have wring your feelings many times by unfeeling acts which I could just as well avoided as not. But my nature is so preverse that I did it and that is an end of it. The only way to mind such things is to ask forgiveness for them and try to do better. I do think if ever I live to get home I will try to repay you for all the love lavished on my unworthy self and try to lead a better life. A more virtuous one I can not. I would give all I possesed to be with you again with the war settled and peace again throughout the land. I have no chance here to buy you presents here and if I had I would not feel justified in spending money for them while my life is hung on so frail a thread and a family to leave unprotected. But I got these pictures from the Christian Commission[2] and concluded to send them to the little ones and have filled up a whole sheet of paper writing about them. Well maybe you will be gratified to get even this. I am sure I am gratified to get any thing at all from you. I must actually close this as the mail will go out in 15 minutes. Before this reaches you I will be at Head Quarters to live. I received orders this afternoon to arrange my affairs in the Co and move up to the adjutant tent for duty. Receive all my love and kiss the children for me. Tell Mary that as soon as I get fixed up I will write to her. I hope you will have a Merry Christmas and when you eat your good things do not regret that I can not get share of them but pray that this war will soon be over so that I can be with you to help provide for your comforts. I must quit.

I remain thine affectionate Taylor

1. Taylor is unusual in his view of corporal punishment. Calvinist doctrine stressed the evil in mankind and that physical punishment was an acceptable means

to repress it. Popular child-care books such as John Abbott's *The Mother at Home* and magazines for mothers in the 1830s and 1840s stressed a child's absolute obedience but cautioned that the parent should remain under control even while ensuring that pain was inflicted. Abbott advised that affection and kindness be applied to correct disobedience, but if that failed, punishment as harsh as necessary was appropriate. Almost all books and magazines advocated the use of a rod, usually made of a birch or apple switch or whalebone from the mother's corset. Prior to the Civil War, reformers did not advocate the abolition of corporal punishment of children, only that such punishment be used in moderation. It is possible that Taylor's Quaker heritage, which opposed brutality, influenced his opposition to corporal punishment.

2. The Christian Commission was organized in New York City on November 16, 1861, by delegates from the Young Men's Christian Association. The commission distributed Bibles, Christian tracts, and magazines; sent soldiers' money to their families; and provided spiritual ministry to the soldiers. Eventually about 5,000 agents were sent to minister to the spiritual and physical needs of the army. Along with the Sanitary Commission, it provided services to the wounded after battles, but it was not until September 1864 that Grant authorized its representatives full access to the Union soldiers. Among the items the commission provided was a "housewife"—a kit that contained needles, thread, and buttons. As late as March 19, 1865, the Des Moines newspaper urged its readers to contribute to the Christian Commission "as the proceeds go to the sick and wounded soldiers."

> Camp Russle Va
> Head Qrs 22n Iowa Inftr
> Dec 25th 1864
> Dear Catharine & Friends

"Good Morning." Christmas Gift and a merry Christmas to you all. I have just had a good breakfast and feel "bully." I went up to the sutlers this morning and bought 2 cans of fresh Oysters $2, one can of condensed Milk 75 cts, one can of Sausage $1.25, 2 lb of butter $1.60, and feasted. You can see what it costs one here to enjoy a little of the luxuries of life. Now I have got my breakfast I do not feel any better than I would if I had just contented myself with hard tack, coffee, and Sow belly. But human nature is always wanting something that it has not got. This $5.60/100 will last 3 of us about 2 days and then we will not be one whit better than as if we had not had it. Except the enjoyment of eating it. This is a beautifull morning and all is quiet on the Potomac. The Shenandoah Valley is white with the snow and the army is enjoying itself in their rude huts with a degree of comfort that they have seldom had the opportunity of experiencing [since] they have left their homes. I am in good health and the favourable news from Rebledom leavs me in good heart. I feel now as if I would get home in the spring when all this bloodshed and devastation of property would cease. But maybe I am too sanguine. However, it seems to me that the leaders of the Rebellion were becoming discouraged and all they want is a few more kicks to make them fall in and behave themselves. The Army lays in just the same condition that it did when I wrote last. Except the 3rd Brigade of our Division has gone to Winchester to guard the town and the 1st to Stephensons Depot 5 miles below to guard the government Stores. Genl Custer took a Brigade of Cavalry and went up the Valley as far as Harrisonburg to see what had become of Early. While encamped near that place the Rebles undertook to capture him by surprising his camp. But they signally failed. As the Rebles making a dash at his head quarters to Capture him they were met by his body guard and instead of Capturing him were nearly all killed or captured themselves. A sharp fight ensued in which the Rebles lost about 140 men while our loss has only 7 men wounded and none killed. After he had cleaned them out he broke up camp and returned to this place having ascertained that no force of Rebles were now in the Valley nearer than 50 miles.[1]

I do not know what the program will be but I hope we will not be compelled to move while this weather is so cold and the ground so damp. I see that old Abe has called out 300,000 new troops[2] and I also see by the Newton papers that Dan Rorabough Enos Sumpter and Jack Scarborough have been drafted and I hope that the next draft will take the Slaughter tribe.[3] I do wish that the cops may be brought to feel that they have a country to protect, as well as a country to protect them. I have had no letter this week but I look for one this morning. But should I be disappointed I will wait patiently till it does come. I am still clerking for head quarters and acting orderly for our own company and have a good time of it. Only I am kept very busy. I am going to try to get some rest to-day, but I do not know wheather I will get it or not. We drew rations of Whiskey this morning and I am going to have some toddy at noon . We got one gill per man. This is the first and I reckon it will be the last. Whisky is not of much account in this army for there is but few who use it any more. The boys had rather have apples or fresh pork. We have a good moral regiment now. The scalawags have all got weeded out and what is left are men of the right stamp. And we feel proud of our Record and all try to deserve it.

The Photographs that I was going to send in my other letter and which I wrote so much about I forgot to do up and so I will send them now. When I found that I had not sent them I thought you would think I was either a fool or drunk. The latter I was not but the former you can judge for yourselves. I could send my money now if I had it but the man who I loaned it to has not returned from Washington and I can not of course send it. But I think he will be back in a few days as his leave of absence is nearly out and as soon as he comes I will get it and send it. We have been looking for Col Stone for the last week but he has not come. What is the reason? Has he Started for Washington or has he gone home? I think Sometimes that he has forgotten his old Regiment and the boys who helped him to his present position. However he may have so much on hand that he has not time to come and see us. I dont know of any thing more of interest to write this morning. When you write to me again let me know how the little ones get along with their lessons and how Cyrus health is and finally everything connected with you welfare and how our old friends the Whites get along in their new home. And if I get home this spring what I can do to make a living for us. For this war has not enriched me any except in feeling that I have done my duty but that is worth something. Kiss the children for me. Give my love to all and write often.

      Yours affectionately

      Taylor

1. On December 19, Custer's Third Cavalry Division began a reconnaissance toward the Confederate army at Staunton. That night he encamped at Lacey's Springs, about nine miles from Harrisonburg. The next morning at about 5:30 his command was attacked by the division of Major General Thomas Rosser. Union losses were possibly two killed, twenty-two wounded, and ten to twenty captured. Rosser lost thirty-two captured and fifty to eighty killed and wounded.

2. On December 19, 1864, Lincoln called for an additional 300,000 men.

3. Newspapers often published the names of men who were drafted, thus adding to the stigma of being drafted rather than volunteering.

Desemoins Iowa Dec 25th 1864

Dear Father

It is with gereate pleasure that I take my pen in hand to let you know that we are all well excpt uncle. But he is better now than he was. He was not in bed atall but he was on the sick list. Well papa thiss Christmass went it well. Papa I wish you a merry Christmass and a happy new year. We have not many borders now.

I wish that you would send home some money for I need a new dress bad. I just now tore the best sunday dress I got. It tore on a trunk in the barroom. Ellis fell and hurt himself and I went to see what was the mater with him. So you see I tore my dress. Mother and aunty had gone to Church to day.

Frank will write some figures for you. I and him are going down on the ice when Mother comes back from Church.

The girls are geting dinner now. I do wish that you could be here and get some of the good corn and potatos and cand tomato too.

I expect it makes thy mouth water to think of such good things. Frank is geting over his mischief now a little. He will write a good many figurs to let thee know that he is learning. Thiss letter is from thy afectionate daughter Sallie A Peirce to her Father Taylor Peirce. Frank will comence to write now.

1 2 3 4 5 6 7 8 9 10 11 12 13 14 15 16 17 18 19 20

Des Moines Dec 25 1864

Dear Taylor

I set down to write thee to day to let thee know that we are all well and in good heart and hope that the soldiers will all get home in the spring. For I do hope that the war will be at an end by that time.

For I can not see for the life of me what the Rebles will have to fight for by the first of May. For they have not had a victory to a mount to any thing since the Red River expidition and our Generels have it the coil of freedom around the great beast of Slavery so that it must die and that soon if it is not already dead. And then the Rebs will or might as well give up if that is what they are fighting. For I see by the Papers that Sherman has made seven thousand freed men of their slaves on his march through Georgia and has not only made freedmen of them but they will become good Union soldiers in a little time with train-ing.[1] That is what I call takeing from the weak and giveing to the strong. But it matters not how we get their men or money just so we get them and put them to use for the cause of freedom and Union so that our officers keep an eye to the good of the country in the future as well as the presant as for as is consistant with their power and hon-ner. But I fear there are a great many in office that look to much to their own intrest to keep a good look our for the country cause. Though I think that our President and some of our most able Gener-als are trying to do all they know to do for the good of the nation now and forever Amen.

Well Taylor I have run on writeing and have not said any thing of what we are doing at home. Cyrus receved thy letter and the Re-comendations allright last week and went to see to it but could not get any thing done until the Gov came home an they could hear from him. So I thougt that he would not write thee just now thinking that thee had seen the Govenor before this time thyself. But just as soon as he can find out anything he will write thee all about it.

Sallie and Frank are out on the ice and are having a gay old time while I sit writeing. Ellis is asleep and I have a good quiet time all to my self for that is some thing I do not get often. Indeed I do not get the chance to read any thing to amount to any knowledge of any kind a bit more than when I was keeping house and had six or eight men to cook for. So thee must excuse my poor letter and hope to better thy-self the next time thee gets married.

Taylor I guess I have pritty nearly run out now. I will close wish-ing thee a merry Christmas and a happy new year hopeing thee is well and that thee will be at home by this time next year. So farewell for the presant.

I remain thy own Catharine

1. As Sherman marched through Georgia, thousands of former slaves followed the army. Sherman's anti-black sentiments were well known and in January 1865 prompted a visit from Secretary of War Edwin M. Stanton. The visit resulted in Sherman's publishing Special Field Order Number 15 on January 16, 1865, which encouraged blacks "to enlist as soldiers in the service of the United States."

South Carolina, North Carolina, Georgia, Iowa

EDITOR'S NOTE. On December 30, 1864, the 22nd Iowa was ordered to march from its winter quarters to Stephenson's Depot, five miles from Winchester, and board a train for Baltimore. The regiment reached Baltimore on January 7, 1865. Four days later the regiment and its equipment embarked on the *Illinois,* but because the ship drew too much water, the regiment had to reembark on the *Manhattan.*[1] The 22nd Iowa then sailed to Annapolis, Maryland, where it again embarked on the *Illinois* and sailed to Fortress Monroe, Virginia, where it took on provisions and departed for Savannah, Georgia.

The regiment remained at Savannah until early March, when it was ordered to Morehead City, North Carolina. The 22nd Iowa returned to Savannah during the first week of May but was then ordered to Augusta, Georgia. In late June the regiment was ordered to return to Savannah, where the soldiers were mustered out in July. The men were then transported to Davenport, Iowa, and arrived there on July 29.[2] By August 3 all the men had been paid and discharged. The next day the company from Newton boarded the railroad but stopped at Iowa City, where they were met with great fanfare and "a bountiful and magnificent dinner." It is not known when Taylor reached Des Moines.

1. Some accounts state that the regiment embarked on the *Marshaltown,* but no record of such a vessel can be found. There was, however, a steamer, *Manhattan,* owned by the U.S. government on a register dated October 15, 1864. The steamer operated in eastern waters and was probably the vessel on which the regiment sailed.

2. Records of the adjutant general of Iowa state that the regiment was mustered out of service on July 25, 1865. Regimental reports and a letter from a soldier in Company F state that the regiment left Savannah on July 22 and reached Baltimore on July 25. A regimental history compiled by Stone states that the regiment reached Davenport on July 27, although other reports and the *Daily Davenport Democrat* indicate that the regiment did not arrive there until July 29.

> Head Qtrs 22 Iowa Inftr
> Camp Carroll Baltimore Md
> Jany 9th 1865
> Dear Catharine & Friends

We are here awaiting transportation to go somewhere. I can not tell you when but we have been ordered to take 15 days rations and there is 5 Steamers laying to receive this Division on board. I am just as busy as I can be and have hardly time to think. The old Adjt has left and I am duly installed in his place but without my commission of course I will not be able to draw pay for the position. But if I can get the commission dated back to the 1st of Jan I may be can get mustered to that date but if I can not I will be satisfied. I have heard nothing from the Governor as yet. I received your letter of the 25t but have not had any since. I am expecting one to-day and if I should not get it before we embark it will be some time before I will hear from home. It will be likely to be some time before you will hear from me but keep in good heart for I am in a good place and comfortable and in good health.

I think we are going to New Orleans but I can not say certain. The 15 days rations denotes a voyage of some length. You can direct your letters as usual 2n Brig 2 Div 19 A.C. by way of Washington untill you hear from me again. I am sorry that I have not received my pay for I fear you will need it. The officer I loaned my 2 months pay to that we drew in the Valley is in New York and I am afraid he will not get back before we embark and I will not be able to get any money either for myself or you. But if you can get along untill my Com Comes I can get my pay on my muster out rolls and I hope that I can have some chance to send it to you. Give my love to all. Kiss the little ones for me and tell them to be good children and write often. I will write another letter if we do not go on board today. I setup all last night getting our reports ready for the War department and do not feel for writing this morning. The 28t Iowa is brigaded with us now[1] and I have many of my old friends with me. We are kept very close here. I have not been in town since we come here but the Col has promised me that I should go this afternoon. I must close.

        I remain Affectionately
        Taylor

1. Between December 31, 1864, and January 9, 1865, the Second Division, Nineteenth Corps, was reorganized from four brigades to three. The 22nd Iowa remained in the Second Brigade. The reorganized brigade consisted of the 22nd Iowa, 28th Iowa, 13th Connecticut, 131st New York, and 159th New York Infantry Regiments.

Des Moines Jan 11th 1865
Dear Taylor

We are all well and are geting along in the same old way with this exception. There is but three boarding now and therefore we do not
have so much to do and Sallie and Frank gose to school so that I am
haveing a good time just now. I see Sallie in her letter asks thee to send
money so she can have a new dress. I will explain to thee how it is I
only got her two dresses this fall one to were to school and a sunday
one and she in her riping round has torn her sunday one so that I will
have to get her another shortly. But I expect to get some money
through John Sumpter in a few days so thee need not be troubled
about us for we have all we realy need. We have plenty to eat and
enough to wear to keep us warm and comfortable and that is more
than a great many of the Soldiers family can say This winter. For thirteen dollars a month will not go far towards keeping family at the
price all things are at this time. I told thee in my last of a dinner that
was given at this place for the benifit of Soldiers familys.[1] It is seen
now that there was cleard over three thousand dollars and also that
there is familys enough in the City and county in need of help to take
it all and then none of them be made very rich. I do realy feel thankfull that I am not in need of help from any thing of the kind and if I
get the money from Dixon this winter when it is due I will have some
to do something else than just to live on. John Sumpter was here yesterday and he says that Dixon will pay it as soon as it is due. John has
sold his place and is on the lookout for an other. He did not say who
got it or the price. He was not here long but he will stop as he comes
back and he said he would pay me the money that Rorabough owes
us yet for the work thee done before thee went a way.

Well Taylor I do not know much to write of. Mary receved a letter
this morning from W Cook.[2] He says the friends are all well and that
Maris Peirce[3] served his time and got home in time to vote for old Abe
and John and Ellis were both at his house at this time. But he said he
had receved two letters from thee since thee went east and he was
going to write to thee in a day or two so I will leave off saying any
more hopeing he will do so.

Mary also got one from Webster Brown[4] from Savanna. He has
been with Sherman in his glorious and victorious march through Ga
and is one that through safe and well but he dose not say any thing

but the same we have seen in the papers. It is not worth my while to write any of the war news for thee will know all that I know and more too if thee has a chance to get a paper.

As to Des Moine it is on a stand still. Just at this time all kinds of business is dull now but the people are makeing big calculation on what will be done in the spring in the way of improvements. [last page missing]

1. Catharine's previous letter was not found. A dinner advertised as a "Grand Festival" was held on January 1, 1865, and raised $4,000 to be donated to soldiers' families.

2. This letter was not found.

3. Corporal Maris Pierce enlisted from Chester County, Pennsylvania. He served in Company C, 97th Pennsylvania Infantry, and was discharged on September 20, 1864, at the end of his three-year term of service. The spelling "Pierce" is as shown in the *History of Pennsylvania Volunteers.*

4. This lettter was not found. Webster Brown was a Pennsylvania native and resident of Guthrie Center, west of Des Moines, when he enlisted December 16, 1861. He was promoted to first sergeant, Company C, 4th Iowa Infantry, on December 16, 1864. He reenlisted January 25, 1865, and was killed at the battle of Bentonville, North Carolina, on March 21, 1865. Census records of 1850 indicate that he was raised in Little Britain Township, Lancaster County, Pennsylvania. In 1850 Cyrus and Mary Milner and Taylor and Catharine Peirce were living in Colerain Township, Lancaster County.

> On board the Steamship Illinose
> Fortress Monroe Jan 13 1865
> Dear Catharine

I take a little time to let you know that we are on the wing and are all right so far. I do not know where we are going too but I think to Savanna.[1] We are getting enough rations to about take us there but the expedition is kept a proper secret. Even our Regimental Officer does not know where we are going. I am well and have a good place. I have a State room and berth and have pleanty of bread and butter to eat. I have my Regimental business all done up so that as soon as we land I will be able to write you a good long letter.

I hardly know what to write for the mail leaves in an hour and I have but little time to spread myself or even to write you an ordinary letter. The 28th Iowa is on board with us and Wright Wilson[2] sends his compliments to thee. There is about 1,700 men on board but the vessle is very large and is not so much crowde as it was comeing from Orleans last summer. The men are generally in good health and in high spirits and feel as if they would like to have a chance at Ft Fisher[3] or Charleston. I tell you if we get at Charleston there will not be one stone left on top of another to tell where the City stood. I received a letter from thee the 10th[4] and was glad to get it for I knew if did not get one before I left it would be some time before I would get one. I wrote you the day we got orders to move and I think I told you that I was duly installed in the adjt place. Well I get along first rate. Col Graham is very kind to me and has the best accomodations going for me. I tell you that I am getting allong a great deal Eisier than I ever done before since I come in the service. Graham gave me a horse and I have him on board. He is a nice one and you know I like a nice horse. So if my Commission only comes so that I can keep my place I am good for another campaign if the rebles does not kill me and I do not believ they will get a chance to do that. If you do not hear from me for some time you need not get out of heart for I expect it will be some time befor the mail will go out from us and may be longer before it comes to us. I am sorry that I did not get paid off before I left but it seemed as if things was so much hurried that we could not get our pay. The only thing that I care about is that I am afraid that you will want some clothing before I can send you the money. I would have sent home a lot of old clothing if I had the money but I could not pay the freight on it. But I have saved it up and will send it as soon as I can. Kiss the little ones for me and give my love to all and I hope the next you hear from me will be the glorious news of the fall of some reble stronghold and maybe their entire government. I would be happy if such should be the case. The mail is about to start so farewell.

> I remain affectionately
> Taylor Peirce

1. The regiment departed Fortress Monroe the night of January 13. Its destination was Savannah.

2. J. Wright Wilson, Company K, 28th Iowa Infantry. See the letter of March 28, 1863.

3. Fort Fisher was at the entrance of the Cape Fear River that led to Wilmington, North Carolina. A December 1864 Union attack to seize the fort had failed, but another assault on January 15, 1865, resulted in the fort's surrender.

4. This is probably Catharine's letter of December 25, 1864.

On Board the Steam Ship Illinois off Cape Hataras N.C.
Jan 14 1865
Dear Catharine & all the rest

We are again out on the rough. Many of the men are sea sick and the crowded state of the vessle makes it very uncomfortable. We have 1,280 men 108 offices the General comd the Brigade and his staff consisting of himself and and 5 or 6 officers and about 50 officers servants that with the ship hands makes about 1,500 men which makes it pretty thick. Our regiment is all on the middle Deck and have berths and are better fixed than we ever were on board of any vessle we have been on. I have a room and berth to myself and am very comfortable fixed. I have my box. Cap got it filled with butter in Baltimore and as I have pleanty of govt rations beside I live very well. The officers mostly eat at the table and pay $2 per day for their board the rooms costing nothing. The 28th Iowa is not so well quartered as we are oweing to their officers not useing proper exertions to procure them comfortable quarters. A portion of them [has] to lay out on the Hurricane Deck and as the weather is cold it is very disagreeable. Major Myres has gone home on leave of absence and their Col has never got back to them Since he was wounded at Cedar Creek.[1] It leaves them without any officers to take proper care of them and of course they get the worst place there is. I feel sorry for the poor fellows for the 28t is as good a regiment (always excepting the 22n) as ever left Iowa.

Well we Sailed or rather Steamed from Los Monroe[2] about 3 oclock this morning with sealed orders. At 9 oclock the orders were opened and we find our destination is Savanna, Georgia.

Well "Hurrah" for Sherman and his conquering host. If the 22n has not done enough for the country I would as soon serve here under Sherman as any of them and you may be sure that whereever the 22n is she will be found doing her duty. I do think that it is the best regiment that I have seen among them all. There is the most brotherly feeling amongst the men and between them and the officers off any set of soldiers that I have yet become acquainted with and there will be many a tie of friendship formed that will only be severed by death.

This will not be very well written for the ship rolls so and I am sitting writing on my knee so you see that I am not in a situation to make very fine display of penmanship. I have very little idea where we will go after we arrive at Savanna but I suppose we will stay there a while and probably go up and help Sherman take Charleston. I want to be at the taking of that hot bed of traitors. You may bet if ever we get into that place there will be no more traitors born there. For we will not leave a stone or brick in a position to protect a traitors head or a hearth stone whereby one can warm himself. Desolation will reign where once the oligarchs of Slavery held their revels and squandered the fruits of the toil of their human brutes. I feel as if I had the will to lay waste their homes and scatter their families to ends of the Earth for the lives they have caused to be sacrificed at the altar of Avarice and the woe and sorrow that hangs like a mist over our once happy land. I feel as if the rebellion was now in the toils and a few more draws on the coils will strangle it. For the sake of humanity I hope it is so. And for the prosperity of the land and the happiness of our people I hope that the Lord will Stop the Effusion of blood and the waste of human life. But I very much doubt wheather nature has yet become calm after her convulsive throws produced by slavery and wheather more blood must not be spilled and more lives offered up as an attonement for the sins which we permitted to lay like an incubus on our free government.

But I hope not and with this hopes I see in my future a peaceful home, a properous country, and a happy family. I am well to-day and have nothing at all to see to so I am feeling quite relaxed from care as this is the first time that I have felt free since we left Baton Rouge last July and a hard time it has been. The Campaign in the Shenandoah valley was a long one and a very severe one. The exposure we were subjected to was very warm on the constitution and none but the best men stood it. I suppose you wonder how I stood it if none but the best stood it. I tell you what, I am about as tough a one as you find and I believe I will yet outlive all our family infirmities and continue to wend my way through the world to a good old age. There is one thing troubles me though. I have got so that I cant drink Whiskey and that makes me feel bad to have to bid a final farewell to an old and valued friend. Finish tomorrow.

1. For John Meyer, see the letter dated April 18, 1863. Bartholomew W. Wilson was an Indiana native and resident of Tama County when appointed captain on July 24, 1862. He was promoted to lieutenant colonel on April 7, 1863, and commanded the regiment at Cedar Creek, where he was severely wounded. He was promoted to colonel on June 15, 1865, and was mustered out July 31, 1865.

2. Fort Monroe, Virginia.

Des Moines Jan 18th /65
Dear Taylor

We are all well and doing well for we have little or nothing to do. We have but two boarders and the children go to school so that leaves the most of the day with not much to concern us only the absent one. Mary receved a letter from Anne M Gibson yesterday[1] saying that my couson Mary Carter died of consumtion at Aunt Lydia Hanses on the second of this month. She said the friends were all well. Aunt Hannah is just the same she has been all summer. Rachel wanted to know how to direct to thee for she has not heard from thee for some time and did not know how to send thee a letter. We will have to wait a day or two to answer her letter untill we hear from thee again. I received thyne of the 9th yesterday saying thee was just about to embark for parts unknown. But I hope we will hear from thee soon and thee will come out right side up with care. I feel rather sorry that you leave the valley this winter but it may turn out all for the best. We poor short sighted mortals do not know what is best for us and therefore we are obliged to put our trust in a power or rock that is higher than I. I feel that I was in need of something to lean on and I do not beleive that I could find anything better than him who made and takes care of all creation. My daily prayer is for thy safety and for the good of my country that there will soon be a peace brought about that will be a lasting one. I see that Mosuria has met in convention and liberated her slaves to be amediately free only four contrary votes being cast.[2] So we see the glorious cause is marching on and we might sing glory to God in the higher and there will soon be peace for all men on this small continant of the United States, hopeing that we will be blest with life to see all men have thair natureal right that belongs to them at thair birth's.

Well Dear I have run on and have not told thee much of what is going on at home. We are all takeing good rest just now geting ready to take Soldiers if there is any comes in on this call. William Scarborough was here the other day. He said that W. Blumford was drafted the other Draft but got off on account of his broken sholder and J Cooms got off for poor health. He also said that Josua Adamson was killed and S D Cole was at home a perold prisoner. B Sumpter was still with his Reg and had the name of being a very good Soldier. He said that John Akins had buried his wife this winter of typhoid fever and he himself had buried his of consumtion after lingering about six month with it. He also said that Harvey J Skift had come home and had bought that timber land that we claimed in the Slaughter grove for the taxes. And as he had not got all the rails he was to have he wanted me to write to thee of it and see how it will be a bout him geting the rails.

Well I bleive I have writen all I can think of at this time. I will close.

      With love I remain forever thy own
      Catharine

1. This letter was not found.

2. On January 11, 1865, the Missouri state convention met in St. Louis and voted to free all slaves in Missouri immediately. There were four dissenting votes.

      Des Moines Jan 25th 1865
      Dear Brother

Not haveing much to do these days I thought I would write to thee and let thee know how we ware all getting along. We are all well. That is something for us to say. The weather as been verry cold for some days and Cyrus is puffing up the banisters to the stairs and is midling well. Catherine has a cough but is not sick with it.

      *   *   *

The children are in their own room playing. Their mother thought it to cold to send them to school. They are well. Sallie and Franky are growing tall and Ellis is growing fat. His face is like a full moon. He is geting to be a verry good child. I do not think he ever felt well till this winter. He can say everything and is like little Mary many ways. We only have three boarders now and the old mare and colts sold and gone and we just have the two cows and two pigs. We expect to subsist solgers if the war does not stopp before the middle of Febuary. We had fourteen recruits here last week but we can barely live keeping boarders this winter for every thing is so high. Flour is six dollars per hun lbs molasses two dollars per gallon sugar to thirty cents per lb coffe sixty butter fourty potatoes two dollars per bushel corn ninety cents and all spices and little things is double or thribbl what they used to be.

By strict economy we all live and have plenty to eat. All wise ones who pretend to see into futurity prophecy a flood next spring but it does not trouble me for I think we are fixed now so that the flood can not disturb us much. Cyrus had a great deal of dirt hauled here last summer. That is one thing that makes us scarce of money this winter trying to fix up as we would be safe if high watter should come. But spring will soon be here and then the expence of liveing will be less. I tell thee that it is a hard winter on the poor in Iowa. Clothing of all kinds ar so high unless people have something laid up for hard times must suffer.

* * *

Cyrus still talks of selling out and going to a warmer climate. If he sells I shall go to Rachels and take care of Aunt Hannah till he finds a place to suit him and then if it suits me I shall go their. If not stay just whare I please.

When thee gets thy commission and niew suit I would like thee to send me thy likeness. Cathrine has two here but one of them neither of us likes and of cours I would not want her to give me the good one because she has the best right. At any rate I wish a good one to keep. If thee never gets home it will be a great comfort and if thee does I will in all likelyhoods be seperated from thee and would like to have a likeness. I hope thee has got thy commission ear this. When Cyrus went to see the govenor about thy commission he said thee was a good slger and he would do all he could for thee there is. But one thing I fear about thy New office. I am afraid it will throw thee in the company of those that are able and willing to drink liquor. It has been with hert felt gratitude to the Father of all that I have learned that thee could not get whiskey. I thought if thee could not get it thee would get accostomed to doing without it and find that thee was better off with out it and conclude to be a free man agen. Oh my dear brother for the sake of thy wife and little ones never touch the hateful thing again. It is the bane of mankind and causes more heartbroken women and scroffuless [scrofulous] and deformed children than all other causes. Do not get offended at my fears. I know that if thee lets liquor alone thee will get along for thy heart is all right.

Their is a great deal of talk of peace here. Some say that the Govenor has sent a dispach that thier will be no draft in Iowa on the fifteenth of next month[1] in contemplation of peace but the most of the men doubt'd. The Irish are leavenig town who are subject to draft in the first ward. The second ward had come out of the draft by hireing substitutes.[2] I would like to see a draft if it would catch the right ones Old Tyrrell and a fiew copperheads. But I would for rather have pease so that the brave ones might return to their homes and familys and rest after their many hardships toils and sufferings.

We herd that Joe Coon [Kuhn] was kiled[3] but it has not been confirmed.

* * *

Their is going to be a great deal of improvement here next summer niew grist mills and dwelling houses.

* * *

It is near supper time and I must close. Please write soon and often. We have not herd from thee since thee left Baltimore. We have serched all battle accounts for mention of the 19th army corps but in vain so we hope thee is still saife. Catherine and the children send their love to thee. I remain thy effetionate sister

Mary

1. On October 6, 1864, the War Department informed Governor Stone that Iowa had credit for 1,281 men in excess of past draft calls to apply to future calls. On December 19 there was a draft call for 300,000 men to begin February 15. Iowa was required to furnish no men under this call.

2. The Enrollment Act passed by Congress on March 3, 1863, allowed a man to either pay a $300 commutation fee to exempt him from the draft or hire a substitute. Commutation was repealed in July 1864. During the two years between the enactment of the draft and the end of the war, 75,429 substitutes were hired by draftees.

3. See the letter of June 14, 1863.

Savannah Ga Jan29/65
Dear Catharine
I again set down to write to you hoping that this may find you all in good health and doing well as far as worldly matters are concerned. I

am well in health and in good Spirits. I am better fixed than I have ever been since I come into the service and am more comfortable. After we arrived at Savannah We took up our quarters in the Banking house of the Charleston and Savannah R Road Co. I had my office in the counting room which had every convenience in it for enjoying ones self hydrants gas lights and stoves all of which I put to use and set back and tried to imagine myself a Southren nabob. But after a trial or two I awakened to the reality that I was not a nabob but a bob what had to bob around at other folks bidding and sometimes had to bob right smartly to keep things going.

Well we luxuriated in that Elysium for several days untill Shermans forces got out of the way when we were moved to the defences around the City. There is only Genl Grovers Division here on duty now. There is some detachments of Shermans troops still near town await- ing orders to march and I expect will all move out in a few days. Our division is composed of 3 Brigades, one Commanded by Col Wash- burn of Illinois and the other by Col Porter of Massachusetts. We be- long to the Brigad now comd by Day formerly Comd by Molineux who is now in command of the Division,[1] Grover being in command of the post of Savannah. We moved out to the lines on the 26th and have got good quarters up for the whole regiment. The men are busy finishing them off to-day. Although it is sunday the noise of the hatch- ets and saw is continuous and no one is resting except those who have their quarters completed. I have a Wall Tent all to myself. I have a good floor in it and a frame work up in the inside to keepe it square and nice and yesterday I went to work and built me a nice little brick fire plac and chimney and put up a pair of bedsteads and got some of the long moss and have just as good a bed as I wish. You had better think I am enjoying myself to-day. No one comes in to bother me and for once I can hear myself think. Oh what a luxury it is to be once in 2 years free from annoyance. I believe that I feel better to-day than I have done since the first gun was fired at Ft Sumpter. I think that we will be likely to remain at this place untill our time is out and if the Yellow Fever does not get us we have a pretty fair prospect of getting through this term of service alive. I seen Bluford Sumpter.[2] His regi- ment is laying about 2 miles from here. He says that Josh Adamson[3] was killed at Altoona and Doke Cole[4] was taken prisoner and par- rolled and went home on furlong. Bluford and Ben Teisdale[5] come to see me two or three times after I first come here. George E Spencer called here to see me yesterday and made inquiries about you and sent his respects to thee. He is colonel of the 2 Alabamma Cavalry and is now commanding a brigade of Kilpatricks Division of Cavalry.[6] He told me that they had orders to march this morning for South Carolina. His Brigade was encamped about 10 miles out of town and when he heard that I was here he come down to see me and offered me a position on his staff. But I thought that as I had seen the Elephant and as there was a prospect of getting to rest some time I would not accept his offer at this time. Although if I thought I would have to go into the field again I would have taken his offer. There is not much change in this town Since the war broke out. It has always been occupied by the reble troops who kept down any loyal demonstrations that showed themselves and things went on quietly untill our troops come in and now we keep down any reble move that is likely to be made. So upon the whole Savanna is a quiet and uninteresting place. It is quite a nice City. The Streets are all Shaded with live oaks whose green foliage makes a pleasing contrast with the withered and frosted forrest surrounding the Town. The wood has a very diversified appearance. Some of the trees having shed their leaves while the evergreens such as the large magnolia live Oak and Pine growing up in the midst gives a very pleasing affect to the view. We had quite a scare night before last. About 12 o clock at night a fire broke out in the upper end of town and not far from where the rebles had an arsenal in which was stored some 2,000 shells and a large amount of powder. We had moved out of town that day and had all got to sleep and was resting finely when the fire got into the building and the shells began to explode which caused us to think we were attacked. In about one minute the whole camp was out ready to meet the rebles but the explosions become so frequent and all in one direction that we began to think what it was and soon went to bed again. The uproar continued for nearly 2 hours killing and wounding Several by the fragments of Shell which flew through the air as thick as the field of battle. The fear of the explosion kept the people away so from the fire that two whole squares was burned before it could be extinguished.[7] The people are destitute of food and the government is feeding several thousand negroes and citizens. No doubt some of them are the very jockeys who sat fire to the buildings for the purpose of destroying our ammunition as a keg of powder was discovered setting at the corner of our magazine with the head knockd out so that the sparks could drop in. Which if it had done the explosion would have set our magazine off where was stored some 50 Tons of Gunpowder and 20,000 rounds of large ammunition for the Siege guns. If this had been destroyed the rebles could have made a successfull raid on us for our ammunition being all destroyed we could not have defended ourselves. But fortunately it was discovered in time to prevent the intended catastrophe and the jails are full of the Suspected ones. To give you an idea of how things worke here I will tell you an incident that occured two days since. Notice was given that letters could go to friends outside of the lines by a flag of truce but they all had to be subjected to official scrutiny before they were put into the mail sack to be sure that they continued no contraband news. One woman sent up 5 and in one of them she wrote her frien that she hoped that Yellow Jack meaning the fever would get amongst the yanks and clean us out and some more such language. She also stated that the Priest was the most loyal confederate in Savanna and some more of the same sort. The Provost martial showed the letter to Genl Grover who imediatly detailed a guard and sent them up and took the lady and Father Pendegrast up and Set them outside the lines with an admonition not to appear in Savannah again during the war or they would both be strung up.[8] I tell you the rebles are quiet here. They have had some pretty severe lessons. And all the boys want is to get them to openly avow their disloyal and he that is hardy enough to do so will need a coffin and a hole in the ground in less than a week. We are putting up Strong fortifications arround the City as one division is a small force to hold a place of this size right in the heart of an enemys country. But I think we are good for it. I am now going to quit telling abut other things and speak of myself and my prospects. I have a good place and get along finely with my reports and all my business. And if I get my commission I am going to be mustered in for three years and if I wish to after our time is out I can be mustered out with the regiment. But if I prefer Staying being a Staff officer the War department will have to assign me to some department where I will be less exposed than in the regiment. The orders are that adjutants who have served faithfully in the field during their term of service will be at their own request assigned to the Staff of Generals Commanding Posts with the rank of

Post adjutant and a recommendation for promotion in case of vacancies. So if I see that I am not going to have money enough to make us a home I will try and get assigned to some post where I can have you with me until I can get enough to do it. "What do you thing of it?" It will be optional with myself wheather I remain in the service after the regiment is discharged or not and want your advice. I have got clear of the graybacks and am dressed up clean once more. I have not been paid yet and what money I loaned is still out. The man has not yet rejoined the regiment but we are expecting him back and also the paymaster. I have 7 months pay due which is 168 dollars and I know you need it but I will have to wait till I get it to Send it. Give my love to all. Kiss the children for me and tell them to be good and try and learn their lessons well.

> Affectionately Thine
> Taylor

1. On January 21 Major General Cuvier Grover was assigned to command the District of Savannah. On February 12 Brigadier General Henry W. Birge took command of the Second Division, Nineteenth Corps, from Grover. The division, assigned to the District of Savannah, consisted of three brigades commanded by Colonel Henry D. Washburn (First Brigade), Colonel Nicholas W. Day (Second Brigade), and Lieutenant Colonel James P. Richardson (Third Brigade). Colonel Thomas W. Porter, previous commander of the 14th Maine Infantry, commanded the First Brigade from October 19, 1864, until early January 1865. He was mustered out of service on January 13, 1865, along with all except four companies of the 14th Maine. Brigadier General Edward L. Molineux officially commanded the Second Brigade until February 17, at which time Day officially took command.

2. Bluford Sumter, Company I, 39th Iowa Infantry, was an Indiana native and resident of Des Moines when he enlisted August 12, 1862. He was mustered out June 5, 1865.

3. Joshua Admonson, Company I, 39th Iowa Infantry, was an Indiana native and Des Moines resident when he enlisted August 22, 1862. He was killed at the battle of Allatoona, Georgia, on October 5, 1864. At that battle, Confederates under General John Bell Hood were repulsed by a Union division commanded by Brigadier General John M. Corse.

4. Samuel D. Cole, Company I, 39th Iowa Infantry, was a Tennessee native and Des Moines resident when he enlisted August 22, 1862. He was captured at Allatoona on October 5, 1864, was paroled, and was mustered out June 5, 1865.

5. Benjamin Teesdale, Company I, 39th Iowa Infantry, was a native of England and a Des Moines resident when he enlisted August 22, 1862. He was mustered out June 5, 1865.

6. Colonel George E. Spencer commanded the 1st Alabama Cavalry. In January 1865 his command was reassigned to the cavalry division commanded by Major General Judson Kilpatrick, and Spencer took command of the Third Brigade. Before the war he served as secretary of the state senate and afterward served two terms as U.S. senator from Alabama.

7. The fire broke out on January 28 and destroyed more than 100 buildings, including the former Confederate arsenal located at West Broad and Broughton Streets. The fire was attributed to either Confederate sympathizers or Union soldiers, but the exact cause was never determined.

8. Reverend Charles Clement Prendergast was the pastor of St. Patrick's Catholic Church in Savannah.

> Head quarters 22 Iowa
> Savannah Ga Feb 4 1865
> Dear Catharine, Cyrus, Mary Sally Frank & Ellis and all
>   whom it may concern,

This is a most beautiful night and my work being all done I concluded to spend an hour or two in writing the news and also in giving you some of the Items of our doings and welfare. In the first place as self is of the greatest importance of any thing that I have to write about I will just give you a short sketch of my wonderful proformance in the defence of this "gallient and Gelorious" Republic. My duty now consists in eating "hard tack" and "Sow belly" and writing dispatches for the Commander of the bully 22n Infantry.

I am in good health and in good spirits but it would revive me or rather exalt my heroics to receive a letter from Some of you about this time, as It has been a month since I have had that felikity [felicity]. It would do you good to see how aristocratically I am fixed. I have a tent to myself with a floor in it and brick fireplace and chimney to it and all the books, papers, and parphanalea of Hd Quarters arround me. In the words of the Poet I am monarch of all I survey.[1] If I dont Survey too much. And am an autocrat of very limited powers. In short I am the biggest bull pup that watches round the Colonels Quarters.

But in sober truth I am comfortably and pleasantly situated. My duties are light and my associations are agreeable for I enjoy the Society of the most inteligent men in the command. And Some of them are men of the best moral character that I have Seen in any Station in life. And my highest aim is to so conduct myself that I may enjoy their friendship through my after life when peace shall once more spread her golden wings over our land.

If I could have you all near me I would be as happy as man ever gets to be on earth. But with all the enjoyments I have here there is still a vacant spot in them that makes me long for other Scenes.

In spite of me my thoughts wander away over river and mountain and plain to my own lovd Iowa: her clear bright Sky her fresh and bracing air and her fertile prairies. And imagination pictures your fireside with you all sitting round and the little ones in their childish glee, Sending joy and gladness all arround with their little sports. Oh how I long to be with you. I feel as if all of earth was centred around your house. Shall I ever again enjoy it? I hope so. I feel that I will soon enfold you all once more in the embrace of affection. Soon will the Sword be hung in the hall. No more will be heard the deep roar of the canon as it hurls its deadly missles through the walls of human flesh. Man will cease to Slaughter his fellow man and the Stars and Stripes will float peacefully from mast and Spire. Then will the reunion of those who still live be unuterably happy. Oh that the hour was come. I am sick of blood and slaughter. Sick of scenes of woe, and want, and misery. Sick of the hardships exposures and depotisms of a state of war. And even our rights and privileges safe. How soon would I bid farewell to the tented field and seek within the bosom of home that quiet and rest that I have been so long a stranger too. Enough of this. Our division is all the troops that are stationed here. Sherman has gone to South Carolinna and is now about 80 miles from here.[2] We are working on the fortifications and erecting quarters. We are well fixed up and the Regiment is in a better condition than its has ever been since it come out. We have only about 325 men here now the rest being absent on detached service and in the hospitals and some of them home on furlough. We have Present and absent 563 men belonging to the regiment. We lost 7 men the last month 6 Discharged and 1 died. So you see that we are gradually wearing away. 6 months more and we will not have more than one half the number that we started out with. Truly this is destructive of human life.

The weather is mild and pleasant. The frogs are Singing and all nature shows the near approach of Spring. There has been fresh shad in the market but I have not been down to town this week although it is not 400 yards off. Yet I like to stay at home so well that I do not go where I have no business. And things are so high that soldier cannot afford to buy them so I do not go to see what is in market.

The people in the country is very poor and hundreds of the poor creatures come daily to get provisions which I am happy to say is liberaly given by the commander of the post. I think when the war is over these people will be very cautious about embarking in another.

I do not know wheather we will get to stay here or not. I think that this division has too good a fighting reputation to get to lay long in such a place as this and I am looking every day to get orders to be ready to march although the opinion seems to prevail that we will get to stay here for some time. I would like to stay here for I have done all the fighting that I want to do if it can be helped. But if the government cannot get along without me I am willing to make another effort.

The city of Savannah has been the seat of wealth and luxury at one time. There is many works of art and the indications are that there had been considerable industry among the inhabitants of late years before the war broke out and ruined them. I will quit to night and try and write some more to morrow.

Feb 5th. I concluded to write some more to day as I hear that the mail will leave this evening and there is a chance of your getting this before a great while. I do not feel in as good condition for writing as I did last night but I will try to write something to interest you.

General Saxton[3] made a speech to the colored population this week which for feeling and sound sense I do not think I have heard Surpassed. The circumstances that called it forth are these. Genl Sherman in his order after he had occupaid Savannah proclaimed the freedom of all the Slaves and at the same time gav them 40 acres of land on the uninhabited Plantations and Islands to each head of a family with the understanding that they would settle on it and cultivate it.[4] Genl Saxton was appointed [to] carry out the measure and entered on his duty last week when he called togather the freedmen and told them what the project was for their benefit. I wish that some of the men who assert that the negroes would rather remain in Slavery had been here. There was not a single damned nigger that did not shout for joy when they found that they were no more a slave. It made many moist eye to see the poor Slave make his joyfull demonstrations. I have no doubt

but that they will [have] many disadvantages to encountre from prejudice on the part of some rascality on the part of others and little to
commence with on their own part will be serious drawbacks. But I
hope to live to see the day when the flag that has protected me will
wav its protecting folds with the same power over them. Those
croakes of the north who are so afraid that they will get mixed up with
niggers I think now might quell their fears and hold their peace for
there is ample room for the negroe here and pleanty for him to do.
And there will be no need of them commingling unless in indeed
"they" like the men of the same stamp who are in the army prefer to
mix. And I suppose there is many who would not let their hatred of
the nigger step in between them and their desires.

When you See old marm Slaughter give her my compliments and
inform her that my children have no relations in the South with
african blood in them but I cannot say so much for some of those who
used to think themselves insulted when they heard me pleading for
the negroes rights.

Sallie & Franky. Bless your little Souls how I would like to See you.
I want you both to be good children and learn your lessons so that
when I get home you will know something that I may feel proud of
you instead of having children that I would be ashamed of. I also want
you to learn to work. For after all industry is the only Sure way there
is for you to get along. You cannot even make good Scholars without you are industrious. You may be Smart and intelligent but if you
are not industrious your intelligence will be of no avail.

The first thing to think of is to find out what you wish to do and
then persevere untill it is accomplished. In order to proform you must
have health. As you are young and have not seen as much as I have I
will tell you something if you will only mind it that I have found out
about preserving health. In the first place you will not think it worth
while to trouble yourselves as you feel well any how. But in order to
keep well you must observe Some rules which you cannot dispense
without suffering for it in the future. Now to preserve your health
you must not confine yourselves to the house altogather nor must you
remain in the open air altogather. But you must take care not to expose yourselves to too great extremes. If you have been in the house
wher it is warm before you venture into the cold you should clothe
yourselves so that the body will not become chilled at once or the

chances are that you will take cold and inflamation will ensue. Neither must you Eat too much for many of the causes of sickness proceeds from foul stomachs. There is another thing. You should always take enough of exercise to make your system active so that nature will not be obliged to take unnatural courses to through off extraneous matter. You should set down a rule to be followd under all ordinary circumstances. First you should get up in the morning as soon as you get awake for laying after you awake makes you lazy. You should then wash and clean yourselves up and walk about or do something untill you get your breakfast. For one half hour after you should not fix your attention to any thing particularly. But after that time you should spend at least 3 hours in labour or study, and so on for the rest of the day.

If you attend to these simple rules you will be likely to enjoy good health and clear minds. With this I will stop.

I had thought of sending you some presents but I have no money and I am not able to get you anything that would be of any use to you at this time. But maybe I will get a chanc to get you something yet before I leave here. I hear that there is a mail in but there is so much of it that if there is anything in it for me it will not be distributed so as to let you know wheather I get a letter or not. I am begining to look for my commission now as I think Gov Stone has had time to send it to me if he ever intends to do it. Well it is nearly time to send out the mail and I must close. If this letter is not as good as it might be it is as good as I can write now.

Affectionately yours
Taylor

1. This verse is attributed to Alexander Selkirk, who was put ashore by his ship's captain on a deserted island and lived there alone for five years. Daniel Defoe evidently drew his inspiration for *Robinson Crusoe* from Selkirk's experience.

2. On January 31 the Fifteenth and Seventeenth Corps began moving from encampments near Beaufort and Savannah into the interior of South Carolina. By the date of this letter Sherman's forces were in the vicinity of Bamberg, where they cut the South Carolina Railroad.

3. Major General Rufus Saxton commanded Union forces near Beaufort, South Carolina, from February 19, 1863, until January 23, 1865. He was then assigned to inspect local settlements and plantations and to recruit Negroes for the army. Saxton was criticized by Major General John G. Foster, commander of the Department of the South, for this speech because he feared that it would lead to a reigniting of Confederate activity in the region.

4. By Special Field Orders Number 15, Sherman gave the Sea Islands off the coast of Georgia and South Carolina and "abandoned rice fields along the rivers for thirty miles back from the sea" to former slaves and prohibited all whites, except government officials, from going there.

> Des Moines Feb 10th 1865
> Dear Taylor

I received thine of the 29th this morning and was very well pleased to know that thee was so well fixed as thee is at this time and hope thee may continue to be in a good situation all the time thee will have to stay in the service. I have nothing to advise abut thee staying in the service another three years. That I will leave to thy will or circumstance to direct. I would be glad to have thee at home as soon as possible for I am very tired of staying in one place so long. I have never stayed three years at one place since I was maried before. So it is no wonder that I want to have a change and I would like thee to get home on account of the children. For they are geting old enough to want some of thy care along with the care I give them. But I will say just do as thee thinks is for the best for all concerned. As for me I can get along some way or other. Of course I do not expect to get a long as well as if thee was at home and allthings were going on in proper order but I have give up makeing my plans for the time to come. There fore I just take all I can get out of the presant and let every day take care of its own wants. God in his might will provide, or at least I feel inclined to trust to him for I think I have got a long as well as meny others have since their husbands have been in the army. I have had less hard work to do and better liveing since thee has been a way than I ever have since we came to Iowa. But with it all I would rather be with thee in a humble home of our own. But enough of this. We are all well with the exceptions of colds. The little ones are quite unwell with colds. The weather is good now. Last week it rained and the rivers broke up and the ice came down and I think that the way the children took cold was being out to look at the ice on Sunday. It is doubtful if we [will have] much more cold wether this winter or not. We have had a very plesant winter this far and I hope it will continue so untill spring. Thee wants to know how the children get along with their study. Well there is a school house on this side and there was one term before new years and they get a long very well. But this last term there has been so much changing in books and so much fuss that I have concluded to keep them at home and make them study with me. I find that they can learn if they are kept to their book. Sallie is very fond of reading and writing and I think she will make a fair scholar in time. Frank learns right along to read and spell with out any trouble. Ellis has learned to talk and he can say any thing he hears said. I would like to send his likeness for thee to see how he has grown since the one thee has was taken. I expect Dixon will pay. If he dose I will send it soon. Well I guess I will quit for I do not know anything new. Things about town go on about the same as usuel. So farewell for this time

     Catharine

     Des Moins iowa Fridy feb 1865
     Dear Fater

Thiss is a Cold blustry day and no School. There was school yester and Frank and I wend and I am sick. Its got a bad Cold by going to. It was wors yesterday because it rained then. My eyes are all swelled up. Bruther will write next Wednesday. Oh papa I wish you would jayhalk us an Accordain. I want to learn to play. There is a lady boards here that has one. You Can send it home in the box with your clothing cant you?

Feb 6. I was asking you for an accordain. My pap we got thy letter of 14 and oh I am so glad for the negros are free. Papa [illegible] something at the last of the letter. Miss Willcot my Teacher gave me some books. She gave all the Children some that had a Father in the army. It is most bed time so as to wash myself. Frank is Makeing some Figures to send to you. I have not got much more to say only that I want to know what kind of work you want me to do. No more at Presante. From Sallie Peirce to her father

     Des Moines Feb 16th 1865
     Dear Taylor

I have set down to write to thee but I am surrounded with the children and their are fussing and Ellis is so cross that no one can any more than stay in the house with him. He has had a very bad cold for the last week and when ever any little thing is the matter with him he is so ill natured that every body wants to get a mile away from him. I do not know what will become of him if dose not improve as he gets older. I had began to think he was a prietty fair child this winter. While he was right well he done well enough but as soon as he took cold and was not very well then I found him as cross as ever. Frank has had a cold and been as bad as Ellis but he takes his out in mischief and in teasing Sallie or some thing of the sort. I am writing with my paper on Sallie slate for S is useing the stand with her lessons. I have stopd them from school all togather for the fact that they were not learning anything there on acount of haveing a teacher that dose not know how to teach. Or has rather to submit to a superintendent of the public schools in town that thinks he knows it all because he came here from Ohio. And I am of the humble oppinion that he dose not know much after all for he make so many new rules and changes the books so often that no child can learn any thing. So at least I found that ours were not and I concluded just to keep them out untill there was a new teacher. I know that I can learn them some and they will not learn so much bad as they would at school. Thee talks of Sallie working. Well I think she will learn to work if there was any thing she could do but there is not much chance for her here. For Mary has to keep a girl and you are not going to get a hired girl that likes to have a little girl bothering round them at their work. I have got Sallie so she can sew right well and if she keeps to her books that is all I can do for her now. Cyrus recived a letter from Alice H Roman and one from Cyrus B Milner yesterday.[1] C is liveing with Alice and her husband at this time. They do not ether of them write much. I guess they wrote on an experiment to see what for an answer they would likely to get. Alice said she was going to write to me and if she dose I will be sure to write in answer immediately. Cyrus says that Jonathan Peirce rented out his farm and came out west last spring. That is about all they say of the folks. We are all well and I guess that we will get along well enough if we only try to be satisfied with what we have. But I believe that is not in human nature. Cyrus wants to sell out and go to some place south of this but wheather he will make it out this spring remains to be seen. I consider them well fixed here and Mary thinks if he would just be contented they could get along well enough. I received the money on the Mortgage from Dixon yesterday so thee need not be any ways uneasy about me. For if a person has plenty of money they can get a long any place. If thee is not likely to get thy pay any time soon just say so and I will send thee some of this if thee need it. My sheet is full. I will close.

> I remain forever thine
> Catharine A Peirce

1. Neither letter was found.

> Head Quarters 22n Iowa Infra
> Savannah Ga Feby 15 1865
> Dear Catharine Cyrus Mary & Children

I set myself to write you once more to let you know how I am getting along and what my prospects are. I am Still at head quarters acting Adjutant but have no Commission nor do I think I will get one. I think Some one is working against me getting it. There has been 3 recommendations sent in for me but I have never heard a word from Either of them yet. We got a notice from Adjutant Genl N B Baker this evening requesting us to forward an official notice of the death of Charles H Huntley Adjutant of the 22 Iowa and also asking if he had Ever been mustered in. There has never been any such a man belonging to our Regiment and what the meaning of it is I cannot tell. But I think that Some one has written to the Adjutant that Some such a man has a commission as adjutant to keep me from getting one untill it is too late to be mustered.[1] Col Graham got me to write to Baker this Evening and requested him to forward the commission without delay. For we have no Adjutant and no Officer to make one and the Regiment will be very much out of fix if we do not get some one. I shall send a letter in this to Stone and I wish Some of you to hand it to him and See what is the matter.[2] If there is any objection to giving me a commission I would like to know it and I would be satisfied but if there is none with him I want to find out what it means. I have my Suspicions that there is a man here that has been sneaking around writing to the department and giving false information. And if so I would like to know it. The Sergeant Major was very angry because I got all the Offices to sign my recommendation and no one would sign his. And I was told then that he would try some underhand scheme to deprive me of the position even if it would not benefit him but I thought he certainly not stoop to anything so low. But since this notice has come, I am convinced that something is wrong.

There is one thing. If I do not get it I have the Satisfaction of knowing that I have more friends in the Regiment than any other man in it Private or Officer. And so I can rest on my reputation without an office but for the sake of you all I would liked to have went home with some mark of favour from the government. But Enough of this.

I am well and in good heart for I think we will all get home this summer.

I received Marys letter this week and it was truly a god send for me for I had not had one from her for so long. I dont know wheather She thinks I ought to write to her seperately or not. I have always wrote my letters for all of you and supposed you understood it. For I have got too old to write love letters to Catherine and as far as affection is concerned although I feel a different kind of affection for you Seperately I can not tell which is the dearest to me. And I wish you all to understand that when I write that I intend you all to receive all my love in its proper way. I feel a different kind of love for Catherine than I do for the Children and different for them to what I do for My Sister and so for Cyrus. But nevertheless I feel a keen sympathy for you all and hope I will soon be able to enjoy your society once more.

I was somewhat Surprised at Some of Marys fears for my Sobriety but may be if I could see myself as others see me her fears are well founded.

The different view I had always taken in regard to intoxicating liquors to what Either of you had probably made my use of it Seem of little consequence to me when in reality it seemed momentous in your eyes. But you can let your fears subside. For I can say with clear conscience that the desire for it never gave me any trouble nor have I tasted it more than 3 or 4 times since I was at home. Although during the fatiguing campaign in the Valley the General ordered one gill per man issued daily but I thought I felt better without it and let the other boys have it if they wanted it. But there was but few of our Regiment took any, and so it was around if one wanted it. But I have found that the Soldiers generally do not want it. I think one reason is that their food is of such a nature that they have no desire to drink liquor. If it will do you any good and make you feel any happier I will promise never to taste it again unless prescribed by the doctor. And will live religiously to my promise although I do not feel that there is or ever was any danger of me becoming a drunkard I think Even if I had have liked it. I thought too much of my family to allow it to get me down.

I have changed in many of my views since I come into the Army and I think if I am Successful in getting through it I will have learned something to my advantage. I have been associated with a different class of men from what reside on Skunk and the motives that urged me to action have been different. And as I am no wiser I feel that I am better and have other and higher aims than I had when I thought of nothing but plodding my life out on skunk bottom!

I would like to write you a good long letter but it is midnight and I have to send in my reports at daylight to morrow and this sheet will have to do for the present. I feel sorry that Cyrus Still thinks of selling out for I had looked forward to the time when I would be out of the Service and would be able to set down and enjoy the Society of you all in a quiet way, free from all the nois and hardships of Camp. And it makes me feel lonesome to look forward to a lone sojourn far away from those I love. I would try and come home to get a place for Catharine if you sell out but it would cost me so much that I would have but little left to do it with. And as my term will soon expire I will have to trust to providence to protect her and the little ones untill I get with her. I had hoped to have got paid before this time but since we got down here the prospect does not seem good. I loaned Lt De Camp[3] $50 when we were at Cedar Green as I could not sent it home and was afraid the rebs would get it and [he] is away sick and I cannot get that Either now. So I have to wait until he gets back again to send you any. I feel anxious about you more so that I ever did since I have been out. I do not know what is the reason unless it is the prospect of your being left without a home. But I have faith that Something will turn up that you will get along comfortable untill I get home.

I do not know what more to write about. I intended to have stoped on the other sheet but I had more to say than it would hold. So I commenced on this and have run out.

We are not doing much now but fortifying. We have no drills nor any military exercise and so we Cook and Eat and Eat and Cook and dig a little and build Shanties and lay round Camp. I have not been in town but once since we came out here although it is not more than a quarter of a mile off. I am kept midling busy in the office and find but little time to idle. I have never played a game of cards since I have been out. I have played a few games of checkers. That is all the amusement I have ever participated in and you may judge that I am pretty civil. I have plenty of books to read and have been trying to improve myself some in Mathematics and grammar. But you will think by the manner in which I write my letters that my grammar does not do me much good. But I write my business letters better for I have not so much to say in them. And when I write to you I feel just like talking to you and grammar falls to the ground. Sallie wanted me to write to her. I wrote her and Frank a page or two in my last and I will write her some more as soon as I get a letter from home if it makes me feel more contented than I do now. But if it does not I can not promise it for I do not wish to write to her unless I feel like it. Cyrus thinks if that he could get to a warmer climate it would be better for his health. It may be so but I am afraid that the climate South would be injurious to him. I have seen no place yet where the health was so good as it is in Iowa generally. Of all the climates that I have been in this is the worst. The cold wet wind fairly drives through one and there is more Sickness in the army here than we have ever had Since we left Rolla.

I think that maybe if he could go to Texas that he might be benefited. But I am Satisfied that outside of that and the Valley of Virginia I have seen no place that will compare with Iowa.

I find that the dampness of the air in all this Southron Country is as bad as the Cold in Iowa. I can not get that full breath of Fresh dry air any where that I can there. Last summer in Louisiana I suffered very much with the damp and heat. The ground would be wet with rain and dew and the hot sun would steam the vapour up of the decaying matter and it was almost impossible for a man to live in it. But I do not pretend to say what would be best for him and if he could go some place where he could enjoy health I would be glad to see him do it. Although I would like to settle down near him for you are all that I have on this earth to care for and there is so few of us that it seems as if I would be alone if you leave. Well I must close. I wish you to hand this enclosed letter to Govornor Stone[4] and See what the matter is about my commission.

I remain as ever

Affectionate Taylor

Put Stones letter in an Infulope and hand to him in person. Do not give it to any other one.

Taylor

1. Charles H. Huntley enlisted in the 32nd Iowa on August 21, 1862, was promoted to adjutant August 13, 1863, and was killed at Pleasant Hill, Louisiana, April 9, 1864. The confusion was probably based on the similarity between the regimental designations.

2. The two letters Taylor refers to were not found. On February 22 Colonel Graham sent Baker another request that Taylor be appointed adjutant.

3. William M. DeCamp was a New York native and resident of Iowa City when he enlisted August 9, 1862. He was promoted to second lieutenant January 8, 1863, and to first lieutenant May 27, 1863. He was wounded at the battle of Port Gibson on May 1, 1863, and was discharged for disability April 26, 1865. After the war DeCamp and Taylor corresponded several times, but there is no indication whether DeCamp repaid the loan.

4. This letter was not found.

Head Quarters 22 Iowa

Savannah Ga Feby 27 1865

Dear Brothe

I concluded to write you a few lines to inform you of what is going on. Mary wrote me that you had some notion to sell out and leave Iowa. Now before you sell and leave I would advise you to gather what mony you can and take a trip down here. If Dixon pays Catharine get it and I will have $200 to send home in a few days and then you can invest it in things that you can more than double your money in. Potatoes sell in this market at $8 per bu butter at $4.00 pr lb onions at $6. Dried fruit would sell high and in fact all such things bring a high price and are ready sale. I am satisfied that you could clear $1,500 this summer if you can get permission to Ship goods. And I think if you would go to Gov Stone he would give you a recommendation that would make you all right. I think the troops will stay here all Summer and there will be a good chance for a man to make money all the time.

There is also a large lot of worn out government Mules & horses that will be sold Some time during the Summer and you might make a good thing by investing in them. But I am not able to give you an adequate idea of all the means there is here for a man like you to make money. I would not advise this unless you think of leaving Iowa for I do not think it worth while for you to unsettle yourself for the mere object of ammassing money. For I find that home is the main thing in this world. But if you do think of leaving this is the best opening that I have seen Since I have been out. And If I get my commission I can be of great service to you in getting along. If you do not sell out and wish to travel and make it profitable I do not see that you could do better than lay up a few hundred dollars worth of butter chees onions Potatoes and Eggs and come to Savannah. If you were here now you could clear $100 per day easy. But you can judge best for yourself what you wish to do.

I am well and am doing well but I have not received my Commission yet and do not care much about it now. We will be paid off in about 2 weeks and I will send my money to you and Catharine and you can fix up about it.

If you sell out I wish you would help Catharine to get a room where she can stay till my time is out. I had hoped that you could have stayed in Iowa, but I suppose that you do not enjoy your health and of course you wish to try some other place. I am unable to advise and will leave you to do whatever you think best and any assistance that I can render I will be happy to do. I have written to Mary and have a part of a letter written to Catharine and will send it by the next mail.

> Give my love to all.
> Yours afft
> Taylor

March 1st Catharine. I did not finish thy letter and probably it is as well I did not for we are again on the wing. All our dreams of comfort have vanished and we have the prospect of another term of Soldering towards the front. I had hoped that the 22 had done its Share in this rebellion but it seems that we are ever destined to either be at the front or so near it that when others fail we can be at hand to turn the tide.

I do not know where we are going but I think to Wilmington N. Carolina. However you can write me as heretofore and the letters will reach me sometime. I feel sorry to leave our comfortable quarters and would be willing if it could be so to rest on the laurels already won. But I feel as I have always done that. If we are needed I am ready to go and assist. However I do not think we will ever have as hard a time of it again as we have had. For the Spirit of the Confederacy is broken and nothing but pride "that Satan like Sin" keeps them from throwing down their arms.

I do not feel disheartened about getting home for I feel full of the faith that this war is about played out. And when the time comes that I can once more rest in the bosom of the loved ones I can feel the conscious pride of haveing done my duty. True I will be worn out some and will not feel as young as if I had loitered my time away in slothful Ease but I think my conscienc will feel clean and I will have seen much that I never would have seen if I had Stayed at home.

> I have seen combat on the tented plains
> And seen the green sword red with many a stain
> The bursting Shell and bayonet glistning bright
> Told of the fierce and well contented fight,
> I've seen the hostile flags above the carnage wane,
> And Friend and foe placed in a common grave
> And days, and weeks and months passed o'er
> Amid the ceaceless battles roar.
> Then all is hushed the Eastern sky is bright,
> With the glow of freedoms dawning light
> [Soudons?] bold peak, amid the sky
> Glows like an amethyst on high
> With rainbow tints her snows are spread
> And sparkles like stars her frost crownd head
> On his bright peak freedom shall take her stand
> And dry her tears and smile upon the lands,

So it seems to me but I am not very poetical to night and this will do. I dont know wheather you can love it or not, but maybe it will not hurt you. I intended to write more but I am so busy that I will have to quit for the preasant and maybe I will get time to write more before the mail goes out.

Well Kitty this is the 2n of March and I have not yet finished my letters and as I received good news all round and have finished my monthly work I concluded to try and finish it up. In the first place we received official news of the capture of Wilmington N.C.[1] and I am in hopes now that the confederacy is about gone up. I think it will burst one of these days with as great a noise as if some of their shells made on the fields of Winchester and Cedar Creek. I am glad to hear that thee has received Some Money as I was afraid that thee would have to do without the comforts of life. But it was impossible for me to make the government pay me any sooner but providence seems disposed to take care of us. As for my needing money I have no use for it here and if I had money things are so high I would not buy anything. So I am glad now that I have not got any money to spend or tempt me to buy any things.

I hardly know what to write thee about. As far as business is concerned I know nothing about the business world. All my knowledge extends to the duties of my position and wheather to advise thee to get the taxes paid or not I am undecided. If I was sure of being at home this fall I would advise thee to get the taxes paid but as it is I think it probable that the best thing thee can do will be to keep thy money or give it to Cyrus and let him try and make something out of it untill I get home. The love of gain or the desire for wealth sinks into insignificance amid the Storm of war. And if I get out of this and have the country safe I feel as if I would be satisfied, even if I have to set me down and toil for our daily bread. When I look back and see from what Source I received my enjoyment I wonder that I have been so blind as not to see it sooner. All of happiness that I have ever experimented has come from the same cause and that was from contentment and love. I often think of Burns's lines.[2]

> We may be poor Rolie and I
> But light's the burden love lays on
> Content and love brings peace and joy
> What more has kings upon the throne

These lines are true and I am astonished at myself for not appreciating when It was within my reach.

> I knew not then what bliss was mine
> Till kneeling at a false shrine

I came near loosing all
For not content with love and health
I fain must seek the bauble; wealth
The Idiots gilded ball.
Now when the spring of life is gone
My feelings scared and colder grow
I see what I have lost
The love I wasted in its bloom
And buried in a sordid tomb
Not heeding what it cost
But still I hope my life may last
So that I may from out the past
Draw pure affection, yet
And tame my heart that I may give
Love for thy love while we may live
to pay for what I get

Dear one how these long lonesome nights throws my mind back on its self. And memorys that I though long since buried arise and crowd arround my heart untill it carries me back to the dear times when thee and I were togather young and joyous with not a cloud to mar our happiness. Can we hope to ever feel so again? I hope so but I fear the young feelings that prevaded our hearts have become calloused by troubles untill they are not susceptable of the intensity of love we felt for each other then. Well I must quit this. I did not intend to write a love letter when I commenced but somehow or other it has run into something very like one and I guess thee will be ashamed to show it. But if thee is thee can keep it all for thyself. I got a letter from Edith McConnell[3] to day. She speaks very kindly to me and asks about thee. Says she will call if she ever gets to Des Moins. She is true to the union and flatters us soldiers very much.

I have written to Cyrus and Mary both and you will all get your letters about the same time. Last night I wrote that we were going to move but there is no motion like it yet. But I expect we will soon be ordered to hold ourselves in readiness to go. I think we will go to Morehead City Near Newbern N.C. as Stores are being movd there and I think an expedition will be fitted out to cooperate with Grant and Sherman against Richmond. I would like to join the Expedition and help to knock that d—d hole into the middl of next week. And if it was not that I do not like the style of shells and bullets the Rebs uses I would try and get there in time to see it go under. However I will not dispair for I have always had the luck to get into all the fights on hand and I may get into this one to my sorrow. But I am good for one more conflict and I think that will clean the thing up.

Well I must close for it is now past midnight and I must get some sleep. I am going to write Sallie and Frank a letter to morrow. So farewell.

> Taylor

Kiss the children for me and tell them to be good. I am glad thee is teaching them thyself.

> thine Affty
> Taylor

1. On February 22 the Confederate army abandoned Wilmington, and Union soldiers entered without opposition.

2. These poems are not by Robert Burns. The authors cannot be identified.

3. This letter was not found.

> Head Quarters 22 Iowa Infa
> Savannah Ga March 9 1865
> Dear Sallie & Frank

I concluded to write a you a letter this morning to let you all know what I am doing and what is going on here.

We are now under marching orders and I suppose we will move to morrow or next day.[1] We do not know certainly where we are going but we understand that we are to go to Moorehead City in North Carolina. Our 3d Brigade left here last Saturday and hear that it is at that place and I suppose that we will go to it.[2] Savannah is going to be Garrisoned by Negro troops.[3] There is about 20,000 of them here and at Hilton Head and they will be quite sufficient to guard these points. We have heard that Sherman and Beauregard has had a great battle near Charlotte in N.C. and that Sherman has whiped him and is still marching on towards Richmond.[4] We hear too that Sheridan is concentrating a large army at Alexandria in Virginia.[5] And you need not be Surprised to hear of us being ordered to take up our line of march at any time for the front. I had hoped that our hard Service was over but while there is any head to this rebellion I am satisfied that we will obtain but little rest. For the service in the Army is like a bad teamster. If they balk thy whip the good horse to make him do his own work and the work of the bad ones too. But there is one thing certain. If we help take Richmond I think it will be the last we will have to do for I think the confederacy after being gutted, quartered and its head cut off will certainly not live much longer. We have had a very pleasant time since we have been here and I have enjoyed myself as well as I could do away from you. But I suppose pleasure is now at an end and another Campaign will be made before our term of service expires. I have not heard any thing from my commission yet and my time is out to day for being mustered as we have only six months to serve. So I will not get any benefit from it. I did not care about it for myself but I thought that it would make you all feel happy to know that I had done my duty to my country and had received a mark of approbation for it. And I also thought that a little additional pay would render you more comfortable. But if I am unfortunate enough to not get it I must try and be satisfied, although it seems hard that after all I have done I should be disappointed.

I am still in the Adjutants Office and I suppose will stay there untill the war is over as I am the only one who can attend to the work. But I will get no more pay than I have done. I have written all this about myself. Now I will write about you. What are we going to do when I get home? Have you thought anything about that? Has Ingersoll paid mother the rest of the money he was to pay her? Has Uncle Sold out or is he going too? I want to know all about it. I want Mother to get all that money from Ingersoll and keep it all togather if Uncle does not need it untill I get home and then I want to get a farm fixed up so that we can live and thee and Frank can have time to get your education and help Mother and me do the work when you are not learning your lessons. I think I can teach you myself better than the racing class of teacher that Straggle through the country without brains.

I think we can live better in Iowa than any place I have seen yet. This country is both poor and unhealthy and much of the South is the same way. And as health is of the greatest importance in insuring happiness I think we had better put up with the clear fresh air of Iowa and rich green Prairies even if it is cold in winter than to live in this poverty stricken miasmatic Sunny South where a man cannot draw a whole breath from the 1st of May untill the last of September without feeling as if he was inhaling gass or heated air. What I meant about thee learning to work was that thee might learn how to sew and knit so that thee could help mother keep house snug and clean and the rest of us clothed and learn to cook so that we could have something good to eat. If thee can learn to work as well as Mother and Auntie thee will make a good housekeeper and will be able to get along in the world even if thee does not have much money.

I want Frank to try and learn and be a good boy so that he may get into a good way of making a living for himself when I and mother will both be called away from you. An Orphan myself[6] I have seen what is needful for one to make his way through the world and if experience will be any advantage to him I will cheerfully give him mine. The first step is to be good. That is what I never was and feel sorry for it now. The next is to be honest and the next is to get a good education and lastly to be frugal and industrious. If these are all accomplished he will come out all right. Well I must quit now for the sheet is full. I will write again as soon as I land at our destination. You can direct as usual but instead of Savannah direct to Morehead City N.C.

> Affa your Father
> Taylor Peirce

1. On March 8the 22nd Iowa was ordered to be prepared to move, but no destination was given.

2. Four regiments (24th Iowa, 38th Massachusetts, 156th New York, 176th New York) were at Morehead City. The other two regiments (128th New York, 175th New York) were repairing roads near Kinston. Taylor writes that the Third Brigade left Savannah on March 4, but another account states that it left on March 5.

3. On March 11 the 102nd Regiment, U.S. Colored Troops, arrived in Savannah. Three days later the 54th Massachusetts Infantry occupied the town. That same day the 33rd Infantry Regiment, U.S. Colored Troops, arrived in Savannah and remained there until June 9. On March 24 the 102nd and the 54th were ordered to Georgetown, South Carolina, and the 103rd Infantry Regiment, U.S. Colored Troops, was ordered to Savannah and remained there until June 30. Although black units had been in Hilton Head previously, from January through May 1865 the town was garrisoned by the 144th New York Infantry. At this stage of the war the regimental strength of the Union army was about 300 men, so Taylor's estimate of 20,000 soldiers occupying the two towns is probably incorrect. When Sherman en-

tered Savannah on December 21, 1864, his army was accompanied by about 10,000 "contrabands." Perhaps this accounts for Taylor's estimate.

4. This is not correct. Sherman was advancing toward Fayetteville, in the eastern part of North Carolina, and reached it on March 11. Charlotte is approximately 120 miles west of Fayetteville.

5. Sheridan was not at Alexandria. His army departed the Shenandoah Valley and reached Charlottesville on March 3. He moved along the north bank of the James River and destroyed vast quantities of cotton, flour, wheat, and salt, along with miles of railroad and several bridges. He would join Grant near Petersburg on March 18.

6. Family records reflect that Taylor was seven when his father died and twenty-six when his mother died.

> Head qrs 22n Iowa Inftr
> Newbern N.C. March 15/65
> Dear Catharine & all the rest

We are again on the move. I do not know at this time what our next move will be. We left Savannah last Sunday and arrived at Morehead City yesterday and last night we got on board the cars and come to this place.[1] It is 36 miles from Morehead on the Neuce River at the confluence of the Trent. It is a very nice place. The Railroad from Morehead to Raleigh runs through it. Gen Schofield is about 40 miles up at Kingston. He had quite a fight there but drove the rebles and when last heard from was moving on Goldsborough where he will form a junction with Sherman.[2] I think it is likely that Sherman will halt sometime at Goldsborough to recruit his army and cloth it as a portion of it was not clothed at Savannah. Morehead will be his base of supplies as the water is not deep enough here to admit of vessels of heavy tonnage to land. If you will look at the map you will see at once what the grand movement of this army will be. Sherman is moving north without any base at present. Schofield is moving west from this place on the railroad and is repairing it as he goes. Terry is moving northwest from Wilmington and the whole will concentrate at Goldsborough or at Raleigh.[3] Then the road direct north to Richmond will be the communication from the base to the army and to maintain and keep it open it will require a considerable force as the safety of an army depends upon quarter Master and Commissary supplies and the length of the rout will be considerable. It will take all the detachments of all Corps to keep it up.

From all these circumstances I conclude that we will have to keep open and guard the communications and supplies. We are at this time under Genl Birge.[4] Our Brigade is Commanded by Col. Graham[5] and the Regt by Lt. Col. White so we have the thing pretty much in our own hands. I am well and in good heat for I think this is the last struggle of the Confederacy.

I have no letter from home since the 16 of last month and am anxious to hear from you. I have not heard from my Commission yet and do not care much about it now as I am probably in a better condition than as if I had it as my position is easy and I have no responsibility. But still I do not have the honor but that is but an empty bauble. As "nigger said when he lost his rabbit" not so berry good after all. Well I must close with some love to you all. I hope soon to see you all once more never again to leave you in this world. I think you will all be glad when the war is over not so much on my account as for the country. For war is a dreadful thing when once you come to contemplate the Suffering and the moral depravity that it produced. We have not been paid of yet nor do I know wheather we will be here but as you have enough to keep you for the present I am better contented. The man I loaned my money to has not returned yet but we are looking for him every day and I can send you some if I do not get paid for I do not need money here. I will express some Clothing for I have more than I can take with me on a Campaign and will have to either throw it away or let it go home by express and I think it better to save it than to throw it away. Kiss the little ones for me and receive my best wishes and affections yourselves. Write to Newbern N.C. 2 Brig 2 Div 19AC and write often.

   Affectionately yours.
   Taylor

1. On March 12 the regiment embarked on the *Yazoo* and steamed for Morehead City. It arrived on March 14 and that same day traveled by train to New Bern.

2. Major General John M. Schofield commanded the Department of North Carolina. On March 8 forces under Braxton Bragg attacked and routed the lead units of the advancing Union army. Schofield brought up reinforcements, and Bragg withdrew after inflicting 1,257 casualties, mostly prisoners. The Confederates lost only 134 men.

3. By March 24 Sherman's army, advancing from Fayetteville, had joined at

Goldsborough with Schofield's from New Bern and a provisional corps commanded by Major General Alfred H. Terry that had marched from Wilmington.

4. Several reorganizations occurred from January through April that involved the 22nd Iowa. In March Major General Henry W. Birge commanded the Second Division, Nineteenth Corps. The 22nd Iowa was part of the second brigade of that division. In April Birge took command of the First Division, Tenth Army Corps, Army of the Ohio. The 22nd Iowa would become part of the First Brigade of that division.

5. Graham took command of the Second Brigade on March 4.

Head Quarters Iowa Infa
Newbern NC March 18, 65
Dear Catharine and all the rest

We are now under marching orders and are fitting up for an active Campeign.[1] Sherman is marching on Goldsborough and Schofield has taken Kinston and will connect with Sherman to-morrow at Goldsbourogh. If the Rebels does not make a stand there I think Sherman will halt and recruit his army and cloth and rearm it. In that case we will not be likely to move from here untill about the first of April. But if the Rebs should make a stubborn resistance at Goldsbourough We are liable to leave here for the front at any time. However I am of the opinion that there will be but little more fighting for I think the spirits of the Jonnies is broken. From the way they are deserting I should say that the greater portion of them was tired of it.

I expressed all my Surplus Clothing day before yesterday and directed to C A Peirce Des Moines Iowa. All the articles in the box were mine except (2) two Overcoats that belong to Asa E. Burtch.[2] You can tell mine by its being a cavalry coat without any piping on the cape and on the Shoulder you will see some grease where the candle droped the melted tallow on it and I never took time to take it off. Burtch has one Cavalry Coat which has a paper with his name pined on it. The other one is an Infantry Coat. The difference is in the Colar and Cape. These two Coats you will give to his wife when she calls for them. I had no money to pay the freight on them here and I want thee to pay it and send me word what it costs to send the whole thing and I will settle with Burtch for the freight here. I sent home all the clothes I could dispence with and all my old letters and the history of the Regiment and I would like you to preserve them for future referance. You will see by my drawers that I am troubled with the bleeding piles. I have never been right well since I was at home. But they do not hurt me much but it is very annoying to me. The doctor has tried to cure me but he says that while I stay in the army it will be impossible to get me cured entirely of them. He says though that when I get home where I can have a change of diet and some rest he thinks I will get better and maybe entirely well of it.

This is a very nice town but it is quite old and there is more negroes around here than I ever seen in one place before. Well I will have to quit writing as the desk is needed for other work. I am in good health and in good heart. I think the War is about played out and we will get home before harvest. I heard yesterday that we were to be paid off on next Wednesday and if so I will be able to send you some $150 which you can use in any way that you think proper. But I think you had better not invest much money in real Estate for as soon as this war is over things will collapse and there will be general break down in financial matters. And those who have money to lay out at that time will be able to do better with it than to lay it out in property at the present rates. If I was at home I would sell out every thing I have at this time and work at days works for a living untill after the crash is over and then I could buy something to do me and settle down. This is only my views. I do not wish to be understood to dictate but I just express my opinion. For while I am attending to the defence of the country you may attend to the things at home and when peace comes I will try and take the comforts of the world during the rest of my life. I sent some books for the children. Some of them I have packed through one Campeign and some of them I got in Savannah. I want the Children bounce on to that greek grammer and learn the letters and how to make them and as soon as they can learn to spell and pronounce the language. I sent some Mathematics for Frank when he is old enough to learn it. Those religious book were presents so I sent them along not because I though them indespensible but because I wished that the children may not be prejudiced against any one creed but contemplate camly all the opinions expressed and judge for themselves which is right. Kiss the little fellow for me and tell them to be good children and I think I will be with them by the time the sun is in the zenith. My love to Cyrus and Mary. And all for thyself (I have no letter yet).

Affectionately Taylor

1. The regiment was ordered to be prepared to move to Goldsborough, but the order was canceled. It remained at New Bern until March 20.

2. Asa E. Burtch was an Ohio native and resident of Vandalia when he enlisted July 28, 1862. He was mustered out July 25, 1865.

Hd qrs 22n Iowa Infty
Morehead City North Carolina
March 25th 1865
Dear Catharine

I concluded to write you a few lines to day to keep you informed as to our where abouts and what we are doing for our country.

I am well and the Regiment is now laying at Morehead City[1] which you will see by examineing the map is near the mouth of the Neuce River at the lower end of Pamlico Sound. This is the great harbour and base of Supplies for Shermans Army. The Rail road running from here to Ralleigh through Goldsborough where Sherman now is having joined Schofield & Terry near that place where they had a battle on last Sunday & Monday. The Rebles attacked the 20th Corps on Sunday and drove them back some distance. On Monday morning the 15th & 17th Corps come up and went into them and give them a sound drubbing capturing 5 Rebel Genl. and Several hundred prisoners and a large amount of Arms and Stores. We have not had the details of the fight as yet but some of the prisoners have been sent in.[2]

Our Regiment and in fact all of our Brigade except the 28th Iowa and 13th Connecticut are at this place doing fatigue duty building Rail Road unloading Vessels and forwarding Q.M. Stores and Subsistance to the Army at Goldsborough.[3]

We have been turned over to the Q Masters Dept for the present and I suppose will be employed at this business untill Sherman cuts loose from this base when we will either join him and accompany his expedition north to Weldon or we will be transported to Norfolk Va to open a new line of Communication from there to Weldon or some other point on the different R Roads running through N Carolina.

When we first came to this place we were sent to New Bern but in a few days we were sent down again and have been at work night and day all this week in Sending out Subsistance and Clothing to the front. There is some talk of sending us to Carolina city to work on the Rail

Road between there and new Bern. If we go it will be tomorrow or next day. There is such vast amts of stuff to send out that it will require another track to be laid to furnish sufficient transportation.

This is a low sandy neck of land laying between Pamlico Sound and Bogue Sound and at the west end of Beaufort inlet and is one of the meanest places we have had the fortune to be encamped. The wind never ceases to blow and the sand is worse than it was in Texas if possible. There is one redeeming quality though. There is plenty of Oysters and Clams here for gathering and if we could only be comfortable we could do very well but I hate to eat sand and breathe sand and look through and hear through sand all the time. The wind off the Sea is damp and chilly and that off the Shore is cold and damp so you may think that the climate and the situation is not delectable. However I belive I would as soon put up with it as it is as to take any more fighting in mine. Troops are continually pouring through here from the north for Sherman and from the number that has landed and went to the front this week it looks as if the North had rolled itself in one vast wave on the South sufficient to swallow it up. The Rebs no more makes a fight. They attack the advance guard of the army and Skirmish with it until the main body comes up when they fall back pell mell and our boys move on. It is said that Robert E Lee was at the battle on last Monday in person[4] trying to inspire his men with courage but was unable to make them stand and fight. The cause is doubtless they have been whipped so often that they are out of heart.

We have not been paid yet. We are looking for the paymaster every day but when we will get to see him is unknown. I have had no letter from home since the 18th of February[5] and am beginning to get anxious to hear from you. I have heard nothing from my Commission either and do not care two Straws wheather I get it now or not. If I do get it I will not be mustered untill I hear from home. I think 3 years is enough to serve the country at least for one who has seen the number of years that I have and had a little family to depend on me for a living. So I guess I will come home this summer and try to get something to do to keep soul and body togather. Mr Roach[6] was here this week and told me of the Coon Bridge being swept away.[7] Tell Dr Turner I am glad of it for if he had been honest and not cheated me out of what I earned god would have been more merciful and maybe let his damnd old Bridg alone.

I wrote you last Saturday and notified you that I had expressed home some clothes. I will write again for fear you do not get that one. I sent for myself one overcoat one pair of pants 2 Blouses some shirts and drawers and a lot of Books and papers and old letters. For Asa E Burtch 2 Overcoats one a Cavalry overcoat with a slip of paper with his name pined on it and one Infantry coat. This was all that was in the box for him. My Coat had some tallow on the shoulder by which you can tell it. I had no money to pay the freight and when thee pays it I want thee to write to me what the cost is so that I can settle with Burch for his share. I wrote to Edith McConnell this week. I received one from her some time ago and if thee will look over my old bundle of letters thee can see what she wrote to me.[8] She is very anxious about me or at least seems so and says that she will be to see thee this summer. Time is lagging along now and I expect that the next 5 months will move slow along as the nearer our term of service is out the more anxious we feel to get out. I already begin to dream about home and its joys and as each day passes and the time approaches I get more anxious. But I will try and be patient and take care of myself and get home.

How is the little ones getting along? Is that young scion as cross as ever? Is he going to be of any use? Is Sallie going to make a good sober steady woman or is she going to be vain and given to folly? As far as Master Frank there is no use talking about him. He will either be a good man or as great a devil as his pap and time will have to intervene to determine which course he will take. I hope to get home in time to get them on a little farm somewhere so that they can be taught industry and economy and at the same time give them a good English Education and if I find they will bear it something more. Kiss the little things for me and try to make them love me. Oh how I wish for their little caresses and some older ones too. But I must not make so much fuss about that or I shall have you all crazy for my return. Give Cyrus and Mary my love and tell them I want them to write me soon and if they sell out there and I can get off I will try and get home sooner to get thee fixed up. But I do not know wheather I will be able to get away untill my time is out. I must close. I hope to get letters from home soon and will write as soon as [I] hear from you.

Affectionately Thine
Taylor

March 28th mail in. Genl Sherman passed through here on his way to City Point.[9] News here that peace commissions at Ftrs Monroe.[10] All well to day. Still unloading vessles and I think will stay here for some time.

> Taylor Peirce

1. On March 19 the regiment was ordered to Morehead City and departed New Bern the next day. Some accounts state that the regiment reached Morehead City on March 20 and others on March 22. The regiment traveled by rail, so March 20 is probably correct.

2. On March 19 the lead division of the Fourteenth Corps encountered the Confederate army commanded by General Joseph E. Johnston. The battle that day resulted in a draw, and little fighting was done again until March 21. Johnston withdrew after sustaining 1,646 casualties while inflicting 2,606. No Confederate generals were captured.

3. The regiment was assigned to assist the quartermaster general in moving supplies from the port at Morehead City to the army near Goldsborough.

4. Lee was not at the battle.

5. Taylor is probably referring to Catharine's letter of February 16.

6. James P. Roach was a Tennessee native and Vandalia resident when he was appointed captain of Company G, 23rd Iowa Infantry, on August 15, 1862. He resigned April 10, 1863, and enlisted in Company F, 47th Iowa Infantry, on May 28, 1864. He became the chaplain on July 21, 1864, and was mustered out September 28, 1864. He was appointed sanitary and military agent for Iowa, and in March and April he visited Iowa troops in North Carolina.

7. Rains in early March caused the Raccoon River to rise, and by March 17 the bridge had been swept away. On March 20 the city council voted to establish a free ferry between the two parts of Des Moines separated by the river. The *State Daily Register* reported on March 28, 1865, that a new bridge would be constructed by November 1.

8. The letters to and from Edith McConnell were not found.

9. On March 25 Sherman left Goldsborough, and on March 27 he reached City Point, Virginia, where he met with President Lincoln, General Grant, and others to discuss the state of the war.

10. What Taylor is referring to is unclear. On February 3, Lincoln met with Confederate vice president Alexander Stephens at Hampton Roads, but no agreement was reached. On March 27 and 28 Lincoln, Grant, and Sherman met at City Point, Virginia, to discuss possible terms of surrender for the Confederate armies.

Head Qrs 22n Iowa lnfty
Morehead City NC April 2 1865
Dear Catharine

It is sunday again and I am ready to write you another letter so that you can know what we are doing down in this God forsaken Rebel Smitten land. I am well except a cold and sore mouth which does not stop me from work.

I received a letter from thee and Sallie this week dated the 5th of March.[1] There must be one out between the 18th of February and the 5th of March that I have not received yet for I suppose that you aim to write once a week. The Regiment is working here in the Q.M. department unloading Vessels and loading up Cars to Send to Goldsborough to the Army. It would astonish you to see the Vast quantities of Subsistance and Clothing that is being sent forward. There was sent from this place in one day 418,000 lbs bread 75,000 pairs pants 80,000 pairs Socks 500 bbls pork and 30 car loads of forage for horses besides other thing in small quantities that are nescessary for the Army. There is a great Army concentrating at Goldsborough. There has been a continual Stream of Recruits and convalescents and reinforcements passing through nearby ever since we come here. And yesterday the cap was put on by the arrival of about 7,000 from the different hospitals and recruiting depots in the country. I am of the opinion that Sherman will have the largest and best army that any General has commanded since the commencement of the war. He must have at this time 140,000 men[2] and the great portion of them are Veterans and have endured all the hardships and shared all the Victorys of the Army of the Tennasee. And of course are not likely to be defeated or driven back by any equal amount of rebels. When Sherman cuts loose from this base and the hosts of the North begin to move you may expect to hear of the fur flying. It is supposed that the movement will commence about the 12th of this month. And I tell you the confederacy must prepare to stand from Under. For of all the men and soldiers I have seen yet the Western troops under Slocum[3] and Schofield seem the most determined to destroy not only the rebellion but impoverish the country so that it will not be able to exist for the next century. North Carolina has not been so sorely visited as some othe States have but still it has come in for its Share of destruction as well as some of the rest. It Seems to me when the Armys of the

Union get in motion that you will almost be able to here the roar to the green plains of Iowa. Just to think of Grant with his 3 lines of battle Each 20 miles in length[4] Sherman with 4 collumns sweeping North covering a track of 40 miles in width Sheridan with 30,000 of the best cavalry that has ever been organized Since Murat led the squadrons of Bonapart, and Kilpatrick with another force nearly equal hovering on Shermans Extreme left[5] protecting the flank from attack and at the same time executing such brilliant movements that one would think that the rebles would throw down their arms and accept the amnesty of the President. And I have no doubt but they would if it were not for their leaders. It makes my heart bound when I look on the vast efforts and almost innumerable hosts of the Government to-gather with the seeming exhaustless Supplies that are being forwarded to the field. It shows to what an unlimited degree the nation has con-fided their cause to the president and congress and what wonderful resources the government is possessed of. I am proud I am a Citizen of the United States and happy that I seen what was my duty and have done it. Well I think we will move to the front in about 8 or 10 days. I hear that we are going to be temporarily assigned to Gen Terry for the coming campeign. But I do not know what truth there is in it. But there is no doubt but that we will take part in the movement about to be commenced.

I was in hopes that we would be assigned to Slocum as he has the Western men and I have no confidence in the eastern troops since the Campeign in the Valley and I would like to get from amongst them if we are going to have to fight any. I suppose we will close up the rear and protect the supplies and keep open the communications untill there is a new base opened. Where that will be I am hardly able to tell. But I Suppose eithe Chowhan [Chowan] River at Pitts Landing or at Norfolk and the interior Base will be at Weldon. I expect a hard battle at Weldon for if the Rebs are going to try to defend their present po-sition they must hold Weldon. If not we will have no fighting in East-ern N.C. or Virginia. And in that case we will be run all over Gods creation again hunting the damnd Rebs to get to shoot them which will cost us more labor and wear out more men than the rebles are worth when we do get them. There is a rumour here that Grant has taken Petersburg[6] but it has not been confirmed by any official report. If it is true I think the rest of the campeign will be light work. For with that it will be easy for Sherman to connect with Grants left and swing his lines westward and completely encircle Lee's Army which will put our forces in such a position that we can afford to wait untill they are Starved out or compell them to come out an fight us in the open field. The result of which must lead to a final winding up of the rebellion.

I have written all about the situation of our affairs and the prospects of the Army wheather it will be interesting to you or not. But I have taken it for granted that you would like to know anything that was going on. So I will write some about myself and my prospects. I am still in the adjutants Office keeping the records of the Regiment. I have not received my Commission nor do I think I am going to. I think Stone does not intend to give me one but what the reason is I am unable to find out. For I know that no man ever had a better recommendation for an office than I had, and none ever had a more earnest petition sent in for an early action to take place in regard the issue of the commission for the reason that we had no Adjutant and no one to fill the place but myself. Hence the reason of my being kept here without any legal authority. I do not know what I will do. Sometimes I think of applying to be releived and sent to my Company again for it is very annoying to me to be here without proper authority although I get along very well and the Officers treat me just as well as though I was actually the adjutant. Yet you know that I never did like to push myself when I had no right. I am also doing the work for $24 per month that I would be entitled to $140 per month for and that is another consideration if not for myself it is for my family.

Time is flying along and 4 months more lets me out of the Service. What am I going to do then for a living? I know as little about the business of civil life now as though I was a child. For the last three years I have given my whole mind and energys to the cause of the country and feel that in a financial view I have lost rather than gained. But I will have the conciousness of having done my duty to my country and my children in protecting their rights and I hope some course will be marked out for me to make a living. What is Cyrus going to do? Is he still going to sell out? I would like to buy his property if I was able so that I could have some place to go to to rest when I am done with war. But of course that is all in my eye unless I can get my commission and then I do not know what the prospect would be for me to pay for it for I do not know what it is worth now. I think Des

Moines will be one of the best points in Iowa and if a person had property there it would eventually be valuable. I expect I can get a little farm fixed up that will do me better than anything else to make a living on for I do not want to hang around a city without I can have a good birth and plenty to do. I see by the papers that goods are coming down and all other things must become lower and when the war is over I look for another term of hard times. I suppose I will be entitled to 160 acres of land when I get through, free from taxation for 5 years.[7] And if I can find it and make a home on it I think we can live very happy. The only thing will be to make the improvements but if I am as well as I am now I can do it. I am glad that the children are trying to learn and it makes me feel happy to know that I have such an affectionate family. For there is many men in the army who has not got that kind of family at home to cheer them. I have often thought if you were as some of the Soldiers wives are that I hear of I would not be worth one damd cent. But I am truly thankful that my ways have been strewn with flowers in that respect. Dear one I hope in a few months to be with you again and taste once more the pleasures and happiness of home. I am glad that Cyrus & Mary are making some money and doing so well. If they can be comfortable in their old days it will give me a great deal of pleasure. I do not see what they can wish for more than a good comfortable home and a living in this world. For my part I have seen so much danger and hardship that I feel as if I could be contented with a very little spot of Gods earth if I could enjoy it in peace. I want Cyrus and Mary both to write to me for I expect after we cut loose from here that you will not get much news from me untill we strike a new base. So you may make calculations for to be at least one month without a letter. But I will keep you posted untill we do leave and will try and inform you where we will come out next and what the prospect is for the future. There is a mail in and I will wait to see if I get a letter. I just got 2 letters, one from thee and one from Mary.[8] I am happy very and will spend this day in better spirits than I have done many of the last days. I did not know that I had written despondingly as Mary thinks for I have not felt so. Nor did I have any fears about my family coming to want. Nor do I want Cyrus to forego his own interests for our welfare. I only request that the family may be assisted in getting located so that they can live comfortable untill I can get home if he should sell out. I want you to understand that I have as deep an interest in his welldoing as my own and not for the world would I do any thing that would injure him in his future if I could help it. I am truly thankful that while I have been soldering that my wife has such comfortable home. For it has been a great help to me in enabling me to bear the hardships of the War. If I had have been placed in the situations of many a poor fellow I expect I would not have done so well as I have.

Tell Sallie and frank I wrote to them and will try and write again. Give my love to all inquiring friends and tell them we are going to knock the bread basket out of the Rebs soon.

> Affectionately
> Taylor

1. This letter was not found.

2. On March 31 Sherman reported an effective strength of 81,140 officers and enlisted men.

3. Major General Henry W. Slocum commanded the left wing of Sherman's army as it advanced north from Savannah. The wing consisted of the Fourteenth and Twentieth Corps.

4. By April 2 Grant's line stretched approximately fourteen miles south and west from the Appomattox River near Petersburg. On April 1 Sheridan defeated Confederate forces at Five Forks, thus depriving them of the use of the Southside Railroad that ran from Petersburg.

5. Sherman's army consisted of four separate forces. The right wing was the Army of the Tennessee (Fifteenth and Seventeenth Corps) commanded by Major General Oliver O. Howard. The left wing was the Army of Georgia (Fourteenth and Twentieth Corps) commanded by Major General Henry W. Slocum. The center was the Army of the Ohio composed of the Tenth and Twenty-third Corps commanded by Major General John M. Schofield. The cavalry division, numbering 4,148 men, was commanded by Major General Judson Kilpatrick. Marshal Joachim Murat was Napoleon's flamboyant cavalry commander and brother-in-law. Sheridan's cavalry command of three divisions (two from the Army of the Shenandoah and one from the Army of the Potomac) totaled 17,658 men present for duty.

6. The Confederate army withdrew from Petersburg during the night of April 2.

7. The Mexican Bounty Act of 1847 provided a quarter section (160 acres) to any soldier other than an officer who had served in the Mexican War for at least one year. In 1855 the act was amended to state that the soldier need have served only fourteen days. That act did not apply to soldiers serving in the Civil War, although many mistakenly believed that it did. On March 21, 1864, Lincoln signed a bill that provided a homestead to soldiers who had served two years. Not until 1870 did Congress legislate that soldiers who had served ninety days could claim 160 acres.

In 1872 the act was again amended to require one year's residency on the land. The act that admitted Iowa to the Union on December 28, 1846, stipulated that land granted for military service was exempt from taxation for three years.

8. Neither letter was found.

Head qrs 22n Iowa Infa
Morehead City, N.C. April 9th/65
Dear Catharine

It is Sunday Morning again and I am Still well and in good heart concerning our military situation. I received a letter from thee this week and was glad to hear that you were all well and happy to hear that Cyrus is doing well. I feel very greatful to him and Mary for their assurance in regard to the wellfare but I would be sorry to know that by thy situation they would be impeded in any of their arrangements from doing better. For I can not ask them to neglect their own interests for my benefit. I think now that I am going to be at home before a great while. Long before you get this you will have heard the glorious News of the discomfiture of the Rebel Army.[1] This I think winds up the Southeren Confederacy and of course our fighting unless there is something more than we know of now. We are still at this place doing fatigue duty, that is Sending Subsistance to Sherman.

Our 3r Brigade was ordered to the front this morning. I expect that they go to hold some point for a base of supplies.[2] It is said here that Sherman occupied Raleigh Friday.[3] One thing certain the capture of Richmond has altered the state of affairs here. Before the news arrived we had commenced to move our things to Norfolk. But Since that every thing has been ordered back and the Vessels are still unlading and subsistance is going forward. Yesterday Wade Hamptons Cavalry cut the rail Road between here and Goldsborugh but did not do much damage.[4]

I can not tell how long we will remain here but I think likely as long as this is Shermans base. I am pretty well fixed up again. I have a floor in my tent and a good bunk to sleep on but our living is poor or at least it is for me. We draw bread fat pork and coffee and sugar. This is all the government furnishes us and we have no money to buy any thing else with. We can gather some oysters but they are small and not very good. There is plenty of fish but we have to pay for them if we get them. It is always the case that the troops in the field fares better than those at posts for the reason that all surplus luxuries are sent forward if there is transportation. If not they are stored untill there is so that we do not get any of them unless some sanitary agent comes along and distributes them to us.

I hardly know what to write about. I think I will wait until afternoon when the mail comes in and see what it brings. I have not received my commission yet and I think I will not be needed in the service much longer. So I think I will be at home and will have to go to work again. It is going to be hard for me get any thing to do that I can make a living at for a time for I am worn out. I do not wish you to think that I am sick or any thing of that kind but I am just worn out. And I can inform you that when a man goes through three years of campaigning Such as our Regt has done he is pretty near used up. But I have always found enough to do and I expect I always will if I am able to do it.

You Seem to think that my letters showed that I was out of heart. Now I do not see what you take it from for when I wrote those letters I was just as contented as ever I was only I did not want to leave our nice quarters in Savannah. But I think if you will read the letters right you will find that they are more ludicerous than Solemn.

I have nothing of any account to do and get out of sorts laying arround. I have about 3 hours work in a week now. I have the affairs of the Regiment up to date and it is easy to keep it so. Well I will stop untill the mail comes in.

Well the mail is in and I received thy letter and one from Sallie.[5] The subject first of my mind is Ingersoll. The contract was that he was to pay thee one Hundred dollars less an order that I gave him for thee to pay him some 37 dollars or thereabouts. The order will show for itself. Thee has the written agreement that if he sold the mill he was to pay thee the money and him and I Settled up and I gave him an order for what I owed him to come out of it and a portion of that order was for the taxes on that land. He has a deed for the land and I have nothing to show that he ever was to deed that land back to me. Although I frequently wished him to give me a bond for a deed and under all the circumstances I concluded to let him keep the land if he done as he agreed. But I want thee to go to him and just tell him that thee wants that money as per agreement. And if he says anything about what I owe him just tell him that his agreement was to pay the 100 Dollars and thee will pay the amount of my order on thee and that is all thee will do. Tell him that as for his and my arrangements thee knows nothing about but thee wants the money and if he will not pay it, go to Some good lawyer then and see if they cannot compel him to pay it. Now I want thee to do this for life is uncertain and I may never live to get home. And another thing I wish to find him out and if he refuses to pay that money. If I live to get home, I do not say what I will do but I have made it a business to kill just such damd hounds as he is these last 2½ years. He justly owes it and agreed to pay it to thee. Thee can tell him that I say that I do not owe him one cent for he has been paid in full for all he has ever done for me. It is true that if he laws that Parker Matter through for me I was to pay him some $250 but he took both sides of the case. He is Parkers lawyer and since he has acted as he has done with my affairs I have no confidence in him and I believe I could disbar him as a lawyer. But this I do not care anything about for things have changed so that I can not tell what I will do when I get home. But he must pay thee that money. I have seen too much hardship to allow a d—d copperhead to swindle my wife. As soon as thee get this letter I want thee to see him and tell him that I have not been able to send thee any money for 10 months and thee needs it and write me the result. And if he will not pay it I will apply for leave of absence to kill cops and we will see if he does not poney.

I was glad to hear that you were all well and tell Sallie that I love to get her letters and tell master Frank that he must be a good boy and try to make a better man than ever his father was.

Our whole Brigade has come down here and we are about the only troops here. I do not know how long we will stay here but I think likely as long as Sherman stays on this line of communications.

David Wrights Son Wilson that used to keep the White Horse Tavern is down here on a cavalry Regiment.[6] He has been to see me but I was not at home as we say when he was here so I did not get to see him.

I think the war is over and I hope 2 months more will see us all mustered out and returned to our homes. The glorious old Flag waving as free as ever and peace and prosperity once more in our land. There is talk of our being paid soon and I hope we will get it for many of the men have not been paid for 10 months and I know that their families must need it. This is all that I think of to night. Give my love to all my acquaintainces and tell the shirks that we will soon have their homes secured for them and their selfish Souls can rest in ease. And we will take the extreme pleasure of feeling the utmost contempt for their diminutiveness. I hope that they may all be drafted and Sent to Mexico. Forgive my ill feelings for I am mad about Ingersole.

> I am affectionately thine
> Taylor

1. Taylor is probably referring to the surrender of Richmond on April 3 after the Confederate army abandoned it the previous night.

2. The 38th Massachusetts and 156th New York (both in the Third Brigade) left Morehead City on April 8 for Goldsborough. The 24th Iowa (Third Brigade) and 131st New York (First Brigade) departed Morehead City for Goldsborough on April 9. The 128th and 175th New York (both in the Third Brigade), near Kinston, were ordered to Goldsborough on April 9. The 176th New York (also assigned to the Third Brigade) apparently remained at Morehead City.

3. This is not correct. The Union army occupied Raleigh on April 13.

4. On April 6 Johnston ordered Lieutenant General Wade Hampton to destroy the railroad near his position at Boon Hill. Boon Hill sat astride the North Carolina Railroad, which intersected the Wilmington and Weldon Railroad at Goldsborough and then ran to Raleigh and westward.

5. This letter was not found.

6. The White Horse Tavern was in London Grove Township, Chester County, Pennsylvania. David Wright was the innkeeper until 1853, which was after Taylor and Catharine moved to Iowa. He had a son, listed in the census as J. W. Wright. John Wilson Wright was the innkeeper until 1856, when he became the keeper of the Pennington Hotel in Sadsbury Township. Sergeant John W. Wright was mustered into Company C, 104th Pennsylvania Infantry Regiment, on January 5, 1864, and was mustered out August 25, 1865. He would have been age thirty-one at the time of his enlistment. The regiment was raised in Bucks County, a few miles east of Chester County. Of the John W. Wrights who served in Pennsylvania regiments, this is the only one who could be the Wilson Wright Taylor mentions. There were no W. Wrights in Pennsylvania cavalry regiments. During the spring of 1865 the 104th Regiment was deployed near Petersburg, Virginia.

> Head Quarters 22n Iowa
> Morehead City NC April 16 65
> Dear Catharine

Again it is Sunday and all looks bright. The soldiers heart is light and I expect the loved ones at home are looking forward to his speedy return to a happy home and their loving smiles.

I am well and feel now as if we would all be at home soon for I think the war is over. Lee and the army of Northern Virginia are prisoners.[1] General Johnson is hemed in by the forces of Sheridan, Sherman and Stoneman,[2] and long before this reaches you he will be a prisoner and his army disbanded. There is a rumour in Camp to night that Jeff Davis was captured at Charlotte by Stonemans cavalry.[3] If this is true I expect to be with you once more before two months more rolls round. Oh what a load is lifted from my mind. Our Country safe the war over and my life spared to once more partake of the joys of home. Dear ones what a world of bright anticipations the near approach of our emancipation from the fiery ordeal gives rise to. How we sit and talk over the pleasures of our meeting with the home circle. We have almost become childish over the prospect. It would make you smile to hear all the calculations that are made amongst the boys about what good times they are going to have when they get home. We are Still at Morehead City and I think we will remain here untill our time comes to take or homeward trip. Sherman is at Raleigh and a portion of his army has gone on to Some point near to Salisbury[4] but there has been no fighting since the news reached Sherman that Lee had Surrendered. It is reported here that dispatches went through to Sherman a day or two Since for him to halt his army and I learn that the Ammunition train was ordered back to New Bern Yesterday. Things is still going forward though as if we still intended to keep the army up in central N Carolina for some time. I suppose Sherman thinks that the Old Serpent of Rebellion is not to be trusted and as long as he keep wiggling his tail he will keep the club raised to strike so that he will have no chance to injure any one in his dying Struggles.

There is a vast Army in this State not less than 150 or 160 Thousand men[5] and many of them Vetterans of all the Campaigns of the war. Heroes whose weather beaten and scared faces are the image of freedom and Independance. We had a review to day while it made me feel proud that we had fought through this dreadful conflict. Yet the well remembered faces of many of the brave men who came to the field with us was missing from the ranks that it filled my mind with Sorrow. I could not help but think of the many acheing hearts that must still ache on for the loved ones whose forms are laying in a Soldiers grave far from his once happy home. Oh how thankful I feel that the great ruler of the Universe has been pleased to allow me to live to see this day. The dear old Flag Still throws its protecting folds around us and the nation purged of the henious curse of Slavery is about to enter a career of greatness and prosperity never equaled by any known on earth. My heart is almost to full to full to write. I can think of nothing but home. While the war was going on and rebellion still existed I was comparitavely contented. But now that it seems as though the strife was over and the Victory won I am impatient to wend my way for the old home and the little ones. I hope no more to be disturbed by the hoarse clarion of the Canons Roar.

When I look back and contemplate the hardships that have been endured and the dangers encountered I shudder at the recolection. I do not believe that all the wealth of the world would hire me to undergo it again and nothing short of the ruin of the country wold ever induce me to take part in another term of service like the one just passed.

I have had no letters from home this week nor in fact from any one. I have been looking for one from William Cook and one from Edith McConnell but have not Received any. I have not got my Commission and I think I will not get it now. The Adjutant General either must have suppressed it from personal feelings or Col Stone never issued it. I am Satisfied there is some sculduggery about it but where it is I am unable to discover. However if I do not get it I will not have to be under any obligations to any one and an Independant Spirit is better than boughten honors. The only thing that bores me is that all the officers wanted me commissiond and I done all I could for the cause and nothing that I am aware of stood in the road and to fail (through neglect of some of the officials) to get what I so justly earned or at least what all thought I earned, it makes me feel bad. But I must bring my letter to a close. We are not going to be paid off I guess untill our term of service expires and I do not care now. Thee has got some money to live on. I would like to have 4 or 500 Dollars to commence with when I get out but I recon I will not have that much unless thee can live on air untill I get home. And I am afraid that thee is not ample enough for that. The night is wearing away and I must close. Kiss the children for me.

> Thine affty
> Taylor

1. On April 9, 1865, General Robert E. Lee surrendered the Army of Northern Virginia to Lieutenant General Ulysses S. Grant.

2. On April 16, Major General George Stoneman's cavalry was astride the railroad between Greensboro and Charlotte, thus blocking the Confederate army under General Joseph E. Johnston from moving southwest. Sherman's army was approaching Raleigh from Goldsborough and Pittsboro. Sheridan had departed Appomattox on April 10 for Petersburg. Upon reaching that city he was ordered to join Sherman in North Carolina, but he did not depart Petersburg until April 24. Johnston's army was between Hillsboro and Goldsborough.

3. This rumor was not true. Davis would not reach Charlotte until April 19.

4. On April 12 Stoneman's cavalry captured 14 artillery pieces and 1,364 Confederates near Salisbury. He then spent two days destroying a portion of the North Carolina Railroad near Salisbury that connected Raleigh and Charlotte.

5. On April 10 Sherman's army consisted of 88,948 men.

> Head Quarters 22 Iowa Infty
> Morehead City NC April 17th 65
> Dear Catharine and all the rest

I wrote you last night full of hope and bright anticipations for the future. But ah how Soon is the brightest prospects clouded. Truly is it said that we know not what a day will bring forth. Amid the general joy and anticipations of an early peace joy a sad and prolonged wail comes from the North and tell us of the death by the assassins hand of one of Earths best men. Lincoln is dead.[1]

Oh what crime has our country been guilty of that it requires that Such men as he must fall. I had thought or hoped at least the sin of slavery had been washed out in the blood of the thousands of the best and bravest of the land but it seems not. The magnitude of the national Sin must nescessarily require proportionate attonement. And when one comes to contemplate it, it only creates wonder that the destruction of life and property has not been greater. We have no particulars of the murder here yet. We have only heard that Lincoln was murdered in the "Theatre" and that Stanton and his son was killed in their own house.[2] This is only in keeping in the principles of the Southeren People. Slavery has divested them of every principle of humanity. They are more like barbarians than civilized beings. While we were in Savannah our Lt Col was invited to a party at the house of a prominent Rebel Lady or at least she called herself a lady when the conversation turned on the relics retained by persons as a momento of the war. When she addressed the Col and told him She had a letter from an admirer of hers sent from the battle field of Chickamanga that She thought a great deal of. He said that it was written with the blood of a dead yankee. Her admirer wrote her that he dipped the pen in the blood as it ran from the wound that caused the yankees death and she was going to preserve it as an evidence of the heroeism of the Chivalry. Another one of the chivalry was captured last fall in the Valley, the Nephew of Gov Letcher[3] who used the jaw bone of a Yankee for a spur. Another lady had a yankee skull for a drinking cup. Now when we think of these things I do not wonder at them assasinating any one that they can get to without being caught.

I would not be surprised to learn that our northern Cops had a hand in it too for men of their avowd principle would stop at nothing to carry out their ends.

I would be in favour of letting the niggers go in now and make a clean shucking of the South. I am in favour of having the South Settled with a better breed of dogs and therefore let the negroes take it. For I beleve they are as much better than the Southeren Whites that they might bear the same comparison to them that the Jews did to the Gentiles. I want you to write to me how the cops behave over the news. If they seem to rejoice over it I am of the opinion that the thing has had its inception in the north among the traitors and Cowards. My lord if I ever hear a man justify or even hint at a justification of such a thing I would send him to hell quicker than ever a cat killed a mouse. What is to become of us now? I have no confidence in Johnson.[4] Seward is not likely to recover and who is there now to manage things to keep us out of the hands of a Military Dictator? I am sure I can not tell. All looks gloomy. I want Cyrus to write and tell me how the cops in Des Moins take the news. And also let me know what the feelings is in the North in regard to the future. We get so little news here that I do not find out much but the war News.

I must close. Kiss the little ones for me and give my love to Mary and Cyrus and all the friends.

> Thine affectionately
> Taylor

April 19th. I am well and am going out to hunt Shells on the beach with the Rev Mr Roach of Des Moines to-day.

I received thy letter of the 4 of April[5] yesterday. Glad to hear hope C will not have any more of his bad spells.

1. President Abraham Lincoln was shot at Ford's Theater in Washington by John Wilkes Booth on April 14. He died the next morning.

2. Secretary of War Edwin Stanton was not attacked, but an attempt to kill Secretary of State William Seward was made. He survived his wounds.

3. John Letcher was governor of Virginia from 1860 to 1864.

4. Vice President Andrew Johnson succeeded Lincoln and attempted to implement a conciliatory policy of Reconstruction in the South. He was opposed by Radical Republicans, who voted to impeach him. He was tried in the Senate and was retained in office by a margin of one vote.

5. This letter was not found.

Head Quarters 22 Iowa
Morehead City NC April 22/65
Dear Catharine and all the rest,

I have not much on hands this morning and concluded to Spend the time in writing to you. Our Regiment is still here or at least the organization is although the members is nearly all away on detached Service.

Our Regiment has the best reputation for honesty and Sobriety of any troops here and are sought after by all the Commanders who are responsible for government property for guards and messingers and this nescessarily leaves but a Small amount of men with the Regiment. Out of 346 men who report for duty we only have 88 Enlisted men and 6 officers with us and some of them are about Starting for Washington with a prisoner who was arrested as being implicated in the plot for the assasination of the president.[1] I am not doing much and am very discontented. Now that the war is over and the Country Safe I want to get home and am more impatient than I have ever been since I come out. I have no letter since the 4th of April. I was looking for one to-day but I did not get it. I feel ready now to leave the army at any time that I can get away. For I think I am not needed here and there is pleanty of men who can do what is to be done that are not so much needed at home and have not so many to draw them to their firesides. There is but little news here. The Shock caused by the anouncement of the murder of Lincoln is wearing off and a deep feeling of retaliation against all concerned in the plot has taken the place of the sorrow that was first felt.

We have been notified that a cessation of hostilities has taken place and negotiations are taking place for the Surrender of all the Rebel forces. What advance is being made but Gen Sherman telegraphed down here night before last for Gen Easton[2] to forward ten days rations for 30,000 men. Which I suppose indicates that he will have to feed the Rebel army and I suppose the preliminaries are agreed upon but we have not been officially notified of it yet.[3]

I have been out looking around some this last week as there was nothing to do. And I expect to go up a Raleigh some time this next week to see that place. I will some time give you an account of my visit to the Islands but have not time to do it justice now. Mr Roach of Des Moines and Col White and our Chaplain made up the party and we had a splendid time of it. Roach has left here for Iowa with 300 sick Iowa Soldiers. He is a good man and full of energy. Gov Stone could not have made a better selection for the place. I am well and hope when you get this that Cyrus will have regained his health. We are tolerably well fixed here and are living pretty well for Soldiers.

I must close to day. My love to all and kiss the little ones for me.

   Farewell
   Taylor

1. None of the principal conspirators in the assassination plot were captured in North Carolina. On April 21, however, H. C. Higginson, who identified himself as a Union army major and Secret Service officer, wrote to Major General Schofield from Morehead City. He stated that he had known some of the parties involved in the plot while he was imprisoned at Andersonville. Higginson had been a member of Company K, 19th Illinois Infantry, prior to his capture. Schofield referred the case to the Union commander at Morehead City, and Sherman ordered Higginson to be sent under guard to Washington. This is probably what Taylor is referring to.

2. Brevet Brigadier General Langdon C. Easton was chief quartermaster, Military Division of the Mississippi. Sherman's title was commander, Military Division of the Mississippi.

3. On April 14 Johnston wrote to Sherman and asked for a suspension of fighting. Sherman agreed, and the two met on April 17. The terms presented were the same as those presented to Lee by Grant, but Lincoln's assassination colored their acceptance. Both generals referred the matter to their respective governments. Stanton, particularly upset over the assassination, opposed leniency for the Confederates.

Head Qrs 22 Iowa Infantry
Morehead City N.C. April 23/65
Dear Catharine

It is Sunday again and a most beautiful day so I concluded to add a little to what I wrote yesterday. The news here this morning is that terms of peace has been agreed upon between Gen Sherman and Jo Johnson and that the rebel Soldiers are all to march to their respectiv States and Stack their arms at the State Capitols to be taken possession of by our authorities.[1] I hope this is true for now that the time approaches I am like a "race horse" impatient to be off. "Home." What pleasant fancies it brings up. Oh had I the wings of the dove how soon should I see you again. Dear One the anticipations of the happy hours that I hope to spend with thee yet renders me happy and tends to make the long wearisome hours more endurible.

Many an hour is spent in weaving the bright pictures of our future loveing life and building Castles in the air to realise in future years. Sometimes the thought comes to me how am I to make a living for we will be very poor. But I hope I get out of the army with good health and I think I will be able to make us comfortable and try to live so that our life may go down in one blissful dream of love and affection. Does thee know that the proudest day of my life will be when I clasp thee once more and feel that I am worthy of thy love and know that I Still possess it? And then to think of our dear little children. What a joy it will be to watch over them and teach them the road to honor and virtue. What can Earth give that we can not enjoy if contentment and love presides over our household? I think before this reaches thee the news will have been Spread that peace is declared and an order for us to return to Iowa to be mustered out will have been given. If thee writes to me I want thee to give me some idea of what there is to do so that I can make up my mind what to work at when I come. Can a man hire to work around Des Moines so as to make a living? If not we can go on to a piece of land and make a little farm? Could there be another butcher shop kept up in Des Moines?[2] If so could Cyrus attend to it if I could get the stock? I do not wish to Stay around there unless I can get into business. This is not to show for I do not want others to see thy love letters. I wish I could send a kiss and get one in return. This is great for an old fellow, isnt it? Well send me some love any how.

Affectionately thine
Taylor

1. On April 23 northern newspapers published accounts of the deliberations and accused Sherman of a pro-Confederate stance. The following day Grant directed him to notify Johnston of the government's rejection of the proposed surrender terms and ordered Sherman to renew hostilities unless Johnston formally surrendered.

2. On December 16, 1865, Mr. A. P. Wood (unidentified) wrote to Governor Stone in regard to Taylor. Wood stated that Taylor owned a butcher "shop on the North side of Court Avenue, directly across from Orwig's old office." According to the city directories of the postwar period, Taylor never opened such a shop. R. G. Orwig was a lawyer with a law and real estate office on 4th Street between Walnut and Court, and later at 219 Fifth Street. In 1869 he became owner and editor of the *Des Moines Bulletin,* which merged with the *State Register* the following year.

Head Qrs 22n Iowa Inftr
Morehead City NC May 2/65
Dear Catharine and all friends

I again set down to let you know how things are progressing in the Department of North Carolina.

In the first place I am in good health and fine Spirits though not so well satisfied with the prospect of getting home as I expected to be when the news first came that Gen Johnson had Surrendered to Sherman.[1]

At that time I hope that the 1st of June would have Seen the Iowa Vols out of the service but other circumstances are transpiring that renders it highly improbable that we will remain in the employ of the government untill the term of our service expires.

We have received orders to report at Savannah Ga again and are preparing to embark to-morrow for that place. It is stated here that General Grover has his head quarters at Augusta and that we are to Garrison Savannah and I suppose that will be our employment untill there is an order from the war department to muster us out. When you write again direct you letters to Savannah. We are now the 1st Brigade 1st Division 10 Army Corps.[2]

There is very little news here. There is a good deal of anxiety in regard to getting out of the service but I think we will be kept movin around untill our time is out so that we will have no time get home sick.

I have had no letter from home since the date of the 16t[3] and am anxious to hear from you. I hope Cyrus will be in better health by the time this reaches you. And I hope soon to be with you again.

I can hardly realize the quiet and relaxation of Military discipline that has taken place since the surrender of the rebel armies. After 4 years of turmoil Strife and Slaughter it seems a relief to all of us to be once more in a situation that we can count upon one moments Safety and comfort. Well it is night now and all is in an uproar getting ready to move. We are ordered to be ready to March at 4 O clock to morrow morning. I am in good heart now for I think I will get to see you soon. I see by the General orders from the war department that the first of June is set for the time to lesson the army[4] and I think by that time that we will all be mustered out of the Service and the country will be at peace. I understand that we go from here to Savannah and remain in Georgia this Spring untill the inhabitants conclude to settle down and obey the laws of the land. After which I expect we will be releived and sent north to New York or else we will be sent South round by the way of Orleans and up the Mississippi River home. I hoped to have received a letter from you before I left here for I cannot tell when one will reach us again after we leave here.

This is a poor letter. I have had so much to do to day that I can not write anything that would be interesting to you. So you will have to put up with it as it is. I expect we will get away about noon and if I have time in the morning I will add something more to it.

Well I have got my commission and have been assigned to duty as adjutant[5] but have not been mustered yet. I intend to be mustered as soon as I can get to some place where there is a mustering officer. We have no time to wait for anything of the kind at this time and I expect will not have any chance untill we get down to Savannah. In fact I do not care much whether I get mustered now or not for the length of time I have Stay in the Service.

Well what am I going to do when I get home for a living? Is their going to be work enough for me to do to keep you or is the times going to be so hard that it will be like it was in 1857?[6] I hope not for I would like to see some easier times than we have seen for the last 12 years. What is the government going to do in regard to the equalizing the pay of the Soldiers? I think that the Soldiers of 1862 ought to have as much at least as the high priced Soldiers of one year that have never been in a fight nor never endured a Campaign.

Well I must stop for it is 12 o clock and I must be up at 3. Kiss the Children for me and give my love to Cyrus and Mary and all inquireing friends. We have not been paid and I am afraid that we will not be untill our time is out but if you can get along it will come in good play some time. The weather is quite warm here and things are growing and the Peach trees have peaches on them as large as a robins Egg. But the winds are damp and disagreeable.

Oh how I was in Iowa to breath once more the dry pure air off the green Prairies.

> My love to all. Good night.
> Affectionately
> Taylor

1. On April 26 Johnston surrendered 39,012 men of the Army of Tennessee to Sherman. Each parolee was provided ten days' rations.

2. On May 2 the 22nd Iowa was ordered to be prepared to move the next morning, when it boarded the steamer *Cassandra* and headed for Savannah. On March 20 the Nineteenth Corps was ordered to be discontinued by War Department General Orders Number 41. On April 19 the 22nd Iowa was assigned to the First Brigade, First Division, Tenth Corps.

3. This letter was not found.

4. The only War Department general order that mentions a date of June 1 is General Orders Number 77, dated April 28, 1865. That order directs the Commissary General to "stop the purchase of supplies ... except for such as may ... be required for forces in the field to the first of June next." General Orders Number 83, dated May 8, 1865, directs the mustering out of volunteers, and General Orders Number 105, dated June 2, 1865, directs the reduction of artillery batteries. Both, however, were issued after the date of Taylor's letter, and neither established a specific date for the actions.

5. Taylor was promoted to first lieutenant and adjutant on April 25 according to the Adjutant General's Office, War Department. The affidavit below and his oath of office, however, give the date as April 22

6. In the 1850s increasing mechanization, overproduction, the layoff of workers, and excessive investments by railroad compaines resulted in a financial crisis known as the panic of 1857.

I Taylor Peirce being duly sworn do say that I have proformed the duties of 1st Leuit and Adjutant in the 22nd Iowa Inft Vol since the 22nd day of April 1865 by virtue of a commission issued by the Governor of the State of Iowa bearing date 22nd of March 1865 and received

by me on or before the 22nd day of April 1865 that I have been borne
on the Rolls Returns and Reports of the said Regiment as a Sergeant
from the 2nd day of August 1862 to the 22nd day of April 1865 that
a vacancy existed in the grade to which I was commissioned at the
time of receiving such commission caused by the promotion of 1st
Lieut Samuel D Pryce Adjutant of the Regiment to Captain and that
I have made every effort to be mustered into the Service of the United
States as a 1st Lieut and Adjutant in the said Regiment since the 22day
of April 1865 without success until the present time So help me God.

> Sworn and Subscribed before me this 9th day of
>> May 1865 at Savannah Ga
>
> J.W. Wilson , 1Lt & Adjutant, 28th Iowa Inft Vols
> Taylor Peirce, 1st Sergt Co C, 22n Iowa Inft

I Ephraim G White Lt Col comd the 22nd Regt Iowa Vol Inft afore-
said do solemnly swear that the statement and date above set forth are
correct to the best of my knowledge and belief. So help me God.

> Sworn to and subscribed before me this 9th day of
>> May 1865 at Savannah Ga
>
> J. W. Wilson, Adjt, 28th Iowa Inft Vols
> E. E.White, Lt. Col. 22nd Iowa Vols Inft, Comdg Regt

> Head qrs 22n Iowa Infantry
> Savannah Ga May 8th 1865
> Dear Catharine and all the rest

I again set down to give you some account of what we are doing and
have done since my last. I think I wrote you a short letter after we had
received marching orders at Morehead. Well we Started from Morehead on the 3rd of the month[1] and after a very rough Voyage of 3 days
arrived again at Savannah. This was the first time during all my water
trips that I got sea sisk and oh how sick I did get. One hour I was so
sick I was afraid I would die. And the next I was so much sicker that
I was afraid that I would not die but I fineally got over it and feel as
if I had renewed life. I think upon the whole it was a fine thing for me
for comeing again into this nest of miasma and pestilence if I had not
have been cleaned out I might have taken some of the diseases preve-
lent and would probably not have escaped so well.

We landed here yesterday afternoon and went into camp in the quarters Evacuated by the 18th Indianna and by noon to day was well fixed up. And I was just beginnig to feel happy with the prospect of Serving out our time here in good quarters when orders came to pack up and move out imediately and give room for some N York troops who were going to stay here and for us to just camp any where for the present as we would only stay 2 or 3 days at this place. You had better believe there was some tall swearing done about that time. But it was no use. Up we had to get and move out bag and baggage and give room for the Irish N. Yorkes and their fine haired officers. And are now squatted down in the sand and sun with just room enough to turn round and ordered to prepare for a march of 150 miles into the interior of the State divested of all superfluous Equipage which means that we are to take nothing with us but what we carry and go without Tents. We are to have 2 waggons with us and one ambulance for the sick and are to carry beside our clothing 5 days rations. So you see our hardships is not over yet. But the Bible tells us that there is a Crown of Righteousness laid up for those who hold out faithful, and I think if any Regiment Ever Earned one the 22n ought to be counted in that catalogue. For if we have not been round "Some" I am misinformed as to what being around means. I was making some calculation about our traveling a few days since and find that we have averaged 13 miles a day ever since we have been in the service and have been in 9 General Battles 5 Campaigns and a number of Skirmishes and have been under rebel fire about 90 days which I believe is more than any other Regiment has been in since the opening of the war. True Some regiments claim to have been in over 100 battles but I know something of this. What they call battles was what we encountered every day in Shanandoah Campaign and called them small affairs. But maybe I am boasting but I do feel as if we had done our share in quelling the rebellion and we would be glad to get home. Yet Still if the country need us I am willing to render my mite towards sustaining her. We are now going to Augusta and it is said that we will stay there some time but I am of the opinion that we will proceede frome thence to Macon thence to Atlanta and home by the way of Chattanooga and Nashville. However I may be mistaken. You will hear from me at least once a week if the letters can reach you. But you need not get out of heart if you do not hear from me for Some time for I think the mail facilities are not very good and it may be that the letters will not go directly. You may still direct your letters to Savannah untill you hear that we are Some where else for they will follow the Regiment.

I am better fixed for a march now than I have ever been before. I have a horse to ride this time and plenty of means to get my traps along without carrying them. I am also in good health except the piles but they do not trouble me so much as they did when I had to march and carry my load. Another thing I think the war is over and the only thing we will have to do will be lean out the Robbers and thieves that have been preying upon both sides during the war. The weather is very warm here and all things seem advanced as much as at home in June or July. Turnips & redishes and beans are all fit to eat grown this Spring. But the country is so poor that there is no surplus raised and of course there is none for us unless we had plenty of money. And as we have had no pay for a long time now 10 months we are all straped. The money I lent to Lt De Camp I have never heard of since. He is still sick in N York and I do not know wheather I will ever see him again. I sent for it by a Captain Cree[2] of our Regiment but he has not got back yet and I do not know whether he will get to see him or not. I expect I might as well run the risk of the rebels getting it as to let him have it with the prospect of ever seeing it again. But so it is.

Tell Mary that I would have sent her my picture but I had no money to have it taken, and so I can not send it now. I will though as soon as possible. I have a great many things to say but they are not of very much consequence So I will only just write what I think will interest you the most. The negroes are doing finely when they have gone to work for themselves and in the opinion of all sound minded men are the best part of the Southeren population. They are less given to Vice and are a more intelligent class than the poor whites are. And as a moral class they are vastly superior to the higher classes if what I hear of the latter is true. I have not become acquainted with any of the aristocracy myself nor do I think I will. But from what those tell me who profess to know Virtue is as scarce here as peaches in Iowa and that is scarcely none as anyone knows of. Things run high if all is true that is talked of. But I do not know that it is so. And maybe I had better not judge. There is going to be some trouble in getting things straightened out in the South yet. There is a class who have been raised in Idleness and tyranny who can not abide the thought of having to go to work for their living. And now their negroes are free and their wealth squandered and no more nigger to work for them they must either beg, Starve, Steal or work. So I suppose as they were in the habit of Stealing the niggers work from him they will have no concientious scruples in stealing from the Yankees. And I look for a large business in that line to be attempted and carried through too if the troops does not keep them quiet. A few days since An Officer in Some of the Eastern Regts who was cutting a swell and had his wife here showing her round to the admiring gaze of his fellow Officers concluded he would take a stiff at Uncle Sams expence and take a pleasure ride down to Hope Island 8 miles below town in an ambulance (which was contrary to regulations to use a public ambulance for private purposes). So he hired a parrolled Rebl to drive him and his beloved out. The parrolled one instead of driving him on the Road to hope Island took another Rout and soon found some more of his acquaintances when they stepped up and halted Mr Officer and Stripped him of all his Clothes but his drawers takeing his wifes gold watch and all her jewelry and Silk dress leaving them in undress uniform minus $1,000 in Greenbacks beside when they set them out of the ambulance and took passage in it themselves. Since which time the parrolled one and his confeds have not been seen. The Affectionate pair marched into town that night when the night had thrown her mantel over the landscape so that the gaping crowd could not behold their delapidated condition and adjorned at once to their peacefull abode. But not to remain in quiet long for Genl Grover hearing of the affair Sent an order for the Officer to report forthwith and pay for the Ambulance. I learn that the whole thing cost him about $1,800. A nice little sum to get to Show his nice wife. Well if that is all she costs him here he is lucky. Well I must actually close this for it is past midnight and I have a big days work on hands to-morrow. Kiss the little ones for me and tell them I want them to be good and learn to behave so well that I will be proud of them when I get home from the war. I have not had a letter for some time but I am hopeing for one before we leave here. I hope Cyrus will have his health better before you get this. I want you to still keep writing to me even if you should not get my letters regularly. And if I do not get yours now I will some time and they will be good when they come. My love to all. Tell the Copperheads the war is over. The Slave is free and the country is Abolitionised against its will. God is just.

>Affty yours
>Taylor

1. Another account states that the regiment departed Morehead City on May 4 and arrived in Savannah on May 6.

2. Alfred B. Cree was a Pennsylvania native and resident of Iowa City when he was appointed captain of Company F on August 7, 1862. He was wounded at Winchester on September 19, 1864, and again at Cedar Creek on October 19, 1864. He was mustered out July 25, 1865.

>Head Quarters 22n Iowa Infa
>Hamburg South Carolina
>May 21st 1865
>Dear Catharine

It is now nearly two weeks since I have had an opportunity to write to thee and I expect you will be very anxious before you get this to hear from me. We left Savannah Ga on the 11th of this month[1] and marched for Augusta when we arrived the day before yesterday the 19th. We were imediately Sent across the Savannah River to this place or at least the 3 Iowa Regiments were.[2] The Eastern troops were kept in the city of Augusta to do the Guard duty in the town. We are encamped on the hills overlooking the City of Augusta and the little town of Hamburg on the South Carolina Side and occupy the ground on which the first rebel troops were organized and drilled that was ever raised in the Confederacy. Here resides the wealthy aristocrats of the South who at the breaking out of the rebellion counted their Slaves by hundreds and lent all their influence and wealth in trying to overthrow that government which our Fathers Erected with such cost of blood and hardships and which has given to her children the most glorious heritage of prosperity and liberty that it has ever been the lot of people to posess. Here too is seen in countless multitudes the creatures of the tyrants will who from the organization has pandered to the passions and the extravagance of their masters. You can see them of all shades from the pure white with clear complexions and most perfect models of physical beauty to the blackest and most degraded

African. Indeed as far as beauty of form and feature is concerned it seems that his admixture of the races has added too rather than detracted from this unfortunate class. The masses of the white population are extremely ignorant and I do not wonder at the course they have pursued under the leadership of such consumate scoundrels and Tyrants as Davis, Toombs, Wigfall, Breckinridge[3] & others. Who if they had succeeded would have reached a heighth of power at which even their ambition might have been satisfied. But thanks to the courage and Patriotism of our murdered President and the brave troops that encircled his power they have been defeated and the Stars and Stripes again wave triumphantly over the land of our Fathers.

Before this reaches you will have heard of the capture of Jeff Davis and his Cabinet and of Govornor Brown.[4] And all that I can write about it will be but old news. However I will State that he was captured and brought to this place before and sent to Savannah before we arrived. Col Washburn was here with his brigade and if he had not have interpose Jeff would have been murdered by his own exasperated soldery. It is truly pitiable to see the poor deluded rebels returning to their ruined homes broken in health by the hardships of their campaigns in a lawless cause, without money or sympathy many of them crippled for life and no prospect for the future but penury and disgrace. And all must be endured for having been the tools used by the unscrupalous leaders to build up a system of despotism. Dear Catharine although I have seen my comrades torn and mangled on the battle field by these feinds in human shape in their exertions to bring ruin on the country and blight on our happy homes, and have undergone hardship and sufferings myself, yet when I see the utter desolation and ruin they are compelled to accept my benevolance will step in and my heart bleeds for them in spite of myself. How different is their lot from ours. Their wives and mothers who have been instrumental in keeping up their hostility to the government has not only the degrading sensation of having to welcoming home a defeated traitor but have the prospect of loosing the elegant and luxurious homes and the further prospect of a life of toil and poverty for which the past education and customs has illy prepared them.

This is a beauttful country around Augusta. And the County of Burk [Burke] through which we passed on our march and which adjoins this is said to be the richest in the State and is probably or has been the wealthiest portion of the South. Within 20 miles of the city the indications of wealth and luxury are numerous. Nearly all the farms are nicely laid out and the buildings are filed up in a style of magnificence that I have seen in no other part of the south. I must say one thing of the Georgia Ladies. That is that they are the most human looking females that I have seen in the confederacy.

While the male portion of the inhabitants are small thin and sickly looking the woman are large and have the appearance of health. What their moral or womanly qualities are, I am not able to say as I have had no chance to become acquainted with any of their ways of thinking or their maners and customs.

They are generaly well and neatly dressed and some of them are pretty though the most of them are rather coarse featured. The land is poor. Wheather it is oweing to the improper method of cultivation or the natural quality of the soil I am unable to determine. The soil is sandy and generally covered with the yellow Pine where it is not cleared off and is generally level. It is well watered and if properly drained I think is the most healthy country I have seen in the South. I will give you some extracts from my journal while on the march.

May 11th. Received orders to march at 8 A.M. with 6 days rations, 3 in our havarsacks and 3 in the wagons. Ordered to turn over all our regimental Equipage but what one team could hall and the men carry. Accordingly movd out at the hour appointed on the Augusta Road. Marched 13 miles and went into camp. The country all covered with Pine and sweet Gum and much of it quite swampy. Only passed 3 small cultivated spots during the day. Rained all night. Revellie at 3 oclock. May 12th. Move out at daybreak and march through a flat sandy barrens covered with chinquipin [chinquapin] bushes Black Jacks and barren Pine. Passed a few plantations which seemed exhausted by bad culture and the natural thinness of soil. Made 18 miles this day. Encamped near Springvill [Springfield] the county Seat of Effingham County. This county was for the Union by one vote at the Election when the Ordnance of Secession was adopted by the State of Georgia. The man who was accused for giving the casting vote was waited on by the Vigilence committee torn from his family and taken out and hung for daring to vote for the Union. After robbing his family of everything they had they were left to starve or live on whatever they could obtain themselves. Col Graham ordered them to be supplied with enough to last them untill they could procure aid from the Aid society at Savannah.[5] May 13. Marched at 4 A.M. Went 8 miles and struck the Savannah River at Sisters Ferry[6] where we found a boat loaded with supplies waiting for us. Here we encamped and drew 4 days rations. While we remained here several of the inhabitants who were absolutely destitute of provision come in to beg assistance. We divided our rations with them receiving their blessing in return for the aid. The Country arround this place is better than it was father back and I seen some fair fields of wheat growing that will probably yield 8 bushe pr acre. The corn looks well but is planted very thin about 5 feet apart and only one stalk in a place. There has been some cotton raised in past years but the land is now planted in corn. At least all that is being cultivated. Much of the land is idle.

May 14th. Movd out at 4 o clock A.M. and marched over much such a country as we passed through yesterday only more open. This is Burk County and is said to be the richest county in the state but looks to me like the old worn out land in Penna. I think it could be improved so that it would be highly productive. The whole country from Savannah up shows that it is an excelent fruit country. We have had all the Dewberries we could eat and the wild plums are getting ripe though they are inferior to the plums of Iowa. I see mulberries Blackberries, Pears, Peaches, Figs, Grapes and cherries but there is very few apples.

Marched 22 miles to-day and encamped at the plantation of an old hypocritical Methodist Preacher who edified us with doctrine that Slavery was upheld by the bible. So we eat his chickens and left him his bible as it was to strong for our digestive apperatus.

May 15th. Movd out a 3 oclock haveing receivd orders for 3 Regiments to move forward to Waynsborough and take the cars for Augusta in order that they might be movd to Milledgevill to prohibit the meeting of the Georgia legislature which had been called on by Gov Brown to meet on the 22n of the month. This day we marched 28 miles. Our rout was through a better country but the land looked as if it had been worked out. The timber alters in its character somewhat the pines being mixed with oak of various kinds and the Streams clear and swift. This region is well watered and with good cultivation I think would be a desireable place to live in. A man could have the luxuries as well as the comforts of life without much labour. Arrived at dark tired and worn out at the Rail Road. The 131st & 159 & 128 N York Inft was taken on the same night to Augusta. The 3 Iowa Regiments viz the 22n 24th & 28 & the 13 Connecticut remained and marched the rest of the way. We lay at this place untill 3 oclock P.M. of the 16th when we again resumed the march through the town of Waynsborough and encamped about 5 miles from the town. The weather very warm and the men foot sore. May 17th. Moved at 4 oclock and marched about 15 miles through a rich country where the appearance of wealth were obvious. Encamped near Spirit creek. A fine body of clear running water. Lay untill 4 oclock the 18th and marched to within 9 miles of Augusta and encamped. The Style of the buildings are magnificent and the yards and gardens are fixed up in a manner that shows taste and a love for the beautiful.

May 19th. Movd out at 4 oclock and marched in to Augusta about 10 A.M. After halting a few minutes in the city we were marched over the South Carolina side and encamped on Coffers Hill overlooking the Town of Hamburg and the City of Augusta. We are getting pretty well fixed up and I expect will remain here for some time as there is much to do before the civil law can be put in motion. [last page missing]

1. The regiment was awakened at 2 A.M. and told to be prepared to march at 6 A.M. They actually began moving at 9 A.M.

2. These were the 22nd, 24th, and 28th Iowa Infantry Regiments, which were encamped on Schultzer's Hill.

3. Jefferson Davis was president of the Confederate States of America. Robert A. Toombs was the first secretary of state of the Confederacy but resigned to become a brigadier general. In March 1863 he resigned his commission but was appointed to the Georgia militia during Sherman's march to the sea. Louis T. Wigfall had been a U.S. senator before resigning to become a Confederate brigadier general. In February 1862 he became a Confederate congressman. John C. Breckinridge had been vice president of the United States under James Buchanan. He became a Confederate major general and then secretary of war on February 4, 1865.

4. On May 10 Davis was captured by Union soldiers near Irwinville, Georgia. Georgia Governor Joseph E. Brown was captured May 9 by soldiers from the cavalry command of Major General James H. Wilson at Milledgeville, Georgia.

5. Soldiers' Aid Societies and Ladies' Aid Societies were organized in both the North and the South during the war to provide bandages, shirts, food, and small bags that contained needles, pin, buttons, and the like (called "comforts" or "hussies" or "housewives"). Societies in the North were often formed from sewing circles and church groups. Although such societies existed in the South, they were less numerous and less effective than their northern counterparts.

6. Sisters Ferry is on the Savannah River approximately thirty miles north of Savannah.

Des Moines May 21 1865
Dear Taylor

We are all well at this time. Cyrus is not well but he is quite as well as he ever will be. He has had but one bad spell this spring and I think that is well for him. Well Taylor I have a great deel to say but I hope so much that thee will be at home soon that I hate to sit down to write any more. I think you will all get home by the fourth of July and that will not be long in comeing round. I am very sorry that you were sent back into the Southern States on account of sickness that I fear any more fighting. But just at this season of the year is it a bad time to change Climate. Persons are more liable to take desese than any other time in the year. But as thee seems to of had such a good cleening up with seasickness and has a better chance to take care of thyself I hope thee will get through safe and I think by the time thee gets home thee will have seen some of those United States, aspecialy if you are sent home by the way of the Miss river. I am glad of thee geting thy commision if it will help thee to have any easyer time than before. At first I did not care if thee got it or not but thee knows that I am as anxious for thy welfare as I think most of wives are for their husbands. And if my letter seems short or cold think what a task it is for me to write and for give. I think if our Children live and we live yet a few years that we may be able to bring them up so that they may never encounter the hardships that has fallen to our lot. But I begin to think that God directs these things to humble us that we may not think too much of this world or be to proud of ourselves. Our children are in good health and are as good behavior as most Children of their ages and I think thee will be well pleased with them when thee gets home. Thee wants to know what there is to do at Des Moines.

I can tell thee there is plenty of work of all kinds and good wages so that no man need to be idle or go without food and cloths. It will take a good little sum of money to set us up when thee gets home. But I feel very sure that there will be a way for us to get along and not so bad as we have had for worse is useless and I think needless. Well I will close with love hopeing thee may get my letters all right after a time. I sent thee amount of the box may not get that I will say it was eight Dollars and twenty five cts. My pen is very bad.

I remain thy afec
Catharine

Des Moins Iowa May 18th 1865
Dear Father

It is with greatest of pleasure that I take my pen in hand to let thee know that we are all well and doing well. I read a letter last night from Garret Smith[1] to president Johnson and it said that we might as well end thiss war in a Christion way. Do good for evil. Mother saw tow Soldiers thiss Morning from the footbridge and go up the river. Uncle is better now than he ever was. He has not sold yet. When thee comes I want thee to by a farm and live like we used to do. I think I would rather live that way than eny other way.

I have nothing more to say so good by form thy efectsonate daughter
Sallie Peirce

Sallie has writen on this half sheet so I thought I would fill it up with some thing. It has been a beautiful day and I must say that I miss thee more than I did in the cold and bad weather. I would like to be making garden and such work if thee was at home to find a place for me to work on. But I will wait in hope that thee will be at home by this time next year and then we can get fixed up to live. And I think if that should ever happen that I will never give up to move or brake up again if every thing or every body go to old scratch but myself. I think I will try to take care of number one from this. The thing of moveing as we have done never did amount to any thing nor never will. Therefore I think it time for us to try and find a place that we can live without having to change from one place to another. There is one thing. We will have more children and I am less able to knock about than I ever was so that we will be obliged to settle down someplace and stay if it suits or not. For I know that I will not be able to attend to the children and do the other work that I have done theretofore.
Catharine

1. Gerrit Smith was a Northern landowner and philanthropist who became a prominent abolitionist. He was vice president of the American Peace Society, which initially opposed abolition through violence. Jefferson Davis remained in prison awating trial until May 11, 1867, when Smith, Horace Greeley, Cornelius Vanderbilt, and others guaranteed bail for the former Confederate president.

> Head Qrs 22n Iowa Infa
> Hamburg S.C. May 28th 1865
> Dear Catharine & all the rest

This is Sunday and a most beautiful and pleasant day. All is quiet and peaceful as was "creations dawn." What a differance between my situation to-day and the day 12 months ago. Then I was on the march in the unhealthy grounds between the Miss. River & the Atchafalaya in Louisiana with my gun and cartridge box on my shoulder the sun beaming down on my head as hot as the vials of wrath. The roar of the cannon and the rattle of musketry all around me weary and disheartned. To day I am setting in my tent on the most beautiful location that we have ever seen. Not a sound but those of peace and harmony breaks on the ear. And am just taking as much comfort as any man can who is absent from a loved and loving family. So you see that I am both well and in good spirits. I might say happy only I do so want to see you all and be with you again.

This is truly the Sabbath with me. All work is now stoped in our regiment on this day of the week except the nescessary military duty which consists in guard mounting and company inspection to see that all the men wash themselves and put on clean cloths. These duties ocupy the time from 7 to 8 in the morning. Then we have dress parade in the evening when we all turn out in our best. You ought to see your humble Servant come out in red sash, white Gloves, and a sword shining like nigger in a harvest fields, and boots blacked till you would think that they had just been brought from the regions of darkness. I tell you what I cut a swell. How do you think I felt the first time I took my place before the Regiment looking as if I had just been spilled from the bandbox? I guess I felt a good bit like a girl does the first time she has been stayd with and thinks every body knows it. However I went through for I thought a man who could face a battery of howitzers ought not to falter before a set of laughing men. Well we are still encamped on the hill North of Augusta on the S.C. side of the river.

That is the Regiment proper as 3 Companies D, F, & G are detached and sent off to diferent parts of Georgia to gather up government property and protect the citizens from their own returned soldiery. Co D is with a battery. Co G is at Waynsborough Burk Co Ga and Co F is at Athens about 70 miles towards Macon. We have 7 companies with us yet but I am looking all the time for more of them to be sent off in some other direction.

I think it quite likely that we will remain here while we are needed in the service which I think will be untill our term of service expires. The old Slaveholders does not like to give up their negroes and are trying to hold them still and some of them have shot some of their slavs because they would go. The returned Soldiers are pitching into the rich since they have come home. Many of them say that the wealthy part of the community promised to become individually responsible to them for their pay if they would only go and fight and they intend to make them divide what they have now they have been forced to surrender and have got no pay. So you see that it is as nescessary to keep troops here to suppress riot and insurection as it was before the Surrender of "Lee & Johnson."

The plums and cherries are ripe. With the dew berries Raspberries & Mulberries we have pretty plenty of fruit. If we only had some money I think we could live so that it would insure good health and cost us but very little. This is the cheapest place we have been in yet. There is a large cotton factory at work here making 15,000 yards of sheeting pr day and is sold for 12½ cts pr yard. If I had a chance I would send two or 3 bales of it home for I know it is needed in Iowa. This mill furnishes labor for 800 hands 600 of which is white females and 200 white males no negroes being employed and is one of the largest establishments of the kind I ever seen. The soil around the city of Augusta I think has been fertile but has been worked out by hard tillage. The climate is delightful and if the war was all settled up it would be a very desirable place to live. This is one of the great places for raising niggers or at least has been and you can see them of all colors from pure white to coal black. A great many of them look as if some body had made them themselves. We had a high time here last monday.

There is a man named Butler living about a mile off who has made a living of keeping blood hounds to hunt the negroes. And when the war broke out he purchased exemption from serving in the rebel army by keeping his dogs to hunt our escaping prisoners. So the boys found out that he had chased some federal soldiers and captured them and on monday morning about 20 of them went over to his house run him and his family in and shot all his dogs 27 in number. In the afternoon he laid in his complaint to the Gen Comdg the post who told him if he would come to the regiment and identify the men he would have them arrested and tried. So him and his son and his wife come over. And the Major got the men out in line and he started along in his buggy but the boys made a raid on him and he had to leave on the double quick. Since then he has had to lay in the brush to save his own life.

Many things occur that I am keeping a minute of but to small to mention in a letter that will make you laugh. I got your letters dated the 25 of April[1] on friday and was glad to hear that you were all well. Our mail is very uncertain and comes but seldom. We have but little duty to proform now. I am in command of the Regiment to day the officers all being out in the country that out Rank me so I run the machine. The crops here look well for this country and the weather is fine. Kiss the children for me and receve my sincere affection yourselves.

 Taylor

1. These letters were not found.

 Head qrs 22nd Iowa Inftr
 Hamburg SC June 11th 1865
 Dear Catharine and Friends

Again it is the Sabbath. Another week has passed into Eternity. The acts in the great drama of life that have been proformed or good or evill have had their effects and are numbered with the things that have been and are now recorded on the book of life ready for judgement. I hope that my deeds whatever they may be may receive that levity that a wise and just providence may accord in his mercy to all his erring children. I have tried to live a moral and virtuous life and if I have failed it is through judgment not from a disposition to do what is right. Few men are perfect and of cours I have my failings but I hope for forgiveness.

I have been very busy this week in writing a history of the Regiment and am tired this morning though not with severe exercise but from constant thought so you will not get much of a letter. I have received nothing from home since I wrote this day week.

Well time speeds on and Still the 22n lays on the hills of South Caroline. All is quiet in the Camp. Not a sound or an incidence occurs to disturb the peaceful monotony of our daily lives. The workings of the Government progress. Wrong is righted in the proper departments. The national property is being collected and cared for. And the national laws are being executed. But all this is done without having any influence on our lives or our actions. We arise at revellie in the morning if we feel like it. Eat our meals and lay down at Tattoo in the evening if we are sleepy.

There is no drill, no military opperations to be proformed, no military etequett enforced and in fact we are laying inactive and passive like a great living body which after having undergone the extreme of physical Exertion and the object accomplish lays exhausted and quiet to recover its wanted vigor.

I have not been out of camp but once this week. We had a grand Review on Tuesday in which I took part was the only time I have been away. I take no pleasure in running around. My all of life is contained within your home. Beyond this I have no desires. Oh how long will it be before I again embrace you. The hours drag their slow length along and at the end of each succeeding one I grow more impatient. Now that the war is over and the nation saved I feel as if my place was not in ranks of battle. Will I be in a situation to enjoy what I have striven for? I fear not. The army with its scenes of excitement, its dangers its dificulties and privations to be endured and overcome by courage and exertion I fear has awakened feeling in me that are incompatible with a live of Ease and quit. I used when the noise and confusion of a campaign was at its hight long for an hour of rest and quiet. But since it has been so quiet and there has been so little to do the time hangs heavy on my hands. I often think of Scotts lay of the captive knight where says

My hawk is tired of perch and hood,
My Idle Greyhound loathes his food,
My steed is weary of his State,
And I am sick of Captive thrall[1]

But maybe when I get home and have my little family around me these feelings will leave me.

I am much troubled about what to do for a living. I know my property will all be swallowed up and I will have but little money to commence with and after 3 years of Soldiering a man of my age will be so much worn out that I do not see what I can do that will make me a living. But I suppose I ought to be thankful that I still live to get home to you at all. For I suppose there will always be something for me to do.

I have not been mustered yet and it is doubtful wheather I can be and if not my commission will be of just as much use to me as so much brown paper in the way of geting pay. If I could have been mustered and receved pay for my services I would have had some money to help me to begin with but as it is I will not have over $250 which will not do much to towards starting in the world again.

I will have however the consciousness of having done my duty to my country. There is no news here and I have nothing to impart that will be interesting to you. When you write give me a good long letter and tell me something about business. We are expecting orders to be mustered out but there is so much to be done that I do not know how soon it will be.

Kiss the little ones for me and keep them in yourselves in good heart for surely it cannot be long untill I will be with you. I have easy times and still act as adjutant of the regiment and am the only man in it that is qualified to fix up the records so as to be mustered out. I do not say this to boast for it is not a pleasant job to work night and day to fix up what the ignorant have done so as to obtain our rights and then receive no pay for it. This is a poor letter but I am tired and do not feel like writing but it will inform you of my condition. The regiment enjoys good health but all are anxious to get home.

  Truly & affty thine

  Taylor

1. From "Lay of the Imprisoned Huntsman" by Sir Walter Scott.

[undated]
Dear Catharine,

I have written all about the country we have passed through and all of interest about the occurrances generally that I can think of. I will now revert to myself and our present location and prospects.

I am in good health and now the war is over and the necessity of keeping Soldiers in the field is not so great. I am anxious to be once more with thee and the little ones. Oh how I do long to see you all again. Now the dangers of battle no longer meneace my life it seems as if the love of home and the society of those I love had grown ten times Stronger than it was. While every day was fraught with uncertainty as to what might be the fate of myself and others These calm and peaceful days while all around is so silent and devoid of the hurry and excitement that I have been used to for the last 3 years it is impossible for me to keep from becoming home sick. I am also far in the interior cut off from mail communications and can hear nothing from home which makes it more unendurible. I have had no letter since I left Morehead City and as there is no direct line of mail I may not get a letter for some time to come. However I will try to be patient.

Col Graham is commanding the Brigade. Lt Col White is detached from the Regiment and has charge of the rebel ordnance in Augusta and Major Gearkee[1] and I run this institution. I am very well fixed and have every thing my own way which thee knows suits my temper better than to be subject to the control of others. In fact if I could be at home I would be as well fixed as I could wish.

I am not mustered in yet as adjutant but have been ordered to take the place and will draw my pay as a 1st Lt Adjutant from the 22n of last month.[2] My pay is the same as a Captain of Infantry which under the new law is $150 per month with some reduction for internal revenew.[3]

The weather is very warm but we have a fine healthy location for Camp and plenty of good water so I think we will be healthy if we can only keep the mind in exercise enough to make their stomachs digest the strong food that the Government supplys us with. If we had money we could live very well and cheap here. Eggs is worth 15 cts butter 25 cents fresh meat 8 or 10 pr lb and every thing is much cheaper than it has ever been in any place since we left Iowa. I do not know why we are not paid. I have had no pay now 10 months and the last two months pay I received I loaned as I think I informed thee before and I have never seen the Officer since he being stile absent from his Co sick. I am becoming anxious on your accounts for I know that if thee does not need the money Cyrus could use it to advantage.

I was much pleased that thee was trying to teach the children at home. For I have a poor opinion of the good to be desired at a common school for such young children as ours. For if it were posible I would like to have them grow up inocent and uncontaminated with the common vices of the world at least untill they were old enough to judge for themselves.

I expect to start for Savannah in a few days to take charge of a party of men and bring up the Regimental Equipage and will write again when I arrive at that place. I expect my letters will be longer in reaching you now than they have ever been before. But as the chances for my Safety are about as 1 to 100 you need not become alarmed if you do not receive them as often as heretofore.

I have written a good bit in this that I expect will not interest you much. But I had nothing else to write so if it is no so good as it might be you must look over it. Take out what interests you the most. I expect that we will remain here some two months and then start for Iowa to be discharged. It is likely that we will go to Davenport to be mustered out and as we will be likely to have to reman there for a week or two while the records of the Regiment is being prepared for our discharge. If such is the case I would like if some of you could come and remain with me a few days for I will be compelled to remain with the regiment untill the last letter is written and the last drum beat and of course you know that I will be very impatient when I once set foot on my own loved Iowa soil to see some of you.

But I wish you to understand that I do not wish any of you to discomode yourselves for my selfishness. Only if one of you could come and meet me it would be a great pleasure. Of cours when I say one of you I mean Either thyself Mary or Cyrus. It would not be prudent to drag the children out in the heat and fatigue of a trip of that kind and subject them to the chance of a spell of sickness though I would like to see them as much as any of the rest.

However I will leave all this to your own convenience and wishes and if you make up your mind to meet me I will send you word when to come. I believe I must close. Give my love to all and kiss the little ones for me and tell them to keep a good heart and I will soon be at home again.

> I remain Affectionately Thine
> Taylor

1. John Henry Gearkee was a Pennsylvania native and resident of Iowa City. He initially enlisted in Company B, 1st Iowa Infantry, on April 18, 1861; he was appointed captain and commander of Company B, 22nd Iowa Infantry, on July 26, 1862; was wounded at Vicksburg May 22, 1863, and was promoted to major May 6, 1864. He was mustered out July 25, 1865.

2. On July 2 Gearkee wrote to Brigadier General Baker and enclosed Taylor's oath of office. He informed Baker that Taylor had not been mustered as a first lieutenant prior to the 22nd Iowa receiving orders to be mustered out of service. He did this "so that if anything occurs in the future it may appear on Record that [Peirce] has complied with the requirements of the State of Iowa." War Department records indicate that Taylor "was mustered into the service of the United States . . . to date April 25, 1865."

3. On August 5, 1861, Congress passed the first federal income tax law in the nation's history. Initially the rate was set at 3 percent income over $800 a year. In 1864 it was increased to 5 percent on income up to $5,000, 7½ percent on income up to $10,000, and 10 percent on income above that. The tax raised $55 million during the war years.

> Hd qrs 22n Iowa Infty
> Hamburg S.C. June 18th 1865
> Dear Catharine

I am in good health this morning and hope this may reach thee in good time and find you all enjoying the Same.

I now have the pleasure of announcing to you that the War is over and the Services of the 22n Iowa Infty is no longer needed. Accordingly at 8 A.M. to morrow we leave this rebellious Soil and march for Savannah Ga to be mustered out of the Service of the United States.[1] I suppose that It will take us some 30 days from this time for us to reach Iowa as it will be ten days before we reach Savanna and it will take us at least 10 more to fix up the papers to be mustered out. It will then take all of 10 days before we can reach Iowa if we get allong without any obstructions. I do not expect to get all fixed up before the 1st of August so as to get out of the service.

We will be mustered for pay and discharge at Savannah and the papers will be all made out and Sent to Iowa where we will receive our pay and discharges and be released. So you may know now that the time is coming when if no accident should happen that I will be with you. You need write no more to me after you receive this untill we reach Davenport for I will be on the wing so that a letter will never reach me.

If anything should happen and you wish to communicate with me you can Send a letter to Davenport with instructions for it to await the arrival of the regiment.

The weather is very warm here and I expect there will be some who will not Stand the march as there always is some but as we are going home now it is likely that the most of them will make it through.

We have about 400 men with the Regiment at this time. More than we have had since we left Orleans or more than We have had since the first fight in the Valley. One man died of debility and was buried here yesterday. He was a man from Iowa City by the name of Barker.[2] He was one of these whining grumbling gluttonous devils that never get enough to Eat and always think some body ought to keep them. And as fruit was plenty and cost nothing he took to eating such loads of it as to kill him to carry it.

The Regiment is enjoying good health generally and are luxuriating in Plums Peaches Apricots and berries of all kinds. This is a Paredise for fruit and niggers but a damnd poor country for poor White folks. Tell the folks that we will soon be with them again. When all those old feelings Settled up I suppose Abolitionists is not so much an abomination as they used to was. Does Copperheads still hold up their heads or do they look like whipped cuss? Well I have but little to write this morning. I hope soon to see you all and can tell it to your face. Kiss the children for me and tell them to be good and that after 3 years of all kinds of hardships I am again to be with them. I want you to find out something for me to work at as soon as I am out of the Service for I will have to hunt up a living for us frome some scource. How would a butcher shop do in Des Moines for 2 men one to go out on a farm and buy and keep and feed the cattle and the other to kill them and sell the beef? But we will see what is to be done when the time comes to do it. I must close. Give my love to Cyrus and Mary.

   I remain affectionately
   Taylor

1. Headquarters Post Augusta General Orders Number 11, dated June 6, 1865, directed that the 22nd Iowa be prepared to march to Savannah to be mustered out of the service.

2. William Barker was a native of Maine and a resident of Iowa City when he enlisted August 6, 1862. He died of disease at Augusta on June 16, 1865.

> Head Qrs 22 Iowa Infty
> Savannah Ga June 27th 1865
> Dear Catharine

We are once more in the "Forrest City." We arrived day before yesterday and I have been so busy preparing to be mustered out that I have not had time to write you untill tonight. I am well and feel as if I would soon see your dear old faces again. We had a very uncomfortable march from Augusta. It rained on us every day. I was wet from the time I started untill I got here. Sleeping in my wet cloths in the drenching rain and wading the creeks and sloughs was any thing but a pleasant occupation but have since stiffness in my joints. I am none the worse. If I had been exposed to this while in civil life I would have expected to have been down for the next six months with fever or some other civilized complaints.

But when a man becomes a savage or a brute he is not likely to be troubled with any of these delicate complaints that kill the fine haird population at home. We are now encamped on our old camp that we had fixed up so beautifully before we left this place the first time. But some of the hounds has cut down our shade trees and demolished our huts and the camp is shorn of all its beauty. Now we are subject to the broiling sun and loose sand of the shores of Georgia.

Well we are just going it now trying to get up our papers to get out of the service of our dear "old Uncles" and I do hope he will never need is Sons again to help him through such an ordeal as the one just passed.

Dear Catharine amid all my joy and bright anticipations of visiting my home and kindred with the little remnant of my brave comrades there is a bitter sorrow at the bottom of it all. Out of the 101 men that came from Jasper County with me only 35 will be able to return to gladden the hearts of those who loved them as well as thee does me. What vacant seats will remain at the board and stand unoccupied around their winter fires and how many a sorrowing heart will send up its daily moans for their gallant dead.

How thankful we ought to feel for our good fortune even if this worlds wealth is denied us. Life and health still remain with the conscience of having done right and bourn up under the trials and hardships during the nations danger. I do not believe I will ever [illegible] at my lot however lowly again. Nor would all the gold of the Rothschilds[1] tempt me to again endure what I have for the last 3 years. Nothing but the same cause could ever draw me into the dreadful scenes of War that I have witnessed.

I lay at night and shudder with fright at the thought of what I have passed through although at the time it seemd of no consequence or at least no more than what would be expected under the circumstances. But it is useless to recur to these things now. Peace has again folded her afrighted wings and perched upon the land. The curse of Slavery that [found] blot on the Nations Escutcheon is wiped out. The Slavholder, the sensual Tyrant his power broken. The creature of his base passions taken from him stands a monument of Shame, and less than littleness a subject of scorn and contempt for all generations of honerable men for time to come. And God be praised I have not only lived to see this day but have given my feeble support for its accomplishment. I received thy letter with one from Sallie in it when I come here dated the 21st of May and none since. I was glad to hear that Cyrus was better this spring and hope he may yet live to enjoy a degree of comfort commensurate with his labour. Some d—d hound Stole my knapsack with all my clothes yesterday and I have only got the Suit I have on. I had two good soldiers suits worth about 35 dollars and they are all gone. I do not know what I am to do for more now for I did not want to draw any more but I expect I will have too. I say damn all thieves. I must quit as the misquittoes is eating me up so that I fear you will not be able to read this and it is now midnight. Kiss the children for me and give my love to Cyrus and Mary and all the friends. I think we will start for Iowa in 10 days or two weeks.

I remain thine affectionately
Taylor

1. The Rothschilds were a European banking family that began to acquire its wealth in the late eighteenth century, much of it as a result of the Napoleonic wars and the industrial revolution.

Des Moines July 9th

Dear Taylor

It is some days since I wrote thee before thinking I would hear of thee comeing home which I did yesterday and I am truly glad that it will soon come to pass. We are all well and are in good spirits at this time. There is nothing wanting but thy loved presents to make all as brigh as a pleasant dream. I thought I had better write a few lines to inform thee how we are situated now. Well in the first place Cyrus and Mary have the house full of boarders that neather of them can leave home to come to meet thee very well and I think it would be useless for me to undertake to come with the children at this time of the year. And allso it will only be a few more days to wait that we must try and be patiant and it will soon pass and then we will be togather never to part again. Any how by the same cause I hope. Well I have so much to say that I do not know what to write so I will just say that Cyrus has a situation picked out for thee if it only will meet thy views. He thinks it will suit as there will not be any hard labor and a good salry at the same time but I will leave the explanation of the concern until thee gets home. It is something connected with the new insurance company that is makeing up in this City.

There is all sorts of work to do here and plenty of money to pay for it with so I feel confident thee will find something to do if thee is only well enough to work when thee gets home. I will just close by saying the children are well and in perfect fit of delight at the thought of thee coming.

I remain truly thine

Catharine

Des Moines July 9th 1865

Dearet Father

It is with the greatest of pleasure that I take my pen in hand to let thee know we are all well. It is a mostly cloudy day. Ada White is here. It is allmoste Dark and I cannot see very well. I am so glad that thee is getting home my dear papa. It is getting dark. I cant see.

so good by

I remain Sallie

Head qrs 22 Iowa lnfty
Savannah Ga July 9th 1865
Dear Catharine & all the rest

I again commence a letter to you as it is Sunday and my regular day for correspondence.

We are still at Savannah. How much longer we will be kept here I do not know.

We have got our papers almost ready to be mustered out, and I think that maybe by the 20t of the month we will leave this rebel Elysium for our homes in the north.

The weather is very hot and now as I write although not yet 6 in the morning the sweat is rolling of me as if I was in a harvest field. There is a great many Sick in the regiment but I think that there is none that are dangerous. We have lost 2 men by death since we come here. Both of them were stout hearty men one week before they died. One died of conjestive chill. His I wrote you about before and the other one died with yellow Fever.[1]

We are liveing very hard now. There is no money in the regiment none of us having been paid off for nearly Eleven months. Of course we are all out of money and have to depend entirely on the Government Rations for our liveing and the hot weathe and the Strong Sow belly is a "leetell" to strong for my stomach.

Since the war is over the agents of the Christian Commission I guess have pocketed whatever funds they had in their hands and sold out the remainder of their stock and have left the fields of their past thieveing and swindling and returned to their homes to live on their ill gotten wealth. I think among the rest of the evils of this war it has prepared about 300,000 thieves and swindlers for "hell." For if there has not been a series of wholesale roberies carried on, I am not able to judge. The Government has been swindled on one hand, and the solders on the other and these damned hounds is now rolling in wealth and Ease on what actually belongs to the Government and the Soldiers.

When I wrote you before I told you that we were going to have a celebration on the 4th. Well it come off. The day was hot so the regiments were paraded on their respective color lines and the declaration of Independence and the Emancipation Proclamation was read to them a short speech given and three rousing cheers went up for the "Old Flag" and the Union and the troops dismissed. One hundred rounds were fired from the fort at noon. And Volley after Volley of musketry was fired during the day and all through the fore part of the night. In the Evening the City was illuminated and a grand display of fire works took place. But one disgraceful thing took place which it becomes my painful duty to record. The negro fire company who have been some time Organized in this city and are said to be a very efficient and orderly Co. was going to have a grand parade around the City with their engine, in accordance with custom of fire Companies. In the Afternoon a lot of low white citizens and boys assisted I am Sorry to say by some drunken soldiers and some others who thinks that a nigger has no rights that a man is bound to respect, but who is found on all occasions when they can get to in bed with the dirtiest wenches that this dirty southern confederacy can produce, Set on the black fire company who did not number over 100 or 150 men beat them with brick bats drove them off from their Engine tore up their Cloths and run their engines in to a mud hole. And what was worse about the whole thing our d—d milk and water Generals who have control here either did not try to stop it or else they were off in the country at some rich rebels taking dinner and so d—d drunk that they were unable to attend to their duty. The fact is our military Officials here are so little force of character that I despair of any thing ever coming to any good from their system of legislating.

The Post is now commanded by Gen Davis. He I know nothing about. The Division is under the command of Gen Birge[2] who is one of your old fogies that knows nothing about anything outside of a Review or line of battle and when his whiskey runs out. The inferior Officers of these eastern Regiments are composed of pimps and saloon keepers and have just as much Idea of what is justice or human rights as a Savage. They are more ignorant less moral and far less religious than the majority of the negros. I hope to God that something may be done soon to get this Southren country into a state of civilization. But I am afraid of Andrew Johnson. I am afraid of any man who has ever been connected with the slave trade in any manner.[3] And I am more particularly afraid of an old Democratic pro Slavery man to day than I am of the worst rebel that treads this Southren land. They are hypocrites by profession, near relations to the Copperheads of the north, and not to be trusted without a guard with them. If the cabinet does not hold old Johnson Straight, I will bet high that he sells the north yet before he is done with his office. I see Gen Sherman has walloped over too. It seems to me that Southren gold will buy the principals of the best men. One year a go Sherman declared for the right of Sufrage. Since his pockets are lined with Southren gold he declares agains it.[4] I see his brother John is all right.[5] And I hope with such men as Sumner, Stevens and Wade[6] the niggers will have their rights protected yet. Well I must stop this political tirade and tell you that I am well, but have been very busy all week. But I expect to get rest to-day. I will have all my papers finished up by tuesday night and soon as the mustering officer comes here after that I suppose we will be mustered out. I have received no letter from you since the 25 of May[7] nearly 2 months ago and I am getting anxious to hear from you. I do not see what is the reason that our letters do not reach us for they can come through in 10 days from Des Moines. I ought to have one as late as the 25 of June any how. I will close this now. As soon as I find that we will start for home I will start a letter so that you will be able to tell about the time I will get home. I do not expect to get home short of 3 years from the time I left.

I will have to cease writing to go to church as the Chaplain is going to make a few dysentary remarks.

> Affectionately
> Taylor

1. Taylor writes in his June 18 letter of the death of William Barker. On July 2 Thomas W. Lindsay died at Savannah. He was a Virginia native and Iowa City resident when he enlisted July 25, 1862, as first sergeant of Company G.

2. Taylor is mistaken. Brigadier General Henry W. Birge was assigned to command the District of Savannah on June 5, 1865, although as early as May 16 he was signing official correspondence from Savannah as "Commanding." Taylor may be referring either to Major General Jefferson C. Davis, who was in command of the Fourteenth Corps in Kentucky but had previously been in Savannah, or to Brevet Brigadier General Edwin P. Davis, who had arrived with his Second Brigade, Provisional Division, from Washington, D.C., in late June 1865.

3. Andrew Johnson owned five slaves before the war when he lived in Tennessee.

4. Sherman had long viewed blacks as inferior and had opposed the Emancipation Proclamation. In January 1865 Sherman wrote to Secretary of the Treasury Salmon P. Chase that he opposed suffrage for free blacks and reiterated that position in May and July 1865. Although the terms he presented to Johnston caused Secretary of War Stanton to question his loyalty, it was not until 1866 that Sherman would become a controversial figure during the Reconstruction era.

5. John Sherman was a U.S. senator from Ohio. He took moderate positions on reconstruction but often voted with the Republicans for radical legislation. He opposed former Confederates having positions of responsibility in the reconstructed South. Initially he supported President Johnson's Reconstruction policies but then voted to convict the president after he was impeached by the House of Representatives.

6. Charles Sumner was an abolitionist U.S. senator from Massachusetts who advocated equal rights for blacks. Thaddeus Stevens, a Republican congressman from Pennsylvania, was the founder of the Radical Republicans. He sponsored legislation to provide civil rights to blacks after the war and favored harsh punishment for Confederate leaders. Benjamin F. Wade, U.S. senator from Massachusetts, opposed Lincoln's Reconstruction plan, which he characterized as too lenient. He also opposed President Johnson's Reconstruction efforts.

7. This is probably Catharine's letter of May 21 that was postmarked May 23.

Head Qrs 22n Iowa Infty
Savannah Ga July 14, 1865
Dear Catharine

I again Set down to write you the last letter that I Expect to write in the Service of the United States. We are now ready to be Mustered out and to morrow morning the Mustering officer commences on the 24th Iowa and I suppose will finish it this week. On monday our turn comes and by Wednesday the 20th inst we will be ready to leave Savannah for the green plains of Iowa.[1] How I long to Start. This has been the longest month that I have seen since I left home. It seemed to me as if it never would come to an End. But time has flown and now all is ready to move as we used to say when we got ready to move out the rebels with our forces. I have to record another sad casualty to day. We had quite thunder Shower to day. And during the time it prevailed one of the solders of the 24t Iowa who was encamped about 200 yards from our head quarters was struck with lightning and killed instantly. His name was Moor[2] from Cedar County and was said to be an excelent man. He leaves no family to moun his loss which is a great consolation. For when the men die or are killed who have families to mourn for them it is always a Sore afair.

Well I am well and am now nearly done my work as a soldeir. I feel satisfied knowing that our country is safe and the work I engaged in is completed. I feel as if my time was out and I wanted to get home. I have had no letter from you since the 24th of May and am very anxious about you. But I hope soon to be in a situation that letters will not be required to keep us informed of Each others welfare.

The weather has been quite warm for some time here and much sickness prevails. Our Regiment though enjoyed better health than It did when we first come here. Yet it might be better.

I have not much to write about to night. I only write this to let you know that you can look for the news of the arrival of the 22n about the 1st of August if nothing happens.[3] We are to be sent to Davenport where some of you can call and see us if you think proper. If you can not spare the time and money I wish you to write me to Davenport as soon as you get this so that I can hear from you as soon as I arrive there. For I will be mighty anxious by that time. Our Organizations are broken up. There is now no more Brigades or Divisions in this department. We are an Independent Regiment and are doing no duty now as Soldiers to amount to anything.

We draw our own rations and guard our own property. The men are lying around camp Spoiling with inactivity and Idleness. I hope that before anothe week rolls round the Sails will be spread that are to waft us north to our homes. Then farewell to hardships and bloodshed and all other Evils of a State of War. Hoping Soon to meet you all in the embrace of affection.

      I remain yours as Ever.

      Taylor Peirce

1. A ceremony was held on July 20 to muster out the men, although the official date on which they were mustered out was July 25. The regiment embarked on the steamer *Fairbanks* on July 22.

2. George Moir was a native of Scotland who resided in Red Oak when he enlisted August 15, 1862. He was struck by lightning and killed July 13, 1865.

3. The regiment arrived at Baltimore, Maryland, on July 25. The next morning it boarded the Pennsylvania Central Railroad and reached Pittsburgh the next afternoon. There it was met by a band and was escorted to city hall for supper. That night the men boarded the train for Chicago and arrived there Friday morning. The regiment reached Davenport at 10 A.M. on July 29 and marched to Camp Kinsman.

Des Moines Aug 2/65

Dear Taylor

I sit down morning to let thee know that we are liveing but none of us are well. Yet none of us are dangerously ill. I guess that is nothing more the matter with us than this effect of the warm weather and biliousness.[1] There is none of us well enough to come to meet thee without it is Cyrus and he can not leave very well while the rest is so complaining. For they have a house full of boarders and it keeps us all busy to get things along.

Well I do not intend to write much only enough to inform thee I have written to Davenport before and not be to anxious to get home. For we are not sick enough to be in bed and are geting along finely every other way and so glad to hear of the boys geting home and So thankfull for thy own Dear self being so near home and in a fair state of health.

All join in love and a welcome home.

I remain as ever thine.

Catharine A Peirce

1. Biliousness is a condition resulting from excessive secretion of bile by the liver.

Appendix

EDITOR'S NOTE. The next two letters refer to Catharine's death and Taylor's marriage to Eliza.

Home 6th mo 23rd 1867
Dear Cousin Mary

When I recieved thy letter and thee asked me so kindly to write I intended to have done it long ere this. The reason I have not done it is not because I have not thought of thee and thy charge. Dear cousin I do sympathize with thee in thy care of those little motherless children. But we should be thankful they have so kind a friend to care for them and they may live to be a great help and comfort to thee. Their willing hands may administer to thy wants in declining years and remember every effort of thine to train their little hearts aright will have its reward from "Him who doeth all things well." Is Taylor with you too now? Thee did not state in thy letter.

How is Cyrus? What did you think was the matter with Catherine? Was it her lungs? I thought from the way thee wrote that perhaps it was them gave out. Poor woman her sufferings are over. She always seemed afflicted since I can remember her. Do write soon. Give my love to Cyrus and all our cousins. As ever thy aff cousin Lizzie H Lincoln

[The letter below was on the back of Lizzie's letter.]

Home 7th mo 7th My Dear Niece

* * *

And I wonder to myself how thee is getting with thy great charge, a sick husband and so many motherless children. I hope thee may be favoured with health, stength, and patience to fillfil thy various duties. And though the body may ofttimes feel weary a sweet peace of mind will be thy reward. How much I would like to come to see you all. I still look forward with hope that I will yet visit all my dear friends in their western homes, if I live.

Des Moines May 16th 1873

Dear Sister

Eliza & I were married yesterday. I had asked her to marry me before there was any one kicked up about it, and she had accepted. I have done what I conceived to be the best interests of all of us and what I was in honer bound to do after having her get ready Even if I had not desired to do so. But I thought a great deal of her and would have married her any how. I lived for the happiness of others for six years without any thought of my own. I now propose to try to enjoy myself a little if I can. The childrens welfare will be as well guarded as ever it was and if they will only alow us to be Kind to them they will have no cause to complain. I do not ask them to love Eliza, nor call her mother but they must treat her with respect. Thee can tell Sallie as I have always told her that She shall still have the control of the house if she so desires it. Eliza does not wish to usurp any of her privileges but desires to live in love and harmony. I would bring her up but I do not know that we would be welcome. So I will wait and see wheather I am to be cut off or not.

I am sorry that thee has met with such an accident and I think thee had better keep Sallie a while to help thee out. It will make no difference in my feelings or actions towards thee and Cyrus wheather you accept Eliza as one of us or not although I would feel much better if you would treat her as my wife. Yet you can always depend upon my assistance to the extent of my ability.

Affectionately

Taylor

[The following letter from Sallie indicates her involvement, along with her sister Catharine (Kitty) Peirce, in the women's movement. In 1893 Kitty (or Kittie) was editor of a Des Moines newsletter entitled *Women's Standard.*]

Jan 22nd 1893

My Dear Sister,

I have wanted to write you a letter for several days but have not had time and I don't know that I am going to get to finish this for Jim has just come in and wants me to take the children and go with him over to Mr Howards. I had been thinking of so much I wished to say but the most important one was to ask you if you did not wish me to contribute an article for your paper on the subject of "woman, woman's own worst enemy." I feel sometimes when I see how indifferent women are in general to the interest of women, as if I could do the subject ample justice.

M. Howards mother an old lady of 86 was buried tuesday. We sent Taylor[1] down monday to get Mr St John to preach the funeral and Mrs St John and Mrs Royal sent me a lot of papers. Among them was two magazines called "The Review of Reviews" one of which contained an article from the pen of W. M. Stead[2] on the Life of Louise Michel, the great french anarchist[3] from which I make the following quotation which expresses my opinion better than anything I have ever seen in print. He is speaking of the assassination of Gambeta[4] and goes onto say, "it is not surprising that women in all ages have distinguished themselves by assassination, like deceit — it is the natural weapon of despairing weakness and women in every age have had more reason to despair than men against the subjection of women. Louise Michel is ever, and justly in passionate revolt. Knowledge and liberty are the boons which woman demands and so far except in a few exceptional cases she has demanded them in vain. To this hour not a single university in Germany has authorized women to study in those seats of learning. Jealously monopolized by the men who after drowning their sisters to ignorance refuse them civic justice and human rights because they suffer from the consequences of their exclusion as a consequence while everywhere in society man suffers woman suffers still more and his sufferings are not to be compared with hers. Woman is trained to be either a housewife or a courtesan. She is excluded from citizenship, deprived of education and defrauded of the wages of her labor and in too many cases bidden to make up the deficiency by the sale or her person. Hence the (iron?) enters the soul of some women and they become rebels. Sometimes if they are Christians like Mrs Butler they become rebels for the Lords sake. If like Louise Michel they have been alienated from the church they become rebels for the sake of sex — Woman who does not realize the injustice of the denial of justice and equal rights in church and in state is becoming the exception rather than the rule and this change will work itself out in a profound social moral and economic revolution before long. And the slower comfortable women are in appreciating the wrongs of her sex, the more will Louise Michel for driven mad by contemplating the hopeless sum of human misery that is involved in the radical injustice in which the subjection of woman is based."

It seems to me the more I see and read that "the cause" has made rapid strides and yet—when I come to narrow myself to the communities in which I have lived and see how few women are really interested in their own best interests—I feel more discouraged than I can say and feel like saying after all it is not really mens fault that womans lot is what it is.

Do you think for one moment slavery would have been abolished even yet if the slave had sat—as do the women of today—as idle carefree children happy if they have a new dress and enough to eat?

Well Kittie, I can not write much more this time and I dont know whether you can read what I have written or not. I found my ink bottle had frozen and my ink disappeared and I was anxious to write so I wrote with pencil. We are all well. I have not heard from Mary since she went back to school. I was very much opposed to her going back and Jim went over the next day and told them if they did not want her there to send her home but she has not come. He said when he came back that it was an imposition to let her be there when they were so poor.

I am coming down this week and going to Sarah Wards for dinner and if things dont look right I shall bring her home for I need her at home anyhow. It is all I can do to get along at all with out her. I am also coming down sometimes while the Mills meetings continue and go to one meeting. If possible will you go with me?

With love to Auntie and a share for yourself I must close. Your afft Sister Sallie

I am going to make one more attempt for the club.

1. Taylor is the son of Sallie and James Edenburn.

2. William Thomas Stead was an English journalist who wrote extensively on social issues such as child prostitution. In 1890 he founded the *Review of Reviews.* He drowned when the *Titanic* sank.

3. Louise Michel was a French anarchist who believed in violence to achieve her socialist goals. During the Commune she fought on the barricades, was wounded, and was subsequently imprisoned for ten years. She was sentenced to prison again in 1883 for six years.

4. Leon Michel Gambetta was a French deputy who, after the surrender of Napoleon III, demanded that France continue the war against Prussia. Despite the opposition of clerics and monarchists who wanted to reestablish a monarchy, he was able to convince the National Assembly to ratify a republican constitution. He died in 1882 from an infected gunshot wound to his hand incurred while cleaning a pistol. There were also rumors that his death was a suicide.

Envelopes from Taylor to Catharine and from Catharine to Taylor.

STATE OF *North Carolina*

Jones **County.**

I, *Taylor Peirce* aged *Forty four* years, a resident of the Town of *Des Moines* and County of *Polk* in the State of *Iowa* and born in the County of *Chester* and State of *Pennsylvania* do solemnly swear that I will support the Constitution of the United States, and the Constitution of the State of Iowa, and that I will faithfully discharge the duties of *1st Lieut & Adjutant* of the *22d Regmt* *Twenty Second*

Regiment Volunteer *Infantry*. of the State of Iowa, during my term of office, according to the best of my skill and ability. So help me God.

Taylor Peirce

State of *North Carolina*

Jones **County.**

Subscribed and sworn to before me *J. W. Wilson 1st Lt & Adjt 28th Regt Iowa's jn Vol* by the said *Taylor Peirce* this *22nd* day of *April* 1865

J. W. Wilson 1st Lt & Adjt 28th Iowa Inf

Taylor Peirce's commission as first lieutenant and adjutant.

*Corner of Third and Jefferson (now the corner of Second and Clay),
Des Moines, Iowa. The site of the Peirces' home on Jefferson Street was
destroyed by the levee.*

*Unmarked gravesite of Catharine Milner Peirce, Woodland Cemetery,
Des Moines, Iowa.*

Grave of Taylor Peirce, Woodland
Cemetery, Des Moines, Iowa.

Grave of Mary Milner, Woodland
Cemetery, Des Moines, Iowa.

Grave of Eliza Peirce, Woodlawn
Cemetery, Las Vegas, Nevada.

Grave of Cyrus Milner, Woodland
Cemetery, Des Moines, Iowa.

Home of Mary Milner and Catharine Peirce (daughter of Taylor and Catharine), 1520 Center Street, Des Moines, Iowa, ca. 1900.

Home of Ellis (son of Taylor and Catharine) and Mabel Peirce, 1357 Pennsylvania Avenue, Des Moines, Iowa, ca. 1920.

Bibliography

NEWSPAPERS

Daily Davenport Democrat, 29 July 1865.
Des Moines Register (also known as *Daily Register* and *State Daily Register*) 21 November 1862–23 December 1865.
Newton Journal, 27 November 1901.
The Morning News (Savannah, Georgia), 19 May 1876.

PRIMARY SOURCES

Barnett, Simeon. *History of the Twenty-second Regiment, Iowa Volunteer Infantry.* Iowa City: N. H. Brainerd, Publisher, 1865.
Bates, Samuel P. *History of Pennsylvania Volunteers, 1861–1865.* 5 vols. Harrisburg: D. Singerly, 1869–71.
Blake, Ephraim E. *A Succinct History of the 28th Iowa Volunteer Infantry.* Belle Plaine, IA: Union Press, 1896.
Brown, Leonard. *American Patriotism or Memoirs of "Common Men."* Des Moines: Redhead and Wellslager, 1869.
Bureau of the Census. *Fourth Census of the United States, 1820.* National Archives and Records Administration. RG 29. M33.
———. *Fifth Census of the United States, 1830.* National Archives and Records Administration. RG 29. M19.
———. *Sixth Census of the United States, 1840.* National Archives and Records Administration. RG 29. M704.
———. *Seventh Census of the United States, 1850.* National Archives and Records Administration. RG 29. M432.
———. *Eighth Census of the United States, 1860.* National Archives and Records Administration. RG 29. M653.
———. *Ninth Census of the United States, 1870.* National Archives and Records Administration. RG 29. M593.
———. *Tenth Census of the United States, 1880.* National Archives and Records Administration. RG 29. T9.
———. *Eleventh Census of the United States, 1890.* National Archives and Records Administration. RG 29. M407.
———. *Twelfth Census of the United States, 1900.* National Archives and Records Administration. RG 29. T623.
———. *Thirteenth Census of the United States, 1910.* National Archives and Records Administration. RG 29. T624.
———. *Fourteenth Census of the United States, 1920.* National Archives and Records Administration. RG 29. T625.
Byers, S. H. M. *Iowa in War Times.* Des Moines: W. D. Condit, 1888.

Civil War Letters of John Walter Lee, 22nd Iowa Infantry, October 1862–December 1862. Special Collections, State Historical Society of Iowa, Iowa City.

Crist, Lynda L., ed. *The Papers of Jefferson Davis.* 10 vols. Baton Rouge: Louisiana State University Press, 1991–1999.

Davis, Jefferson. *The Rise and Fall of the Confederate Government.* 2 vols. New York: Thomas Yoseloff, 1958.

Des Moines City Directory and Business Guide, 1866–1867, 1869, 1881–1882.

Des Moines Resident and Business Directory, 1871, 1873, 1874–1875, 1876–1877.

Donaldson, Thomas. *The Public Domain: Its History with Statistics.* Washington, D.C.: Government Printing Office, 1884.

Duffy, Edward. *History of the 159th Regiment, N.Y.S.V.* New York: n.p., 1890.

Emilio, Luis F. *History of the Fifty-fourth Regiment of Massachusetts Volunteer Infantry, 1863–1865.* Boston: Boston Book Company, 1894.

Fire Insurance Maps of Des Moines, Iowa. New York: Sanborn Perris Map Co., 1884, 1891, 1901, 1920.

Hewett, Janet B., ed. *Supplement to the Official Records of the Union and Confederate Armies.* 80 vols. Wilmington, N.C.: Broadfoot, 1994–1999.

Index of General Orders, Adjutant General's Office, 1865. Washington, D.C.: Government Printing Office, 1866.

Ingersoll, Lurton D. *Iowa and the Rebellion.* Philadelphia: J. B. Lippincott, 1867.

Iowa State Census, 1885.

Jones, Samuel Calvin. *Reminiscences of the Twenty-second Iowa Volunteer Infantry.* Iowa City: n.p., 1907.

Kautz, August V. *The 1865 Customs of Service for Non-commissioned Officers and Soldiers: A Handbook for the Rank and File of the Army.* 2d ed. Philadelphia: J. B. Lippincott, 1865.

Land Records. Jasper County Courthouse, Newton, Iowa.

List of Pensioners on the Roll, January 1, 1883. 5 vols. Washington, D.C.: U.S. Pension Bureau, 1883.

McMyler, James J. *History of the 11th Wisconsin Veteran Vol. Inf.* New Orleans: James J. McMyler, 1865.

Official Army Register of the Volunteer Force of the United States Army for the Years 1861, 62, 63, 64, 65. Part I: *New England States.* Washington, D.C.: Adjutant General's Office, 1865.

Petty, A. W. M. *A History of the Third Missouri Cavalry.* Little Rock, Ark.: J. W. Demby, 1865.

Pickard, Samuel T., ed. *Life and Letters of John Greenleaf Whittier.* 3 vols. Cambridge: Harvard University Press, 1975.

Powers, George W. *The Story of the Thirty-eighth Regiment of Massachusetts Volunteers.* Cambridge, Mass.: Dakin and Metcalf, 1866.

Proceedings of the Twenty-second Regiment Iowa Volunteers at Its First Reunion. Iowa City: Republican Publishing Company, 1887.

Record and Pension Office, War Department. *Organization and Status of Missouri Troops (Union and Confederate) in Service during the Civil War.* Washington, D.C.: Government Printing Office, 1902.

Records of the 22nd Iowa Volunteer Infantry. Record Group 101. State Archives of Iowa. State Historical Society of Iowa, Des Moines, Iowa.

Reed, David W. *Campaigns and Battles of the Twelfth Regiment Iowa Veteran Volunteer Infantry.* N. p., n. d.

Report of the Adjutant General and Acting Quartermaster General of the State of Iowa, January 11, 1864, to January 1, 1865. Des Moines, Iowa: F. W. Farmer, 1865.

Roster and Record of Iowa Soldiers in the War of the Rebellion. 6 vols. Des Moines, Iowa: Emory H. English, 1908–1911.

Sheridan, Philip. *Civil War Memoirs.* Edited by Paul A. Hutton. New York: Bantam Books, 1991.

Sheriff's Census, Poweshick Township, Newton Township, Jasper County, Iowa, 1852, 1856.

Sherman, William T. *Memoirs of General William T. Sherman.* Westport, Conn.: Greenwood Press, 1972.

Stevens, George T. *Three Years in the Sixth Corps.* New York: D. Van Nostrand, 1870.

Stone, William M. "History of the 22nd Iowa Volunteer Infantry." Iowa Department, Daughters of the Union Veterans of the Civil War, 1987.

Tiemann, William F. *The 159th Regiment Infantry, New York State Volunteers, in the War of the Rebellion, 1862–1865.* Brooklyn, N.Y.: William F. Tiemann, 1891.

War of the Rebellion. Official Records of the Union and Confederate Armies. 70 vols. in 128. Washington, D.C.: Government Printing Office, 1880–1901.

Whiteman, William E. S. *Maine in the War for the Union.* Lewiston, Me.: Nelson Dingley Jr., 1865.

Zilversmit, Arthur, ed. *Lincoln on Black and White: A Documentary History.* Malabar, Fla.: Robert E. Krieger, 1983.

SECONDARY SOURCES

Amann, William F. *Personnel of the Civil War.* Vol. 2, *The Union Armies.* New York: Thomas Yoseloff, 1961.

American Council of Learned Societies. *Dictionary of American Biography.* 22 vols. New York: Charles Scribner's Sons, 1943.

Andreas, Alfred T. *Illustrated Historical Atlas of the State of Iowa, 1875.* Chicago: Andreas Atlas Co., 1875.

Antrim, Earl. *Civil War Prisons and Their Covers.* New York: Collectors Club, 1961.

Barnes, Joseph K. *The Medical and Surgical History of the War of the Rebellion.* 15 vols. Washington, D.C.: Government Printing Office, 1870.

Belser, Thomas A. "Military Operations in Missouri and Arkansas, 1861–1865." Ph.D. diss., Vanderbilt University, 1958.

Boatner, Mark M. *The Civil War Dictionary.* New York: David McKay, 1959.

Bowman, John S. *Who Was Who in the Civil War.* New York: Crescent Books, 1994.

Briggs, John E. "The Enlistment of Iowa Troops during the Civil War." *Iowa Journal of History and Politics* 15 (July 1917): 323–92.

Brigham, Johnson. *Des Moines, the Pioneer of Municipal Progress and Reform of the Middle West, Together with the History of Polk County, Iowa, the Largest, Most Populous and Most Prosperous County in the State of Iowa.* 2 vols. Chicago: S. J. Clark, 1911.

Burton, E. Milby. *The Siege of Charleston, 1861–1865.* Columbia: University of South Carolina Press, 1970.

Calhoun, Arthur W. *A Social History of the American Family from Colonial Times to the Present.* 3 vols. Cleveland, Ohio: Arthur H. Clark, 1918.

Capers, Gerald M. *Occupied City: New Orleans under the Federals, 1862–1865.* Lexington: University of Kentucky Press, 1965.

Carson, Gerald. *One for a Man, Two for a Horse.* New York: Doubleday, 1961.

Casdorph, Paul D. *Prince John Magruder: His Life and Campaigns.* New York: JohnWiley and Sons, 1996.

Caskey, Willie M. *Secession and Restoration of Louisiana.* Baton Rouge: Louisiana State University Press, 1938.

Clark, Dan E. "Frontier Defense in Iowa." *Iowa Journal of History and Politics* 16 (July 1918): 315–86.

———. *Samuel Jordan Kirkwood.* Iowa City: State Historical Society of Iowa, 1917.

Clark, Olynthus. *The Politics of Iowa during the Civil War and Reconstruction.* Iowa City: Clio Press, 1911.

Cogan, Frances B. *All-American Girl: The Ideal of Real Womanhood in Mid-Nineteenth Century America.* Athens: University of Georgia Press, 1989.

Cotham, Edward T. *Battle on the Bay: The Civil War Struggle for Galveston.* Austin: University of Texas Press, 1998.

Cresap, Berner. *Appomattox Commander: The Story of General E. O. C. Ord.* San Diego, Calif.: A. S. Barnes, 1981.

Dahl, Orin L. *Des Moines: Capital City.* Tulsa, Okla.: Continental Heritage, 1978.

Dannett, Sylvia G. L. *Noble Women of the South.* New York: Thomas Yoseloff, 1959.

Davis, William C. *Jefferson Davis: The Man and His Hour.* New York: Harper Collins, 1991.

Delderfield, R. F. *Napoleon's Marshals.* New York: Stein and Day, 1980.

Dixon, J. M. *Centennial History of Polk County.* Des Moines, Iowa: State Register, 1876.

Donald, David. *Lincoln.* London: Jonathan Cape, 1995.

Donehoo, George P. *Pennsylvania: A History.* 5 vols. New York: Lewis Historical Publishing Co., 1926.

Drake, Thomas E. *Quakers and Slavery in America.* New Haven, Conn.: Yale University Press, 1950.

Drury, George. *Historical Guide to North American Railroads.* Waukesha, Wis.: Kalmbach Publishing Co., 1986.

Dyer, Frederick H. *A Compendium of the War of the Rebellion.* 2 vols. Dayton, Ohio: National Historical Society, 1979.

Eaton, Clement. *Jefferson Davis.* New York: Free Press, 1977.

Fellman, Michael. *Citizen Sherman: A Life of William Tecumseh Sherman.* New York: Random House, 1995.

Foner, Eric. *Reconstruction: America's Unfinished Revolution, 1863–1877.* New York: Harper and Row, 1988.

Frank, Joseph A. "Measuring the Political Articulateness of United States Civil War Soldiers: The Wisconsin Militia." *Journal of Military History* 64 (January 2000): 53–78.

Fullbrook, Earl S. "Relief Work in Iowa during the Civil War." *Iowa Journal of History and Politics* 16 (April 1918): 155–274.

Gibson, Guy J. "Lincoln's League: The Union League Movement during the Civil War." Ph.D. diss., University of Illinois, 1957.

Glatthaar, Joseph T. *The March to the Sea and Beyond: Sherman's Troops in the Savannah and Carolinas Campaign.* New York: New York University Press, 1986.

Glenn, Myra C. *Campaigns against Corporal Punishment: Prisoners, Sailors, Women and Children in Antebellum America.* Albany: State University of New York Press, 1984.

Greenbie, Marjorie B. *Lincoln's Daughters of Mercy.* New York: G. P. Putnams's Sons, 1944.

Greven, Philip. *Spare the Child: The Religious Roots of Punishment and the Psychological Impact of Physical Abuse.* New York: Alfred A. Knopf, 1991.

Grimsley, Mark. *The Hard Hand of War: Union Military Policy toward Southern Civilians, 1861–1865.* New York: Cambridge University Press, 1995.

Grinnell, Joseph B. *Men and Events of Forty Years.* Boston: D. Lathrop, 1891.

Gue, Benjamin F. *History of Iowa from the Earliest Times to the Beginnings of the Twentieth Century.* 4 vols. New York: Century History Company, 1903.

Harlan, Edgar R. *A Narrative History of the People of Iowa.* 5 vols. Chicago: American Historical Society, 1931.

Hechtlinger, Adelaide. *The Great Patent Medicine Era.* New York: Madison Square Press, 1970.

Hibbard, Benjamin H. *A History of the Public Land Policies.* Madison: University of Wisconsin Press, 1965.

Hicken, Victor. *Illinois in the Civil War.* 2d ed. Urbana: University of Illinois Press, 1991.

Hill, Louise B. *Joseph E. Brown and the Confederacy.* Westport, Conn.: Greenwood Press, 1972.

History of Jasper County, Iowa. Chicago: Western Historical Company, 1878.

History of Newton and Jasper County, Iowa. 7 vols. N. p.: 1936.

The History of Polk County, Iowa. Des Moines, Iowa: Union Historical Company, 1880.

Horn, John. *The Petersburg Campaign, June 1864–April 1865.* Conshohocken, Pa.: Combined Books, 1993.

Howard, Perry H. *Political Tendencies in Louisiana.* Baton Rouge: Louisiana State University Press, 1971.

Hussey, Tacitus. *Beginnings: Reminiscences of Early Des Moines.* Des Moines, Iowa: American Lithographing and Printing Co., 1919.

Irwin, Richard B. *History of the Nineteenth Army Corps.* Baton Rouge: Elliot's Book Shop Press, 1985.

Jackson, Ronald V. *Iowa 1852.* North Salt Lake, Utah: Accelerated Indexing Systems, 1988.

Kellogg, Sanford S. *The Shenandoah Valley and Virginia, 1861–1865.* New York: Neale Publishing Company, 1903.

Kelly, Orr, and Mary Davies Kelly. *Dream's End: Two Iowa Brothers in the Civil War.* New York: Kodansha International, 1998.

Kimball, E. L. "Richard Yates: His Record as Civil War Governor of Illinois." *Journal of the Illinois State Historical Society* 23 (April 1930–January 1931): 1–83.

Kinsley, James, ed. *The Poems and Songs of Robert Burns.* 2 vols. London: Oxford University Press, 1968.

Kleinberg, S. J. *Women in the United States, 1830–1945.* New Brunswick, N.J.: Rutgers University Press, 1999.

Klement, Frank L. *Dark Lanterns: Secret Political Societies, Conspiracies, and Treason Trials in the Civil War.* Baton Rouge: Louisiana State University Press, 1984.

Kriedberg, Marvin A., and Merton G. Henry. *History of Military Mobilization in the United States Army, 1775–1945.* Washington, D.C.: Department of the Army, 1955.

Lawrence, Alexander A. *A Present for Mr. Lincoln.* Macon, Ga.: Ardivan Press, 1961.

Lawton, Frederick. *The Third French Republic.* London: Grant Richards, 1909.

Lendt, David L. "Iowa and the Copperhead Movement." *Annals of Iowa* 40 (Fall 1970): 412–26.

Linderman, Gerald F. *Embattled Courage: The Experience of Combat in the American Civil War.* New York: Free Press, 1987.

Lokken, Roscoe L. *Iowa Public Land Disposal.* Iowa City: State Historical Society of Iowa, 1942.

Lyftogt, Kenneth L. *From Blue Mills to Columbia: Cedar Falls and the Civil War.* Ames: Iowa State University Press, 1993.

Lystra, Karen. *Searching the Heart: Women, Men, and Romantic Love in Nineteenth Century America.* New York: Oxford University Press, 1989.

Magnusson, Magnuo, ed. *Larousse Biographical Dictionary.* New York: Larousse Kingfisher Chambers, 1990.

Massey, Mary Elizabeth. *Women in the Civil War.* Lincoln: University of Nebraska Press, 1966.

McElroy, Edith W. *Years of Valor.* Des Moines: Iowa Civil War Centennial Commission, 1969.

McMillan, Malcolm C. *The Disintegration of a Confederate State.* Macon, Ga.: Mercer University Press, 1986.

McPherson, James M. *Battle Cry of Freedom.* New York: Oxford University Press, 1988.

———. *For Cause and Comrades: Why Men Fought in the Civil War.* New York: Oxford University Press, 1997.

Moir, William J. "Enoch Worthen Eastman." *Annals of Iowa,* 3rd ser., vol. 6 (July 1904): 416–24.

Moore, Frank. *Women of the War: Their Heroism and Self-Sacrifice.* Hartford, Conn.: S. S. Scranton, 1866.

Moore, Frank, ed. *The Rebellion Record: A Diary of American Events.* 12 vols. New York: Arno Press, 1977.

Morris, Roy. *Sheridan: The Life and Wars of General Phil Sheridan.* New York: Crown Publishers, 1992.

"Mrs. Ada North, Librarian." *Annals of Iowa* 2 (October 1896): 540–49.

Neal, Diane, and Thomas W. Kremm. *Lion of the South: General Thomas C. Hindman.* Macon, Ga.: Mercer University Press, 1993.

Nelson, Jacquelyn S. *Indiana Quakers Confront the Civil War.* Indianapolis: Indiana Historical Society, 1991.

Osborne, Charles C. *Jubal: The Life and Times of General Jubal A. Early, C.S.A., Defender of the Lost Cause.* Chapel Hill, N.C.: Algonquin Books, 1992.

Parks, Joseph H. *General Edmund Kirby Smith, C.S.A.* Baton Rouge: Louisiana State University Press, 1954.

Parrish, William E. *Turbulent Partnership: Missouri and the Union, 1861–1865.* Columbia: University of Missouri Press, 1963.

Petersen, William J. *The Story of Iowa: The Progress of an American State.* 4 vols. New York: Lewis Historical Publishing Co., 1952.

Quarles, Benjamin. *The Negro in the Civil War.* New York: DeCapo, 1989.

Ramsdell, Charles W. *Behind the Lines in the Southern Confederacy.* New York: Greenwood Press, 1969.

Randall, J. G., and David Donald. *The Civil War and Reconstruction.* Lexington, Mass.: D. C. Heath, 1969.

Robbins, Roy M. *Our Landed Heritage: The Public Domain, 1776–1936.* Princeton, N.J.: Princeton University Press, 1942.

Robertson, James I. *Soldiers Blue and Gray.* Columbia: University of South Carolina Press, 1988.

Robertson, William G. *Back Door to Richmond: The Bermuda Hundred Campaign, April–June 1864.* Newark: University of Delaware Press, 1987.

Robinson, Charles M. *Shark of the Confederacy: The Story of the CSS Alabama.* Annapolis, Md.: Naval Institute Press, 1995.

Sage, Leland. *A History of Iowa.* Ames: Iowa State University Press, 1974.

Sanchez, Kaye, comp. *Buried in Woodland.* Des Moines, Iowa: author, 1998.

Scudder, Horace E., ed. *The Complete Poetical Works of Sir Walter Scott.* Boston: Houghton Mifflin, 1900.

Shannon, Fred A. *The Organization and Administration of the Union Army, 1861–1865.* 2 vols. Cleveland, Ohio: Arthur H. Clark, 1928.

Smith, Donald A. *The Birth of Colorado: A Civil War Perspective.* Norman: University of Oklahoma Press, 1989.

Stackpole, Edward J. *Sheridan in the Shenandoah.* Harrisburg, Pa.: Stackpole Books, 1992.

Straus, Murray A., and Denise A. Donnelly. *Beating the Devil Out of Them: Corporal Punishment in American Families.* New York: Lexington Books, 1994.

Stuart, Addison A. *Iowa Colonels and Regiments: Being a History of Iowa Regiments in the War of the Rebellion, and Containing a Description of the Battles in Which They Fought.* Des Moines, Iowa: Mills, 1865.

Taylor, Frank H. *Philadelphia in the Civil War: 1861–1865.* Philadelphia: Dunlap Printing Co., 1913.

Thorne, Mildred. "C. C. Carpenter in the 1858 Iowa Legislature." *Iowa Journal of History* 52 (1954): 31–60.

Tunnell, Ted. *Crucible of Reconstruction: War, Radicalism and Race in Louisiana, 1862–1877.* Baton Rouge: Louisiana State University Press, 1984.

Tuttle, Charles R. *An Illustrated History of the State of Iowa.* Chicago: Richard S. Peale, 1876.

Uglow, Jennifer S. *The International Dictionary of Women's Biography.* New York: Continuum, 1982.

Urwin, George J. W. *Custer Victorious: The Civil War Battles of General George Armstrong Custer.* Rutherford, N.J.: Fairleigh Dickinson University Press, 1983.

Wall, Joseph F. *Iowa: A History.* New York: W. W. Norton, 1978.

Warner, Ezra A. *Generals in Blue: Lives of the Union Commanders.* Baton Rouge: Louisiana State University Press, 1964.

Weaver, James B., ed. *Past and Present of Jasper County Iowa.* 2 vols. Indianapolis: B. F. Bowen, 1912.

Wector, Dixon. *When Johnny Comes Marching Home.* Boston: Houghton Mifflin, 1994.

Welcher, Frank J. *The Union Army, 1861–1865: Organization and Operations.* 2 vols. Bloomington: Indiana University Press, 1989.

Welter, Barbara. *The Woman Question in American History.* Hinsdale, Ill.: Dryden Press, 1973.

Wert, Jeffrey D. *From Winchester to Cedar Creek.* Carlisle, Pa.: South Mountain Press, 1987.

Whitehouse, Joseph W. A. *The Battle of Cedar Creek.* Washington, D.C.: U.S. Army Center of Military History, 1992.

Wiley, Bell I. *The Life of Billy Yank: The Common Soldier of the Union.* Baton Rouge: Louisiana State University Press, 1978.

———. *The Life of Johnny Reb: The Common Soldier of the Confederacy.* Baton Rouge: Louisiana State University Press, 1978.

Wilson, Margaret G. *The American Woman in Transition: The Urban Influence, 1870–1920.* Westport, Conn.: Greenwood Press, 1979.

Winters, John D. *The Civil War in Louisiana.* Baton Rouge: Louisiana State University Press, 1963.

Wubben, Hubert H. *Civil War Iowa and the Copperhead Movement.* Ames: Iowa State University Press, 1980.

Young, Agatha. *The Women and the Crisis: Women of the North in the Civil War.* New York: McDowell, Obolensky, 1959.

Index